The Keystone Library

THE KEYSTONE LIBRARY contains many of the notable works published during recent years. The subjects embrace:

Memoirs and Biography, Travel and Sport, History and Egyptology, Belles Lettres and Poetry.

Wherever possible production is identical with the original editions; illustrations are included; individuality is retained and not lost in the uniformity of a series.

5s. NET, ILLUSTRATED

The Autobiography	MARGOT ASQUITH
Two volumes, sold separately.	
Alexander the Great	ARTHUR WEIGALL
The Life and Friendships of Dean Swift	STEPHEN GWYNN
Baghdad : The City of Peace	RICHARD COKE
Egyptian Tales and Romances	SIR ERNEST A. WALLIS BUDGE
A Very Gallant Gentleman	COMMANDER L. C. BERNACCHI
My Early Life	WINSTON S. CHURCHILL
Thoughts and Adventures	WINSTON S. CHURCHILL
The Regent and his Daughter	DORMER CRESTON
Myself and My Friends	LILLAH MCCARTHY
Sarah, Duchess of Marlborough	KATHLEEN CAMPBELL
Genghis Khan: Emperor of All Men	HAROLD LAMB
The Crusades : Iron Men and Saints	HAROLD LAMB
Six Famous Living Poets	COULSON KERNAHAN
The Life and Times of Akhnaton	ARTHUR WEIGALL
Nero: Emperor of Rome	ARTHUR WEIGALL
Marc Antony	ARTHUR WEIGALL
Nuda Veritas	CLARE SHERIDAN
Life of Horace Walpole	STEPHEN GWYNN
Florence Nightingale	I. B. O'MALLEY
Selected Poems	SIR WILLIAM WATSON
Anatole France Himself	JEAN JACQUES BROUSSON
South America	KASIMIR EDSCHMID

3s. 6d. NET, ILLUSTRATED

Men and Horses I Have Known	GEORGE LAMBTON

Other volumes will be added from time to time

A selection from the
works of the same author

EXPERIENCES OF A LITERARY MAN
SAINTS AND SCHOLARS
THE MASTERS OF ENGLISH LITERATURE
COLLECTED POEMS
THE LIFE OF SIR WALTER SCOTT
THE LIFE OF HORACE WALPOLE
THE LIFE OF CAPTAIN R. F. SCOTT
THE LIFE OF MARY KINGSLEY

SWIFT

From the bust by VAN NOST *in the National Gallery of Ireland*

THE
LIFE AND FRIENDSHIPS
OF
DEAN SWIFT

BY
STEPHEN GWYNN

KEYSTONE

LIBRARY

LONDON
Thornton Butterworth Ltd.

First Published 1933
First Impression in the Keystone Library . . 1935

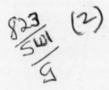

CONTENTS

CHAP.   PAGE

PREFACE 9

BOOK I
THE APPRENTICE TO LITERATURE

I   PARENTAGE AND EDUCATION 13
II   SWIFT'S SERVICE UNDER SIR WILLIAM TEMPLE . . 24
III SWIFT'S EARLY POEMS 33
IV LAST YEARS OF DISCIPLESHIP 45

BOOK II
THE WIT AND PAMPHLETEER

V   ENTRY INTO THE WORLD 69
VI   A TALE OF A TUB 84
VII 1704–9 : LITERARY LONDON 93
VIII BEGINNINGS OF THE PAMPHLETEER 112
IX   IN THE MINISTRY : LONDON, 1710–13 122
X   WINDSOR AND LONDON, 1711–13 143
XI   SWIFT'S RETURN TO COURT 163
XII QUEEN ANNE DIES 183

BOOK III
THE DEAN

XIII DUBLIN : 1714–20 199
XIV 1717–23 : SWIFT'S IRISH CIRCLE 209
XV   THE DRAPIER 228

5

CONTENTS

CHAP.   PAGE

XVI   ENGLAND REVISITED 249

XVII   *GULLIVER'S TRAVELS* 260

XVIII   SWIFT'S LAST VISIT TO ENGLAND AND STELLA'S DEATH   270

XIX   THE IRISH PATRIOT 283

XX   THE END 298

INDEX   317

6

LIST OF ILLUSTRATIONS

TO FACE
PAGE

SWIFT . . . . *Frontispiece*

JONATHAN SWIFT, AGED 42 106

ROBERT HARLEY, EARL OF OXFORD AND MORTIMER . . 126

EXTRACT FROM THE "JOURNAL TO STELLA" 160

JOHN ARBUTHNOTT, M.D. (*in the text*) 188

JOHN GAY 216

MATTHEW PRIOR 216

STELLA 246

VANESSA 246

POPE 258

BOLINGBROKE. 258

DEAN SWIFT, AGED ABOUT 65 272

DEATH-MASK OF DEAN SWIFT (*in the text*) 313

PREFACE

THIS is an account of Swift, as man and as writer. I have not attempted to follow out the politics in which he was involved, in England or in Ireland ; but I trust that such indications have been given as are necessary to understand the formation and development of his extraordinary powers.

The account is constructed almost entirely from Swift's own writings and the vast correspondence, collected and edited by Mr. Elrington Ball, in six volumes. Mr. Ball's work is dedicated to the memory of Cæsar Litton Falkiner, whose death in early middle age took from Irish historical scholarship one of its most discerning students, and deprived many of a friendship which put at their disposal not only rare charm of intercourse, but the resources of a fine library and great knowledge, offered with a generosity beyond praise.

Mr. Ball gives Falkiner the monument that he deserved. I have never before, in much study, been privileged to use an edition where research was so complete or conveyed with such lucid brevity. It is with deep regret that I offer this tribute to a man who can no longer receive it.

There have been many biographical studies of Swift, compiled, like this one, solely from written records. Sir Walter Scott's is the first of them, and among the best ; the last, Sir Henry Craik's, is generally regarded as the standard work. But even for Craik, research was a main object ; he inherited and carried out the admirable beginnings which Forster left unfinished. Since then Mr. Ball's work has been completed and also Mr. Temple Scott's definitive edition of the works ; and whoever writes now need not greatly interrupt narrative with discussion of new details.

But every biographer must study and estimate the various biographies written by men who had seen and known Jonathan Swift. Lord Orrery's was the first of them, composed in the Chesterfieldian form of letters to his son ; it was so vehemently resented that the next two were written expressly to correct the impression it conveyed. The first of these was by Delany, who had known Swift intimately for twenty-seven years, before the final wreckage of his brain. That wreckage had begun when Orrery came into his circle. Deane Swift, a zealous champion, knew even less of him than Orrery. Thomas Sheridan was only a boy when he saw the great man, infirm and passionate; but he transmitted the tradition gathered from his father, whose friendship was as long as Delany's and even more intimate.

The testimony of these four first-hand witnesses must be judged with reference to their personal quality. Orrery was conceited and an ass; so, unluckily, was Deane Swift, though, unlike Orrery, neither a snob nor malicious. Delany was a scholar and an honest gentleman; the limitation to his judgment is suggested by the fact that he wished Swift had not written *Gulliver*; but he is by far the best of the four. It is impossible to say how accurately Sheridan, writing nearly fifty years after his father died, reproduces what his father told him.

Mrs. Pilkington's gossip does not go beyond gossip, but is good contemporary stuff of its kind.

Yet when all is said, it is in the Letters and in the published writings that we must find Swift. Even on the vexed question of his relations to the women who loved him, essential truth will be found only in the letters to Vanessa and the poem on their early alliance; in the *Journal* and in the long series of birthday verses dedicated to Stella.

The late Charles Whibley, a writer whose prose had not a little of Swift's quality, has deprecated in one of his best essays all inquiry into these intimate relationships; and indeed, though no biographer of Swift can avoid this side of his subject, none, I think, can escape some sense of prying indiscretion. But genius has its penalties. By what he wrote to them, of them and for them, Swift lifted a veil for us to look through; and we see there, even in the meaner of these attachments, much of what made him beyond all ordinary measure loved and lovable.

My thanks for courteous assistance are specially due to the Very Rev. H. J. Lawlor, Dean of St. Patrick's: to Dr. R. R. Leeper, Superintendent of Swift's Hospital; and to the staff of the London Library. Messrs. Bell and Son have generously given me a general permission to use Mr. Ball's edition of the correspondence, of which they are the publishers, as far as their control extends over this work. For a general sense of the period I owe more to Mr. F. S. Oliver's historical essay, " The Endless Adventure," than to any other modern work.

Book I

THE APPRENTICE TO LITERATURE:

MOOR PARK, 1689–98

CHAPTER I

PARENTAGE AND EDUCATION

IN the august company of great writers there are some who, for one reason or another, so affected popular imagination in their lifetime that a ghost of them survives, vaguely familiar to thousands who in reality know nothing but the name. Dante perhaps : Heine, Goethe, Balzac, Dumas *père* certainly, among foreigners : of our own stock, Johnson, Burns, Sir Walter, Byron and—less clearly —Dickens. They people the dim domains of our common culture, they bring a breath of life among the shades. Loving research has sought to build up beside them a figure of Shakespeare, but has not really fixed any lineament : nothing results but some fleeting image of a young man holding horses outside a theatre. The others are different : we recognize them as they pass, we know their gesture and carriage, as the citizens of a little town know its chief men. Yet, I think, Jonathan Swift has a distinction of his own, the only man of letters who became a legend in his lifetime.

It began in Ireland, where he was what he still is, the great " character " who would say and do the most astonishing things, whose wisdom always bore its own peculiar and eccentric imprint. " Very classical, ma'am, as classical as Dean Swift " is a phrase I have heard from an old Dublin woman, such a one as Mr. O'Casey writes his plays about. In the wider world, his name always carries another in its company ; he and Stella still fascinate curiosity with the unsolved riddle of their romance. More than curiosity is moved ; a presence is evoked that can still almost intimidate. Setting apart Shakespeare and Milton, there is, I think, no English writer for whom greatness can be claimed more assuredly than for Jonathan Swift. Yet the word as applied to him bears a peculiar significance. He was, it is true, the creator of a work which endowed the whole European race with a set of eloquent symbols ; *Gulliver's Travels* ranks with *Don Quixote*. But the imagination of his own country has been affected less by his writings than by his personality, which in them survives imperishably. Other men, for example his contemporaries, Dryden and Pope, may rival him as writers; but we do not think of them as Titans. They do not appear as he does, in sinister ascendancy, only the greater if baffled and tormented.

Such a man will inevitably be many times the subject of a biographer's study, all the more because through succeeding generations his character has made for itself as many enemies as friends. There is no use in pretending to impartiality: you must be for Swift or against him; just as nobody was ever impartial about Parnell, the man in many ways most truly comparable. Gifted writers, admirably equipped by knowledge, Macaulay and Thackeray, have experienced the repulsion far more than the attraction of Swift's genius, and have blackened his image. Such pens bite deep. If I venture to attempt an interpretation very different from theirs, it is because we can base our judgment on what was thought of the man by his intimates; because we can show how he dealt by his friends, great and small, and by his near neighbours; how much enduring affection he received and he gave.

It is a further inducement that to write of Swift involves amassing some considerable knowledge of his time. Few men of letters have touched life at so many points. The image of a Titan appropriates itself only to his fierce and lonely old age; in the fullness of his powers he was a man eminently social, gregarious and even clubbable, as much a centre and rallying point as Samuel Johnson.

What I am attempting is merely interpretation. Research has been done, and with rare thoroughness. All the documents are to hand: yet I think that the story of his life—more especially in its early stages—does not stand out so clear as it should. The formation of his mind, the direction and the limitation of his interests, above all the development of his supreme craftsmanship in writing, afford a critical theme which no one is likely to handle exhaustively. I profess no more than to give one student's account of him, of his works and of his friends.

Jonathan Swift was born in Dublin on November 30, 1667, and was brought up in Ireland till he reached the age of twenty-one. But his parents were English, only a few years settled in the country, and he always regarded himself as an Englishman. He meant by an Irishman one of the race whom the Normans conquered; and though probably he might have extended the term to Fitzgeralds, Burkes, Butlers, and the other Norman strains long and deeply interfused with Gaelic blood—especially if they had remained Catholic—there is no evidence that such speculations interested him. What should be made clear is that when he was born the type which we call Anglo-Irish scarcely existed, and was not recognized, but that before he died, it was strongly developed, beginning to be organized, and conscious of its own separate interest and allegiances. In fact, he created it. This Englishman was the first who taught the Anglo-Irish to think of themselves as a nation; he was their acknowledged leader. Indeed, all Ireland acknowledged him—the first non-military leader to whom Ireland ever did homage.

Even before his period of leadership in Ireland he had given proof in England of a new power, characteristic of the modern world; for he stands at the transition. During the seventeenth century in which he had his apprenticeship to life, matters even of internal policy were still in the main settled by the sword. In the eighteenth, on which he set his mark imperishably, other weapons prevailed; the appeal to what we call public opinion in some degree superseded the appeal to arms. Argument was not omnipotent, but he proved, in two countries, how much argument could do. He believed almost to exaggeration in the power and the right of reason to control conduct and government. Yet, since he was even more than is usual among mortals, a complex of contradictions, reason in him was remarkably affected by tradition and transmitted loyalties. The history of his family illustrates and accounts for this clash of tendencies.

In the reign of Charles I, after Naseby had been fought and lost, an elderly clergyman came riding to Raglan Castle which was held for the King. He demanded to be brought to the Governor, who asked him, " What service can you render to His Majesty ? " " He shall have my coat," said the Reverend Thomas Swift, throwing off a weather-beaten garment. The Governor feared that this could be of no great use. " Then will he have my waistcoat ? " and that also was thrown off, and fell heavy on the floor. Three hundred gold pieces were quilted into it. Mr. Swift, whose property had been plundered some forty times since the troubles broke out, had mortgaged his small estate at Goodrich, in Herefordshire (where he also held the living), and so raised this welcome subsidy. For this and other actions which became known to the Parliamentarians, he was imprisoned as a malignant, saw his livings sequestered, and died a poor man in 1658, but still an ardent and active clergyman of the Church of England. This old militant was to Jonathan Swift the glory of the Swift family though it had not lacked other distinguished names. All that was traditional and instinctive in the Dean of St. Patrick's followed on the example of the Vicar of Goodrich; but events which happened in the next generation limited that hereditary allegiance.

Thomas Swift left five sons, of whom only one, his namesake, followed the family tradition and took orders. The eldest of the five, Godwin, was already a student of Gray's Inn when his father died, as was also his younger brother Dryden. The other two, William and Jonathan, became solicitors: and it appears that William first had the thought of seeking his fortune in Ireland, where he went in the year after the Restoration, taking with him Jonathan, then only twenty. The two barristers followed; Godwin Swift was called to the Irish Bar in 1663. There was then in Ireland (however difficult it is to believe now) a shortage of lawyers, because for twelve years, from 1641 onwards, the country had been devastated by a war of extermination, at the end of which most men surviving had become soldiers, while more than half the land was transferred to new owners and claimants in respect of services to the Parliamentary cause. All Catholics were pushed into the province of Connaught. After the Restoration, these confiscations were naturally questioned by those who had fought on the King's side; and the titles of half Ireland were in question, making a field of fame for lawyers. The Swift brothers got ahead rapidly, especially as they had the countenance of the great Ormond family. Godwin and William earned considerable estates. Dryden (whose name came from his mother, a Huntingdonshire lady, aunt to the poet) died young. So also did Jonathan, who was only five-and-twenty when he left his widow with an orphan daughter and the prospect of another child. This posthumous infant, born on November 30, 1667, inherited nothing but his father's name, Jonathan.

In a fragment of autobiography, written when he was about sixty, Swift has a comment on the union which resulted in his birth too characteristic not to be given in full:

This marriage was on both sides very indiscreet; for his wife brought her husband little or no fortune, and his death happening so suddenly before he could make a sufficient establishment for his family, his son (not then born) hath often been heard to say, that he felt the consequences of that marriage not only through the whole course of his education, but during the greatest part of his life.

The Dean himself must be blamed for the exaggerated belief that he grew up in penury, dependent on the niggardly charity of relations. Nothing could be less true. He was indeed born an orphan and portionless; but he was the child of young parents who had made a love match, and there is no suggestion that it was disapproved by their relations. Two of his uncles were well able to mitigate the consequences of such a bereavement; and the eldest of them, Godwin Swift, who undertook the charge, was affluent.

There is a story current that once at a dinner-table in Dublin Swift spoke disparagingly of this uncle, and was interrupted by another clergyman who asked, "Did he not give you your education?" "Yes," Swift is reported to have answered, "he gave me the education of a dog." "Then, sir, you have not the gratitude of a dog." To me this story bears all the appearance of a retort invented by one who would like to have made it. The outline of Swift's education was familiar to everybody in Dublin. He was sent to Kilkenny school for eight years, and then for seven more he was a student in Trinity College, Dublin. His cousin, Thomas Swift, son of an English rector, received practically the same upbringing. So for that matter did Congreve, Swift's schoolfellow. These were the Irish equivalents for Winchester and Oxford. I do not believe that Swift ever said in company a thing so grotesquely contrary to the facts as to call this a dog's upbringing.

Nevertheless, it is true that Swift "never loved his uncle Godwin, nor the remembrance of his uncle to the hour of his death." There was a sourness in his nature, and he had not a grateful heart. He could lavish affection and loyalty; but a pride which amounted to disease made him an ungracious receiver of benefits. Yet in the account which he has left of his uncle Godwin there is one point which may account for antipathy; it concerns the part of Swift's mind which was not reasonable. "He married a relation of the Marchioness of Ormond, and upon that account, as well as his father's loyalty, the old Duke of Ormond made him his attorney-general in the palatinate of Tipperary. He had four wives, one of which, to the great offence of his family, was co-heiress to Admiral Deane, who was one of the Regicides."

There breaks out the resentment of a Royalist, all the bitterer because the man who allied himself with the family of a Regicide had been greatly assisted by the greatest of the Stuarts' subjects. The remaining lines of the account should be added. "Godwin left several children who have all estates. He was an ill pleader but dextrous in the subtle parts of the law." So the passage stood at first; later, before 'dextrous,' were interlined the words "perhaps a little too."

The *Account* was certainly written after Swift had lost Stella, and the venomous interlineation may have been added in his lonely, savage old age. Whatever the cause, his memories of youth were darkened by an old resentment. We have no word, good or bad, about his schoolboy life at Kilkenny, to say whether he was happy or unhappy. Two incidents of it rest on the best authority—his own. The first indeed is not related of Kilkenny; but as the school is on the banks of the Nore, and Swift was there from six to fourteen, one may fairly assign it to that place.

I remember, when I was a little boy, I felt a great fish at the end of my line, which I drew up almost on the ground, but it dropped in, and the disappointment vexes me to this very day, and I believe it was the type of all my future disappointments.

Many of us can sympathize, especially if it was a salmon; but this might have happened to the happiest schoolboy and been remembered with tears of the spirit to his dying day. The other detail is specific, and if we are to press it for biographical information, it tells us that Swift while a schoolboy sometimes had several shillings in his pocket:

When I was a schoolboy at Kilkenny, and in the lower form, I longed very much to have a horse of my own to ride on. One day I saw a poor man leading a very mangy lean horse out of the town to kill him for the skin. I asked the man if he would sell him, which he readily consented to upon my offering him somewhat more than the price of the hide, which was all the money I had in the world. I immediately got on him, to the great envy of some of my schoolfellows, and to the ridicule of others, and rode him about the town. The horse soon tired, and lay down. As I had no stable to put him into, nor any money to pay for his sustenance, I began to find out what a foolish bargain I had made, and cried heartily for the loss of my cash; but the horse dying soon after on the spot gave me some relief.

On the other hand, it may never have happened and been simply an apologue invented to discourage imprudent marriages—for it is said to have come in a letter addressed to a young clergyman. In any case there is no complaint here of anyone but himself. It is very different when we come to the account of his college career.

He was admitted to Trinity on April 24, 1682—aged fourteen and a half—as a " pensioner," that is, neither one of the privileged fellow-commoners, nor among the sizars, who in return for cheap education did certain menial duties, which Goldsmith half a century later found very irksome. He had in fact exactly the same status as his cousin and contemporary, Thomas Swift. None the less he wrote in his old age:

> By the ill treatment of his nearest relations, he was so discouraged and sunk in his spirits that he too much neglected his academic studies ; for some parts of which he had no great relish by nature, and turned himself to reading history and poetry : so that when the time came for taking his degree of bachelor of arts, although he had lived with great regularity and due observance of the statutes, he was stopped of his degree for dulness and insufficiency ; and at last hardly admitted in a manner, little to his credit, which is called in that college *speciali gratiâ* on the 15th February, 1685, with four more on the same footing : and this discreditable mark, as I am told, stands upon record in their college registry.

According to Swift's younger kinsman Deane Swift (grandson of Godwin), the unkindness complained of amounts simply to this, that Godwin Swift kept his nephew short of money during his college life. It is possible that the rate of his allowance may have been curtailed, for the lawyer, not content with his professional earnings, speculated in various ventures unsuccessfully and embarrassed himself before he died in 1688—the last year of Swift's academic career. But there is no reason to believe that Swift knew, as Johnson did at Oxford or Goldsmith at Trinity, actual hardship. He had two other uncles, one of whom, the solicitor William Swift, he himself called " the best of my relations." The other, Adam Swift, also a solicitor, owned property in Down and in Antrim, and may not have been so accessible. But there were also elder cousins, one of whom, Willoughby Swift, son of Godwin by his first marriage, was settled in Lisbon and is said to have been very liberal to his relations. One of his half-brothers, Deane Swift (called after the regicide), joined him in Portugal. This man's son, Deane Swift junior, nephew to Willoughby, was Jonathan Swift's second biographer, and it is he who tells a surprising tale. Swift in his college rooms, with pockets very empty, observed from his window a seafaring man peering about him in the square, and thought to himself, " How happy I should be if that were a messenger from my cousin Willoughby." Whereupon, the man entered his staircase, knocked at his door, asked if he were Jonathan Swift, produced a great leather bag and poured out its contents on the table—refusing to take the share of it which was offered by the lucky collegian. The story goes on that from that time forward Swift declared he " became a better economist and never was without some little money in his pocket."

At all events, if Swift never knew what it was to be in want of a dinner or without clean linen, he grew up with a bitter dread of penury. Like all satirists, he dreaded ridicule, and youth is the time when a man feels and resents most the contempt of those who are richer; and it is the young who are readiest to let this contempt be seen. He went out into the world determined to avoid anything that would drag him down even to an appearance of inferiority.

Whoever provided it, money was forthcoming to enable him to complete his college curriculum—the full course of seven years. The B.A. degree was given at the end of the fourth year, and technically Swift might have been refused it, for his answering had been defective in the third year's examination. Forster's research has shown that he was marked ' bad ' in philosophy, ' good ' in Greek and Latin, ' negligent ' in theology. But even up to this day a student in Trinity threatened with failure can go to his tutor and plead for reconsideration. Swift—most unlike Goldsmith—was on the friendliest terms with his tutor, St. George Ashe, an important person in the University and later in the Church. One may fairly assume that Ashe knew enough of his man to make a good case for overlooking the shortcomings and giving the degree by " special indulgence." Throughout his life Swift showed distaste not only for the formal pedantry of scholastic logic (then a great part of the curriculum) but for all abstract speculation.

When the difficulty was surmounted, he continued to read for his master's degree, having graduated bachelor at eighteen, the age when most students now matriculate. The final examination was due at Easter, 1689: but in the winter before that, the bottom suddenly dropped out of the Protestant world in Ireland to which the Swift clan belonged.

At the close of 1688 the Revolution drove James II from the throne in England. But in Ireland the Catholic Viceroy, Tyrconnell, was in control, with an army largely Catholic and a parliament bent on undoing the work which was done under Cromwell and established by law with little modification under Charles II. At the beginning of 1689 matters looked so threatening for Protestants that the authorities of Trinity College liberated all men from their academic obligations. Swift's tutor Ashe set the example of going to England; the pupil followed it, abandoning the near prospect of his M.A. degree.

These events shaped Swift's political attitude for life. Had his lines been cast in England from the first, he might, like his friend Atterbury, have been a Jacobite. But inevitably from his upbringing he looked at the actions of James II with the eyes of the race who had effected a conquest in Ireland and profited by it; whose property as well as their ascendancy was now threatened with a confiscation reversing that by which they were installed. His own folk were not among those who got land in Ireland by grant; they had paid for their purchases, and the title of what they had bought under the law's sanction was now challenged. Yet that was not all. Swift was by interest loyal to the cause for which his grandfather suffered, the cause of Church and King—but of a king who belonged to the Church of England. An alien religion divided this loyalty. If the King's creed changed, a subject, Swift held, must remain loyal to the Church, which was constant.

Then and thereafter Swift was a monarchist, firmly attached to the Protestant succession on reasoned judgment. The Battle of the Boyne re-established all these interests with which his hopes were bound up : for his prospects lay in Ireland. He was inevitably a partisan of King William, who had rescued his kith and kin and all his friends from the risk of ruin, and who had prevented the re-introduction of Popery, for whose trappings he had then and thereafter a savage contempt. But the completeness of William's victory put fear of a Roman Catholic ascendancy beyond the bounds of reason. What remained with Jonathan Swift was an instinctive and hereditary abhorrence of the other extreme. The Church of England, with its reasonable religion, still needed to be defended against enemies ; and they were lodged within the Protestant gates. Swift intellectually despised Catholics ; but with all the instincts of his nature he hated dissenting sectaries, whose hands were, to his eyes, sacrilegiously bespattered with the blood of a martyred king.

In the generation of his grandfather men had been Cavalier or Roundhead. That distinction was confused when the Round-head Monk put Charles II back on the throne. In the generation which succeeded, men had learnt to call themselves Whig or Tory, and Swift found himself entering on manhood a Whig perforce. Moreover, the convulsion that pitched him upon the world brought it also to pass that he should be apprenticed to life under a most distinguished Whig master. After a few months spent with his mother at Leicester, he entered the household of Sir William Temple at Moor Park, being then in his twenty-second year. Probably his mother had arranged this employment for him.

His relations with his mother were in some ways limited. It was never in her power to give him a home ; and even as an infant he was separated from her in an extraordinary way which he himself has related. When he was a year old, his nurse, a woman from Whitehaven, found herself obliged to see a relation who was sick and from whom she had expectations. Being extremely fond of her charge, she " stole him on shipboard unknown to his mother, and carried him with her to Whitehaven where he continued for almost three years ; for (his *Account* says) when the matter was discovered, his mother sent order by all means not to hazard a second voyage till he would be better able to bear it. The nurse was so careful of him that before he returned he had learnt to spell ; and by the time he was three years old, he could read any chapter in the Bible."

Swift's *Account* is never to be trusted for exactness as to dates, even in things that happened during his manhood. But on general lines, we can take his word for the story and for his early precocity in education ; on which comment has often been made. I am more concerned to point out that in the earliest span of his conscious existence, another woman was to him his mother : and this also. Many and many an English child born in Ireland has been almost made Irish by its nurse : but Swift's first impressions came from an Englishwoman.

When the child was brought back, he and his mother appear to have lived in Godwin Swift's house ; but at six he went to the boarding-school at Kilkenny, where according to the old custom the years were broken only by two holidays and these not long ones. At some date, we do not know when, but quite possibly when the boy went to school, Mrs. Swift moved her abode to Leicester. We know only that from the beginning of 1689, when he first came to stay with her as a young man, he wrote to his mother constantly when away from her, and made her a yearly visit, even when it meant two or three days' travel on foot or by carrier's waggon. Deane Swift has left this description of her :

Her conversation was so extremely polite, cheerful, and agreeable, even to the young and sprightly, that some of the family who paid her a visit near fifty years ago at Leicester, speak of her to this day (1754) with the greatest affection. . . . She was a very early riser ; was always dressed for the whole day at about six o'clock in the morning, in a mantua and petticoat, which according to the fashion of those times she constantly wore ; and her chief amusements were needlework and reading. . . . She declared in her latter days (for indeed she was a woman of an easy, contented spirit) that she was rich and happy, and abounded with everything.

The difference in age between her and her son can only have been some twenty years, for she was the young wife of a man who died at five-and-twenty. Swift himself told a story that when he settled in to his first living, a parson of thirty-three, she came over and took lodgings near him, and amused herself by telling the housekeeper she was come there to receive the addresses of a lover. She even let her son appear in that character before she ended the mystification.

This is really all we know, except that when he came to stay with her fresh from Trinity, she was much perturbed by the excessive interest he showed in one Miss Betty Jones—apparently his second cousin. " My prudent mother," he told his friend Worrall, " was afraid I should be in love with her ; but when I went to London she married an innkeeper in Loughborough by whom she had several children."

It has been often alleged that Mrs. Swift was related to Dorothy Osborne, whom Sir William Temple had married. If that were so, I think Swift would certainly have stated the fact ; for his account extends itself upon her descent from " the most ancient family of the Ericks who derived their lineage from Erick the Forester." Since the days of this Saxon who opposed William the Conqueror, the Ericks, he said, had lasted on in Leicestershire, " but declining every age and are now in the condition of very private gentlemen." Mrs. Swift was the daughter of a country parson and her sister, Mrs. Kendall, was married to one.

Yet probably it was she who, having her son on her hands, stirred up the Swift family in Ireland to use what influence they could ; and for reasons which must be examined in the next chapter, Sir William Temple was a man to whom they were entitled to apply.

CHAPTER II

SWIFT'S SERVICE UNDER SIR WILLIAM TEMPLE

AS soon as we are done with the shadowy period of Swift's boyhood and student days, biography has material to work on, not copious, but solid and full of sap. But since Swift was Swift, mythology begins immediately from this period. The years that he passed in Temple's household have been represented as years of abject humiliation in which the half-menial underling played a contemptible part. Nothing could be farther from the truth. The most fortunate thing that ever happened in Swift's life was the storm that drove him to that shelter. He was a young man, needing to be formed for the world; chance made him an inmate of the most cultivated household in Great Britain. He wanted to be a writer, and for ten years he was writing for, and with, the most admired master of English prose. He was interested in history and politics; there he was, living beside a man who for twenty critical years had lived at the focal centre of European diplomacy. These were privileges, implied in the very nature of his situation. But Fate added to them the beginning of a connection which, however we may interpret it, or his conduct in it, brought into his cloudy life the best sunshine it was to know.

For the misapprehension of the Moor Park period, which is to be found even in Sir Walter Scott—to say nothing of the misrepresentation in which Macaulay outdoes all the perverters of truth —two men are chiefly to blame : Swift and Temple. I have said already that Swift had not a thankful heart ; but any clever and poor young man is commonly disposed to think whatever falls to him less than his deserving, and it is not possible to say that this young man overvalued his own talents. But we have full knowledge that Swift was capable of gratitude, and that later in life he paid it in the fullest measure, even beyond the bounds of reason, to a great man who gave him what he most desired—recognition of his intel-

lectual rank. Temple never earned this gratitude. Long before
he died, he had certainly seen what is at least a little masterpiece produced by the young man who was his daily associate:
he probably saw what is by consent of critics a masterpiece without
qualification; yet there is no trace that he accorded to genius the
invaluable stimulus of adequate commendation. The truth probably is that he was not of a nature to recognize a masterpiece when
he saw it. Meredith's Sir Willoughby Patterne was a most
accomplished and cultivated English gentleman, who would have
made good Lord Melbourne's saying that an English gentleman is
qualified for any post which he has influence enough to secure.
Yet Meredith does not think it important to demonstrate this.
What he does demonstrate is that Sir Willoughby fell short in
essential generosity, and did not willingly admit anything that
disparaged his own ascendancy. I do not think Temple ever knew
that Swift was intellectually even his equal. Had he known it,
we should have had from Swift, what we have not, the acknowledgment of what Temple was worth to him—incomparably more than
any mere money obligation.

The best that Temple gave was access to a rich and cultivated
experience, and a mind fully equipped to discourse on what it had
known. Almost forty years divided the employed from the
employer, the secretary from his chief. Swift was twenty-two when
he came to Moor Park, Temple sixty-one. Admitting that men
aged earlier then than now, and that Temple had not escaped the
gout (though his temperance and active habits kept him clear of
it till nearly fifty), he was still short of the grand climacteric, and
probably had never at any time been better worth knowing. He
had grown up among the Civil Wars, son of a moderate parlia-
mentarian, but educated in England by his grandfather, Dr. Hammond, a royalist divine; he had spent two years in France during
the early period of the *Grand Monarque's* reign, and had learnt to
use French like a witty Frenchman; he had travelled in the Low
Countries and Germany, and in Flanders had made himself master
of Spanish also. Then came years in London, the life of a well-
provided young man with literary tastes, as well as conspicuous
prowess at tennis, and a taste for deep play; but at twenty-seven
a romantic attachment which had lasted since he was twenty ended
in a happy marriage and he settled down in County Carlow near
the seat of his father, Sir John Temple, Master of the Rolls. After
the Restoration, father and son jointly represented County Carlow,
till Charles prorogued the Irish Parliament, and William Temple

with his family came over to London, strongly recommended by Ormond to the King's chief ministers. Clarendon never liked the fine young gentleman, but Arlington did, and it was Arlington who first gave him in 1665 what he had always desired, diplomatic employment. The nature of it makes one realize that a generation later he could describe adventures of his own that might belong to the D'Artagnan saga.

In 1665 England was at war with Holland. Between the Dutch and the growing power of France lay Flanders, on which Spain's hold was weakening, and also a huddle of tiny states. One of these, Münster, was governed by a Prince Bishop who, by his geographical situation, was well placed so as to fall upon the rear of the Dutch. This potentate sent a mysterious envoy looking like a carter, and speaking bad English, yet nevertheless an English gentleman who had turned Benedictine monk and had known Clarendon when he and Charles were at Cologne during their wanderings. The message was that for a matter of half a million rix-dollars the Bishop would invade the United Provinces with twenty thousand men. Encouragement was given; next came the Baron Wreden, a leading person at the Bishop's court, and with him the matter was arranged. There was hope of bringing in also a couple of allies, the Elector of Brandenburg and the Duke of Neuburg; but all was to be strictly secret. Is it not like an opening chapter in Dumas, setting the scene for the second, in which at four o'clock one morning, a messenger from Arlington calls Temple out of his bed, to come to Whitehall? There he is asked if he would undertake a secret service, not named, on which he must start in three or four days (Dumas would have made it hours). Temple answered that he could not decide without a friend's advice, but that if Arlington, as his friend, would advise him to accept, he was willing. " Accept then," said the Minister; and so the mission was unfolded. But Temple declined to take charge of anybody's money but his own, and a London alderman was found for this part of the job—who bought two ship-loads of tin which, sold at Antwerp, would provide the needful. A first instalment was paid, and when Temple, journeying by Brussels, met the Bishop, he found him anxious for a second. Matters were complicated, because half the tin with its ship foundered. Still, the invasion took place, though it did not produce startling results. Next year, France, friendly to the Dutch, declared war on England, and matters grew ticklish for England's allies. The Bishop began to think of a separate peace, and his Baron

Wreden ran across to England. This gentleman and Temple had seen a good deal of each other at Brussels ; Temple describes their intercourse :

The Baron of Wreden was, I think, twice a day of some old drunken philosopher's opinion, that the world was round, and in no further care for his master than drinking his health. . . . For my part, I came off still with colours flying, as every man may do that will fly with them himself. I am, I confess, ashamed to think how little honour our master will get by me ; but this infirmity God only can help, as Sancho says of his parents, for malice your Lordship could not believe it, if you knew how much pains I have taken with myself in this kind since I came over.

Temple, who loved wine like a Frenchman, had all a Frenchman's distaste for pottle-deep potations ; but he was too good a diplomat not to humour his colleagues, and here is a letter from him to Wreden then in England :

BRUSSELS. *Dec.* 10, 1665.

I Received yours, and am glad of your arrival at Court, where I never doubted the good Reception so honest a Gentleman would find, who came from so brave a Prince. I am sorry for your bad Wine and Lodging at Oxford. . . . In the mean while, take my word for the matter, 'tis but half a dozen glasses more, and good or bad, comes all to the same thing. As for your Lodging, in Troth, I believe the Crowd is so great at present in every House, that you will hardly find an opportunity of making Love to your Landlady. But, Sir, you must have a little Patience, and not think of succeeding in all Amours, at the rate you did with *Mademoiselle* Isabella ; besides, if you remember, it cost you dear enough then, by the Fright you were in, of losing your great Diamond. Love, like other things, is good for nothing when one makes too much haste in it ; and our English Ladies don't care that men should be over violent in beginning this game for fear they should be so in concluding it. . . . And is not this now a very fine Letter for two grave Ministers of State ? But come, we must talk a little of Business, if it be only for the good Grace of the Matter : And yet I am confident, if Sr *Bealing* would entertain you at this Rate but once a Month and unbend himself a little from his serious way, you would reckon him as your only Friend and think no more of me.

The letter was written in French and the original is better; yet the English is Swift's, who translated it for Temple's posthumous *Memoirs*. But is it not very clear that a clever young man would value infinitely the society of a chief who had so pleasant a wit, or such a tale to tell as followed in the correspondence ? For in April, 1666, Temple, under orders to go and see the Bishop, set out for Münster, secretly, as he had to cross several territories ; and

once more we are in full tide of Dumas or Sir Walter. Temple
wrote to his father :

BRUSSELS, *May* 10, 1666.

I went into *Dortmund,* and hearing there, that for five or six Leagues
round all was full of Brandenburg troops, I dispatcht away a *German*
Gentleman I had in my Train with a Letter to the Bishop of *Münster*
to let him know the Place and Condition I was in, and desire he would
send me Guards immediately, and strong enough to convey me. The
Night following, my messenger returned, and brought me Word, that
by Eight a-Clock the Morning after, a Commander of the Bishop's would
come in Sight of the Town at the Head of twelve hundred Horse, and
desired I would come and join them as soon as they appeared : I did
so, and after an easie March till four a-Clock, I came to a Castle of the
Bishop's, where I was received by Lieutenant General *Gorgas,* a *Scotchman*
in that Service, who omitted nothing of Honour or Entertainment that
could be given me. There was nothing here remarkable but the most
Episcopal Way of Drinking that could be invented. As soon as we
came to the Great Hall, where stood many Flaggons ready Charged ;
the *General* called for Wine to drink the King's Health ; they brought
him a formal Bell of Silver gilt, that might hold about two Quarts or
more ; he took it empty, pulled out the Clapper, and gave it me who
he intended to drink to, then had the Bell filled, drank it off to His Majesty's
Health, then asked me for the Clapper, put it in, turned down the Bell,
and rung it out to show he had playd fair, and left nothing in it ; took
out the Clapper, desired me to give it to whom I pleased, then gave his
Bell to be filled again, and brought it to me. I that never used to drink,
and seldom could try, had commonly some Gentlemen with me that
served for that Purpose when 'twas necessary ; so I had the Entertainment of seeing this Health go current through about a dozen Hands,
with no more Share in it than just what I pleased.

Next day he was met by the Bishop at the head of four thousand
horse, and conducted to Münster with such ceremony that he
suspected a disappointment ; and before the night was out, he had
learnt the secret. The Bishop under pressure from France had
made peace with the Dutch, but wanted to keep Temple " amused "
till the final payment of rix-dollars should be completed. Learning
this, the envoy kept his own counsel, slipped out of the palace
at night, got his horses, rode five-and-twenty miles to a village on
the frontier and pretended to go to bed (as indeed he would have
wished to do, the Bishop having constrained him to drink fair
with all the rest) ; but, getting fresh horses brought to the back
door, he rode till midnight so as to reach the territory of Neuburg.
Next day he made Düsseldorf by noon and borrowed a coach
from the Duke which got him to Brussels in time to stop the
payment.

This was adventure leading to nothing : but high politics

followed. In the intricate dealings of those years Temple grew clear that England's danger was from France, and that her interest lay in friendship with the Dutch, rivals though they were on the sea and in trade. The difficulty was that Charles II thought otherwise. But Temple had more than a moment of triumph, when by swift resolute action he put through the Triple Alliance between the Protestant powers of England, Holland and Sweden. Even though the work was undone in three years, Temple's prestige in the Low Countries lasted, and he was hardly less in favour with William Prince of Orange than with the Great Pensionary, de Witt.

But the reversal of all that his policy stood for caused his withdrawal from The Hague ; and there followed a period of retirement at Moor Park which he occupied by various literary works. Then he was sent again to the Congress of Nimeguen and in 1677 was fetched home to receive from Charles an offer of the Secretaryship of State—which he declined. Not many young men have found themselves, as Swift did, conversing with a statesman who has refused the highest office in his country.

Under James II Temple naturally could not serve, but there were friendly and loyal relations between him and his Sovereign. Probably for this reason he was not among those who dealt with the Prince of Orange to come over. Yet it was he who had made the match which gave William his chance ; and the new King, who would gladly have had his service as a minister, always treated him as a friend and counsellor.

Nothing could be more natural than that an ambitious youth coming as a dependent into the household of such a man should regard his patron with profound admiration, and there is not the least trace in Swift's correspondence that the dependency was made disagreeable, still less humiliating, to him. It is true that dependency of any sort was irksome to that savage pride ; but equally true that after he had secured a very decent competence in Ireland, he resigned it to return to Moor Park. How any intelligent man who ever read the pages of Swift's writings can believe that he not only submitted to but courted a menial situation, passes my comprehension ; but Macaulay either believed it, or wrote as if he did.

It is really necessary to get rid of some of the lumber—beginning with the legend that Swift was Temple's son. Swift was born in Dublin in 1667 when his mother had been for two years married. During these two years Temple was in the Low Countries chasing after the Bishop of Münster. So much for that. Why, then, did

Temple assume the charge of this young man in April, or May, 1689 ? In the first place, Swift was an Irish Protestant fleeing from the threat of what might happen when Catholics got the upper hand. People remembered only too well what had happened in 1641, not fifty years earlier : indeed they remembered it with wild exaggeration ; and Temple's father, Sir John, had written one of the lurid accounts. On the face of things, fugitive Protestants had a claim on English hospitality stronger than that of the Belgians in 1914. But Temple was not simply English. His branch of the family had settled in Ireland in the last days of Elizabethan conquest ; he drew revenues from land there ; he even held the post of Master of the Rolls, inherited from his father, though its duties were discharged by deputy. In all probability, during the years he lived in Carlow, he must have known Godwin Swift, who was Attorney-General in Ormond's palatinate—which included Carlow. His father, as Master of the Rolls, must also have come across the other Swift brothers of whom William and Adam were solicitors doing large business, one in Dublin, the other in Ulster. This is exactly borne out by Swift who in the *Account* says that he " was received by Sir William Temple, whose father had long been a great friend of the family " : it is also confirmed by Temple himself in a letter to which some preface is needed.

Symptoms of the disease which dogged Swift through life and finally destroyed him appeared during the first period of his residence at Moor Park. Doctors agree now that it was otosclerosis, a thickening in the labyrinth of the ear which causes dizziness and pain, " labyrinthine vertigo." But he himself attributed the trouble (in the *Account*) to a " surfeit of fruit before he was twenty years which caused him to contract a giddiness and coldness of stomach that almost brought him to his grave." (Elsewhere he is more specific and says that he ate a hundred golden pippins at a sitting.) Physicians in England " weakly imagined that his native air might be of some use to recover his health," and in 1690 he went back to Ireland with a letter from Temple to Sir Robert Southwell, who was then accompanying William III to Ireland as Secretary of State for that country.

Commending the young man, Temple wrote :

He was born and bred in Ireland, though of good family in Hereford-shire, was near seven years in the College of Dublin, and ready to take his degree of master of arts, when he was forced away by the desertion of that College upon the calamities of the country. Since that time he has lived in my house, read to me, writ for me, and kept all accounts as far as my small occasions required. He has Latin and Greek, some French, writes a very good and current hand, is very honest and diligent, and has good friends, though they have for the present lost their fortunes, in Ireland, and his whole family having been long known to me obliged me thus far to take care of him. If you please to accept him into your service, or upon any establishment of the College to recommend him to a fellowship there, which he has a just pretence to, I shall acknowledge it as a great obligation to me, as well as to him.

This letter was dated May 29, 1690—a month before the Battle of the Boyne restored the fortunes of the Swifts, as of all Protestants in Ireland. Southwell received the recommendation, which survived among his papers ; but nothing came of it, nor do we know anything of this visit to Ireland. Most probably Swift went north to his uncle Adam. All that his *Account* tells us is that " growing worse, he soon went back to Sir William Temple, with whom, growing into some confidence, he was often trusted with matters of great importance."

He had been in Ireland about a year and a half when he returned to his mother in Leicester, about August, 1691 ; stayed there, amusing himself (as will be seen) till December, when he set out for Moor Park, taking occasion on the way to stop at Oxford with his cousin, Thomas Swift, who, having also fled from Trinity College, had gone on to complete his academic career at Balliol. For the next two years and a half Swift was a member of the Moor Park household.

The heads of that household were Temple, his wife and his widowed sister. About Lady Temple, as Lady Temple, we know little ; but Mistress Dorothy Osborne is an adorable figure. She and her future husband met first in the Isle of Wight, when he was on his way to the Continent and she and her brother were bound for Guernsey to join her father who held it for the King—the King being at that moment Colonel Hammond's prisoner on the island. Young Osborne wrote with a diamond on the pane of the inn-window this verse : " And Haman was hanged on the gallows that he had prepared for Mordecai." Before they got away, the malignant sentiment was noted and reported to Hammond who arrested the party. Dorothy Osborne, trusting to a gentleman's gallantry, stepped forward and took the writing on herself. She got them off and that was the beginning of Temple's admiration. We have a series of the letters she wrote to him during their long attachment, full of gaiety, wit and devotion. Since then, forty years had gone by ; she had lost all her children, the last of them, her only son, most tragically, by suicide, only in the very summer before Swift first came to Moor Park. But it is hard to believe that anything could have altered that lovely nature in its essentials ; and if to have high-placed friends makes a woman worth knowing, she was the close ally and correspondent both of William and Mary.

Lady Giffard, Temple's sister, was her brother's adoring intimate. Indeed the household revolved in worship about its centre, who, as Lady Giffard wrote in her " Character " of him, " was all the life of his family, that looked as if they had no life when he was out of it, which no man, I believe, ever was so seldom." This a little suggests Letitia Dale writing of Sir Willoughby. Yet by a consent of testimony, the man had charm, which lingers in his writings, and kindness—which his treatment of a most difficult inmate does not contradict.

If we try to see Swift against this background, through the help of his own writings, we must remember that then, and at no other period of his life, we see him posturing : trying to get outlet for something formidably strong in him that seeks expression. Later, when he has found his medium, one would as soon talk of a blacksmith posturing with his hammer, or a swordsman with his sword. But for the moment he was writing verses and something of the poetaster disfigured even his letters. He was long coming to himself, like the best wine, which is the least palatable before time mellows it. Yet the expert can detect even in its crudity what is to come.

CHAPTER III

SWIFT'S EARLY POEMS

NOBODY has hitherto been able to read with pleasure Swift's early poems. Yet their turn may come ; they are completely intellectual, devoid of spontaneous emotion, and destitute of lyrical flow. Commending them for these qualities to lovers of recent verse, I propose to consider them as biographical material : for Swift, like all young poets, was thinking always about himself when he wrote.

The first of them was, the title says, " written at Moor Park in June, 1689," when Swift had been for some few weeks an inmate of Temple's house ; and it has been construed as a needy youth's attempt to win favour with his patron. Those who think so must be odd judges of human nature. Neither at two-and-twenty nor at two-and-forty was Swift capable of interested adulation ; but at two-and-forty he showed himself easily, perhaps too easily, drawn into hero-worship, and what he admired then was the honest statesman, the man who understood subtleties of government, but was personally incorrupt. It would be strange indeed if the same admiration had not kindled when he met for the first time a man of European reputation whose whole way of life gave example of indifference to the rewards of power. The " Ode to the Hon. Sir William Temple " shows us what was moving in the young man's mind and what the elder man was pouring into it.

Temple piqued himself on virtue and on philosophy, which in that age meant moral philosophy of a Roman cast ; a philosophy derived from the practice of life, but inspired by the ancient classics. He had always been bookish, but always contemptuous of book learning divorced from experience. Cambridge pleased him so little that he left the University after two years—a bond of sympathy with the Dublin student whose bachelor's degree came only *speciali gratiâ*.—So the Ode begins with lusty denunciation of " mere learning " :

Nature's fair table-book, our tender souls,
We scrawl all o'er with old and empty rules,
    Stale memorandums of the schools :
    For learning's mighty treasures look
      Into that deep grave, a book ;
    Think that she there does all her treasures hide,
And that her troubled ghost still haunts there since she died ;
Confine her walks to colleges and schools ;
    Her priests, her train and followers, show
    As if they all were spectres too !
    They purchase knowledge at th' expense
    Of common breeding, common sense,
    And grow at once scholars and fools ;
    Affect ill-manner'd pedantry,
Rudeness, ill-nature, incivility.

First and last, Jonathan Swift had no use for the abstract, and its votaries the schoolmen ; but not less was his distaste for ignorance. It was not easy to find the accomplished gentleman who was also scholar and statesman ; yet at the very gate of entry on to life, that marvel met him.

    Those mighty epithets, learned, good, and great,
    Which we n'er join'd before, but in romances meet,
    We find in you at last united grown.

A young man's hero-worship is not less real because its expression sounds bombastic ; and we learn clearly for what qualities Temple wished to be admired. Not for martial heroism : the old Roman

    saved his country by delays,
      But you by peace.
    You bought it at a cheaper rate ;
    Nor has it left the usual bloody scar,
    To show it cost its price in war.

First and last, Swift had no admiration for the soldier as soldier, and no satire in *Gulliver* is better directed than that against military glory. Yet he was Marlborough's contemporary.

It was not with tales of war that Temple charmed his pupil, but with exposure of

    The wily shafts of state, those jugglers' tricks,
    Which we call deep designs and politics. . . .

    Great God ! (said I) what have I seen !
      On what poor engines move
    The thoughts of monarchs and designs of states !

Swift was to say that again in *Gulliver*, in a very different fashion.

But for my present purpose, importance lies in the close of the poem, since that has to do not with Temple, but with Swift. He offers to his patron the tribute of admiring envy:

> Shall I believe a spirit so divine
>   Was cast in the same mould as mine?
> Why then does Nature so unjustly share
> Among her elder sons the whole estate,
>   And all her jewels and her plate?
> Poor we! cadets of Heaven, not worth her care,
> Take up at best with lumber and the leavings of a fare.

It will be noted that the poet writes much better when he is writing about himself; and also that his complaint is not of his endowment from Nature but of the occupation to which he is consigned:

> Some she binds 'prentice to the spade,
>   Some to the drudgery of a trade:
> Some she does to Egyptian bondage draw,
> Bids us make bricks, yet sends us to look out for straw:
>   Some she condemns for life to try
> To dig the leaden mines of deep philosophy:
> Me she has to the Muse's galleys tied;
> In vain I strive to cross the spacious main,
>   In vain I tug and pull the oar;
>   And when I almost reach the shore,
> Straight the Muse turns the helm, and I launch out again:
>   And yet to feed my pride,
> Whene'er I mourn, stops my complaining breath,
> With promise of a mad reversion after death.

Here we have it: a furious ambition for fame, and the conviction that if fame is to be achieved he must achieve it as a poet.

> Nature the hidden spark did at my birth infuse,
> And kindled first with indolence and ease;
>   And since too oft debauch'd by praise,
> 'Tis now grown an incurable disease:
> In vain to quench this foolish fire I try
>   In wisdom and philosophy:
>   In vain all wholesome herbs I sow,
>   Where nought but weeds will grow;
>   Whate'er I plant (like corn on barren earth)
>   By an equivocal birth,
>   Seeds, and runs up to poetry.

We seldom think of Swift as a poet; but he himself always did; as one—so he put it in "A Rhapsody" (written when he was sixty-six)—"Whom Phœbus in his ire Has blasted with poetic fire," and so debarred from all hope of advancement. But to come back to 1689: it is very probable that Temple accepted with indulgent complacency "this worthless verse, the tribute of a humble Muse"; and not at all probable that he discerned (as we can do, who know the finished outcome) the strength of an athlete, with no ear for music, attempting a complicated dance. In any case, the long discipleship had begun. It went on uninterrupted for a year, during which the young man, in Temple's own words, "read to me, wrote for me, and kept all accounts as far as my small occasion required"; acted in short, as what Temple recommended him for to Southwell—"a gentleman to wait on you." The words are misleading to our ideas or notions. Very much the same would have been asked of a domestic chaplain—or of Will Wimble in Sir Roger de Coverley's household (that is, supposing that Will Wimble could read and write). Such positions were accepted in those days without a thought of degradation. In this case the idea of a menial status cannot be reconciled with what appears in a letter from Swift, written in May, 1692, which speaks of frequent conversation with "the unhappy Bishop of Ely about two or three years ago," as a result of which "half a promise" had to be given to the Bishop that a poem should celebrate Archbishop Sancroft. This can only have been at Moor Park in Swift's first year there.

There is also in the same letter (to his cousin, Thomas Swift, then at Balliol) this curious phrase: "I remember when I used the Court above two years ago, I heard very much the complaint you make of too many foreign counsellors about the King." Elrington Ball infers that "Swift had been one of the crowd of solicitants who hung about Court circles in the hope of obtaining employment." This again could only have been from Moor Park and with some kind of introduction from Temple.

The relation between Swift and his employer changed after the young man's first absence in quest of health; he was more on the footing of a confidential secretary. The first letter of his which is preserved dates from after his return, and it contains much that is of interest—including the glimpse of an episode which fills up the picture of his youth.

In the summer of 1691 he had gone to his mother in Leicestershire and had once more, it would seem, made her so anxious by a flirtation, that her brother-in-law, the Rev. John Kendall, Vicar of Thornton, ten miles from Leicester, wrote to him about it. Swift's reply begins with a very definite declaration:

As to that of my great prospects of making my fortune, on which as your kindness only looks on the best side, so my own cold temper, and unconfined humour, is much greater hindrance than any fear of that which is the subject of your letter, I shall speak plainly to you, that the very ordinary observations I made with going half a mile beyond the University, have taught me experience enough not to think of marriage till I settle my fortune in the world, which I am sure will not be in some years ; and even then myself I am so hard to please that I suppose I shall put it off to the other world.

One need not take too seriously such resolutions of a gentleman not yet four-and-twenty ; but they are worth remembering. What follows tells a great deal more.

How all this suits with my behaviour to the woman in hand you may easily imagine, when you know that there is something in me which must be employed, and when I am alone turns all, for want of practice, into speculation and thought ; insomuch that in these seven weeks I have been here, I have writ, and burnt and writ again, upon almost all manner of subjects, more perhaps than any man in England. And that is it which a person of great honour in Ireland (and who was pleased to stoop so low as to look into my mind) used to tell me, that my mind was like a conjured spirit, that would do mischief if I would not give it employment. It is this humour that makes me so busy when I am in company, to turn all that way ; and since it commonly end in talk, whether it be love, or common conversation, it is all alike. This is so common, that I could remember twenty women in my life, to whom I behaved myself just the same way ; and I profess without any other design than that of entertaining myself when I am very idle, or when something goes amiss in my affairs. This I always have done as a man of the world, when I had no design for any thing grave in it, and what I thought at worst a harmless impertinence. But, whenever I begin to take sober resolutions, or, as now, to think of entering into the Church, I never found it would be hard to put off this kind of folly at the porch.

First of all, then, in the seven weeks since his return to Moor Park, he had been writing furiously—stimulated, perhaps, by the days spent at Oxford with his cousin Thomas Swift, another would-be poet. Secondly, it is, I think, implied, that when he returned to Ireland he had been regarded with interest as the associate of King William's intimate friend. Whoever the " person of great honour " may have been, he was at least a person of discernment. Thirdly, we have it here set down that Swift always sought women's society as an amusement and had the usual young man's desire to be distinguished by particular notice.—Fourthly, this dates for us his definite choice of a profession.

There is no indication that his studies at the university had any particular purpose beyond that of obtaining a degree. All his Irish kindred were in the law, but he never appears to have looked that way. The obvious career for him lay in the Church ; his father's father, grandfather and great-grandfather had all been clergymen, and also one of his father's brothers : but Temple's recommendation of him to Southwell does not suggest that in 1690 he had the Church in view. It would be insincere to say that he had begun to feel a vocation ; and just as misleading to hint that he was conquering a reluctance. What seems plain is that he felt the need of employment.

The rest of the letter must now be given. Youthful though its wisdom sounds, it makes plain that the grim realism of " household thoughts " was with this young man from the beginning.

Besides, perhaps, in so general conversation among that sex, I might pretend a little to understand where I am when I go to choose for a wife ; and though the cunningest sharper of the town may have a cheat put on him, yet it must be cleanlier carried on than this which you think I am going to top upon myself. And truly, if you knew how metaphysical I am that way, you would little fear I should venture on one who has given so much occasion to tongues ; for, though the people is a lying sort of beast, and I think in Leicester above all parts that I ever was in, yet they seldom talk without some glimpse of reason, which I declare, so unpardonably jealous I am, to be a sufficient cause for me [not] to have any woman any farther than a bare acquaintance, except all things else were agreeable, and that I had mathematical demonstration for the falsehood of the first, which if it be not impossible, I am sure is very like it. Among all the young gentlemen that I have known to have ruined themselves by marrying, which I assure you is a great number, I have made this general rule, that they are either young, raw, and ignorant scholars, who, for want of knowing company, believe every silk petticoat includes an angel ; or else they have been a sort of honest young men, who perhaps are too literal in rather marrying than burning, and so entail a misery on themselves and posterity, by an over-acting modesty. I think I am very far excluded from listing under either of these heads. I confess I have known one or two men of sense enough, who, inclined to frolics, have married and ruined themselves out of a maggot ; but a thousand household thoughts, which always drive matrimony out of my mind whenever it chances to come there, will, I am sure, fright me from that ; besides that I am naturally temperate, and never engaged in the contrary, which usually produces those effects.

The truth is that Swift was of a cold temper, and never ridden by any of the various desires which push men into marriage. What possessed his mind was literary ambition, and it took now the oddest outlet. John Dunton, a speculative bookseller, publisher and writer, had launched an "Athenian Society" for the general advancement of learning—issuing periodically the *Athenian Mercury* —a sort of "Notes and Queries." Some talk of the venture had reached Swift in Ireland, but during his visit to Oxford, "a very learned gentleman" produced two or three of the numbers; and at Moor Park he found all four with their supplements. Indeed, Dunton says that Temple had corresponded with him. At all events, Swift decided to honour the Society with an Ode, which he hoped (not in vain) to see prefixed to its next publication. It was, so far as I can ascertain, his first appearance in print; and if tradition is right, this effusion came to the notice of Dryden, then the acknowledged literary dictator. Dryden was nephew to Elizabeth Dryden, Swift's grandmother, and it may be that on the strength of this relationship, the younger man ventured to call his attention to this work, and came to town for a verdict. He got it—whether at Wills's coffee-house or elsewhere: "Cousin Swift, you will never be a poet." If indeed it was this Ode that Dryden saw, one may excuse him for a failure to detect any kind of promise. Nothing else in Swift's early poems is so fit to be scoffed at.

The rebuff rankled, as was inevitable, for, incredible as it seems now, the young man had flung his whole energy into this absurd composition. I must give almost in full a letter to his cousin at Oxford, dated May 5, 1692, which seems to me of capital importance to a biographer. Incidentally it discloses the hero-worship of Temple, and also a state of relations between the secretary and his chief which gives the lie direct—if indeed that were necessary—to Macaulay's rhetoric. But the main interest is the glimpse of a great writer in the making.

It makes me mad to hear you talk of making a copy of verses next morning, which though indeed they are not so correct as your others are, is what I could not do under two or three days, nor does it enter into my head to make anything of a sudden but what I find to be exceedingly silly stuff, except by great chance. I esteem the time of studying poetry to be two hours in a morning, and that only when the humour sits, which I esteem for the flower of the whole day, and truly I make bold to employ them that way, and yet I seldom write above two stanzas a week—I mean such as are to any Pindaric ode—and yet I have known myself in so good a humour as to make two in a day, but it may be no more in a week after, and when all is done I alter them a hundred times; and yet I do not believe myself to be a laborious dry writer, because if the fit comes not immediately, I never heed it, but think of something else. And besides, the poem I writ to the Athenian Society was all rough drawn in a week, and finished in two days after, and yet it consists of twelve stanzas and some of them above thirty lines, all above twenty, and yet it is so well thought of that the unknown gentlemen have printed it before one of their books, and the bookseller writes me word that another gentleman has in a book called the *History of the Athenian Society* quoted my poem very honourably—as the fellow called it—so that perhaps I was in a good humour all the week ; or at least, Sir William Temple speaking to me so much in their praise made me zealous for their cause, for really I take that to be a part of the honesty of poets that they cannot write well except they think the subject deserves it.

But that itself will not always hold, for I have had an ode in hand these five months inscribed to my late Lord of Canterbury, Dr. Sancroft, a gentleman I admire at a degree more than I can express, put into me partly by some experience of him, but more by an unhappy reverend gentleman, my lord Bishop of Ely, with whom I used to converse about two or three years ago, and very often upon that subject, but I say, I cannot finish it for my life, and I have done nine stanzas and do not like half of them. . . .

I have a sort of vanity or *foiblesse*, I do not know what to call it, and which I would fain know if you partake of it : it is—not to be circumstantial—that I am overfond of my own writings ; I would not have the world think so, for a million, but it is so, and I find when I write what pleases me I am Cowley to myself and can read it a hundred times over. I know it is a desperate weakness, and has nothing to defend it but its secrecy, and I know farther that I am wholly in the wrong, but have the same pretence, the baboon had to praise her children, and indeed I think the love in both is much alike, and their being our own offspring is what makes me such a blockhead. I am just the same to yours, and though I resolve to be a severe critic yet I cannot but think I see a thousand beauties, and no faults in what you take any pains about, for as to the rest I can easily distinguish when either of us have been idle. I am just so to all my acquaintance : I mean in proportion to my love of them, and particularly to Sir William Temple. I never read his writings but I prefer him to all others at present in England, which I suppose is all but a piece of self-love, and the likeness of humours makes one fond of them as if they were one's own. . . .

We have the Ode on Sancroft, carried to the end of a twelfth stanza and stopping there unfinished. I incline to think that what stopped it was Dryden's *obiter dictum*. Swift did not then or thereafter accept Dryden's verdict ; he continued to write verse, but there were no more Pindarics. What is more, he took example from the hand that chastened him. His " Ode to King William," though dull, is at least straightforward stuff written in the ten-syllabled quatrain which Dryden had used in his " Annus Mirabilis." Swift's only other poems of this period employ the heroic couplet with which Dryden's fame is specially associated ; and in one of these we begin to discover the man of genius.

These were verses " To Mr. Congreve," and they illustrate much more than Swift's slow development as a writer. In the maturity of his powers he had such a generous freedom from jealousy as is rare and edifying; yet it is more surprising to find it here in the ambitious young man of genius who had been completely out-distanced by one younger still. Two years divided their ages and when Swift left Kilkenny at fourteen it is not likely he knew much of Congreve, the youngster of twelve. When Congreve entered Trinity as a freshman Swift was already in his fourth year; but sixteen is much nearer eighteen than twelve to fourteen, and the gap was always lessening through the four years they were in college together. Then the Revolution scattered them, and Congreve went to London and the law—but not much more seriously than Thackeray's Mr. Pendennis. He wrote and success came prompt and dazzling; Dryden had a greeting for his verses very different from what was given to " cousin Swift." He was fully established as a poet before his comedy *The Old Bachelor* was accepted—just about the time when Swift's unlucky verses to the Athenian Society were making their bow to the world. By November, 1693, when Swift sat down (for the third time) to accomplish " this offering long designed to Congreve's fame," the *Double Dealer* had been produced, and met a somewhat doubtful reception. Rumour of this reached Moor Park and Swift wrote to his cousin, then in London, to know " how it succeeded; because my sending these to Mr. Congreve depends upon the issue."

" These " were meant to be printed in front of the play, but it does not appear that they were ever sent. Possibly Swift learnt that the *Double Dealer*, when it came to be printed, would have no less a man than Dryden blowing the preliminary trumpet. What we do know for certain is that friendship between the old schoolfellows never weakened and that later, when Congreve had become simply an amiable man about town, much concerned to hold on to a Government place, Swift, rapidly rising not only into fame but power, could serve his friend, and did so.

The Swift of 1710 was indeed almost incredibly different from the writer of these " two hundred and fifty lines, not Pindaric " —about Congreve. Yet already in this poem the unsuccessful poet knew himself a satirist; already indeed he was proving himself one, when he sketches for his friend " those you so ignobly stoop to fear "—

> For, could you think? the fiercest foes you dread,
> And court in prologues, all are country bred;
> Bred in my scene, and for the poet's sins
> Adjourn'd from tops and grammar to the inns;

Those beds of dung, where schoolboys sprout up beaux
Far sooner than the nobler mushroom grows ;
These are the lords of the poetic schools,
Who preach the saucy pedantry of rules.

Apparently one such had made his way back to his native Farnham
and roused Swift's fury by modish prate.

Last year, a lad hence by his parents sent
With other cattle to the city went ;
Where having cast his coat, and well pursued
The methods most in fashion to be lewd,
Return'd a finish'd spark this summer down,
Stock'd with the freshest gibberish of the town ;
A jargon form'd from the lost language, wit,
Confounded in that Babel of the pit. . . .
What bungling, rusty tools are used by fate !
'Twas in an evil hour to urge my hate,
My hate, whose lash just Heaven has long decreed
Shall on a day make sin and folly bleed,
When man's ill genius to my presence sent
This wretch, to rouse my wrath, for ruin meant ;
Who in his idiom vile, with Gray's-Inn grace,
Squander'd his noisy talents to my face ;
Named every player on his fingers' ends,
Swore all the wits were his peculiar friends ;
Talk'd with that saucy and familiar ease
Of Wycherly, and you, and Mr. Bayes :
Said, how a late report your friends had vex'd,
Who heard you meant to write heroics next ;
For tragedy, he knew, would lose you quite,
And told you so at Wills's but t'other night.

Two of these lines have often been quoted :

My hate, whose lash just Heaven has long decreed
Shall on a day make sin and folly bleed.

This is good rhetoric, and it may be granted freely that no man
ever wielded a fiercer lash than Swift. Yet, did sin and folly bleed
for him ? Three or four years later, when this same writer had
found his proper medium, and discovered with it his supreme
quality of humour, which persistently applies to rhetoric the dis-
concerting contact of realities, here is how we find him writing
in *A Tale of a Tub*—

I have observ'd some Satyrists to use the Publick much at the Rate
that Pedants do a naughty Boy ready Hors'd for Discipline : First
expostulate the Case, then plead the Necessity of the Rod, from great
Provocations, and conclude every Period with a Lash. Now, if I know

any thing of Mankind, these Gentlemen might very well spare their Reproof and Correction : For there is not, through all Nature, another so callous and insensible a Member as the *World's Posteriors*, whether you apply to it the *Toe* or the *Birch*.

That is the genuine Swift; what we meet in the lines to Congreve is only a poor foretaste. Indeed throughout the greater part of the poem we find much of the earlier " Pindaric " exaggeration, though expressed in the more disciplined form. Yet there is also unmistakable the real voice. " An old unvanquished pride, That looks with scorn on half the world beside," and " my resentment's weight "—these were to be the characters, the stigmata, by which Swift's shade would go always marked among the immortals.

One more of these poems remains to be considered, and it is almost of the same date, December, 1693, and " occasioned by Sir William Temple's late illness and recovery." As so often happens in literary life, the Muse holds dialogue with her servant. Why should he look doleful when everyone is rejoicing ? There had been a bad moment :

> Mild Dorothea, peaceful, wise, and great,
> Trembling beheld the doubtful hand of fate ;
> Mild Dorothea, whom we both have long
> Not dared to injure with our lowly song ;
> Sprung from a better world, and chosen then
> The best companion for the best of men :
> As some fair pile, yet spared by zeal and rage,
> Lives pious witness of a better age ;
> So men may see what once was womankind,
> In the fair shrine of Dorothea's mind.

That, one may say incidentally, is the only allusion made by Swift to Lady Temple, and the most significant thing it conveys is that he liked her too well to write Pindarics about her. But the poem goes on :

> Grief flung sables on each menial look ;
> The humble tribe mourn'd for the quick'ning soul,
> That furnish'd spirit and motion through the whole.

This is exactly, though in Pindaric phrase, Lady Giffard's account of Temple's position in his household. Why then, since Temple has recovered, does his secretary look sad ? Now the poet has his innings, and if I construe it rightly, here is a farewell to poetry ; at all events, it is a disenchanted, disillusioned young man who girds at the Muse.

> Malignant goddess! bane to my repose,
> Thou universal cause of all my woes;
> Say whence it comes that thou art grown of late
> A poor amusement for my scorn and hate.

What has she to do, lingering perversely?

> Wert thou right woman, thou shouldst scorn to look
> On an abandon'd wretch by hopes forsook. . . .
> For let Heaven's wrath enlarge these weary days,
> If hope e'er dawns the smallest of its rays.
> Time o'er the happy takes so swift a flight,
> And treads so soft, so easy, and so light,
> That we the wretched, creeping far behind,
> Can scarce th' impression of his footsteps find.

His farewell to the Muse was bringing him much nearer to attainment of poetry than he had come before:

> To thee I owe that fatal bent of mind,
> Still to unhappy restless thoughts inclined;
> To thee, what oft I vainly strive to hide,
> That scorn of fools, by fools mistook for pride;
> From thee whatever virtue takes its rise,
> Grows a misfortune, or becomes a vice.

Two more lines stand out:

> Since thy few ill-presented graces seem
> To breed contempt where thou hast hoped esteem.

It is not surprising to learn that a breach with his patron impended; but for the moment Swift must only vent his spleen upon his imaginary mistress:

> Madness like this no fancy ever seized,
> Still to be cheated, never to be pleased;
> Since one false beam of joy in sickly minds
> Is all the poor content delusion finds.
> There thy enchantment broke, and from this hour
> I here renounce thy visionary power;
> And since thy essence on my breath depends
> Thus with a puff the whole delusion ends.

It was a painful separation: but Swift and the Pindaric Muse were well rid of one another.

CHAPTER IV

LAST YEARS OF DISCIPLESHIP

SWIFT'S second residence at Moor Park, though it ended in discontent, began happily. The letters to his cousin at Oxford are those of a young literary aspirant free to follow his bent. Moreover, in the first summer after his return, a pleasant way was found to complete his equipment for a profession. The universities of Oxford and Cambridge have always accepted students from Dublin *ad eundem gradum*, and Swift therefore was in a position to get his master's degree without crossing the channel. Certain formalities had to be fulfilled : Dublin must provide a *testimonium* showing that his terms of residence and examinations entitled him to sit for the degree. St. George Ashe, his old tutor, was now returned from Vienna and had been promoted to the Provostship ; yet it seems that friendly offices were needed to stir up the authorities, and on November 29, 1692, Swift wrote a grateful letter to his uncle William. The letter tells so much that it must be given in full :

SIR,
My sister told me you was pleased (when she was here) to wonder I did so seldom write to you. I hope you have been so kind to impute it neither to ill-manners or want of respect. I always have thought that sufficient from one who has always been but too troublesome to you. Besides, I knew your aversion to impertinence ; and God knows so very private a life as mine can furnish a letter with little else, for I often am two or three months without seeing any body besides the family ; and now my sister is gone, I am likely to be more solitary than before. I am still to thank you for your care in my *testimonium* ; and it was to very good purpose, for I never was more satisfied than in the behaviour of the University of Oxford to me. I had all the civilities I could wish for, and so many showed me favours, that I am ashamed to have been more obliged in a few weeks to strangers, than ever I was in seven years to Dublin College. I am not to take orders till the King gives me a prebendary ; and Sir William Temple, though he promises me the certainty of it, yet is less forward than I could wish, because I suppose he believes I shall leave him, and, upon some accounts, he thinks me a little necessary [at present]. If I were [affording] entertainment, or doing you any satisfaction by my letters, I should be very glad to

perform it that way, as I am bound to do it by all others. I am sorry my fortune should fling me so far from the best of my relations; but hope that I shall have the happiness to see you sometime or other.

On June 14, 1692, Swift was incorporated a member of Oxford University from Hart Hall (now Hertford), which from its antiquity enjoyed a precedence in the right of inscribing strangers on its books. Three weeks later, on July 5, he received his master of arts degree. Some oral examination or disputation had to be passed, and in May he had written to his cousin of Balliol, "I have got up my Latin pretty well and am getting up my Greek, but to enter upon courses of Philosophy is what I protest I will rather die in a ditch than go about." Few people who contemplate this way of decease are called on to undergo it, and Swift was not one of them. On the contrary, he was evidently treated as a brilliant young man coming from an elder statesman's household, to which William III was an occasional visitor.

When or how often William came to Moor Park, we do not know. But, as most people have heard, he offered Temple's secretary the captaincy of a troop of horse—and also taught him the Dutch way of eating asparagus. This story rests on the authority of Deane Swift and may be believed, not because Deane Swift is a good witness, but because he is very unlikely to have invented the asparagus. If, however, by November, 1692, Swift had, as he told his uncle, the promise of a prebend from William, one may fairly assume that the military offer had been made earlier; had the two been offered as alternatives, Swift's sense of humour would have preserved the fact.

There is, however, one instance in which we know definitely that there was a meeting between the King and this seeker for preferment, and it did not take place at Moor Park. In the spring of 1693 there was serious perturbation at Court because a Bill for Triennial Parliaments had passed and only needed the royal assent, which the King was afraid to give. Portland, the most trusted minister, was sent down to Moor Park where Temple lay at this time in the illness which occasioned Swift's poem. Temple's argument against those who had persuaded Portland "that King Charles the First lost his crown and his life by consenting to such a bill," failed to convince the Dutchman; accordingly, being unable to leave his bed, he decided to put the case to William through his secretary. "Whereupon," says Swift's *Account*:

Mr. Swift was sent to Kensington with the whole account of the matter in writing to convince the King and the Earl how ill they were informed. He told the Earl, to whom he was referred by his majesty (and gave it in writing), that the ruin of King Charles the First was not owing to his passing the triennial bill, which did not hinder him from dissolving any parliament, but to the passing of another bill, which put it out of his power to dissolve the parliament then in being, without the consent of the house. Mr. Swift, who was well versed in English history, although he was under twenty-one years old, gave the King a short account of the matter, but a more large one to the Earl of Portland; but all in vain. For the King by ill advisers was prevailed upon to refuse passing the bill. This was the first time that Mr. Swift had ever any converse with courts, and he told his friends it was the first incident that helped to cure him of vanity.

"Twenty-one years old" is wrong: he was then over five-and-twenty. But we may trust entirely his recollection of the shock to his confidence in his power of reasoning, and the disappointment to high hopes. Every young man builds castles, and doubtless Swift set out that day for the ride to London counting on the achievement of an important mission, beyond which lay ample fulfilment of promises that were slow to mature.

He was not good at forgetting, and till far on in life he was again and again to expect and be deceived. But specially then, living at Moor Park, and seeing nobody but the family for months on end, he had too much chance to brood. A healthy young man need not have been pitied for such a period, but Swift was never healthy. His body was strong enough, and he had a passion for violent exercise; Temple, a great enthusiast for riding and walking, must have approved of a secretary who made little of tramping the thirty-eight miles to London and who at this time and later frequently made his journeys to Leicester or Oxford on foot, sleeping where he found a cheap lodging (but, for he was always fastidious in cleanliness, paying twopence for clean sheets). At Moor Park he used twice a day to leave his books and run up a hill some distance from the house, covering the half-mile in six minutes. This was the only break in reading for far too many hours a day. Many young men live just as unwisely and thrive on it; but the fits of giddiness and deafness to which Swift had been subject since he grew up were, as we know now, symptoms of structural malformation near the brain. Whether long-continued and intense mental activity heightened the sufferings which resulted, or whether the most lethargic blockhead similarly malformed would have been condemned to the same slowly increasing tortures, doctors may decide: but one thing is certain. All the miseries of Jonathan Swift's life, and they were many, came from his brain. That is true in more senses than one, yet how far they are connected, again the doctors must determine. The complex of cells which housed that powerful intellect had grit in its machinery : yet the mind-force which drove the machine poured power in ceaselessly, observing, grouping, deducing, always confident that clear reason could reach a practical conclusion, yet always angry, seeing reason thwarted by flaws in the very stuff of humanity.

Naturally enough, with such a disposition Swift throughout his life avoided solitude. He loved company ; and at Moor Park the only adult society was that of three people, all of them forty years older than he. They could teach him much, but they could not give him companionship. He found that, however, in the strangest way.

Lady Giffard kept in her employment one Mrs. Johnson, widow of a man who had been Temple's confidential servant. With Mrs. Johnson lived her two daughters, of whom the elder, Esther (called Hetty), was only eight years old when Swift first came to Moor Park.[1] Whether as one of his duties, or by his own inclination, the young man of two-and-twenty began teaching the pretty, clever child her lessons. " I think," he says, in his *Journal* to her (chaffing her because Harley had taken her hand for his), " I was MD's writing-master." This is Macaulay's " flirtation in the servants' hall." The only justification for the phrase is that first and last Swift loved playing tutor to women, young or old. His own recollection is inaccurate, as so often, about dates, but is none the less significant : he thought she was six years old when they first grew acquainted. That stamps this impression of their early relationship. When he came back after his first absence, she was between ten and eleven, and until she was thirteen he had the teaching of her—a plump little black-haired creature, with big eyes. But manifestly the fondness had been there from the first ; the " little language," kept up forty years later (" Nite deelest logues," and so forth), belongs to a time when Stella had difficulty not only about spelling words, but even about saying them.

God only knows what springs of tenderness were let loose in that strange young man who had, properly speaking, never had a home ; who never had a child, and who, so far as we know, never even tolerated any child but this one. God only knows what this outlet in baby talk was worth to his fierce, chafing intelligence. What it was worth to the other human being concerned, is another

[1] The name Stella was invented much later. For reasons which are considered later (at p. 80), it seems probable she was Temple's child.

reckoning; she paid in heart-burning. But he gave her immortality, and if she stands the test of that formidable gift better than many heroines (even when we know them in far less detail), it is surely fair to say that he deserves some credit for her instruction. Her praise comes to us with most authority from her teacher and her lover, who tells us nearly all we know about her—except the thing which is of all the most eloquent. She went to her grave carrying a secret that he wished her to keep, and not all the innumerable researches of curiosity have been able to wrest it from her, dead or living.

There is no secrecy about their early days at Moor Park; it is only Macaulay's imagination that disfigures so simple a relation. Still, we do not know a great deal; but when Jonathan Swift departed in anger from Moor Park, he left, one may be sure, a small girl crying her big eyes out. One may be pretty sure also that the young man of seven-and-twenty was too much engrossed with his own anger to take notice.

The break was made early in May, 1694, and it is not hard to account for. Swift chafed, not unnaturally, to find himself still at seven-and-twenty a dependant with no profession. Only one profession was really in his mind—the Church; and Temple was probably loath to press the King for a fulfilment of the promise —if indeed promise there had been. Plainly there was a scene of expostulation, and Temple met the demand by an offer. His father had been granted the Mastership of the Rolls in Ireland for two lives (according to a practice frequent in that age) and Temple, now Master, though discharging the duties by deputy, held the patronage. There was a clerkship worth £120 a year vacant; Swift could have this. Thereupon the young man answered that this offer removed a scruple. " Since he had now an opportunity of living without being driven into the Church for a maintenance, he was resolved to go to Ireland and take holy orders." These are his own words in the *Account*. It seems unreasonable to assume that Temple made the offer expecting a refusal. The equivalent in our money would be about three hundred a year, a very useful provision for a man without ties who desires to be a writer. But at all events on June 3 Swift wrote to his cousin Deane, who had joined Willoughby in Portugal, a letter which makes it plain that the parting was on bad terms, and that the plunge was a desperate one; since he expressed a wish to obtain even a chaplaincy to the settlement at Lisbon.

After a stay of some weeks with his mother in Leicester, this candidate for orders crossed the channel. But difficulties presented themselves. Marsh, then Archbishop of Dublin, demanded testimony of the candidate's behaviour in the years since he left the University and the city in which he was brought up; and would take no man's word but Temple's—as indeed was not unreasonable. Swift had to humble himself, and he did so with an abasement that gives the measure of the wound to his pride.

> The sense I am in, how low I am fallen in your Honour's thoughts [he writes] has denied me assurance enough to beg this favour, till I find it impossible to avoid.

Then, after a statement of the reasons which make it necessary, comes this:

> I entreat that your Honour will consider this and will please to send me some certificate of my behaviour during almost three years in your family; wherein I shall stand in need of all your goodness to excuse my many weaknesses and follies and oversights, much more to say anything to my advantage. The particulars expected of me are what relate to morals and learning, and the reasons of quitting your Honour's family, that is, whether the last was occasioned by any ill actions. They are all entirely left to your Honour's mercy, though in the first I think I cannot reproach myself any farther than for infirmities.
>
> This is all I dare beg at present from your Honour, under circumstances of life not worth your regard. What is left of me to wish, next to the health and felicity of your Honour and family is, that Heaven would one day allow me the opportunity to leave my acknowledgments at your foot for so many favours I have received, which, whatever effect they have had upon my fortune, shall never fail to have the greatest upon my mind, in approving myself, upon all occasions.
>
> Your Honour's most obedient and most dutiful servant.
>
> J. SWIFT.

This, preserved among Temple's papers, was endorsed by Lady Giffard, or her nephew, "Swift's penitential letter." We have not Temple's reply, but he sent speedily what was desired. Had he rubbed salt into the sore, it is not believable that the two could have met again. Neither is this "penitential" letter to be judged by our standards. The usage of the day sanctioned if it did not prescribe an extravagance of deference in expression; Temple himself on his first mission to Flanders, after begging Arlington to take particular care of his concerns, ends a letter with this surprising sentence:

> The reason which must bear me out in all troubles I give you is, my lord, to tell you a truth that you are one of those great persons whom I do not only honour and esteem but love too, if you will give

me leave to say so, and you must esteem it no presumption since God Almighty himself commands we should love him as well as honour him and serve him.

In short, I believe that Temple did not consider Swift's tone unsuitably abject: the young man had administered discipline to himself, and undoubtedly smarted under it; but what followed later proves, I think, that neither the young man nor the elder lost the other's respect. Without an apology Temple would certainly not have opened his doors again to Swift; but when the apology was made, he accepted it like a gentleman, and in so doing made reconciliation possible.

For the present, however, Swift was thrown on his own resources. These must have included some influence with the Irish government; for within a fortnight after his ordination as priest he was appointed (on January 28, 1695) by the Lords Justices, of whom Lord Capel was the chief, to the prebend of Kilroot, comprising three parishes on the northern shore of Belfast Lough, beyond Carrickfergus. Antrim is now the most Protestant of Irish counties; the proportion of Catholics was probably even smaller then. But the mass of the people were dissenters of one type or another, and the Episcopalian clergy had small congregations. There is a tradition that Swift tried to gather them by inviting them to see him skip stones in the sea: and possibly legend has preserved some early touch of his irony. It would have been like him to say, and even to prove, that a hundred would come to watch him play the fool when scarcely a dozen would muster for his preaching. In any case, as Craik has justly said, the story is worth referring to because it shows the effect of Swift's personality in Ireland. Wherever he went he was remembered; and if memory failed, legends were built up to replace it.

What we actually know about this period of his life concerns itself chiefly with the family of the Rev. Roger Waring, rector of Donaghcloney. Two young Warings, nephews of this man, had been Swift's contemporaries in Trinity, and acquaintance may have come through them; or again during his first absence from Moor Park, he may have met the son, Westenra Waring, who entered college in 1691. At all events, it is indisputable that he fell in love with Miss Jane Waring, and wanted her to marry him. She, however, was a lady who enjoyed delicate health (the old phrase exactly expresses it) and also conformed to the fashion of the time, which prescribed that lovers should be treated scornfully. So much we can gather from the letter dated April 29, 1696, in

which Swift demanded that she should make up her mind definitely.
Such at least is the purport of the epistle : but frankly the impression
produced is that of playacting :

> Would to Heaven you were but a while sensible of the thoughts
> into which my present distractions plunge me ; they hale me a thousand
> ways, and I not able to bear them.   It is so, by Heaven : the love of
> Varina is of more tragical consequence than her cruelty.

He too wanted to be in the fashion ; this was the style of lovers
in contemporary romances—just as the poems he had been writing
were drenched in the dregs of Cowley's popular vintage.   However,
it was plainly an offer of marriage, with every suggestion that he
had received encouragement, and with hints that only his lack of
means made him unsure of acceptance.   There is no allusion to
the fact that the lady had a small fortune of her own ; but Swift
certainly would not have risked himself so far had he not known
this.   Yet I do not for an instant believe that he expected anything
to come of the letter.   It was the romantic and poetic way of conveying that he meant to accept an invitation to return to Moor Park.
At this point the letter leaves heroics and becomes lucidity itself.
He awaits her answer " with a world of impatience," since he is
prepared to set out for England in a fortnight.

> How far you will stretch the point of your unreasonable scruples
> to keep me here, will depend upon the strength of the love you pretend
> for me.   In short, Madam, I am once more offered the advantage to
> have the same acquaintance with greatness that I formerly enjoyed, and
> with better prospect of interest.   I here solemnly offer to forgo it all
> for your sake.   I desire nothing of your fortune ; you shall live where
> and with whom you please till my affairs are settled to your desire, and
> in the meantime I will push my advancement with all the eagerness and
> courage imaginable, and do not doubt to succeed.

Long pages more of rant follow ; but through them pierces the
conviction that if " in one fortnight he must take eternal farewell
of Varina," he is resigned to the sacrifice.

But, as there was no formal engagement, so there was no formal
rupture : and persons who knew them both, including Swift's
uncle Adam, who had a house in Waring's parish, believed that
some attachment or understanding continued.   In any case the
last was not heard of the matter for a long time, and I shall have
to return to an episode which shows us the least likeable aspect of
a great man.

On the other hand, a very different trait of Swift's character
now got the first chance we know of to disclose itself.   First and

last, he never neglected an opportunity to serve a friend. It is true, he seldom omitted to strike an enemy when he could; yet this was generally with the pen : his marks of friendship were more substantial. In this case, the letter to Varina tells us that if Lord Capel, who was reported ill, did not die, Swift would make his journey by Dublin and pay " a visit of leave." Since he owed his preferment to Capel, that was a proper courtesy; but almost certainly he had in mind to secure the reversion of his prebend to Mr. Winder, a neighbouring clergyman, who, he says in his *Account*, " was reckoned a man of sense and piety and was besides encumbered with a large family." At all events, through whatever means, he accomplished the object, and could write to Winder from Moor Park, showing his satisfaction and also much practical kindliness. Most of his library had been left, to be sent on later, and he wanted Winder to keep some volumes—among them Temple's *Miscellanea* " which is a good book, worth your reading." A bundle of sermons also had been left and these Winder proposed to forward, having taken copies. Swift pooh-poohed this. " They were what I was firmly resolved to burn and especially some of them, the idlest trifling stuff that ever was writ, calculated for a church without a company, or a roof." He never valued himself on his pulpit eloquence. Also, Winder had come on certain " letters to Eliza. They were writ in my youth. Pray burn them." (Mr. Ball conjectures that the heroine may have been Miss Betty Jones, to whom during his stay at Leicester, before he first went to Moor Park, he paid attentions which made his mother anxious.)

Out of all this we may build up some picture of the young clergyman to whom in his thirtieth year, had come, as he told Varina, an offer " to have the same acquaintance with greatness as I formerly enjoyed, and with better prospect of interest." The letter proves that he had not outgrown certain affectations and even egregious absurdities. Intellectually he was still unripe; the fruit had not developed its savour and was full of crude juices. His ambition was dominant as ever; the very offer to surrender those prospects as a proof of his devotion makes it plain how he rated them; it was the most romantic gesture he could conceive. Yet in itself it showed that the form of that ambition was altering. If he was to be a poet, why not follow poetry in the seclusion of Kilroot? Something was now in view for which " acquaintance with greatness " would be of service. In short, at the back of his mind, there was dawning the idea of power.

All this is young-mannish; but one of the letters to Winder, concerning money due from his glebe tenants, shows already a shrewd capacity to deal with business, strictly but generously. In such matters his judgment was mature. What is more, one feels a new tone in the correspondence. He is a man standing on his own feet, invited to be Temple's companion and assistant, but no longer dependent on him. Without Temple's help he had gained a secure competence; at Temple's request he had given it up. One of the letters refers to this " resignation and the noise it made among you," which shows that it seemed to others a rash step; but he was obeying the impulse of his own ambition, yet without the fear that he put himself at any man's mercy. At Moor Park he would certainly meet people who could be of use to him, and if Temple failed to secure him material advantages—as he did fail—Swift knew by this time that his personal qualities would make their own way—as they made it. We are far now from the mood when his Muse must hear of " ill-presented graces " that " bred contempt where they had hoped esteem." Belfast, then a country town of third order, even for Ireland, offered little choice of society, but its great folk were the Chichester family, and the letter to Varina makes plain that he was already on friendly terms with Lady Donegal—whom long after he was to celebrate in verse.

Moreover, although we do not know the terms of Temple's invitation, one fact, whether it was mentioned or not, must have been present to Swift's mind. Lady Temple had died in 1695, and she was not one who could pass away and leave no gap. There was a chance to do kindness merely by giving the widower the companionship he desired. Under these conditions, Swift could be content and even happy in Temple's house. Beyond doubt it added to his happiness that Stella was now a young woman, so much a new creature that long after he could write :

> Since first I saw you at sixteen,
> The brightest virgin on the green,

as if the early childish association had been blotted out; and, indeed, doubtless, in a sense it was. Later still when her dead body lay in another house, and he found what solace he could in recollection, he recalled her as being counted " one of the most beautiful, graceful and agreeable young women in London—" only " (he adds with characteristic ruthlessness) " a little too fat."

All we know about these London doings is what can be inferred from a letter written in the early spring of 1698 when Czar Peter the Great was on his visit to England. Swift was at Moor Park while the family was at Temple's house in "the Pell Mell." The letter has come down to us without an address, and the best opinions hold that it was sent to Stella's mother; but beyond all doubt it was meant for Stella's reading. It is how Swift wrote to Stella and to nobody else—though all his letters to her were, so to say, written to be read in company. It is not so intimate in its foolishness as the *Journal* of 1710, but already there are touches of the same whimsical tenderness. You can see him already, as he describes himself later, pursing up his mouth for a kind of baby talk about Lady Giffard's pet bird:

> I received your kind letter from Robert by word of mouth, and think it a vast condescension in you to think of us in all your greatness. Now shall we hear nothing from you for five months but "we courtiers." Loory is well and presents his humble duty to my Lady, and love to his fellow-servant; but he is the miserablest creature in the world, eternally in his melancholy note, whatever I can do, and if his finger does but ache, I am in such a fright you would wonder at it. . . .
>
> Nothing grows better by your absence but my Lady's chamber floor, and tumble-down Dick. . . . Mr. Mose and I desire you will remember our love to the King, and let us know how he looks. Robert says the Czar is here, and is fallen in love with you, and designs to carry you to Muscovy; pray provide yourself with muffs and sable tippets, &c.
>
> Æolus has made a strange revolution in the rooks' nests; but I say no more, for it is dangerous to meddle with things above us. I desire your absence heartily, for now I live in great state, and the cook comes in to know what I please to have for dinner: I ask very gravely what is in the house, and accordingly give orders for a dish of pigeons, or, &c. You shall have no more ale here unless you send us a letter. Here is a great bundle and a letter for you; both came together from London. We all keep home like so many cats.

That is a happy letter, the first in his correspondence which could be called so. He had now companionship of a creature he loved, and it was no longer a child's company. Passages in the *Journal to Stella* imply that there was an equality of friendship even in those days. "I am thinking," he writes to her in 1710, "what a veneration we used to have for Sir William Temple because he might have been Secretary of State at fifty." Again in 1711: "Don't you remember how I used to be in pain when Sir William Temple used to look cold and be out of humour for three or four days and I used to suspect a thousand reasons? . . . I have plucked up my spirits since then, faith: he spoiled a fine gentleman." I doubt whether at any time Swift would have let any other person but Stella know that he was "in pain" for any such reason. These few careless words tell us that to her his most intimate mind lay always open, as much when he was still to some degree in tutelage, and she only a girl in her teens, as a dozen years later when he was fiercely asserting himself among ministers of State.

Such passages have often been quoted for another purpose, to illustrate Swift's feeling towards his patron; and it is clear that even in the later period the younger man was never wholly at his ease. But it seems to me not less clear that the cause was not fear of anger, but in reality an excess of veneration, which it is implied that Stella shared. The old potentate kept his household in subjection, yet not, I think, by severity. He imposed himself; he created an adulatory atmosphere. If this was the defect of his qualities, his qualities were real; and there is no reason to doubt that when he was in good humour he could be excellent company. One glimpse of the household at Moor Park must be quoted from these stray recallings of common memory in the *Journal.* Swift had been seeing much of the Lord Treasurer Harley, in October, 1712. " I was playing at one-and-thirty with him and his family t'other night. He gave us all twelve pence apiece to begin with. It put me in mind of Sir William Temple." For once Scott, of all men, puts the wildest misconstruction on Swift's meaning. " Sir William's stingy patronage seems," he wrote, " to have justified this sarcasm." The last thing in the world that Swift would have done would be to accuse Harley of meanness. What he does convey is the picture of a pleasant intimate family gathering when the head of the household insists that they shall have a flutter and he will set them up in stakes. Old times at Moor Park were brought back to Swift's mind, by an evening spent in the house of the man who beyond all men—rightly or wrongly—he loved and admired.

But in plain truth, the best proof of Swift's feeling towards Temple is the tribute of discipleship, shown in trivial matters as well as things that go down to the very roots. Their minds were congenial, though their tempers were not. Temple imparted to Swift his own very remarkable culture and much that was wise in his philosophy of government. Negatively, too, the completeness of the influence may be traced in a recurrence of the same limitations, in culture and in speculative thought.

I take first the similarity of tastes. It was probably with Temple that Swift acquired his admiration for the French genius : it must certainly have been there that he gained a command of the French language remarkable in one who never set foot on the Continent. This was equipment. In a matter of mere liking (which indeed connected itself with the cult of France) they were both temperate men, but Temple, so Lady Giffard notes, " loved the taste of good wines, and those that were least kind to him, and drank them constantly, though not above three or four glasses." Swift was always fastidiously interested in what he drank ; Moor Park was a good school for that. Another characteristic, unmistakably acquired, was the taste for gardening and the form it took. Temple laid out at Moor Park a garden in the Dutch style with canals and other ornamental water ; we find Swift doing the very same thing as soon as he got a piece of ground at his disposal ; later in life, when he was not planning the like for himself, he was pressing it on the friends to whose houses he paid long visits. With the disciple as with the master, horticulture was, in the first instance, garden planning ; in the second, it was the care for procuring choice vegetables and fruits. Flower-beds, Temple tells us, might be left to the ladies ; but the pride of his heart were his grapes, his apricots and his walls with trees trained to a perfection that Evelyn has commemorated. Swift according to the measure of his opportunity sought to emulate these excellencies on his little glebe at Laracor, in ' Naboth's Vineyard ' outside the Deanery of St. Patrick's, and later, at Sheridan's house in Cavan.

What he learnt to admire at Moor Park he never ceased to admire ; what he did not learn to admire there, he never noticed. Temple, who had travelled widely, wrote amongst other things of architecture ; but you may search his writings for one word about Rouen or Chartres or Nôtre Dame. He might conceivably have developed in Swift what was by nature deficient there, a sense of beauty ; what he did foster was a sense of order and of elegance, and also an extreme fastidiousness. He was, his sister notes, " sensible extremely to good air and good smells, which gave him so great an aversion to the town that he once passed five years at Sheen without seeing it." Swift could not imitate this avoidance, but in the abominations which his satire so copiously recorded there is even a disgusting insistence on stench.

On the intellectual side, Swift owed much to his patron's political philosophy, which is most succinctly expressed in the Maxims included in the second volume of Temple's *Miscellanies*.

Avoid innovations in ancient and established Forms and Laws, especially those concerning Liberty, Property and Religion, which are the possessions men ever have most at heart.

This is the creed of a Tory, but a Tory who values liberty. "Strenuum pro virili libertatis vindicatorem" was the description of himself which Swift, a Tory assuredly, desired to be set over his grave.

Again in Temple's "Essay on the Origin and Nature of Government" we read:

"The ground upon which all government stands is the consent of the people, or the greatest and strongest part of them."

Swift was to give Temple's principle unforgettable expression when he wrote in the Drapier's famous Fourth Letter: "Government without the consent of the governed is the very definition of slavery."

Lastly, we can form some notion of Temple's philosophy of life from the "Heads designed for an Essay on Conversation," which Swift as his literary executor included in the third volume of *Miscellanea*. These counsels were certainly not lost on the man whom Addison, Arbuthnot, Harley and Bolingbroke took to be the best company rather than the most brilliant talker of his time.

In conversation, Humour is more than Wit, Easiness more than Knowledge; few desire to learn, nor think they need; all desire to be pleased, or if not, to be easy.

Of excellencies that make Conversation, good Sense and Good Nature the most necessary, Humour the pleasantest.

A little Vein of Folly or Whim pleasant in Conversation, because it gives a Liberty of saying things that discreet men, tho' they will not say, are willing to hear.

Then comes a word of guidance which assuredly Swift laid to heart.

Bluntness and plainness in a Court, the most refined Breeding. Like something in a Dress that looks neglected and yet is very exact.

Finally, and at the core of the matter, we have these two sentences:

The greatest Pleasure of Life is Love; the greatest Treasure is Contentment; the greatest Possession is Health; the greatest Ease is Sleep; and the greatest Medicine is a true Friend. Something like Home that is not Home, like Alone that is not Alone; to be wished and only found in a Friend, or in his House.

Swift had a genius for friendship hardly second to his genius for literature; and such expressions of Temple's mind are sufficient assurance that the admiration for his patron which Swift publicly expressed was a most genuine sentiment. If the petulant fits and starts of a fierce-tempered and impatient young man show us the seamy side of their companionship, I think Swift meant no less than he said when, introducing Temple's literary remains, he spoke of this "great and good person."

As to the more technical side of their association, Swift was learning his trade as a writer in the workshop of an admitted master, to whom he paid full tribute. " It is generally believed," he wrote, " that this author has advanced our English tongue to as great a perfection as it can well bear."

Yet long before he set down the words in the Introduction to Temple's work, Swift himself had given Temple evidence of a prose style entirely beyond the elder man's compass. For in the years between 1696 and 1699, he was writing his *Tale of a Tub*. Whether Temple saw it, is uncertain ; but undoubtedly he was shown a smaller masterpiece, since that formed part of a controversy into which he had been drawn.

In 1690 the second part of Temple's *Miscellanea* was published, containing an essay on " Ancient and Modern Learning " which spoke disparagingly of the moderns. In 1694 there came a reply from Wootton and three years later a second edition of Wootton's book appeared with an appendix by Bentley, who proved that the Fables of Æsop and the Epistles of Phalaris, which Temple had chosen as the fine flower of classic literature, were not " classics " at all, but mediæval forgeries. Thereupon the Honourable Charles Boyle entered the lists against Wootton and his more formidable ally. The whole episode has been carefully discussed (for instance in Jebb's ' Bentley '), and need not be elaborated here. Yet it should be observed that Temple's controversy shows him to have been without appreciation of real learning. Swift's mind was infected with the same slighting attitude towards knowledge that lay outside his own range of study. On this particular occasion, however, recognition of the strong points in his opponent's case was no more to be expected from Swift than from an advocate in the law courts. He plunged lightheartedly into the fray, caring no more for argument than Aristophanes did when he wrote the " Frogs."

What I propose to consider is not the quarrel, in which (to use Swift's phrase) " whole rivulets of ink have been exhausted," but this triumphant *jeu d'esprit*, where, quite literally, a great wit is at play. It is the transition from a would-be poet to a genius whose true medium was prose, yet who had developed in the practice of verse that power of fertile illustration which never left him. Indeed, when he set himself to write " Thoughts " in the manner of La Rochefoucauld, what we get is nearly always an image condensed into a witticism ; for instance ' Old men and comets have been reverenced for the same marks, their long beards and their pretences to foretell events.' Nothing goes to waste in a born writer's self-imposed apprenticeship, and Swift, an omnivorous reader, had found at last the true way to utilize all that had fed his wide-ranging curiosity. Later, life itself was to supply the material on which his imagination worked; but here he comes capering like a young race-horse from his pasture among books: every motion instinct with energy and grace.

Let us come to the plot of this excellent invention, beginning with the causes of the battle:

This Quarrel first began (as I have heard it affirmed by an old Dweller in the Neighbourhood) about a small Spot of Ground, *lying* and *being* upon one of the two Tops of the Hill *Parnassus*; the highest and largest of which, had it seems, been time out of Mind, in quiet Possession of certain Tenants, call'd the *Antients*; And the other was held by the *Moderns*. But, these disliking their present Station, sent certain Ambassadors to the *Antients*, complaining of a great Nuisance, how the Height of that Part of *Parnassus*, quite spoiled the Prospect of theirs, especially towards the *East*; and therefore to avoid a War, offered them the Choice of this Alternative; either that the *Antients* would please to remove themselves and their effects down to the lower Summity, which the *Moderns* would graciously surrender to them, and advance in their Place; or else, that the said *Antients* will give leave to the *Moderns* to come with Shovels and Mattocks, and level the said Hill, as low as they shall think it convenient. To which, the *Antients* made Answer: How little they expected such a Message as this, from a Colony, whom they had admitted out of their own Free Grace, to so near a Neighbourhood. That, as to their own Seat, they were *Aborigines* of it, and therefore, to talk with them of a Removal or Surrender, was a Language they did not understand. That, if the Height of the Hill, on their side, shortened the Prospect of the *Moderns*, it was a Disadvantage they could not help, but desired them to consider, whether that Injury (if it be any) were not largely recompenced by the *Shade* and *Shelter* it afforded them. That, as to the levelling or digging down, it was either Folly or Ignorance to propose it, if they did, or did not know, how that side of the Hill was an entire Rock, which would break their Tools and Hearts; without any Damage to itself. That they would therefore advise the *Moderns*, rather to raise their own side of the Hill, than dream of pulling down that of the *Antients*, to the former of which, they would not only give Licence, but also largely contribute.

In that should be observed first of all the indirect compliment to Temple, who in his " Essay on Ancient and Modern Learning " had laid down that all knowledge came from the East—(out of Chaldæa into Egypt and so to Greece and Rome); and next, the ingenuity and ease with which the metaphor is followed into all its applications. The same completeness of imagination was ultimately to make Lilliput and Brobdingnag as present to our minds as if we had visited them. Then remark the writing. There is trace of Temple in the measured, deliberate movement; but we come on the greater master when suddenly the tone changes and a sort of growl comes into the voice, which, taking a few words from the commonest speech, warns the pioneers that they will "break their Tools and Hearts."

But to pick up the story: "There appearing no end of the Quarrel, the Books in St. James's Library, looking upon themselves as Parties principally concerned, took up the Controversie," because the Librarian, Bentley, had maltreated the Ancients and even threatened to throw some of them, (Æsop to wit, and Phalaris), on the dust-heap. For it must be remembered:

In these Books, is wonderfully instilled, and preserved, the Spirit of each Warrior, while he is alive; and after his Death, his Soul trans-migrates there, to inform them. This, at least, is the more common Opinion. But, I believe, it is with Libraries, as with other Cœmeteries, where some Philosophers affirm, that a certain Spirit, which they call *Brutum hominis*, hovers over the Monument, till the Body is corrupted, and turns to *Dust*, or to *Worms*, but then vanishes or dissolves: So, we may say, a restless Spirit haunts over every *Book*, till *Dust* or *Worms* have seized upon it; which to some, may happen in a few Days, but to others, later.

There is an echo here of the most famous passage in Milton's *Areopagitica*; but the *Brutum hominis* comes from Thomas Vaughan's *Anthroposophia Theomagica*. This young man had no taste for meta-physics, but he had dabbled in the cabalists and other strange stuff.

While the angry volumes come bursting from their shelves, and the Ancients, advised by Temple (chief of those Moderns who fled over to that party, in which he had "been educated and long conversed"), were drawing together, there happened the incident of the bee caught in a spider's web which is described in an apologue so famous that one need hardly quote from it. The spider, who stands for the moderns, claims that "this large castle (to shew my Improvement in the Mathematicks) is all built with my own Hands, and the Materials extracted altogether out of my own Person"; while his intruding adversary has nothing but "a pair of wings and a Drone-Pipe." "I am glad," answered the Bee, "to hear you grant at least, that I am come honestly by my Wings and my Voice, for then, it seems, I am obliged to Heaven alone for my Flights and my Musick."

Is not that a poet's answer?—is it not a poet who completes it in the last sentence of the apologue, putting it into the mouths of the Bee's party?

For the rest, whatever we have got, has been by infinite Labor, and search, and ranging thro' every Corner of Nature: the Difference is, that instead of Dirt and Poison, we have rather chose to fill our Hives with Honey and Wax, thus furnishing Mankind with the two Noblest of Things, which are Sweetness and Light.

Then we come to the battle, which after epic fashion begins with a scene at the Court of Jupiter, who, having decided on his purpose, transmits his message to " certain of those light nimble Gods, his ministring Instruments in all Affairs below."

They travel in a Caravan, more or less together, and are fastened to each other like a Link of Gally-slaves, by a light Chain, which passes from them to *Jupiter's* great Toe: and yet in receiving or delivering a Message, they may never approach above the lowest Step of his Throne, where he and they whisper to each other thro' a long hollow Trunk. These Deities are call'd by Mortal Men, *Accidents* or *Events*; but the Gods call them, *Second Causes*.

And now the fight begins, and the young race-horse curvets and gambols. Homer is at the head of the ancient cavalry, but Virgil shines on the left wing and seeks an object worthy of his valour:

When behold, upon a sorrel Gelding of a monstrous Size, appear'd a Foe, issuing from among the thickest of the Enemy's Squadrons; But his Speed was less than his Noise; for his Horse, old and lean, spent the Dregs of his Strength in a high Trot, which tho' it made slow advances, yet caused a loud Clashing of his Armor, terrible to hear. The two Cavaliers had now approached within the Throw of a Lance, when the Stranger desired a Parley, and lifting up the Vizard of his Helmet, a Face hardly appeared from within, which after a pause, was known for that of the renowned *Dryden*. The brave *Antient* suddenly started, as one possess'd with Surprize and Disappointment together: For, the Helmet was nine times too large for the Head, which appeared Situate far in the Hinder Part, even like the Lady in a Lobster, or like a Mouse under a Canopy of State, or like a shrivled Beau from within the Pent-house of a modern Periwig; and the Voice was suited to the Visage, sounding weak and remote. *Dryden* in a long Harangue soothed up the good *Antient*, called him *Father*, and by a large deduction of Genealogies, made it plainly appear, that they were nearly related. Then he humbly proposed an Exchange of Armor, as a lasting Mark of Hospitality between them. *Virgil* consented (for the Goddess *Diffidence* came unseen, and cast a Mist before his Eyes) tho' his was of Gold, and cost a hundred Beeves, the others but of rusty Iron. However, this glittering Armor became the *Modern* yet worse than his own.

That was how Swift paid back his cousin : and apart from the buffoonery there is a real stab, in the description of Dryden's high-trotting steed, the heroic couplet.   Another literary debt is paid, but one of gratitude.   Pindar, " never advancing in a direct line, but wheeling with incredible Agility and Force," made terrible Slaughter, " till Cowley advanced on the other Side, imitating his Address and Pace, and Career, as well as the Vigour of his Horse and his own Skill would allow."   This availed the modern nothing ; a monstrous javelin cast would have done Cowley to death; but he had divine attendance ; and even when the Ancient had " cleft the wretched Modern in twain," Venus picked up one half of the severed volume, " and wash'd it seven times in Ambrosia, then struck it thrice with a sprig of Amarant ; upon which, the Leather grew round and soft, and the Leaves turned into Feathers, and being gilded before, continued gilded still ; so it became a Dove, and she harness'd it to her Chariot."

This of course implies the verdict that Pope summed up later in a couplet on Cowley—

> Forgot his epick, nay, Pindarick Art,
> Yet still we love the language of his heart.

Temple perhaps was of Pope's opinion, and Swift here conforms to it in what was written as a superb compliment to the Champion of the Ancients.   But when he published this performance, a note was added—

I do not approve the Author's Judgment in this, for I think Cowley's Pindaricks are much preferable to his Mistress.

Though he had renounced Pindaricks for himself, he was constant in devotion to the model which he had failed to imitate.   It is worth remarking that in the mock heroic passages of this effusion, he still writes poetry, but conceals it.   The concluding simile, which describes the fate of Bentley and Wootton, impaled together on Boyle's lance, is almost continuously in blank verse.

As, when a skilful Cook has truss'd a Brace of Woodcocks, He, with Iron Skewer, pierces the tender Sides of both, their Legs and Wings close pinion'd to their Ribs ; So was this pair of Friends transfix'd, till down they fell, joyn'd in their Lives, joyn'd in their Deaths ; so closely joyn'd that *Charon* would mistake them both for one, and waft them over Styx for half his Fare.

Manifestly this exquisite piece of invention was undertaken for the author's own delight; but it was designed to please Temple, and we may suppose it pleased him. Yet we must also suppose that Swift wished it to be published; and published it was not till six years later. There is only one conceivable reason for the delay, —that Temple wished it. In March, 1698, writing to a friend, in high praise of Boyle's answer to Bentley, he alludes to something " undertaken without my knowledge which I afterwards diverted, having no mind to enter the List with such a mean, Dull, Unmannerly Pedant."

Now, Swift had here a real grievance. Literary reputation was what he desired for its own sake and what would be of most use to him. Yet nowhere in his Letters is there any trace of a complaint. He was as little disposed to quarrel about his own work as any author that ever lived; moreover, he was never in a hurry. By his own account, the much more important work which now occupied him was completed before Temple died; but he kept it by him another six years.

Meantime, he lived at Moor Park, transcribing and revising Temple's manuscripts, writing, reading enormously, and bursting out of doors, once before dinner, once after, to race up his hill and back again; until by the end of 1698, the old man's health failed and the secretary kept a journal of his illness. The last entry reads : " He died at one o'clock this morning, the 27th of May, 1699, and with him all that was good and amiable among men."

As Forster says, Swift never altered that estimate, though once more it has to be said, a meaner man would have paraded grievances. His sister wrote :

My poor brother has lost his best friend Sir William Temple, who was so fond of him whilst he lived, that he made him give up his living in this country, to stay with him at Moor Park and promised to get him one in England. But death came in between, and has left him unprovided both of friend and living.

All the positive benefit that Swift received was under Temple's will which " beside a legacy, left him the care, trust and advantage of publishing his posthumous writings." The works brought him an appreciable sum, but after labour spread over some years; and they brought him unpleasantness with Lady Giffard and Temple's heir.

He left Moor Park in short at two-and-thirty little richer than he had come there at two-and-twenty; but intellectually and socially having acquired priceless advantages. Perhaps, considering all things, he was not sorry to be able to say that materially he owed Temple little; pride was always on the defensive in this relation.

Yet it is true that Temple was the first of Swift's notable friends, and perhaps the one of all who did most for him. He sent him out into the world accomplished and mature for all life's uses.

Thirty years later, when *Gulliver* had brought Swift to the height of fame, Mr. Flower, afterwards Lord Castledurrow, recalled in a letter his own schoolboy impression of Temple's secretary. Flower, whose mother was a Temple, had been staying at Sheen in Temple's house, and was committed to Swift's care from Sheen to London. " We took water at Mortlake," he writes; " the commander of the little skiff was very drunk and insolent, put us ashore at Hammersmith, yet insisted on his fare, which you courageously refused; the mob gathered "—and the boy expected every moment to see the parson stripped of his gown and tossed in it for want of a blanket; " but " (and he quotes Virgil about a crowd submitting to a man *pietate gravem ac meritis*) " by your powerful eloquence you saved your bacon and money, and we happily proceeded on our journey." It is a first glimpse of the dean who could stop a faction fight in Dublin simply by appearing in the street. Authority was Swift's natural inheritance.

CHAPTER V

ENTRY INTO THE WORLD

TEMPLE'S death left Swift provided with the modest legacy
of a hundred pounds, a literary job of importance and profit,
the publication of his patron's posthumous works, and, further,
with expectations of preferment. How far these last were justified
cannot be ascertained; the significant fact is that they were disappointed, and that for the next fifteen years, the most brilliant
period of his existence, disappointment continued to be his portion.
The reason lay in his character; pride was at the root of all. Very
justly he rated his own abilities high; but a sanguine temper led
him to count on material rewards to match them. Thus he was
never in reality disinterested; yet in an age when all rewards came
by interest, he was too proud to solicit, believing ingenuously
that other men would do for him, to their own credit, what he
could not do for himself without a sense of degradation. Men
of energy and active imagination often make the same mistake.
Benevolence for them is what Hobbes called it, "a love of
power and delight in the exercise of it," and to Swift himself the
sight of a young man with talent needing help was a positive
temptation which he never resisted when he had power at command.
Naturally then, convinced of his own genius, he was convinced
that others would make efforts to give it full scope. Cynics could
have taught him that energy of any kind is uncommon, and benev-
olent energy much rarer; but Swift, like the gentleman in Molière,
expected too much of human nature and ended in misanthropy.

It is best to follow his own account of what happened, because,
even if inaccurate in some respects, it lets us see into his mind.
Upon Temple's death, according to the *Account*, " Mr. Swift removed to London and applied by petition to King William upon
the claim of a promise his Majesty had made to Sir William Temple
that he would give Mr. Swift a prebend of Canterbury or Westminster." This petition was entrusted to the Earl of Romney
who promised to second it, but " said not a word to the King. . . .
Mr. Swift having totally relied on this lord's honour and neglected

to use any other instrument of reminding his Majesty of the promise, after long attendance in vain, thought it better to comply with an invitation given him by the Earl of Berkeley."

The Lord-Lieutenancy being then in commission, Berkeley had been appointed one of the Lords Justices in whom it was vested, and went to Dublin early in September, 1699, having Swift with him; so that the "long attendance in vain" may have lasted six months. The first and worst part of the disappointment was that this Irish-born lover of England was constrained to fall back on the country of his birth. But though he came there under distinguished auspices, having his residence either in the Castle or at the Lodge in Chapelizod, which was the official residence out of town, there were more rebuffs. He had counted on being secretary. The *Account* says :

Another person had so far insinuated himself into the earl's favour, by telling him that the post of secretary was not proper for a clergyman, nor would be of any advantage to one who aimed only at church preferments, that his lordship after a poor apology gave that office to the other.

In some months the Deanery of Derry fell vacant; and it was the Earl of Berkeley's turn to dispose of it. Yet things were so ordered that the Secretary having received a bribe, the Deanery was disposed of to another, and Mr. Swift was put off with some other church livings not worth above a third part of that rich Deanery; and at this present time, not a sixth: namely the Rectory of Agher, and the Vicarage of Laracor and Rathbeggan in the Diocess of Meath; for which his letters patent bear the date 24th February following. The excuse pretended was his being too young, although he was then thirty years old.

In the following year, Marsh, Archbishop of Dublin, added to these preferments the small prebend of Dunlavin and on October 22, 1700, Swift first took his seat in the Chapter of St. Patrick's Cathedral, whose name he was to make famous throughout the whole world.

It was not riches, as the deanery would have been; and he thought that riches were his due. But it was a settlement in life, Laracor and its allied parishes bringing in about £200 a year, and Dunlavin adding another £60. The equivalent to-day would be at least £750. Report of it, perhaps exaggerated, spread to County Antrim, and Varina once more appears. She and Swift had continued to exchange letters, and their relations were still undefined. Now, some two or three months after his appointment to the livings in County Meath, she wrote complaining, got an answer which did not give her satisfaction, complained again, and received an icy ultimatum, which comes to this : "I will marry, if you are prepared to face cheerfully a difficult union; but I have no wish to persuade you into it." The best-natured man could hardly say such a thing agreeably and Swift when angry was anything but good-natured. A biographer who suppressed his reply would undoubtedly be leaving out a disagreeable wart on the countenance. Yet, knowing only of the lady what we can read through the lines of this letter and the earlier one, I think Varina must have been a very trying person. Here are the essential passages:

The letter you desired me to answer I have frequently read, and thought I had replied to every part of it that required it; however, since you are pleased to repeat those particulars wherein you desire satisfaction, I shall endeavour to give it you as well as I am able. You would know what gave my temper that sudden turn, as to alter the style of my letters since I last came over. If there has been that alteration you observe, I have told you the cause abundance of times. I had used a thousand endeavours and arguments, to get you from the company and place you are in; both on the account of your health and humour, which I thought were like to suffer very much in such an air, and before such examples. All I had in answer from you, was nothing but a great deal of arguing, and sometimes in a style so very imperious as I thought might have been spared, when I reflected how much you had been in the wrong. The other thing you would know is, whether this change of style be owing to the thoughts of a new mistress. I declare, upon the word of a Christian and a gentleman, it is not; neither had I ever thoughts of being married to any other person but yourself. I had ever an opinion that you had a great sweetness of nature and humour, and whatever appeared to the contrary, I looked upon it only as a thing put on as necessary before a lover; but I have since observed in abundance of your letters such marks of a severe indifference, that I began to think it was hardly possible for one of my few good qualities to please you.

What follows indicates that in the earlier letters he had inquired as to her means, and that she now reproached him with fortune-hunting and further accused him of understating his own. It shows also that the company from which he desired her to withdraw was that into which her mother had re-married.

Then comes the alternative that he puts before her:

My uncle Adam asked me one day in private, as by direction, what my designs were in relation to you. The answer I gave him was to this effect: that I hoped I was no hindrance to you; because the reason you urged against a union with me was drawn from your indisposition, which still continued; that you also thought my fortune not sufficient, which is neither at present in a condition to offer you; that if your health and my fortune were as they ought, I would prefer you above all your sex; but that, in the present condition of both, I thought it was against your opinion, and would certainly make you unhappy; that, had you any other offers which your friends or yourself thought more to your advantage, I should think I were very unjust to be an obstacle in your way. Now for what concerns my fortune, you have answered it. I desire, therefore, you will let me know if your health be otherwise than it was when you told me the doctors advised you against marriage, as what would certainly hazard your life. Are they or you grown of another opinion in this particular? Are you in a condition to manage domestic affairs, with an income of less perhaps than three hundred pounds a year? Have you such an inclination to my person and humour, as to comply with my desires and way of living, and endeavour to make us both as happy as you can? Will you be ready to engage in those methods I shall direct for the improvement of your mind so as to make us entertaining company for each other, without being miserable when we are neither visiting nor visited? Can you bend your love and esteem and indifference to others the same way as I do mine? Shall I have so much power in your heart, or you so much government of your passions, as to grow in good humour upon my approach, though provoked by a ——? Have you so much good-nature as to endeavour by soft words to smooth any rugged humour occasioned by the cross accidents of life? Shall the place wherever your husband is thrown be more welcome than courts or cities without him? In short, these are some of the necessary methods to please men, who, like me, are deep-read in the world; and to a person thus made, I should be proud in giving all due returns towards making her happy. These are the questions I have always resolved to propose to her with whom I meant to pass my life; and whenever you can heartily answer them in the affirmative, I shall be blessed to have you in my arms, without regarding whether your person be beautiful, or your fortune large. Cleanliness in the first, and competency in the other, is all I look for. I desire, indeed, a plentiful revenue, but would rather it should be of my own; though I should bear from a wife to be reproached for the greatest.

I have said all I can possibly say in answer to any part of your letter, and in telling you my clear opinion as to matters between us. I singled you out at first from the rest of women; and I expect not to be used like a common lover. When you think fit to send me an answer to this without ——, I shall then approve myself, by all means you shall command, Madam,

Your most obedient humble servant
JONATHAN SWIFT.

Whatever else one may think of that letter, it marks a vast change from the young gentleman who wrote only four years earlier, " O Varina, how imagination leads me beyond myself and all my sorrows! It is sunk and a thousand graves lie open." There was a mature man now to deal with; and I cannot but think that the lady on her part was still in the mood for Pindaricks. Anyhow, with that letter she vanishes: but certain affirmations in it need to be borne in mind. Swift regarded a sound economic basis as necessary for happiness in married life ; that is many times made clear, and this letter clearly proves that he did not at any time regard himself as physically disqualified for marriage. But chiefly we are bound to believe, " upon the word of a Christian, and a gentleman," that Stella was not then in his mind as a possible wife, or mistress of his fancy. She was in fact at this time in her eighteenth year, and, I believe, to his imagination no more than a charming child who had grown up under his eyes and under his care : while he conceived of himself as a person " deep-read in the world " and rather middle-aged. It is not an uncommon pose at three-and-thirty. Yet, in point of fact, he was in a certain sense only beginning to be young. It is only from this time on that he comes into possession of the gaiety which made him delightful company and which is there still, lighting up page after page of the *Journal* to Stella.

Perhaps the company that first called it out was that of Lord Berkeley's household ; for in spite of angry beginnings, lasting friendships were made there. Swift resented furiously his disappointment over the secretaryship first, and then over the deanery, and a lampoon on Berkeley and the intriguing Bushe, entitled " The Discovery," was the result. This did not see the light in Swift's lifetime, but was preserved by him, as seems to have been his habit from the first. So was another set of verses, of which also Lord Berkeley was the subject, and the title, " The Problem," is inoffensive enough. But as to its substance, Deane Swift fifty years later thought the thing indelicate—as it most certainly is ; though when Swift means malice there is no mistaking it, and I cannot but think that he considers Lord Berkeley's propensity to break wind as a natural subject for raillery. It is gross, but gross in a good-humoured way that might have been tolerated in an old-fashioned mess-room.

At any rate, " The Problem " requires to be noted because it shows us Swift as a versifier in possession of the manner which was to be his henceforward. He discarded the heroic couplet for the less pompous octosyllable, in which no doubt Butler was his master—he is said to have known " Hudibras " by heart ; but he used it with a finish that Butler never attained. His first essay in it, or at least the first that comes down to us, was written in 1698—probably while he was dancing attendance at Court in London. In these " Lines written in a Lady's Ivory Table-book," the brilliant opening is disfigured by quite unnecessary nastiness at the end :

Peruse my leaves thro' ev'ry part,
And think thou seest my owner's heart,
Scrawl'd o'er with trifles thus, and quite
As hard, as senseless, and as light;
Expos'd to ev'ry coxcomb's eyes,
But hid with caution from the wise.
Here you may read, "Dear charming saint;"
Beneath, "A new receipt for paint:"
Here, in beau-spelling, "Tru tel deth;"
There, in her own, "For an el breth:"
Here, "Lovely nymph, pronounce my doom!"
There, "A safe way to use perfume:"
Here, a page fill'd with billets-doux;
On t'other side, "Laid out for shoes"—
"Madam, I die without your grace"—
"Item, for half a yard of lace."
Who that had wit would place it here,
For ev'ry peeping fop to jeer?
To think that your brains' issue is
Exposed to th' excrement of his,
In pow'r of spittle and a clout,
Whene'er he please, to blot it out;
And then, to heighten the disgrace,
Clap his own nonsense in the place.

Swift throughout life was fastidious about sweetness and cleanliness; he was nice to excess over them. Yet throughout all study of him, one is perplexed and haunted by his propensity to disgusting images. One of his own 'Thoughts' applies to himself: "A nice man is a man of nasty ideas." It is, in his case, the very opposite to prurience, and less natural: an ugly abnormality. Doctors may be able to decide whether it was in any way connected with the latent disease in his brain; but laymen must be content to note that it was already here when the man was young, strong, merry and enjoying himself—as can be plainly seen from another handful of verses belonging to this same place and time. The first of these is "A Ballad on the Game of Traffic," written at the Castle of Dublin, 1699, and has no merit at all except as a light-hearted stringing of names together, through half a dozen quatrains, at the end of which comes this:

With these is Parson Swift,
    Not knowing how to spend his time,
Does make a wretched shift,
    To deafen them with puns and rhyme.

This, needless to say, was by another hand: Lady Betty Berkeley, the Earl's second daughter, found the verses lying unfinished in

Swift's room and scribbled in this conclusion. Thereupon came another " Ballad to the Tune of the Cut-purse " :

> Once on a time, as old stories rehearse,
>   A friar would need show his talent in Latin ;
> But was sorely put to't in the midst of a verse,
>   Because he could find no word to come pat in ;
>   Then all in the place
>   He left a void space,
>   And so went to bed in a desperate case :
> When behold the next morning a wonderful riddle !
> He found it was strangely fill'd up in the middle.
>   *Cho.*   Let censuring critics then think what they list on't ;
> Who would not write verses with such an assistant ?

That was how they amused themselves at Dublin Castle; and Lady Betty after scandalizing the world a good deal (as is recorded by the Duchess of Marlborough amongst others) lived on to be much courted for her wit, her memories and her amazing possessions, more than sixty years after this. She was noted then by Horace Walpole as the friend of Swift—and not without reason, for he and she maintained their alliance and correspondence till the last spark was out of the invention that in 1699 set them all laughing with " The Humble Petition of Frances Harris."

Mrs. Harris, housekeeper at the Castle, had lost her purse and was making her lamentation.

> 'Tis not that I value the money three skips of a louse :
> But the thing I stand upon is the credit of the house.

And so on : Here are the humours of the servants' hall observed and crystallized by the man who was afterwards to suggest to Gay a " Newgate Pastoral."

That very lighthearted production is entirely characteristic of one aspect of Swift's mind. Thirty years later Lady Betty Germain was quoting it at him ; and later still, he was at work on completing a sketch begun in these days, his " Advice to Servants." The humours of life below stairs were always amusing to him ; and when he was master he never forgot that his servants were human beings. They knew the rough side of his tongue and the soft side of his nature.

These trifles belong to what he never gave up, the pursuit of *la bagatelle* ; it occupied him as crossword puzzles nowadays occupy the learned. But oddly enough from the same year, which marks his independent establishment in the world, there comes down to us a document which shows much that was hidden from the world : a set of " Resolutions for when I come to be old," of which the original manuscript is reproduced in Forster's *Life* from the paper found by Swift's cousin, Mrs. Whiteway, after the Dean's death, but dated 1699 :

Not to marry a young woman.

Not to keep young company, unless they really desire it.

Not to be peevish, or morose, or suspicious.

Not to scorn present ways, or wits, or fashions, or men, or war, &c.

Not to be fond of children, or let them come near me hardly.

Not to tell the same story over and over to the same people.

Not to be covetous.

Not to neglect decency or cleanliness, for fear of falling into nastiness.

Not to be over severe with young people, but give allowance for their youthful follies and weaknesses.

Not to be influenced by, or give ear to knavish tatling servants, or others.

Not to be too free of advice, nor trouble any but those that desire it.

To desire some good friends to inform me which of these resolutions I break or neglect, and wherein ; and reform accordingly.

Not to talk much, nor of myself.

Not to boast of my former beauty, or strength, or favour with the ladies, &c.

Not to hearken to flatteries, nor conceive I can be beloved by a young woman ; *et eos qui hæreditatem captant, odisse ac vitare.*

Not to be positive or opiniative.

Not to set up for observing all these rules, for fear I should observe none.

This, it will be agreed, is an extraordinary table of commandments ; not because the resolutions are in themselves—with one exception—eccentric or indeed other than wise, but because it is astonishing to find a man of thirty-two so taking stock for the future. I cannot agree with Forster that the first of them has any special application, or that he had Stella in mind. It is a resolution for the time " when I come to be old." Now, by the time he was even fifty, Stella would be six-and-thirty, which in that period was certainly not accounted young. But the resolutions tell us this at least—that Swift thought of himself as likely to marry, though not till he had acquired some degree of wealth ; and that he thought himself likely to acquire this and so to be the mark for legacy-hunters whom he determines (in forcible Latin) to hate and shun. They inform us that he was aware of a temptation to covetousness —unless indeed we believe this to be set down by him among the usual failings of old age, against which the other resolutions were directed. All these are normal enough ; but there remains the startling resolution about young children, which so shocked those who first published this paper that they scratched out the latter half. What is one to make of it, coming as it does from a man who taught Stella to form her letters and kept up the " little language " from that day on till he was a middle-aged divine and she a mature young woman ? Forster says, very justly, that a man does not warn himself against that to which he feels no inclination. I add that there was seldom any man fitter to amuse and delight children than this maker-up of stories, complete in all the little details that children in all ages have clamoured for; the proof is in *Gulliver*, that outrageous satire on the human race which has so often been a nursery treasure. Yet in the whole of Swift's writings I cannot remember one mention of children which has the least suggestion of the charm of childhood. They are always squalling brats, whose parents against all reason think them attractive.

There I think one gets the key to what is most abnormal in this strange intellect. Conservative though he was to the bone, Swift set up Reason on a high altar and trampled on instinct with every imaginable insult. Above all, the two instincts which mankind has been most anxious to idealize, the procreative and the parental, were the objects of his satire. A man caressing his mistress, a mother fondling her child, had been perennially the theme of poetry ; he made it his business to show that ugly variants of the same phenomena were observable among the beasts. Reason ordained that marriage should be made on quite other principles than those of simple inclination ; reason ordained that children should be brought up separate from their unreasonably indulgent parents. We find it all set out, where we find the whole of this philosopher's philosophy, in *Gulliver*. All that need be said here, and said by way of compassionate excuse, is that for a man " deep-read in the world," as Swift thought himself, he lacked one of the commonest among human and humanizing experiences : he had never known a home.

It will be noted that none of the resolutions refer to his duty as a clergyman. We shall find him later taking stock of his position in that regard. He had certainly no aspiration after saintliness, and from the first, externally at least, he wished to be as little of a clergyman as possible. Even " Mrs. Harris's Petition " makes that clear :

So, as the *devil* would have it, before I was aware, out I blunder'd,
" *Parson*," said I, " can you cast a *nativity*, when a body's plunder'd ? "
(Now you must know, he hates to be called *Parson*, like the *devil* !)
" Truly," says he, " Mrs. Nab, it might become you to be more civil."

But from the first he accepted the obligations of his profession and did his duty. He might joke about it, but he was never a parson *pour rire*.

The proof of this was to be seen, not only in his own lifetime, but for a century and a half after it. Absenteeism was then rather the rule than the exception in the Church of Ireland; the incumbent of a living sublet his duty to a curate for forty pounds a year, or thereabout, and spent his time and the balance of the money as it suited him. Swift had to make it plain from the first that he intended to be a resident, and on that ground secured the Primate's consent to his holding of Rathbeggan with Laracor, on the ground that the joint income would be " but a comfortable support for your petitioner and encourage his residence and due performance of his duty." The first thing to be done was to build a parsonage; for there was no lodging for the rector in this parish about a mile and a half from the little old town of Trim. The glebe was only an acre in extent; before Swift died, he had acquired twenty acres in addition by which his successors benefited till the disestablishment of the Church. But his first care was the rectory, little more than a cottage, and the garden, for which walls were built to be covered with fruit-trees in a manner worthy of Temple's pupil; and the little stream which ran near by was to be dammed, ditched up, straightened out and transformed into a canal after the fashion of Flanders, with a row of willows planted on each bank.

Meanwhile, he took the place in hand ecclesiastically also, and announced that prayer would be read every Wednesday and Friday. Orrery preserves a story that when the first of these services was held, the only congregation was his clerk and bellringer named Roger. It is a situation with which many an Irish parson has often been confronted; but Swift notified his perception of it by beginning his service " Dearly beloved Roger, the Scripture moveth you and me in sundry places."

Having three parishes, Swift had of course always a curate; and while Berkeley was in Dublin, he needed to be in constant attendance as chaplain. This tie, however, ceased early in 1701, for Berkeley, a Whig, was superseded by the Tory Rochester. Great changes were in the air, political passion ran high against William and his Whig advisers; and when Berkeley returned to England, in April, 1701, Swift accompanying his Chief, found London in a ferment over the impeachment by the House of Commons of Somers, Portland and Halifax. The House of Lords, in which Whigs still had the majority, resisted the impeachment and matters looked ugly.

Up till this date, Swift says, " although I had been for many years no stranger to the court, and had made the nature of government a great part of my study, yet I had dealt very little with politics." But now discussion with Berkeley suggested a parallel : and he wrote his first pamphlet. In it he avoided direct personalities and veiled the controversy under a review of *The Dissensions in Athens and Rome*. It is to me the least readable of all his discourses —and no political pamphlet is very readable to anybody after a lapse of two centuries. The discipleship to Temple is marked by a parade of learning and by an avoidance of humour ; but the central doctrine, which is Temple's, was one to which Swift permanently gave allegiance : that country should come before party. The thing, however, caught the taste of the times, and, as Craik points out, was singularly opportune in its appearance ; for within a few days after its publication, James II died at St. Germain, and Louis XIV publicly recognized the Pretender as legitimate heir to the English throne. There was a violent anti-Jacobite reaction ; a new general election in November, 1701, put the Tories out and the Whigs in. Somers and Halifax, whose services to the State had been magnified by Swift (under a thin disguise of Roman names), were much pleased with their timely champion—though for the moment they did not know who he was.

It must be remembered that up to this time Swift was only known to the public as the editor of Temple's posthumous *Letters* and *Miscellanea*. His pamphlet came out anonymously, and after its publication he returned to Ireland where people were reading it and speculating on the authorship. Some even assigned it to Somers ; and Burnet was obliged to disown it. " Returning next year to England," Swift continues, " and hearing the great approbation this piece had received (which was the first I ever printed), I must confess, the vanity of a young man prevailed with me to let myself be known for the author." Thereupon not only Somers and Halifax, but Burnet, " desired my acquaintance with great marks of esteem and professions of kindness." They " were very liberal in promising me the greatest preferments I could hope for, if ever it came in their power."

But in the meantime much had happened. William III died in March, 1702, and after Anne's accession a new parliament was chosen, again largely Tory, and a ministry in which Swift's Whig friends had no ascendancy. The preferment, to which nothing in his record then presented any obstacle, was no longer in the gift of either Somers or Halifax. Before they had the power again, a work of genius rose up against him.

Meantime his private life had taken on the ambiguous shape which it was to wear for quarter of a century. During that summer of 1701 he had presumably paid a visit to Moor Park where Stella was now living in lodgings with a poor relation of Temple's, Rebecca Dingley. Her mother either had remarried, or was about to remarry, with Temple's steward, Mr. Mose, and she herself inherited under Temple's will a small fortune of about £1,500, part of which came from land in County Wicklow. Swift pointed out to her that interest for money was higher in Ireland, and living cheaper, and suggested her moving to be near him—a proposal which, as he admits, " was also very much for my own satisfaction." Mrs. Dingley, a good lady then in her later thirties, who had on her part a very small income, agreed to be the companion; and the thing was settled. Before Swift had left England that autumn, they were settled into lodgings near him at Trim. When he went over to England in the spring of 1702, they entered upon occupation of the vicarage and kept it in order till his return : when his head-quarters were in Dublin, the same routine was observed, the ladies taking a Dublin lodging. They met constantly, probably daily, but so far as can be known, Stella and Swift were never alone together. In a sense all the world knew that she was under his protection ; but her conduct and his were such that the society in which he moved—even when his enemies were many—never put any construction on the word protection but the one to which it is very seldom limited.[1]

---

[1] A remarkable instance is afforded by a letter of July, 1723, from Dr. Evans, Bishop of Meath, to Archbishop Wake, communicating with much venom the gossip occasioned by Vanessa's death. It contains this sentence : " In April last she discovered that the Dean was married to Mrs. Johnson (a natural daughter of Sir W. Temple, a very good woman)." Dr. Bernard, who unearthed this important letter, relies on it to support his view that a marriage between Swift and Stella took place. But he adds that Dr. Evans " is undoubtedly wrong about Stella's parentage," and says elsewhere that there " is no shadow of evidence for the unworthy suggestion." As to the unworthiness, we have to consider the manners of that age. Lady Giffard in her eulogy of her brother says that he had extraordinary command of his passions, except those which he did not think it worth while to control. One may fairly conclude that she would not have been scandalized if she found that he was about to become the father of an illegitimate child. She, although an inmate of his household, had her separate status there. Stella was baptized at Richmond on March 20, 1681, as the child of Edward Johnson. " He was," Swift says, " a younger brother of a good family in Nottinghamshire." Her mother was " of a lower degree ; and indeed she had little to boast of in

Discretion was carried so far that during Swift's long absences, his correspondence was addressed to " the ladies " jointly. We know this from the only solid source of information about these early years of his settlement at Laracor—his correspondence with the Reverend William Tisdall, a clergyman of some pretensions to wit and learning. An intimacy had grown up in which " the ladies " were included. Swift who had been in England from April to September in 1701, and from April to October in 1702, went across again in November, 1703, and did not return till May, 1704 ; the ladies meanwhile having lodgings in William Street (between Grafton Street and Dame Street), close to the newly enclosed Stephen's Green, beyond which Dublin did not extend southwards. He wrote to Tisdall a month after his arrival, describing the opening of a controversy over the sacramental test for dissenters, with which he was to be much concerned, though on this matter he and the Whigs were far apart. But the rest of the letter consists of messages to " the ladies." He had called upon Stella's mother as directed, and he had gone into questions concerning the investment of her money upon which he was the recognized adviser. Finally, Tisdall was to explain to Mrs. Johnson " a new-fashioned way of being witty, they call it a *bite.*" It was establishing a sort of permanent April Fools' Day.

You must ask a bantering question, or tell some damned lie in a serious manner and then she will answer or speak as if you were in earnest ; and then cry you, " Madam, there's a *bite.*" I would not have you undervalue this, for it is the constant amusement in Court, and everywhere else among the great people ; and I let you know it, in order to have it obtain among you, and teach a new refinement.

Stella, who by all accounts was equally good at sense and nonsense, took kindly to all such instruction, and the next letter

---

her birth." This does not seem inconsistent with the view that Temple married his mistress to a young man in his employment. There would, however, be no reason to form that view were it not that Temple by his will left £20 a year to Mrs. Johnson, £1,500 to Stella, and nothing at all to her sister, or to the brother of whom there is mention in the *Journal*. It seems also clear, since before her move to Ireland Stella had set up house with Mrs. Dingley (a kinswoman of Temple's) that she was regarded as somewhat apart from the rest of her family. Swift's influence would encourage this, for he set astonishingly low value on the ties of blood, insisting on those formed by rational preference.

It is impossible to know whether he attached belief to the rumour which made Stella Temple's child—and which he must have foreseen from the dispositions of Temple's will. But for the same reason he would have been curiously indifferent in his personal feeling as to whether they were true or no. If Stella had been Temple's natural daughter, she would still have had (as he says of her), " little to boast of in her birth."

replies to some account from Tisdall of how she emerged from a fit of choking with a pun for her first word. Another passage shows how freely Swift encouraged this intimacy.

> I am mightily afraid the ladies are very idle, and do not mind their book. Pray put them upon reading; and be always teaching something to Mrs. Johnson, because she is good at comprehending, remembering, and retaining.

It is not very surprising that the next letter, dated April 20, 1704, should deal with a serious development. Tisdall had written asking that Swift should put before Stella's mother a proposal for her daughter's hand; Swift's reply had seemed to Tisdall "unfriendly, unkind and unaccountable." Swift wrote his mind in a letter so characteristic that it must be given in full.

> In answer to all this, I might with good pretence enough talk starchly, and affect ignorance of what you would be at; but my conjecture is, that you think I obstructed your insinuations, to please my own, and that my intentions were the same with yours; in answer to all which, I will, upon my conscience and honour, tell you the naked truth. First, I think I have said to you before, that, if my fortunes and humour served me to think of that state, I should certainly among all persons on earth, make your choice; because I never saw that person whose conversation I entirely valued but hers; this was the utmost I ever gave way to. And, secondly, I must assure you most sincerely, that this regard of mine never once entered into my head to be an impediment to you; but I judged it would, perhaps, be a clog to your rising in the world; and I did not conceive you were then rich enough to make yourself and her happy and easy. But that objection is now quite removed . . . by what you have at present, and by the assurances of Eaton's livings. I told you indeed, that your authority was not sufficient to make overtures to the mother, without the daughter's giving me leave, under her own or her friend's hand; which, I think, was a right and prudent step. However, I told the mother immediately, and spoke with all the advantages you deserve. But, the objection of your fortune being removed, I declare I have no other; nor shall any consideration of my own misfortune of losing so good a friend and companion as her, prevail on me against her interest and settlement in the world, since it is held so necessary and convenient a thing for ladies to marry; and that time takes off from the lustre of virgins in all other eyes but mine. I appeal to my letters to herself, whether I was your friend or no in the whole concern; though the part I designed to act in it was purely passive, which is the utmost I will ever do in things of this nature, to avoid all reproach of any ill consequence, that may ensue in the variety of worldly accidents. Nay, I went so far both to her mother, herself, and I think to you, as to think it could not be decently broken; since I supposed the town had got it on their tongues, and therefore I thought it could not miscarry without some disadvantage to the lady's credit. I have always described her to you in a manner different from those,

who would be discouraging ; and must add, that though it hath come in my way to converse with persons of the first rank, and of that sex, more than is usual to men of my level, and of our function ; yet I have nowhere met with a humour, a wit, or conversation so agreeable, a better portion of good sense, or a truer judgement of men and things, I mean here in England ; for as to the ladies of Ireland, I am a perfect stranger. As to her fortune, I think you know it already ; and if you resume your designs, and would have farther intelligence, I shall send you a particular account.

I give you joy of your good fortunes, and envy very much your prudence and temper, and love of peace and settlement ; the reverse of which has been the great uneasiness of my life, and is like to continue so. And what is the result ? . . . I find nothing but the good words and wishes of a decayed Ministry, whose lives and mine will probably wear out before they can serve either my little hopes, or their own ambition. Therefore I am resolved suddenly to retire, like a discontented courtier, and vent myself in study and speculation, till my own humour, or the scene here, shall change.

Readers must judge the man, for all the man is there. Swift was certainly not by his own standard rich enough to make himself and Stella " happy and easy " in marriage. If such marriage would perhaps be a clog to Tisdall's rising in the world, the same was much more probably true for himself; and, knowing as he did, his own restless and ambitious temper, he knew also how great would be the danger of unhappiness for a woman who should find herself considered as a clog.

There is some mythology in Deane Swift's book about the subsequent development, but surely nothing can be plainer than the facts. Stella put aside the chance of marriage with a man younger, richer, and better established in the world for the sake of preserving her relations, ambiguous, disparaging and unsatisfactory as they were, with the man who would certainly choose her " among all persons in the earth " if he were in a position to make that choice with prudence.

A month after this letter was written, Swift returned to Dublin, having committed an imprudence by comparison with which marriage to Stella would have been high wisdom. He had published *A Tale of a Tub*. The die was cast now ; he took all the risks inseparable from giving full play to his peculiar genius.

CHAPTER VI

A TALE OF A TUB

SWIFT, however we take him, was a very odd man ; but oddest of all perhaps in regard to his writings. He was furiously ambitious, not only of literary distinction, but of that as a means to advancement : yet up to the age of thirty-seven he had published hardly anything. Temple may have been responsible for the suppression of his *Battle of the Books*, but from 1699 onwards that obstacle was removed. He can hardly have thought that the moment for publication of the *jeu d'esprit* had been missed, since in 1701 Atterbury (who helped Boyle largely in the rejoinder to Wootton and Bentley), published a " Short Review " of the whole controversy. Yet Swift may very well have been indisposed to make his first venture with so light a piece when he had already by him a work vastly more ambitious. For *A Tale of a Tub* was no less than a general satire on " the numerous and great corruptions in Religion and Learning." " The greatest part of that book was finished above thirteen years since, in 1696, which is eight years before it was published," he wrote in the " Apology " prefixed to the fifth edition—dated 1710. It almost looks as if he had taken literally Horace's precept and kept his masterpiece under lock and key till the ninth year of its mellowing. Undoubtedly the book has the stamp of having been built up over a very long period, *à petits coups*, as Balzac says of another work with which the author had continuously amused himself ; yet in the main, it dates from the Moor Park period, and may even have been begun during the year and a half in County Antrim.[1] But he was at Moor Park for the latter half of 1696, and beyond doubt he was at work on it in 1697 ; for we have a list in his hand of his reading for that year ; plainly he had been impressed by its multifariousness. Though he always ranged wide, I cannot believe that he would

---

[1] Deane Swift has a story that Westenra Waring, Varina's brother, saw a great part of it in manuscript, when he and Swift chummed together in Trinity. This cannot be true, because Waring did not matriculate till two years after Swift went down ; but it is possible enough that Swift wrote some of it at Kilroot and showed what he was writing to the brother of his lady love.

have studied, for instance, the Comte de Gabalis except as a repertory of strange learning. The only part of the whole which must be dated after Temple's death is the dedication to Lord Somers; and that, as I think, belongs to Swift's later and more fully characteristic manner.

Why, then, was publication so long withheld? Certainly not because Swift doubted of his work's quality. I think the answer is that there was a long struggle between discretion and the natural desires which impel an author to publish. I think also that during his stays in London between 1701 and 1704, growing intercourse with men of letters whetted those desires. He attempted compromise, and published, but anonymously: and at first, the cloak hid him. On June 15, 1704, Atterbury wrote to Bishop Trelawney of Exeter: " I beg your worship (if the book is come down to Exon) to read the *Tale of a Tub*; for bating the profaneness of it, it is a book to be valued, being an original of its kind, full of wit, humour, good sense and learning. The town is wonderfully pleased with it." A fortnight later he writes. " The authors of *A Tale of a Tub* are now generally supposed at Oxford to be one Smith, or one Phillips, the first a student, the second a canon of Christ Church." But three days later he writes: " The real author of *A Tale of a Tub* will not as yet be known; and if it be the man I guess, he hath reason to conceal himself, because of the profane strokes in that piece, which would do his reputation and interest in the world more harm than the wit can do him good."

I take these extracts from Beeching's *Atterbury*, but owe to Mr. Tugwell's *Life of Prior* the reference to another letter from Atterbury to Robert Harley which completes the tale. " I cannot close this without expressing the satisfaction I had last night in perusing Mr. Swift's book, which Mr. Prior showed me. 'Tis very well written, and will do good service, but I am afraid by the peculiar manner of writing he will be too easily discovered."

Thus, though Atterbury, a High Church Tory, was delighted by Swift's attacks on the dissenters, he made no question but that certain passages were profane. Further, Prior was in the satirist's confidence; and Harley was already interested in Swift. Moreover, though Atterbury was deeply concerned in the Boyle-Bentley controversy, he had yet never seen Swift's contribution till it appeared now along with the *Tale*. The only previous example of his " peculiar manner of writing " was to be found in the *Dissensions in Athens and Rome*; and even of that the authorship was not publicly avowed. It was natural, then, that there should be much guessing as to the writer of a satire which had to be twice reprinted in 1704 and once again in the following year. Neither was the debate soon settled. Six years later, when a fifth edition appeared (in 1710), it was prefaced by an " Apology," which complained much that authorship had been assigned to a particular name ; and ended with a Postscript angrily resenting a pamphlet issued by Curll in which the volume was represented as the joint work of Jonathan Swift and his cousin Thomas, who also had for a period been an inmate of Temple's house. " The Author asserts that the whole work is entirely of one hand, which any Reader of Judgment will easily discover." [1] In short, Swift would not allow himself to be described as the author, and was furious if the book was attributed to anyone else. Yet he had courted such errors by an elaborate mystification. The original edition was furnished with a bewildering array of preliminary matter. It had (taking them in order backwards) an Introduction, constituting Section I of the actual book, and being preliminary to the *Tale*, which opens in Section II. Before the Introduction was the Preface, which discourses amongst other things on the varying chances of Wit according to Circumstances of Time, Place and Person.

Being extremely sollicitous, that every accomplished Person who has got into the Taste of Wit, calculated for this present Month of *August*, 1697, should descend to the very *bottom* of all the *Sublime* throughout this Treatise ; I hold fit to lay down this general Maxim. Whatever Reader desires to have a thorow Comprehension of an Author's Thoughts, cannot take a better Method, than by putting himself into the Circumstances and Postures of Life, that the Writer was in, upon every important Passage as it flow'd from his Pen ; For this will introduce a Parity and strict Correspondence of Ideas between the Reader and the Author. Now, to assist the diligent Reader in so delicate an Affair, as far as brevity will permit, I have recollected, that the shrewdest Pieces of this Treatise, were conceived in Bed, in a Garret : At other times (for a Reason best known to myself) I thought fit to sharpen my Invention with Hunger ; and in general, the whole Work was begun, continued and ended, under a long course of Physick, and a great want of Money.

Here is mystification, for in that month of August, 1697, Swift was comfortably lodged in Temple's very handsome residence ; yet there is no doubt that the date was exact. Before this comes an " Epistle Dedicatory " which is dated at the end, December, 1697 : and I should guess that the Conclusion had been written before the author turned back to work in the other fashion the

---

[1] I must refer the curious in such matters to Mr. Nichol Smith's admirable critical edition, published by the Clarendon Press in 1921, for full details.

still abundant vein. Here is the opening of this epistolary address
" to his Royal Highness, Prince Posterity."

SIR,

  I here present *Your Highness* with the Fruits of a very few leisure
Hours stollen from the short Intervals of a World of Business, and of
an Employment quite alien from such Amusements as this : . . . For
altho' *Your Highness* is hardly got clear of Infancy, yet has the universal
learned World already resolv'd upon appealing to Your future Dictates
with the lowest and most resigned Submission : Fate having decreed
You sole Arbiter of the Productions of human Wit, in this polite and
most accomplish'd Age. Methinks, the Number of Appellants were
enough to shock and startle any Judge of a Genius less unlimited than
Yours : But in order to prevent such glorious Tryals, the *Person* [1] (it
seems) to whose Care the Education of *Your Highness* is committed,
has resolved (as I am told) to keep you in almost an universal Ignorance
of our Studies, which it is Your inherent Birth-right to inspect.

  It is amazing to me, that this *Person* should have Assurance in the
face of the Sun, to go about persuading *Your Highness*, that our Age is
almost wholly illiterate, and has hardly produc'd one Writer upon any
Subject. I know very well, that when *Your Highness* shall come to
riper Years, and have gone through the Learning of Antiquity, you
will be too curious to neglect inquiring into the Authors of the very
Age before You : And to think that this *Insolent*, in the Account he is
preparing for Your View, designs to reduce them to a Number so
insignificant as I am asham'd to mention ; it moves my Zeal and my
Spleen for the Honor and Interest of our vast flourishing Body, as well
as of my self, for whom I know by long Experience, he has profes'd,
and still continues a peculiar Malice.

  'Tis not unlikely, that when *Your Highness* will one day peruse what
I am now writing, You may be ready to expostulate with Your *Governour*
upon the Credit of what I here affirm, and command Him to shew You
some of our Productions. To which he will answer, (for I am well
informed of his Designs) by asking *Your Highness*, where they are ?
and what is become of them ? and pretend it a Demonstration that there
never were any because they are not then to be found : Not to be found !
Who has mislaid them ? Are they sunk in the Abyss of Things ? 'Tis
certain, that in their own Nature they were *light* enough to swim upon
the Surface for all Eternity. Therefore the Fault is in Him, who tied
Weights so heavy to their Heels, as to depress them to the Center. Is
their very Essence destroyed ? Who has annihilated them ? Were they
drowned by *Purges* or martyred by *Pipes* ? Who administred them to
the Posteriors of —— ? "

In front of this brilliant piece of irony comes the actual dedication
to Somers, where the same gift is converted to the opposite use,
and under the appearance of disparagement, the last refinement of
eulogy is bestowed. Again I quote a few lines :

[1] " Time " is the Person.

I expected, indeed, to have heard of your Lordship's Bravery, at the Head of an Army; Of your undaunted Courage, in mounting a Breach, or scaling a Wall; Or, to have had your Pedigree trac'd in a Lineal Descent from the House of *Austria*; Or, of your wonderful Talent at Dress and Dancing; Or, your Profound Knowledge in *Algebra*, *Metaphysicks*, and the Oriental Tongues. But to ply the World with an old beaten Story of your Wit, and Eloquence, and Learning, and Wisdom, and Justice, and Politeness, and Candor, and Evenness of Temper in all Scenes of Life; Of that great Discernment in Discovering, and Readiness in Favouring deserving Men; with forty other common Topicks: I confess, I have neither Conscience, nor Countenance to do it. Because, there is no Virtue, either of a Publick or Private Life, which some Circumstances of your own have not often produced upon the Stage of the World; And those few, which for want of Occasions to exert them, might otherwise have pass'd unseen or unobserved by your *Friends*, your *Enemies* have at length brought to Light.

This again is datable, for the impeachment from which Somers emerged honourably acquitted, was in 1701.

But between the dedications to Posterity and to Lord Somers was sandwiched in yet another document, headed " The Bookseller to the Reader."

It is now Six Years since these Papers came first to my Hand, which seems to have been a Twelvemonth after they were writ: For, the Author tells us in his Preface to the first Treatise, that he hath calculated it for the Year 1697, and in several Passages of that Discourse, as well as the second, it appears, they were written about that Time.

As to the Author, I can give no manner of Satisfaction; However, I am credibly informed that this Publication is without his Knowledge; for he concludes the Copy is lost, having lent it to a Person, since dead, and being never in Possession of it after; So that, whether the Work received his last Hand, or, whether he intended to fill up the defective Places, is like to remain a Secret.

This was of course a deliberate challenge to curiosity and when Swift wrote this in 1704 he wanted to set the world guessing; quite possibly he plotted the mystification with Prior. I can believe also that when the book was coming out, he bolted from London, partly from fear lest he should give away his secret, and partly from an attack of nerves; for he must have known that a great many people would be shocked by that brutality of ridicule, which Atterbury called profanity.

The *Tale*, as many readers will know, concerns the fortunes of three brothers, born equal at one birth, to whom their father, dying while they were young, left coats apiece, of such virtue that they would last as long as the wearer lived, and would grow in proportion to the body, " lengthening and widening of themselves, so as always to fit." His will gave "full instructions in every particular concerning the wearing and management of the coats." By the Will was meant, according to a Note, the New Testament; and by the Coats "the Doctrines and Faith of Christianity, by the Wisdom of the Divine Founder fitted to all Times, Places and Circumstances." [1] The three brothers who in various ways departed from the injunctions of the Will came to be called Peter, Jack and Martin. Here, in a passage concerning the actions of Peter after he had come to be called "Lord Peter," is Swift's delicate raillery of the confessional:

A third invention, was the Erecting of a *Whispering-Office*, for the Publick Good and Ease of all such as are Hypochondriacal, or troubled with the Cholick; as likewise of all Eves-droppers, Physicians, Mid-wives, small Politicians, Friends fallen out, Repeating Poets, Lovers Happy or in Despair, Bawds, Privy-Counsellours, Pages, Parasites and Buffoons; in short, of all such as are in Danger of bursting with too much *Wind*. An *Asse's* Head was placed so conveniently, that the Party affected might easily with his Mouth accost either of the Animal's Ears; which he was to apply close for a certain Space, and by a fugitive Faculty, peculiar to the Ears of that Animal, receive immediate Benefit, either by Eructation, or Expiration, or Evomition.

Not less refined is the banter on the superstitious regard for the Bible shown by Jack, who stands for the followers of John Calvin:

Jack had provided a fair copy of his Father's *Will*, engrossed in Form upon a large Skin of Parchment; and resolving to act the Part of a most dutiful Son, he became the fondest Creature of it imaginable. For, altho', as I have often told the Reader, it consisted wholly in certain plain, easy Directions about the management and wearing of their Coats, with Legacies and Penalties, in case of Obedience or Neglect; yet he began to entertain a Fancy, that the Matter was *deeper* and *darker*, and therefore must needs have a great deal more of Mystery at the Bottom. *Gentlemen*, said he, *I will prove this very Skin of Parchment to be Meat, Drink, and Cloth, to be the Philosopher's Stone, and the Universal Medicine.* In consequence of which Raptures, he resolved to make use of it in the most necessary, as well as the most Paltry Occasions of Life.

The rest of this passage really does not bear quoting. Nor, if I am to be candid, does any part of this work which concerns the religious disputes of those days give me pleasure to read. Its interest has evaporated. But in days when men remembered vividly how a Catholic king had tried to force Catholicism on England and when his heir was still actively the Pretender, there was great

---

[1] These Notes were added by Swift to the Edition of 1710, after the character of the book had been called in question.

appetite for ridicule of Popery. Not much dimmer was the memory of Cromwell and his image-breaking followers, whose partisans were still strong in parts at least of the land.

But nowadays pleasure is to be found chiefly in those parts of the work which are set in, by way of Digressions, between the Sections containing the Tale proper; for these have to do with various literary absurdities and affectations that nobody objects to see roughly handled. Yet even here, the pleasure to be got from the book is enjoyment of its sheer virtuosity; the perpetual ingenuity, the happy mastery of phrase and the grave-faced irony that never relaxes a muscle sliding always in and out. It is easy to believe that, as we are told, Swift hardly ever laughed. His humour lay inward, inextricable from the processes of thought, never indulging the easy physical explosion.

All critics agree as to the quality of the writing. It is the prose of a master; but it has not always been noted that it is, here in this early work, a poet's prose. The Dedication to Prince Posterity could easily be converted into a poem of the Cowleian type, with its elaborate conceits; and the image of Time, Posterity's guardian, with " his large and terrible Scythe, his long sharp Nails and Teeth and baneful abominable Breath, Enemy to Life and Matter, infectious and corrupting " would have done well in Pindaricks. When Swift, as we have seen, bid farewell to the Muse about the end of 1694, it did not mean that he had renounced literature, but only that he had got a new pen, a much more formidable implement. Humour and irony can be achieved in verse and Swift produced notable examples; but this is not easily done in the heroic couplet and not at all in Pindaricks. For humour some measure of the colloquial touch is needed, and Swift only became himself when he brought this into his range of tones.

The case is not without parallel. Walter Scott, for instance, never discovered his master-faculty of humorous creation till he wrote *Waverley* at the age of forty; in the poems by which he first earned fame he was like a man fighting with a hand tied behind him. Still, Scott had a medium in verse through which many of his latent talents developed themselves freely; it was not so with Swift, and for that reason the inevitable break with the Muse came earlier, and the relief must have been incomparably greater.

Yet service to the Muse had not been for nothing. This early masterpiece is in reality a piece of prose fantasy; at many points, as in the Digression on Madness, a kind of rhapsody in prose;

and both in the choice of words and the turns of thought, he uses again and again the colours of poetry, of which there is no trace in *Gulliver*. Here is one passage about the ravages of Time :

His inveterate Malice is such to the Writings of our Age, that of several Thousands produced yearly from this renowned City, before the next Revolution of the Sun, there is not one to be heard of : Unhappy Infants, many of them barbarously destroyed, before they have so much as learnt their *Mother-Tongue* to beg for Pity. Some he stifles in their Cradles, others he frights into Convulsions, whereof they suddenly die ; some he flays alive, others he tears Limb from Limb. Great Numbers are offered to *Moloch,* and the rest tainted by his Breath, die of a languishing Consumption.

Yet the difference between this early work and all that comes from Swift's maturity lies in essence rather than in expression. Here a young man, bred among books, thinks the thoughts that books have suggested to him. The work is not less original ; Swift here, as later, invented a type for himself ; but *Gulliver*, and of course the greater pamphlets, spring from direct contact with life.

And yet, among the miscellaneous preliminary matter, one more piece of mystification tells us that the author of *Gulliver* was already present, as it were, in the germ. Facing the title-page is a list of " Treatises, wrote by the same Author . . . which will be speedily published." These include " Lectures upon a Dissection of Human Nature," " A Panegyrick upon the World," " A Description of the Kingdom of Absurdities," " A Voyage into England, by a Person of Quality in *Terra Australis incognita,* translated from the Original." So far back was this sinister imagination brooding grimly on the animal called Man ; and here and there comes a single stroke which anticipates the searing force of his later irony.   " Last week I saw a woman flayed, and you will hardly believe how much it altered her person for the worse." That is the literary manner which reaches its full development in the *Modest Proposal*.

But in the main, *A Tale of a Tub* gives us wit much more amenable to deterioration by Time, Place and Circumstance—less universal in its appeal—than even *The Drapier's Letters*. The same feuds that lent spirit to the *Battle of the Books* rage here also. Dryden is pilloried once more with every ingenuity of insult. Swift's Notes to the later edition attempt a justification (not, I think, wholly sincere) by denouncing those like " Dryden, L'Estrange, and some others, who after having past their Lives in Vices, Faction and Falshood, have the Impudence to talk of Merit and Innocence and Sufferings." But if his enmities last, so do his friendships, and in the conclusion there is a compliment to Congreve, characteristically so arranged as to be an insult to D'Urfy.

Yet when all is said, nothing preserves *A Tale of a Tub* but its style, which is a pickle more trustworthy than that which a passage in it attributes to Lord Peter : and nobody who reads it now can be surprised that Queen Anne, a pious lady, should have disliked the idea of seeing its author on the bench of bishops. Swift would have done well to remember a passage from an author to whom he owes much, as will appear from the passage in question. It is the opening of Andrew Marvell's *Mr. Smirke, or the Divine in Mode* :

It hath been the good-nature (and politicians will have it the wisdom) of most governors to entertain the people with publick recreations ; and therefore to incourage such as could best contribute to their divertisement. And hence doubtless it is, that our ecclesiastical governours also (who as they yield to none for prudence, so in good-humour they exceed all others), have not disdained of late years to afford the laity no inconsiderable pastime. . . . They have ordained, from time to time, several of the most ingenious and pregnant of their clergy to supply the press continually with new books of ridiculous and facetious argument. . . . And from hence it proceeds, that to the no small scandal and disreputation of our church, a great arcanum of their state hath been discovered and divulged ; that, albeit wit be not inconsistent and incompatible with a clergyman, yet neither is it inseparable from them. . . . For admitting,—though I am not too positive in it,—that our episcopacy is of apostolical right, yet we do not find that among all those gifts then given to men, that which we call wit is enumerated ; nor yet among those qualifications requisite to a bishop. . . . And as they come by it as do other men, so they possess it on the same condition : that they cannot transmit it by breathing, touching, or any other natural effluvium, to other persons ; not so much as to their most domestick chaplain, or to the closest residentiary. . . . Which if it be the case, they cannot be too circumspect in their management, and should be very exquisite,—seeing this way of writing is found so necessary,— in making choice of fit instruments. The Church's credit is more interested in an ecclesiastical droll, than in a lay chancellor. It is no small trust that is reposed in him to whom the bishop shall commit *Omne et omnimodum suum ingenium, tam temporale quam spirituale* : and however it goes with excommunication, they should take good heed to what manner of person they delegate the keys of Laughter. It is not every man that is qualified to sustain the dignity of the Church's jester.

CHAPTER VII

1704-9: LITERARY LONDON

AFTER the publication of *A Tale of a Tub*, Swift behaved like a man who has launched his bomb successfully and prefers to contemplate the results from a retired position. He had achieved literary fame of the first order, for no book in English prose comparable in importance had appeared within his lifetime; and he was now seven-and-thirty. All the glory of such a success was his if he chose to claim it; yet on the other hand there was an element of scandal attaching, which in itself he would certainly despise, but which would hamper his chosen career. Moreover, he was intellectually an aristocrat to the point of arrogance. The only praise he cared about came from those whom he regarded as his peers; and they were in no doubt as to the authorship. Later, when popular fame meant power, he valued it; but as to the writer's normal rewards, whether in cash or credit, no man that ever wrote was more careless. He never earned a halfpenny by anything he published, till *Gulliver*, and then only because Pope arranged the transaction. He made his work as good as he could; he gave years to finishing the two books that were built to last, and even his pamphleteering was wrought with conscience. He supervised the press carefully; but publication was always anonymous—except in the later editions of *Gulliver*,—and in the *Miscellanies* published jointly with Pope. The collected issues of his writings were put together, first at the bookseller's discretion and, later, at Pope's; and there was very little of it in either case. Everything was jumbled together higgledy-piggledy. But the *Tale* and *Gulliver* when at last they were ready, got as fair a chance as print and paper could give them. These were works of art, by which he made his bid for lasting reputation. The poems which he continued to write were amusements—at times, something more, an outlet for the craving after expression. In most of the rest, the pen was a weapon, an instrument of attack or propaganda, employed to serve purposes other than those of art.

It seems to me clear that once the *Tale* was launched, Swift felt that he had had his fling, had thrown his stake in fame's lottery and been a winner; and that now he must attend seriously to the business of getting on in the world. His pen must help him to become a bishop; consciously or sub-consciously, he knew that for this purpose the less he was identified with the *Tale of a Tub*, the better. So for a long period—from June, 1704, to December, 1707—he stayed away from England; and during that time he busied himself with ecclesiastical matters.

These were not parochial. Part of his time was no doubt spent at Laracor, but he always had lodgings in Dublin; when he was there, his usage was to go down every second Saturday and take the Sunday services, riding back on Monday. But, as he wrote to Archbishop King, what work was there for a man in a parish with a congregation of ten hearers? His real services to the Church in Ireland must be rendered as the prebendary of St. Patrick's who was an accomplished man of letters, and in close personal touch with the Government. After Lord Berkeley's withdrawal, he was no longer Chaplain to the Castle; but the new Viceroy was the Duke of Ormond. With his family the Swifts had been connected since they came to Ireland: Godwin Swift was Attorney-General for the great Duke's palatinate under Charles II; and the present Viceroy was of course well known to many of Swift's friends in the Ministry. There can be no doubt but that the close friendship with all the members of this illustrious family, which Swift maintained even when that friendship had more of danger than of honour, began in these years. Ormond, as was only natural, seeing the origin of his family and the vastness of his Irish estates, spent much more time in Ireland than other Lord-Lieutenants of that period. Yet we do not find any suggestion that Swift had personal influence with him at a point where it might well have been exercised.

It is neither wise nor fair to attribute mean motives, and throughout his career Swift showed an active desire to get justice done for its own sake. But when he pitched upon a boon fairly due to the Irish clergy as a whole, and made himself forward in pressing the demand, I believe he felt also that credit in the Church was to be earned by this means. At all events the course of his life was largely determined by the mission he now undertook. Queen Anne had remitted to the English Church for the benefit of the poor clergy the first-fruits of tithes on livings formerly payable to the Crown. This was done in the beginning of 1704 when Swift was in London, and to his knowledge the like favour had been solicited for Ireland. The matter was left for the Duke of Ormond to see through, and there it hung. In December of that same year, Swift wrote from Dublin to his Archbishop, who had gone to London, urging him to take the matter up.

I have no hesitation in numbering Archbishop King among Swift's friends, though Orrery says he heard Swift say: " The Archbishop is a wit and a scholar, but I hate him as I hate garlic." The remark has the genuine ring about it: but it has always to be borne in mind that Swift throughout his life, and increasingly as he grew older, affected a growling way of expression. Moreover, dean and bishop are by nature cat and dog, and in Swift's old age when Orrery was of his acquaintance, the presumption with him would have been that any bishop was a scoundrel and a blockhead. What the saying really does mean is that even when Swift was crossest with King, he respected his brains. The men were never congenial; yet they wished for common ends, had much in common (including detestations), and knew each other's value. Both were high churchmen, and to that extent Tories by sympathy; but King, who was twenty years the elder, had been put in jail for resistance to some of James II's measures, and he was no more of a Jacobite than Swift, or any other Protestant Irishman.

Another letter addressed to King during his visit to England shows Swift forward in Church affairs. The Dean of St. Patrick's had died, and the Chapter at once proceeded to elect a successor, John Stearne. A letter to the Archbishop, urging him to get this choice confirmed, lest the Crown should interfere and nominate another person, was signed by Swift jointly with the Archdeacon of Dublin ; and, no doubt, he drafted it, and set the whole in motion. Here Swift's concern had been shown, most justifiably, for a scholar and a man of saintly life. Friendship began in the country, for Stearne was rector of Trim, only a couple of miles from Laracor. They had a common taste for books ; and Temple's disciple had been busy here, as so often, preaching the adornment of gardens. After Stearne had settled into his new office, and begun to build the deanery house which his correspondent afterwards made famous, we find Swift writing from London : " I reckon . . . you are now beginning with upholsterers. But pray keep the garden till I come."

But perhaps a stronger reason for Swift's lasting attachment to his good man was the constant kindness he showed to Stella and her companion. There was no better claim to his gratitude, and Stearne shared it with Archdeacon Walls, also a neighbour to Laracor. Walls, with his wife, was on the most familiar terms with

Swift's ménage ; they furnished the company for card-parties and took a hand in the pursuit of puns, which raged at this moment. But the chief leader in that hunt was Dillon Ashe ('Dilly' to his friends), rector of Finglas, on the outskirts of Dublin. He was a brother of St. George Ashe, Swift's college tutor, who had now become bishop of Clogher, and who, with yet another brother, was a constant companion.

All these folk belonged to the college set. Dublin, in those days little bigger than Cork is now, was the seat of the Government and the seat of the University. Cultivated society was chiefly to be found in these two groups. There was not then, as later, a hierarchy of the Civil Service, nor another, equally august, attached to a world-famous brewery : nor was there, what made so great a part of Dublin society in the nineteenth century, a large element from the military garrison. In the days that we all remember, twenty-five thousand troops was about the average stationed in Ireland ; but in 1708 King wrote to Swift on the scare of a Jacobite invasion that there were not above 4,500 soldiers in the country, and no militia. In any case, Swift had no interest in military men, he hated war, and, except Lord Peterborough, seldom seems to have been on terms with any soldier.

But the society of the Castle was much to his mind. Whatever concerned government interested him passionately for itself ; and also, there lay the path to promotion. The Duke of Ormond, as has been seen, was congenial in many ways ; but Lord Pembroke, who succeeded him in the summer of 1707, was more of a companion for men of literary tastes ; indeed, it is said that a happy pun first brought Swift into close alliance with him, his family, and his friend Sir Andrew Fountaine, a famous virtuoso from Norfolk, who came over in Pembroke's train as Usher of the Black Rod. Fountaine so relished the society which he found in Dublin that Swift could write from London to Dean Stearne : " Sir Andrew will never be satisfied till he gets into the little room with the three Ashes, the Bishop of Killala and myself, to be happy at the expence of your wine and conversation."

So close indeed was the alliance, that when Pembroke embarked on November 28, " under convoy of Her Majesty's ships, the *Speedwell, Shoram* and *Seaford,* being attended to the seaside " (at Howth) " with a numerous train of Nobility and Gentry," Swift was privileged to travel with him. But on landing at Parkgate, near Chester (the usual port for Dublin), he found that the Lord-Lieutenant must wait for his equipage which was in another vessel, and

so made the best of his way to Leicester on a visit to his mother
—designing to attend Pembroke in London, where he was invited
to stay at Fountaine's house in Leicester Fields.

The purpose of his journey was to push the petition for remission
of the first-fruits and tithes, especially through the influence of
Somers and of Sunderland, whom he had known at Moor Park :
and this absence from Ireland lasted for above a year and a half,
till June, 1709. We have a good deal of his correspondence for
this period, but mostly addressed to Archbishop King ; and all
this is concerned mainly with the varying fortunes of the cause he
pleaded. No intimate picture of his life can be given, such as
the *Journal to Stella* makes possible for the later years of Queen
Anne's reign ; and one reason is, that in 1708, and never again,
Stella revisited England. On January 22 a letter to Archdeacon
Walls gives greetings from " the ladies of St. Mary's "—so described
because they had changed their Dublin lodging to Capel Street,
which is in St. Mary's parish. " But Mrs. Johnson cannot make
a pun if she might have the weight of it in gold." Irish air, it
seems, promoted this facility. In the middle of April they were
still over, for Dean Stearne is told of an outing : " Pug is well
and likes London wonderfully, but Greenwich better, where we
could hardly keep him from hunting down the deer." After that
we do not know exactly when they went back ; but the list of
letters sent and received which Swift began to keep on November 1
of this year, notes on November 12, " M.D. 10 " among the written,
and on the same day " M.D. 9 " received. Before he came back,
the figure had run up to " M.D. 23 " sent, and " M.D. 18 " of hers
received.

In other words, there was a journal to Stella which, if we only
had it, would tell us all about those years when Swift, still a Whig,
was becoming the ally of Addison and Steele, and dining with
Somers and Halifax. For it is safe to assume that then, as in
1710-12, he kept for this companion of his life, in journals written
up morning and evening, and posted every fortnight or so, a
complete account of all he did, thought and hoped for and feared,
sprinkling it with silly, tender, endearing phrases of their " little
language." Whatever the relation of these two, we know that
when it had lasted ten years, he did perhaps more than any other
man has ever done to make a woman feel that, absent or present,
she was perpetually with him. Three years earlier, is it likely
that he was less devoted ?

However, we must collect what we can. The story begins

with a disappointment. The bishopric of Waterford was vacant and Swift had hoped for it; but it went to Dr. Miller, a scholar who had come over to Ireland in Pembroke's train. A letter to Walls suggests that if Fountaine had been in London, he might have altered the decision. Another to King says that " the Court and Archbishop of Canterbury were strongly engaged for another person, not much suspected in Ireland," meaning himself. The authorship of the *Tale of a Tub* was not then known to Archbishop Tenison or the Queen.

Archbishop King's observation on the whole matter is to be noted: " If a new Lord-Lieutenant be thought on, pray be early to come in his family, for you see that is the only merit." He and Swift strongly agreed in holding that a life spent in Ireland ought to be an advantage to the seeker for Irish preferment, but in fact was rather a disqualification.

Meanwhile, Swift was pressing on King his claims to a Dublin living—not unnaturally, since, as he wrote in 1706 to John Temple, Sir William's heir, his little revenue from Laracor was " sunk two parts in three and the third in arrear." The early letters of 1708 show him still eager in the hunt for preferment. " Pray send me an account of some smaller vacancy than a bishopric in the Government's gift." For he still had faith in the Whig Government's effective goodwill: and as a Whig he was reckoned, and among Whigs he found most congenial associates—but not for the sake of their whiggishness. Joseph Addison comes now into the circle of his friends and there is a letter from him asking Swift's company " at the George in Pall Mall about two in the afternoon," when, the note goes on, " I may enjoy your conversation at more leisure. Mr. Steele and Frowde will dine with us." That was in February, 1708. In July there is a letter to Ambrose Philips—a young man of Addison's circle whose *Pastorals* earned him from Pope the name, which of course stuck, of Namby Pamby Philips. But Swift liked him, and liked the literary atmosphere; it is plain that he was pleased with what Philips had suggested, when he replied to him:

The triumvirate of Mr. Addison, Steele, and me, come together as seldom as the sun, moon and earth: I often see each of them, and each of them me and each other; and when I am of the number, justice is done you as you would desire.

The letter goes on to indicate one of the tastes which the triumvirate had in common. Philips, who seems to have had a commission in the army (but this is no contradiction to what was said above of soldiers), was at this time serving in York, and Swift implores him to come South.

I have always had a natural antipathy to places that are famous for ale. Wine is the liquor of the Gods and ale of the Goths ; and thus I have luckily found out the reason of the proverb—to have guts in one's brain ; that is, what a wise man eats and drinks rises upwards, and is the nourishment of his head, where all is digested, and, consequently, a fool's brains are in his guts, where his beef, and thoughts, and ale descend.

However, these meetings were not merely bacchanalian. Forster had in his library a copy of Addison's *Italian Travels* inscribed : " To Dr. Jonathan Swift, the most Agreeable Companion, the Truest Friend, and the Greatest Genius of the Age, This Book is presented by his Humble Servant the Author." There is no date, unluckily, but it may probably be assigned to the year of their first acquaintance. Political differences later lessened the frequency of their intercourse, but I do not think Addison ever would have wished to go back on his words ; and Swift had occasions to prove his truth in friendship. For the moment, however, the important thing was agreeableness in conversation and Swift's letter to Philips gives one sidelight on that. Frowde, he says, " has brought his poems to perfection, and I have great credit with him because I can listen when he reads, which neither you nor the Addisons nor Steeles ever can." This was part of the good-nature which counted for much in Swift's composition, little though he gets credit for it. It was allied to his complete lack of self-assertiveness in literature ; he was never jealous of any man's literary achievements or pretensions ; and from the same causes he was never a monopolizer of talk.

Yet this is not to say that he underrated his own value. Addison's phrase, " the greatest genius of his age," he may have deprecated ; but he thought himself the equal of any of his contemporaries, until Pope appeared, and then he was infinitely more concerned to exalt the younger man's fame than to assist his own. About Addison, he wrote in another letter to Ambrose Philips :

That man has worth enough to give reputation to an age ; and all the merit I can hope for with regard to you will be my advice to cultivate his friendship to the utmost, and my assistance to do you all the good offices towards it in my power.

It is not certain that Philips knew how great a man was making this offer ; but beyond yea or nay Addison knew the authorship of the *Tale*. Apart from that, to have spoken of Swift as the greatest genius of his age would have been absurd flattery. And after the society of Dublin where all mention of his masterpiece must be shunned like the plague (even in writing to Stella, he always alludes to it as "the you know what"), it must have been supreme relief to be among men who had it in their mind, inseparable from the thought of him.

The natural result of this companionship was that he turned back to writing. It is not clear that between 1704 and 1707 while in Ireland he wrote anything; but we have a whole shower of verses from the time of his landing in London: and with the exception of some angry lines on the Union with Scotland (Swift hated the Scots) all were light-hearted stuff. Some of it was devoted to the ladies; he had resumed his old intimacy with the Berkeley household, and there are two sets of verse to Miss Biddy Floyd, who lived in that family and had much beauty to commend her. The first is called "The Receipt to Form a Beauty," and a very pretty compliment it is :—

> When Cupid did his grandsire Jove entreat
> To form some Beauty by a new receipt,
> Jove sent, and found, far in a country scene,
> Truth, innocence, good nature, look serene :
> From which ingredients first the dext'rous boy
> Pick'd the demure, the awkward, and the coy.
> The Graces from the court did next provide
> Breeding, and wit, and air, and decent pride :
> These Venus cleans'd from ev'ry spurious grain
> Of nice coquet, affected, pert, and vain.
> Jove mix'd up all, and the best clay employ'd ;
> Then call'd the happy composition FLOYD.

Nearly a generation later, Lady Betty Germain ends an invitation thus: "'the happy composition' shall exert her skill in ordering dinner." For Miss Floyd remained always Lady Betty's companion.

But in 1707, as I should guess, the Berkeley household began to chaff Swift on his turning flatterer; and perhaps some day Miss Floyd displeased him; at all events, he produced what he called "The Reverse, or, Mrs. Cludd"—and at once we find him dabbling in nastiness. Then there are other verses to Miss Finch, afterwards Countess of Winchelsea, who is celebrated as Ardelia; and it looks, from one set of them, as if she and Lady Worsley had written verses to him, putting forward the attractions which should keep him in town instead of packing off to the country "when Nature would invite us down."

Better known than this is a piece of ingenious fooling in prose. Lady Berkeley, who could relish a joke, was none the less pious, and she had a weakness for the *Meditations* of the Honourable Mr. Boyle. She liked Swift to read to her. One day when the reading was asked for, Swift took up the volume, and concealing a paper between its covers read her " A Meditation upon a Broomstick," which after tracing the stick from its birth in the forest, ended with an application—" Surely Man is a Broomstick." It passed current with her ladyship and the story went abroad. Anthony Henley, a Whig member of parliament and one of the wits in Addison's circle, was eager to get a copy of the *Meditation* in November, 1708. But Swift would not oblige him.

He was not chary of admitting the public to a much more famous mystification. John Partridge, combining the trade of shoemaker with the pretensions of a " philomath," used to bring out a yearly almanack of predictions supposedly based on astrology to which were annexed advertisements of remedies for disreputable diseases. Swift's miscellaneous reading qualified him well to ridicule such impostors and the first thing he put his hand to on reaching London was a paper of *Predictions for the Year 1708*, which opened with a survey of the subject, conducted with the gravity and air of conviction always assumed when he had something preposterous to say. The Predictions announced a project for " a large and rational defence of this art " :

> Nor am I at all offended, or do I think it an injury to the art, when I see the common dealers in it, the *students in astrology*, the *philomaths*, and the rest of that tribe, treated by wise men with the utmost scorn and contempt ; but I rather wonder, when I observe gentlemen in the country, rich enough to serve the nation in parliament, poring in Partridge's almanack to find out the events of the year at home and abroad ; not daring to propose a hunting-match, till Gadbury or he have fixed the weather.

After a good deal of this, we come to the forecasts of which the first " is but a trifle " :

> Yet I will mention it, to shew how ignorant those sottish pretenders to astrology are in their own concerns : it relates to Partridge the almanack-maker ; I have consulted the star of his nativity by my own rules, and find he will infallibly die upon the 29th of March next, about eleven at night, of a raging fever ; and therefore I advise him to consider of it, and settle his affairs in time.

Then followed a solemn list of predicted public events ; but of course before any of these could be discussed, another paper appeared, written with equal gravity and describing in minute detail the circumstances of Mr. Partridge's death as predicted by Mr. Bickerstaff: how the poor man repented of his frauds and (here is a touch Swift could not miss adding when he impaled quackery) " declared himself a nonconformist and had a fanatic preacher to be his spiritual guide." Then with exquisite accuracy the precise hour of death is fixed, " by which it is clear that Mr. Bickerstaff was mistaken almost four hours in his calculation."

By this time the town was buzzing with the joke and there appeared another pamphlet, *Squire Bickerstaff Detected*, assigned to " John Partridge, Student in Physic and Astrology," which describes the dreadful inconveniences the astrologer was subjected to by persons who had brought him a coffin and the like. This was not Swift's work. But next year when the genuine Partridge's Almanack appeared, with complaint of the slanderous attack, Swift took the field again, and points out, first that with two inconsiderable exceptions, no denial of the truth of his predictions has appeared. One relates to the foretold death of the Cardinal de Noailles, who, according to a Frenchman is still alive : " but how far a Frenchman, a *papist*, and an *enemy* is to be believed in his own cause against the English *protestant*, who is *true to the government*, I shall leave to the candid and impartial reader." The other objection relates to Mr. Partridge's death, which the said Partridge " is pleased to contradict absolutely." This contradiction Bickerstaff goes on to overthrow, appealing in support of his argument, to Mr. Partridge himself—and, making a digression to resent the imputation of inaccuracy by which he was supposed to have been four hours out in his reckoning. In short, the fooling was carried out to the top of Swift's bent, and to conclude the matter he published *A Grub-Street Elegy* :

> Strange an astrologer should die
> Without one wonder in the sky ;
> Not one of all his crony stars
> To pay their duty at his hearse !
> No meteor, no eclipse appear'd !
> No comet with a flaming beard !
> The sun hath rose and gone to bed,
> Just as if Partridge were not dead.

An epitaph at the end nailed down the coffin :

> Here, five feet deep, lies on his back
> A cobbler, starmonger, and quack ;
> Who to the stars, in pure good will,
> Does to his best look upward still.

If Swift had meant to signalize his arrival on the literary scene, he could not have done better; the whole grave farce was so entirely characteristic of his humour, and so congenial to the rather brutal taste of that age, that he was still named and known by it, long after greater titles had been added.

> O thou, whatever titles please thine ear,
> Dean, Drapier, Bickerstaff, or Gulliver,
> Whether you take Cervantes' serious air,
> Or laugh and shake in Rabelais' easy chair.

So Pope, twenty years later, invokes this friend at the opening of the *Dunciad*. But a compliment even more decisive was paid almost at once when Steele, resolving to start the *Tatler*, needed a name for his imaginary Man about Town : he decided for one already illustrious, Isaac Bickerstaff.

It happened very luckily that a little before I had resolved upon this design, a gentleman had written predictions, and two or three other pieces in my name, which had rendered it famous through all parts of Europe ; and by an inimitable spirit and humour, raised it to as high a pitch of reputation as it could possibly arrive at.

In fact it was probably as Bickerstaff that Swift established his place in the circle which had no local habitation—or rather, had several; for in the *Tatler* it was settled that "all accounts of gallantry, pleasure and entertainment" should be dated from White's Chocolate House ; of poetry, from Wills's ; of learning from the Grecian ; of foreign and dramatic news from St. James's Coffee-house. The last appears also to have been specially the place of resort for Irish visitors (who then, as later, generally hoped to get redress of something from the government) and it is with the St. James' that we are most inclined to associate Swift's figure beside Addison's ; for Addison was also, and more officially, though less temperamentally, engaged in politics. Indeed a story has come down, on the authority of Ambrose Philips, which tells how day after day an unknown clergyman would enter, lay his hat on the table, and stride up and down the room, speaking to no one— while Addison and the rest observed with amazement. Finally, however, a country gentleman came in and sat down, to whom the strange clergyman suddenly came up with a question, "Pray, sir, do you remember any good weather in the world ?" The squire looked about, dumbfounded, but recovering himself answered, "Yes, sir, thank God I remember a great deal of good weather in my time." "That is more than I can say," was Swift's answer; "I never remember any weather that was not too hot or too cold; too wet or too dry: but however God Almighty contrives it, at the end of the year 'tis all very well," and with that he left his hearers gaping. True or not, the story is in keeping with those characteristics in Swift which Steele in closing the *Tatler*, acknowledged to have been of great service to him: "a certain uncommon way of thinking and a turn in conversation peculiar to that agreeable gentleman", which "rendered his company very advantageous to one whose imagination was to be continually employed upon obvious and common subjects, though at the same time obliged to treat of them in a new and unbeaten way."

Anthony Henley, replying to a letter about Swift's friend Colonel Hunter, observes that he had "never seen him in so good company as that into which you have put him, my Lord Halifax, Mr. Addison, Mr. Congreve, and the Gazetteer (Steele)." That suggests something of the circle—and Halifax implies Prior. Congreve's name does not appear in the letters of this time, but that was an old and constant friendship: though Swift probably knew, what we gather from a letter of Congreve's to another dramatist, Kelly, that Congreve had not shared the general enthusiasm for *A Tale of a Tub*. It was natural that the man whose model was Molière, whose art lay in the terse, incisive phrase, should not be attracted by a work so inspired by Rabelais' ampler, looser outpouring. But Swift was as little likely to resent the lack of appreciation as any man that ever wrote. Another member of the society was Sir John Vanbrugh, as we know from two poems of this year, in which Swift laughs at the house which Vanbrugh was building for himself out of the ruins of Whitehall then just burnt down, and which surprised by its littleness, all the more since—"the Duke has wisely ta'en him, To be his architect at Blenheim." But the king of the company in these times was Addison, and the proof of his ascendancy is that Swift, having written his "Baucis and Philemon," showed it to his friend, who in less than two hundred lines "made him blot out fourscore, add fourscore and alter fourscore."

We can check the revision, for Fountaine with a true collector's instinct got hold of the original; Forster found it at Narford (Fountaine's home) and the two versions are printed in Temple Scott's edition. Whichever we take, the piece ranks among Swift's best verse; and if his prose works were out of the question, he would survive by this and a few other poems, in the class with Prior and Gay—but above them. It is the story of "two wandering hermits, saints by trade," who on a foul winter evening came to a village and begged shelter. Swift, in the original, let himself go on the details of their entreaty and of the rough answers; but Addison cut this down to " not a soul would let them in." Finally, they reached a small cottage where yeoman Philemon and his Goody Baucis gave them hospitable welcome: and again Swift revelled in details, telling how the hosts tapped " a small kilderkin of beer, brew'd for the good time of the year"; and again gives the essential, which is that the jug went round twice, and still was full measure. Whereupon, followed dismay, appeased by explanations. The churlish village should be drowned,

> Whilst you shall see your cottage rise,
> And grow a church before your eyes.
> Scarce had they spoke when fair and soft,
> The roof began to mount aloft;
> Aloft rose ev'ry beam and rafter;
> The heavy wall went clambering after.

Addison altered it—" The heavy wall climbed slowly after." Yet Swift's is the better piece of sound-suggestion. All the rest is admirable and gets little rehandling, but when Swift wrote—

> The groaning chair began to crawl,
> Like a huge insect, up the wall,
> There stuck, and to a pulpit grew,

Addison touched again and altered for the better—

> Like a huge snail, half up the wall.

The transmutation of the old couple into parson and wife gives Swift's picture of the country clergy in that age and here it is as he wrote it: we can ill spare some of the strokes that Addison rubbed out.

> Presently he feels
> His grazier's coat reach down his heels;
> The sleeves new border'd with a list,
> Widen'd and gather'd at his wrist,
> But, being old, continued just
> As threadbare, and as full of dust,
> A shambling awkward gait he took,
> With a demure dejected look,
> Talk't of his offerings, tythes, and dues,
> Could smoke and drink and read the news,
> Or sell a goose at the next town,
> Decently hid beneath his gown;
> Contriv'd to preach old sermons next,
> Chang'd in the preface and the text;

At christ'nings well could act his part,
And had the service all by heart;
Wish'd women might have children fast,
And thought whose sow had farrow'd last;
Against dissenters would repine,
And stood up firm for " right divine " ;
Carried it to his equals higher,
But most obedient to the squire.
Found his head fill'd with many a system;
But classic authors,—he ne'er mist 'em.

In short, this was holiday time with Swift and there is no bitterness in any writing of this first year of the long stay. Jervas painted his picture then, and we have Pope's word that it was very like him. It looks like a sprightly gentleman, plump and pleased with the world; if it is very unlike a parson, that was how Swift looked. But I confess that none of the portraits or busts give me any clear image of the man. It is always difficult to translate those periwigged images into common flesh and blood; the only way I have found is to pitch on some modern face approximately conforming to the style, and then invest it with the eighteenth-century furniture. Take, for instance, a clergyman—if possible a witty dean—whose face is fleshy but firmly modelled, with full cheeks and strong squared-off jaw; whose nose, not long, but prominent in the visage, is aquiline without being hooked, and, perhaps most important of all, whose lips are not thin but firmly compressed, as if determined against laughter. That is why Pope says that the Jervas picture " has a look of dulness." If we were successfully to complete the picture by a modern anti-type, the eyes must be " very particular " (again it is Pope's phrase) " quite azure as the heavens, with a very uncommon archness in them." Swift's eyes, one may be sure, were allowed to light up, after the jest, from under his bushy black eyebrows which could be formidable. He was of average height, or slightly above it, and had now in the beginning of his forties put on flesh; he complains of it to John Temple in 1706, a year or two earlier, and it was his ceaseless preoccupation to keep down corpulence by violent walking. According to the custom of the day, he wore generally a black gown with pudding sleeves; but his manners were those of an accomplished man of the world, inclining indeed to be self-assertive. One trait of this humorist is notable; he scarcely ever laughed. It was a theory of his, referred to in one of his *Tatlers* (No. 66), that " a certain insensibility in the countenance recommends a sentence of humour and jest." But indeed we scarcely need to

JONATHAN SWIFT, aged 42
From the portrait by JERVAS *in the National Portrait Gallery*

be told this, for the whole style of his humorous writings is what he French call *pince-sans-rire* : and whether in conversation or in print, success never failed it from this time forward.

Yet already the curse of his life was making itself felt; that 'labyrinthine vertigo,' which is felt at first in intermittent fits of giddiness and headache, and gradually wears a man out by sheer torment. The first allusion to it in his correspondence comes in the beginning of 1704 when he says to Tisdall: "I have been so long and frequently poisoned with a little paltry ailment of noise in my ears that I could never get humour and time to answer your letter." A similar excuse is sent to Archbishop King at the beginning of 1709: he would have written if he had not been 'persecuted with a cruel distemper, a giddiness in my head, that would not suffer me to write or think of anything and of which I am now slowly recovering." But the true tale is given in his memoranda book from which Forster prints these entries :

1708. "Nov. From 6th to 16th often giddy. G^d help me. So to 25th, less. 16th. Brandy for giddiness 2^s Br^{dy} 3^d. Decr. 5th. Horrible sick. 12th much better, thank God and MD's pray^{rs}. 16th. Bad fitt at Mrs. Barton's. 24th. Better; but dread a fitt; Better still to the end." 1709. "Jan. 21st. An ill fitt; but not to excess. 29th. Out of order. 31st. Not well at times. Feb. 7. Small fitt abroad. Pretty well to the end. March. Headache frequent. April 2. Small giddy fitt and swimming in head. MD and God help me. August. Sick with giddiness much." 1710. "Jany. Giddy. March. Sadly for a day. 4th. Giddy from 4th. 14th. Very ill. July. Terrible fitt. G^d knows what may be the event. Better towards the end."

"MD and God help me." That is the cry of this brilliant and admired man at the moment when he had perhaps fewest enemies.

Meantime the business on which he had been sent over made no advance. Power rested with the combination of Godolphin and the Marlboroughs; and though in this year Harley made a first attempt to upset the Duchess's control of Queen Anne, it ended in repulse. Harley was put out of office and the Government was more firmly Whig than ever: and the Whig policy was for repeal of the Sacramental Test—a measure equally detested by Swift and by the Archbishop for whom he was acting. In June, after six months of waiting on great men, Swift persuaded Sunderland to procure him a personal hearing from the Lord Treasurer Godolphin. We have his account to King. Godolphin said that the first-fruits in Ireland were an inconsiderable thing, little over a thousand a year, which he would agree to the Queen's granting

provided he were assured of due acknowledgments from the clergy
Pressed as to what this meant, he would only say, " better acknow
ledgments than those of the clergy of England "—and again " suc]
acknowledgments as they ought." Both King and Swift under
stood this to mean that the clergy should withdraw their opposition
to repeal of the Test, and by August 28, Swift was of opinion " tha
the progress made is just the same with that of making me Genera
of the Horse."

Now accordingly, he set to work with his own tools, seekin,
to go beyond individual great men to a wider audience. On
September 14 he writes to Ambrose Philips about certain " by
speculations in my chamber." These certainly comprised th
pamphlet which is entitled *A Letter concerning the Sacramental Te.s*
and is written as from a member of the Irish House of Common
to one of the English House. But the phrase may have included
the whole group of publications dating from this period (between
the summers of 1708 and 1709), which first showed the world th
weapon that he had forged for himself. Two of these are give.
as " written in the year 1708," namely *The Sentiments of a Churc*
of England man with Respect to Religion and Government; and *An Argu*
ment to prove that the Abolishing of Christianity in England may, a
Things now stand, be attended with some Inconveniences. The third
A Project for the Advancement of Religion and the Reformation of Manners
is dated 1709 and appeared early in that year. The discussion o
these must be held over for another chapter; here I complete th
biographical outline.

The special reason for anxiety concerning the Test was tha
Swift's friend, Lord Pembroke, had been replaced as Viceroy b
Wharton, a man of notorious profligacy, probably chosen in hope
that he could effect a change in the disposition of the Irish parlia
ment by means which Pembroke would have disliked. He wa
a very active manager of elections at a time when seats and vote
were bought—though this traffic was less thoroughly organized
than it became at a later date. Yet Swift was able to promise som
service, for Addison was to go over as Chief Secretary. " Being
my most intimate friend, I shall use all my credit to set him righ
in his notions of persons and things," he wrote to King.

Naturally, Addison had pressed his friend not to leave him with
out familiar company in Dublin, and " half persuaded " Swift " to
have some thoughts of returning to Ireland "—after more than :
year's absence. But at this time Swift's expectations were sun]
so low that he entertained a very different suggestion. Berkeley

ad been suggested as an envoy to Vienna, and proposed that Swift
should accompany him as chaplain, with the prospect of other
employment. A passage in his letter to King, of January 8, 1709,
tells the inducements :

I agree with your Grace, that such a design was a little too late at
my years ; but, considering myself wholly useless in Ireland, and in a
parish with an audience of half a score, and it being thought necessary
that the Queen should have a Secretary at that Court, my friends telling
me it would not be difficult to compass it, I was a little tempted to pass
some time abroad, until my friends would make me a little easier in
my fortunes at home.   Besides, I had hopes of being sent in time to
some other Court, and in the meanwhile the pay would be forty shillings
day, and the advantage of living, if I pleased, in Lord Berkeley's family.

He had doubtless in mind the example of Matthew Prior.
Sackville, Earl of Dorset, eating in the Rhenish Tavern in Covent
Garden, noticed a small potboy with a book, asked what it was,
and hearing that it was the Odes of Horace, demanded a translation,
and took the clever lad under his patronage : sent him to Westminster and Cambridge where he made friends with Charles
Montagu.   So began a career which led to high diplomatic employment.   There was no reason why any man who knew French and
Latin, the two languages needed for diplomacy, should not rise
as Prior had risen and very possibly he and Swift talked the matter
over.   Prior had just published a volume of Poems dedicated to
his patron's son, the younger Dorset, and Swift thought well of
them.

But things drifted on : health came back—it was in the worst
of his dizzy fits that Swift thought most of leaving both London
and Ireland—and the publication of his " Letter on the Sacramental
Test " renewed his interest in life.   He tried to mystify King about
its authorship, but that old scholar refused to be put off.   " But
you need not be concerned," King wrote : " I will engage you
will lose nothing by that paper."

This was only fair, for it contained warm defence and eulogy
of this Archbishop, who was so good a Churchman, yet so little
a Jacobite.

Meanwhile, Pembroke and the other magnates had so managed
that both King and Swift were persuaded that the business of the
first-fruits was done ; but by March Swift himself went to the
Treasury and found that no order had been made for any grant ;
whereupon he decided for the first time to attend Wharton's levee,
secured an interview, and finally elicited that Wharton expected

the whole process to be begun again. There had been promis
of a grant; this was admitted; but to make a grant was a ver
different thing. And so, with Addison urging him to make hast
to Dublin, and Berkeley pressing for a last visit to Cranford, an
Pembroke sending a final batch of puns, he turned his back o
London and set out for Leicester.

In what humour he departed, a letter written from Leiceste
will show. In it Swift after his fashion pays his compliment t
Halifax in the form of a reproach:

> I must take leave to reproach your Lordship for a most inhuma
> piece of cruelty, for I can call your extreme good usage of me no better
> since it has taught me to hate the place where I am banished, and raise
> my thoughts to an imagination, that I might live to be some way usefu
> or entertaining, if I were permitted to live in town, or, which is the highes
> punishment on Papists, anywhere within ten miles round it. Yo
> remember very well, my Lord, how another person of quality in Horace'
> time, used to serve a sort of fellows who had disobliged him; how h
> sent them fine clothes, and money, which raised their thoughts and thei
> hopes, till those were worn out and spent; and then they were ten time
> more miserable than before.

There is earnestness behind the jesting; the more Swift was i
London, the more Ireland became to him a place of banishment
and in the latter sentence, the reproach is more real than the char
acteristically invented compliments which make it plain that thi
Mæcenas at least did things handsomely:

> They have in Ireland the same idea with us, of your Lordship'
> generosity, magnificence, wit, judgement, and knowledge in the enjoy
> ments of life. But I shall quickly undeceive them, by letting them plainl
> know that you have neither interest nor fortune which you can call you
> own; both having been long made over to the corporation of deserving
> men in want, who have appointed you their advocate and steward, whic
> the world is pleased to call patron and protector. I shall inform them
> that myself and about a dozen others kept the best table in England, t
> which because we admitted your Lordship in common with us, mad
> you our manager, and sometimes allowed you to bring a friend, therefor
> ignorant people would needs take you to be the owner.

The pith of the letter lay in a postscript which reminded Halifax
that William had promised him a prebend of Westminster. "Pray
my Lord, desire Dr. South to die about the fall of the leaf."

In reply, Halifax wrote:

> I am quite ashamed for myself and my friends, to see you left in a
> place so incapable of tasting you; and to see so much merit, and so grea
> qualities unrewarded by those who are sensible of them. Mr. Addison

nd I are entered into a new confederacy, never to give over the pursuit,
or to cease reminding those, who can serve you, till your worth is
laced in that light where it ought to shine.

We have also Swift's endorsement. "I kept this letter as a
rue original of courtiers and Court promises." Halifax, for all
is hospitality, was not serviceable; and for all his wit, he had
ot the wit to see what Swift's pen might be worth in politics.
)ther men were soon to make that discovery. But they also were
o get no farther than thinking it a shame that he should be left in
:reland.

CHAPTER VIII

BEGINNINGS OF THE PAMPHLETEER

THE four pamphlets which Swift wrote in the last years durin[g] which he was still ranked as a Whig deserve attention fo[r] several reasons. They are a general exposition of his mind o[n] religion and government—subjects which to him were close[ly] allied ; and in two of them—possibly for reasons of prudence—[h]e puts aside his characteristic humour. But irony flashes angri[ly] through *The Letter on the Sacramental Test*. That this Englis[h] interest should come first, is, he says, implicitly accepted by Iris[h] men :

There is in some of Mr. Cowley's love verses, a strain that I thoug[ht] extraordinary at fifteen, and have often since imagined it to be spoke[n] by Ireland :

> " Forbid it Heaven my life should be
> Weigh'd with her least conveniency."

" But," adds the Irish spokesman, " it is hard you will not acce[pt] our services, unless we believe at the same time that you a[re] only consulting our profit, and giving us marks of your love."

There follows a notable reply to those who would conciliat[e] the Dissenters on the ground that " popery is the main dange[r], and all hands should be joined to keep it under."

If we were under any real fear of the Papists in this Kingdom, [it] would be hard to think us so stupid, not to be equally apprehensiv[e] with others, since we are likely to be the greatest, and more immediat[e] sufferers ; but on the contrary, we look upon them to be altogether a[s] inconsiderable as the women and children. Their lands are almo[st] entirely taken from them, and they are rendered incapable of purchasin[g] any more ; and for the little that remains, provision is made by the lat[e] act against Popery, that it will daily crumble away : To prevent which some of the most considerable among them are already turned Protes[t]ants, and so in all probability will many more.

That is Swift's permanent attitude towards the Catholic Iris[h.] There is no protest in any of his writings against the elaborat[e] structure of penal laws which was still being perfected ; but neithe[r] is there any demand for these additions. He was no persecuto[r]

The persecutors were those for whom toleration was claimed. Let the Presbyterians become qualified for office, it will be seen " at what a rate this faction will drive when it gets the whip and the seat." A sketch, sharply bitten in, of the Scottish settlers swarming in upon " the fruitful vales of Down and Antrim " conveys, under thin disguise of compliment, the dislike of " that noble nation " which he had inherited from his grandfather, and increased by residence in Ulster. With one of the vivid images by which he clenched his arguments, he contrasted the two enemies which the Church in Ireland had to fear :

'Tis agreed among naturalists that a lion is a larger, a stronger, and more dangerous enemy than a cat ; yet if a man were to have his choice, either a lion at his foot, bound fast with three or four chains, his teeth drawn out, and his claws pared to the quick, or an angry cat in full liberty at his throat ; he would take no long time to determine.

The other two pamphlets avoid irony and show the more serious workings of Swift's mind. In the *Sentiments of a Church of England Man,* he is evidently concerned to prepare for a change of allegiance from Whig to Tory. Extreme party spirit is deplored ; but when " the two parties that divide the whole commonwealth come once to a rupture," it is every man's duty to choose a side ; and a Church of England man must be led by the interests of his Church—which to Swift was menaced by the Whig alliance with Dissenters.

His *Project for the Advancement of Religion and the Reformation of Manners : by a Person of Quality* is more important. It is dedicated to the Countess of Berkeley, because " the easiest and politest conversation, joined with the truest piety, may be observed in your Ladyship, in as great perfection, as they were ever seen apart in any other person." She is a great lady, distinguished for her virtues, yet none the less at home in the world : and what he proposes is a worldly remedy for the world's corruption. Immorality and contempt of religion are rife among people of quality, fraud and cozenage among traders, the law is " an insatiable gulf of injustice and oppression." How should this be remedied ? By the Prince, but example will not suffice ; no one was ever more exemplary than Queen Anne. If the Queen insisted on at least outward conformity to religion in the persons employed—if piety and virtue were necessary qualifications for preferment, and notorious vices a bar—there would surely be a change. He goes so far as to propose inspectors of morals, a drastic censorship of the stage for indecency, and of the press for writings contrary to the State religion, which is that of the Prince.

Two concrete proposals are of interest : one was to close all taverns at midnight—but he goes further than the Victorian age and would forbid them to all women. The other demanded the building of new churches in London—and this was carried out before the reign ended.

But the pith of his concern is with the financial corruption—" the open traffic for all civil and military employments—I wish it rested there " he adds with a significant glance at the Church. In this matter, he never desisted from preaching ; he set a scrupulous example ; and he gave the main devotion of his life to a statesman who, in the age of the Marlboroughs, left office poor and, whatever his other failings, was honourably parsimonious with the common purse.

It has been suggested that when Swift wrote this tract he was making a bid for a bishopric. That may be ; at the time his thoughts and ambitions were painfully bent on ecclesiastical preferment. But in fairness it should be said that the pamphlet says nothing in the least degree inconsistent with his inmost beliefs. The only difference—and it is a great one—between this and his other writings lies in the manner of putting forward his views. He wrote here, as he preached in his sermons (to use his own words), " plain honest stuff " ; for once in a work designed for print he abandoned his characteristic irony.

And yet in these very months—we cannot date it exactly—he was employing that congenial device to assail the very abuses which he denounced in the *Project*. Here for instance is one passage in *An Argument to Prove that the Abolishing of Christianity may, as things now stand, be attended with some Inconveniences, and perhaps not produce those many good Effects proposed thereby.*

It is further objected against the Gospel System, that it obliges men to the belief of things too difficult for free-thinkers, and such who have shaken off the prejudices that usually cling to a confined education. To which I answer, that men should be cautious how they raise objections which reflect upon the wisdom of the nation. Is not every body freely allowed to believe whatever he pleases, and to publish his belief to the world whenever he thinks fit, especially if it serves to strengthen the party which is in the right ? . . . And is any man worse received on that score, or does he find his want of nominal faith a disadvantage to him in the pursuit of any civil or military employment ?

Here indeed the irony does not go beyond what might be permitted to a bishop to whom the Church might safely entrust the keys of laughter. But in other passages the biting tool has dangerous edges : for instance :

The curious may please to observe, how much the genius of a nation is liable to alter in half an age. I have heard it affirmed for certain by some very old people, that even in their memories a project for the abolishing of Christianity would have appeared as singular, and been thought as absurd, as it would be at this time to write or discourse in its defence. . . .

But here I would not be mistaken, and . . . I hope no reader imagines me so weak to stand up in the defence of real Christianity, such as used in primitive times (if we may believe the authors of those ages) to have an influence upon men's belief and actions. To offer at the restoring of that would indeed be a wild project; it would be to dig up foundations; to destroy at one blow all the wit, and half the learning of the kingdom; to break the entire frame and constitution of things; to ruin trade, extinguish arts and sciences with the professors of them; in short, to turn our courts, exchanges, and shops into deserts. . . .

Or this again:

One great advantage proposed by the abolishing of Christianity is, that it would very much enlarge and establish liberty of conscience, that great bulwark of our nation, and of the Protestant Religion, which is still too much limited by priestcraft, notwithstanding all the good intentions of the legislature.

The candidate for a bishopric would have been wise to deny himself some of this free scope—if it were only the touch about the Protestant religion. But there are temptations which no artist can resist, and that stroke was irresistible to the man who conceived it.

Yet it is evident that he had taken thought upon the consequences of wit out of control; for before he left England he wrote the Apology which was to precede the fifth edition of *A Tale of a Tub*. The work remained anonymous and the fiction was still maintained which represented its publication as having taken place without the consent of the writer:

The Author was then young, his Invention at the Height, and his Reading fresh in his Head. By the Assistance of some Thinking, and much Conversation, he had endeavour'd to strip Himself of as many real Prejudices, as he could; I say real ones, because under the Notion of Prejudices, he knew to what dangerous Heights some Men have proceeded. Thus prepared, he thought the numerous and gross Corruptions in Religion and Learning might furnish Matter for a Satyr, that would be useful and diverting: He resolved to proceed in a manner, that should be altogether new, the World having been already too long nauseated with endless Repetitions upon every Subject. The Abuses in Religion he proposed to set forth in the Allegory of the Coats, and the three Brothers, which was to make up the Body of the Discourse. Those in Learning he chose to introduce by way of Digressions. He was then a young Gentleman much in the World, and wrote to the Tast of those who were like himself; therefore in order to allure them, he gave a Liberty to his Pen, which might not suit with maturer Years, or graver Characters, and which he could have easily corrected with a very few Blots, had he been Master of his Papers for a Year or two before their Publication. . . . He will forfeit his Life, if any one Opinion can be fairly deduced from that Book, which is contrary to Religion or Morality.

Why should any Clergyman of our Church be angry to see the Follies of Fanaticism and Superstition exposed, tho' in the most ridiculous Manner? since that is perhaps the most probable way to cure them, or at least to hinder them from farther spreading. Besides, tho' it was not intended for their Perusal; it raillies nothing but what they preach against. It contains nothing to provoke them by the least Scurillity upon their Persons or their Functions. It Celebrates the Church of England as the most perfect of all others in Discipline and Doctrine, it advances no Opinion they reject, nor condemns any they receive. If the Clergy's Resentments lay upon their Hands, in my humble Opinion, they might have found more proper Objects to employ them on.

A strident acrimony throughout this document makes us certain that when Swift was preparing this definitive edition of his work (for which Sir Andrew Fountaine, his virtuoso friend, had undertaken to find illustrations) he was in no happy mood. He was disappointed for himself; he was hurt in his pride. After all the favour shown him by great men and great ladies, after a year and a half spent frequenting the Court, he was going back to Ireland vicar of Laracor and nothing else. After pressing the business of his Church on all the great, and receiving encouragements till finally he wrote to Archbishop King that the thing was done, he found in the end that nothing had passed but words; he came back a failure. No doubt this is why, landing at Ringsend in Dublin on Thursday, June 30, at seven in the morning, he "went straight to Laracor without seeing anybody," and did not return to Dublin till the following Monday.

Yet Addison, his most intimate friend, now Chief Secretary for Ireland, was at the Castle and had offered him passage in the government yacht: yet Stella and Dingley, his beloved MD, were in their Dublin lodgings. Nothing is so eager to hide itself as a hurt pride.

From the small materials we have to judge by, it looks as if Swift recovered much of his spirits in the thirteen months that followed before he again crossed the channel. Addison was in Ireland, and was happy there; he had made close alliance with Swift's oldest friend, Ashe the Bishop of Clogher, who lived mostly at Finglas. " I have just now come from Finglas," he writes to

Swift in June, 1710, "where I have been drinking your health and talking of you with one who loves and admires you better than any man in the world, except your humble servant. We both agree in a request that you will set out for Dublin as soon as possible."

But Swift was happier at Laracor, among his willows and his walks, and his canal and the pike and trout he had put into it, with MD somewhere near by, to ride out and find him in his morning gown in the garden. None the less, his desire was still for a permanent abode in England: "I reckon no man is thoroughly miserable unless he be condemned to live in Ireland," he writes. And yet (he adds) "I have not the spleen, for I was not born to it." It was in his nature to find means to amuse himself; and for the time Laracor and the fruit trees and its congregation of fifteen, "mostly gentle, and all simple," provided these means.

But by the close of 1710 the waters of English politics were troubled enough to tempt an angler. Sunderland, Marlborough's son-in-law, was dismissed from his Secretaryship of State. Addison set sail, and Swift, writing to him on the 22nd, supposed that in a little time he would be left without one friend in London "that had any credit." From his point of view, the chance of preferment had lain for him with the Whigs; and the Whigs were falling fast. In these conditions, he asked Addison, would it be "of any account" for him to come to England? Since Addison had asked him to name plainly what he had in mind, he stated it: "Dr. South's prebend and sinecure, or the place of Historiographer."

For more than a year Addison as Chief Secretary had been well placed to assist, and had repeatedly given assurances of his desire to see Swift placed according to his merit. Nothing had come of it. Later, in a moment of natural vexation when good offices of his own were slighted, we find Swift saying of Addison, "I never owed him anything." Yet he never bore this friend ill-will for failing to carry out good intentions. The intimacy between them was as close and affectionate when Addison fell from office as it was when he had power, or before it.

It would not have been surprising if Swift had said to himself that, given such opportunities to serve Addison as Addison had to serve him, he would have done more with them. Of the two, he was certainly the more zealous and efficient friend. Yet I do not find the least trace of even a subconscious resentment in this letter; though there is no mistaking what lurks under the phrase addressed to one who had more power and made more professions. "Pray let Lord Halifax know the sense I have of the favour he intended me." " Sense " is deliberately ambiguous : the past tense " intended " is deliberately significant. Halifax had only such credit as goes to good intentions that have not been realized.

At this point, Swift regarded the game as finished for the present, and he resisted the call to go to England. Yet within little less than a week after his letter to Addison, he was despatched, under protest, to see what could be done for the Irish clergy under a changed government. The Primate and bishops of Ireland gave him credentials to two of their order who were then in London ; but since when he arrived on September 9, the bishops in question had already left for Ireland, the affair rested solely in his hands. It led him to entirely new fortunes, and new associates. These must be studied in another chapter : but here it is necessary to clear up Swift's position.

He was, as has been shown, necessarily not a Jacobite ; no man who valued the privileged position of the Church in Ireland could be. By all the associations of his life, he was a Whig, yet by his training under Temple and his own formed opinions, as little of a party man as he found it possible to be. Obligations and attachments to his friends he recognized, but not to any party for its own sake. When Godolphin conveyed to him that the Church in Ireland should, out of loyalty to the Whig government, withdraw opposition to the Test, he found himself quite unable to agree.

I look upon myself, in the capacity of a clergyman, to be one appointed by Providence for defending a post assigned me, and for gaining over as many enemies as I can.

So he wrote in a paper of " Thoughts on Religion " which was found after his death among his papers. Whenever written, it expresses exactly the principle which governed his action at this juncture. The Whigs, in his opinion, asked him to betray the post he was defending ; they would even bribe him and others publicly with the first-fruits to an act of betrayal.

It is well to set down here those others of these *Thoughts* which best interpret Swift's course of action throughout life, and the policy that underlay his writings.

I am in all opinions to believe according to my own impartial reason ; which I am bound to inform and improve, as far as my capacity and opportunities will permit.

It may be prudent in me to act sometimes by other men's reason, but I can think only by my own.

If another man's reason fully convinceth me, it becomes my own reason.

To say a man is bound to believe, is neither truth nor sense.

Every man, as a member of the commonwealth, ought to be content with the possession of his own opinion in private, without perplexing his neighbour or disturbing the public.

The want of belief is a defect that ought to be concealed when it cannot be overcome.

I am not answerable to God for the doubts that arise in my own breast, since they are the consequence of that reason which He hath planted in me; if I take care to conceal those doubts from others, if I use my best endeavours to subdue them, and if they have no influence on the conduct of my life.

Liberty of conscience, properly speaking, is no more than the liberty of possessing our own thoughts and opinions, which every man enjoys without fear of the magistrate: But how far he shall publicly act in pursuance of those opinions, is to be regulated by the laws of the country. . . . Cromwell's notion upon this article was natural and right; when, upon the surrender of a town in Ireland, the Popish governor insisted upon an article for liberty of conscience, Cromwell said, he meddled with no man's conscience; but, if by liberty of conscience, the governor meant the liberty of the mass, he had express orders from the Parliament of England against admitting any such liberty at all.

These sentences make clear the governing principles in Swift's conduct as a clergyman, which also governed his action as a politician. It will be seen that in all these there is an appeal to reason, which is regarded as a faculty divinely implanted. But another of these *Thoughts*—the last—throws light on what is much harder to understand than either the clergyman or the politician—Swift the man.

Although reason were intended by Providence to govern our passions, yet it seems that, in two points of the greatest moment to the being and continuance of the world, God hath intended our passions to prevail over reason. The first is, the propagation of our species, since no wise man ever married from the dictates of reason. The other is, the love of life, which, from the dictates of reason, every man would despise, and wish at an end, or that it never had a beginning.

The limitation to Swift's wisdom was his overrating of what he called reason. At its dictate, he schooled himself to undervalue both love and life. Rabelais, whom he praised so often, could have taught him a better philosophy. But since he was what he was, let us take stock of him.

He had convinced himself that intercourse of the sexes was at best a concession to what was implanted in man by providence, but none the less at war with the superior element, reason.

Marriage was only tolerable under conditions which lessened all the things that reason shunned in it : lessened, in a word, the consequences of penury, of which Swift had a morbid detestation. But, as is evident from the records of his life, he loved not only the company of women, but that intimate companionship into which there must always enter some degree of foolishness ; and in all the love letters that the world knows, none are so rich in adorable nonsense as his to the woman who devoted her life to him. Yet he had so far mastered instinct as to subdue the element of physical desire, and had brought her—it would seem—to live on this footing, year in, year out, until things could be so arranged as to remove the objections to marriage. This was probably the more possible because their relations had begun so far back that they were in some degree like brother and sister. Yet no brother and sister were ever on such terms as the *Journal* discloses. No sister ever gave a brother the kind of happiness he speaks of again and again, when from the rush of London life he turns back, as he does so often, to the thought of Laracor. Moreover, again and again it is made plain that—though she was now in her twenty-eighth year and he in his forty-second—their joint life was represented as a period of waiting. His whole desire is " to make little MD and PDFR easy "—in a word again, to secure an establishment adequate to marriage. This was not to be reckoned by the standard of their friends : his income was probably not less than that of their constant intimate, Archdeacon Walls, and in any case their expenses were not like to be so great, for the Archdeacon's quiver was full ("Will Goody Walls never have done breeding ? " he writes to Stella.) Everything must be handsome about them. Possibly, he convinced himself that this was really the end of his desire.

Yet marriage on the income of his vicarage would have meant tying him to Ireland and perhaps to Laracor for life. Unmarried, he had the road to London always open ; and he knew by this time that in London he became a different man. After those two prolific years in London, he had spent another between Laracor and Dublin and had written nothing. It was true the main work of his early life had come out of solitary application, just as the far greater masterpiece which lay yet undreamt of was conceived and matured in loneliness ; but for all that he was now tempted to do, contact was needed with other keen intelligences and with a stronger current of life than stirred in the Ireland of that submerged period. Like many another man, he cheated himself with words and attributed to reasoned policy what was sheerly instinctive. He had in him the instinct for expression—the more potent, because it was allied to the instinct for power; and he very soon had means to gratify both to the utmost. Once the hunt was up, he never gave a moment's serious thought to the other and nearer object which reason had dictated—his own settlement in the world.

Yet in the very heat of the chase, day by day, morning and evening, we find him stretching out both hands to keep touch with that other for whose happiness and easiness it was his declared purpose to provide.

Artists make good lovers but bad husbands; and Swift was as much a slave and master of his art as any that has lived—none the less because the art he worked in at this time was the decried art of journalism.

CHAPTER IX

IN THE MINISTRY: LONDON, 1710-13

" I AM perfectly resolved to return as soon as I have done my
Commission, whether it succeeds or no. I never went to
England with so little desire in my life." So Swift wrote from
Chester on September 2, 1710, in the first of the letters which make
up the *Journal to Stella*; and it represents faithfully the frame of
mind in which he set out on the journey which was to alter the
whole shape of his life.

He had come back from England a year before, having been
fed full on the sweet pudding of celebrity, with the relish of brilliant
society, in which there was also congenial companionship : but
these had not satisfied him. He wanted preferment, a secure and
dignified position free from the anxieties about money which galled
his pride. He had solicited, not an easy thing for such a man ;
had used skilful flattery, and been put off with fair words. In his
errand of business for the Church he had been brought to the edge
of accomplishment, had even been made to believe himself successful,
and then had been forced to write back to the archbishop, his chief
employer, that they had been deceived. It irked him the more
because the change of decision, in so small a matter, had been
brought about by the new Lord-Lieutenant, Wharton, whom he
abominated and despised. Justice and generosity, sought by every
persuasion of eloquence and adroitness, had been denied by a man
whose corruption stank to heaven, but to whom birth, wealth, and
a formidable jobbish energy gave the reality of power. There,
I think, lay the sting. Swift believed passionately in the rights of
genius ; he had been made to feel that wit and celebrity, however
fully displayed and applauded, counted in the last resort for nothing
solid. So, humiliated and savage, he came home and hid himself
at Laracor, avoiding alike the man whom he liked best—Addison
—and the woman whom at all times and in all places was first in
his thoughts.

Since then, she and his willows at Laracor had brought healing,
but not content. He was afraid of a new attempt ; afraid of new

disappointment to a desire which perhaps hardly had definite shape to him then, but is plain enough to us now.   There were powers in him such as no other man then living possessed ; and until he used them, saw and proved their effect, he could not have outlet and expression.   Yet there was every reason at that moment for him to feel that his chances had gone.   All his connections were on the Whig side, and the Whig ascendancy was crumbling.   When his friends were in power they had done nothing for him ; even less was to be looked for under the Tories, so far as he was personally concerned.   But, there were possibilities for the Church ; and he lost no time on the way, riding along with Lord Mountjoy straight through from Chester in five days—" weary the first, almost dead the second, tolerable the third and well enough the rest."

The *Journal* proper begins on September 9, 1710.   It was posted off about once a fortnight.   The ladies are addressed as MD, which needs no explanation.   Sometimes Stella alone is " Ppt "— poor pretty pet—and he is PDFR—poor dear fond rogue.   I print as it was written ; but the first publication Deane Swift put in " Presto," a name they never used, and " Stella " which was not invented till long after.

All his first visits were to Whigs ; his letters were to be addressed to Steele, the Gazetteer, whose office was at the Cockpit near Whitehall.   " I have not yet gone half my circle ; but I find all my acquaintance just as I left them," he told Stella.   But both to her and to Archbishop King he repeated that the Whigs treated him " as a sort of bough for drowning men to lay hold of."   There was, however, one notable exception.   Godolphin, who with the Marlboroughs had controlled the government, resented his removal so fiercely that when the Queen bade him break his staff of office (as less painful than surrendering it) he waited till the Chancellor of the Exchequer came in and then in his presence snapped the white wand and threw the pieces in the fire.   It is not very surprising that when Swift called on this angry magnate, his reception was " short, dry and morose—altogether different to what I ever received from any great man in my life ! "   So, the next day, which was a Sunday, Swift, coming home at midnight (after a long sitting with Addison and Steele and then in the St. James's Coffee-house with a discontented Whig, Lord Radnor), fell to " rolling resentments " in his mind, and " framing schemes of revenge," after which (" having written down some hints,") he went to bed ; but not before posting up his *Journal* and adding the last word : " I am afraid MD dined at home, because it is Sunday ; and there was the little half-pint of wine; for God's sake be good girls, and all will be well."

A short letter posted that same day hoped they were now peaceably settled in his Dublin lodgings. " But I resolve to turn you out by Christmas, in which time I shall either do my business or find it not to be done."

His business was officially to secure the grant of Queen Anne's Bounty for the Irish Church; unofficially, perhaps to seek preferment for himself. But definitely he writes as one looking ahead to an early return; and she on her side pressed for it—though perhaps not so soon. So he writes on Michaelmas day:

Yes, faith, I hope in God PDFR and MD will be together this time twelvemonth; what then? Last year, I suppose, I was at Laracor; but next I hope to eat my Michaelmas goose at my little gooses' lodgings. O Lord, how much Ppt writes; pray don't carry that too far, young woman, but be temperate to hold out.

Then comes the notice of what proved decisive. " To-morrow I go to Mr. Harley."

Swift had reconnoitred the position of things, which was " a universal uncertainty," though Harley was " looked upon as first Minister "; and he wrote to Archbishop King, " Mr. Harley formerly made some advances towards me; and unless he be altered, will I believe, think himself in the right to use me well." That matter was not long in doubt, though Swift waited till October for further instructions and credentials from the bishops. Meantime he was beset with hospitalities:

It has cost me but three shillings in meat and drink since I came here, as thin as the town is. . . . 'Tis good to see what a lamentable confession the Whigs all make me of my ill usage; but I mind them not. I am already represented to Harley as a discontented person, that was used ill for not being Whig enough; and I hope for good usage from him. The Tories dryly tell me, I may make my fortune if I please; but I do not understand them, or rather, I *do* understand them.

On October 3, after Swift was in bed, a servant of Halifax's came to him with an invitation to go down to his house next day and dine. " But I sent him word that I had business of great importance that hindered me,"—an answer to the deceiving Whig that must have given extraordinary satisfaction to the sender. Next day Erasmus Lewis, secretary to Lord Dartmouth, Secretary of State, brought Swift to Harley.

A letter to King describes the meeting:

I had got myself represented, which I might justly do, as one extremely ill-used by the last Ministry after some obligations, because I refused to go certain lengths they would have had me. This happened to be in some sort Mr. Harley's own case. He had heard very often of me, and received me with the greatest marks of kindness and esteem, as I was whispered that he would; and the more, upon the ill usage I had met with. I sat with him two hours among company, and two hours we were alone; where I gave him a history of the whole business, and the steps that had been made in it; which he heard as I could wish; and promised with great readiness his best credit to effect it.

If Swift had known then, as he came to know, the man with whom he was dealing, he might have reported less hopefully; for Harley was of all politicians the most dilatory, by temperament and by policy. Indeed his employer was slow to believe in the completion of a business which had been seven or eight years in the mishandling. Other bishops had been averse from giving Swift the commission—for the reason, King wrote, that he was "under the reputation of being a favourite of the late party in power"; and they were even slower than King to give credence and insisted that steps should be taken to approach Ormond, the new Viceroy. The *Journal* lets us know how Swift resented this reception of his good news. He insisted on regarding the concession as due solely to Harley's intervention with the Queen, whose personal act it was to be; though Harley himself proposed to bring him into company with St. John, now Secretary of State, and advised he would "speak to others were it but for form and seemed to mean as if he would avoid the envy of doing things alone." But a friend who was an old courtier advised Swift to continue as he had begun and let Harley know that he "relied wholly upon his good inclinations and credit with the Queen."

The truth is that Swift was forcing an open door. Harley had good reason for departing from his dilatory usage. So far as Swift's official commission was concerned, he might have very easily fulfilled his project of being back by Christmas; but long before that, it was plain that business was in the wind far more important than the securing of a few hundreds a year for the Irish clergy. On November 30 the *Journal* has a first guarded avowal of it:

O Lord! does Patrick [his footman] write word of my not coming till spring? insolent man! he know my secrets? No; as my Lord Mayor said, No; if I thought my shirt knew, &c. Faith, I will come as soon as it is any way proper for me to come; but, to say the truth, I am at present a little involved with the present ministry in some certain things, (which I tell you as a secret;) as soon as ever I can clear my hands, I will stay no longer: for I hope the First-Fruit business will be soon over in all its forms. But, to say the truth, the present ministry have a difficult task, and want me, &c. Perhaps they may be just as grateful as others : but, according to the best judgment I have, they are pursuing the true interest of the public : and therefore I am glad to contribute what is in my power. For God's sake, not a word of this to any alive.

Less than two months had passed since his first interview with Harley ; but for more than four weeks already he had been plunged into the new task in which his powers for the first time got full play to an immediate and practical purpose. The exhilaration of it was intoxicating and those first months of the *Journal* might have been written with champagne.

This was the position. Harley through his influence on Mrs. Masham had induced the Queen to get rid of ministers whose policy she disliked, and disliked specially as a churchwoman ; the prosecution of Sacheverell for a high-church sermon had given the chance. But when Swift came over, although the Whig magnates were out, the new elections had still to be held, and when he met Harley first, their result was uncertain. The Tories won, but even so things were dangerous. For seven years Marlborough had accustomed the country to victorious war ; the Whig ministry had associated themselves intimately with the prestige of his name ; and war had, as usual, produced strong vested interests desiring its continuance. Harley and St. John both realized that they must mobilize the stronger force of popular feeling, and they had set about it in a way that marks the advent of modern institutions : they sought to create opinion through the press. A weekly paper, the *Examiner*, had been started before Swift left Ireland, and the ablest pens the ministry could find were set to work. St. John himself wrote, Prior wrote, Atterbury wrote ; but an opposition organ, *The Whig Examiner*, had Addison among its writers and more than countered them. St. John and Harley did not think of Swift till he came to London ; but once his presence there gave the suggestion, they knew they had their man. It was St. John who a few weeks later told Swift that they had been " determined to have him " ; it may have been St. John who had the divination of what that pen could be worth—for Harley's instinct for literature, though it was lively, could not be compared with that of his brilliant colleague. But it was Harley who saw the way to bind to his party the man whose help he desired. Swift came to him as a petitioner : he was treated as one whom it was a Prime Minister's interest to oblige. In one word, the chief holder of power treated him from the first as an equal, and almost from the first as an intimate. He was dealing with a man whose only fortune was his modest benefice, and whose

ROBERT HARLEY, EARL OF OXFORD AND MORTIMER

From the portrait after KNELLER *in the National Portrait Gallery*

only power lay in his pen; yet a man who always asserted that genius should give nobility and should be entitled to power. Harley conceded these claims with a willingness and suddenness that fairly took his new associate's breath away.—Here is the account of twenty-four hours in the life of a country parson come from Laracor to London—as recounted to MD by PDFR.

Oct. 7.—I wonder when this letter will be finished: it must go by Tuesday, that is certain; and if I have one from MD before, I will not answer it, that's as certain too! 'Tis now morning, and I did not finish my papers for Mr. Harley last night; for you must understand PDFR was sleepy, and made blunders and blots. Very pretty that I must be writing to young women in a morning fresh and fasting, faith. Well, good morrow to you: and so I go to business, and lay aside this paper till night, sirrahs.—At night. Jack How told Harley, that if there were a lower place in hell than another, it was reserved for his porter, who tells lies so gravely, and with so civil a manner. This porter I have had to deal with, going this evening at four to visit Mr. Harley, by his own appointment. But the fellow told me no lie, though I suspected every word he said. He told me his master was just gone to dinner, with much company, and desired I would come an hour hence, which I did, expecting to hear Mr. Harley was gone out; but they had just done dinner. Mr. Harley came out to me, brought me in, and presented me to his son-in-law, Lord Doblane, (or some such name), and his own son, and among others, Will Penn the Quaker: we sat two hours, drinking as good wine as you do; and two hours more, he and I alone; where he heard me tell my business: entered into it with all kindness; asked for my powers, and read them; and read likewise a memorial I had drawn up, and put it in his pocket to show the Queen; told me the measures he would take; and, in short, said every thing I could wish; told me he must bring Mr. St. John (Secretary of State) and me acquainted; and spoke so many things of personal kindness and esteem for me, that I am inclined half to believe what some friends have told me, that he would do every thing to bring me over. He has desired to dine with me, (what a comical mistake was that), I mean, he has desired me to dine with him on Tuesday; and after four hours being with him, set me down at St. James's Coffeehouse, in a hackney coach. All this is odd and comical if you consider him and me. He knew my christian name very well. I could not forbear saying thus much upon this matter, although you will think it tedious. But I will tell you; you must know, 'tis fatal to me to be a scoundrel and a prince the same day: for being to see him at four, I could not engage myself to dine at any friend's; so I went to Tooke, to give him a ballad and dine with him; but he was not at home; so I was forced to go to a blind chophouse, and dine for tenpence upon gill ale, bad broth, and three chops of mutton, and then go reeking from thence to the first minister of state. And now I am going in charity to send Steel a *Tatler*, who is very low of late. They may talk of the *you know what*,[1] but, gad,

---

[1] *A Tale of A Tub.*

if it had not been for that, I should never have been able to get th
access I have had ; and if that helps me to succeed, then that *same thir*
will be serviceable to the church.   But how far we must depend upo
new friends, I have learnt by long practice, though I think, amon
great ministers, they are just as good as old ones.   And so I thin
this important day has made a great hole in this side of the paper ; an
the fiddle faddles of to-morrow and Monday will make up the rest ; and
besides, I shall see Harley on Tuesday before this letter goes.

I must tell you a great piece of refinement of Harley.   He charge
me to come to him often ;   I told him I was loth to trouble him in so
much business as he had, and desired I might have leave to come at hi
levee ;   which he immediately refused, and said, That was not a plac
for friends to come to.   'Tis now but morning, and I have got a foolis
trick ;   I must say something to MD when I wake, and wish them a goo
morrow ;   for this is not a shaving day, Sunday, so I have time enough
but get you gone, you rogues ;   I must go write : yes, 'twill vex m
to the blood if any of these long letters should miscarry : if they do
I will shrink to half sheets again ;   but then what will you do to mak
up the journal ? there will be ten days of PDFR's life lost, and that wil
be a sad thing, faith and troth.

Was there ever such a letter-writer ?   Was there ever a strange
love letter ?   Was there ever a letter more full of the essence of a
love letter, which is to share life to all its fullness, in defiance o
time and space ?

The *Tatler* was his poem " The Shower," a piece of verse equa
to Hogarth's paintings.   Steele printed it with enthusiastic com
ment.   Swift had no thought of breaking with his Whig friends
though the ballad for Tooke was his lampoon on Godolphin
" Sid Hamet's Rod ".   But the days of alliance with the *Tatler*
were numbered, for Steele, a furious politician, could not keep
from attacking the new ministry in it, though Harley had given
him his post as Gazetteer.   The Ministry could not be expected
to employ a declared opponent to edit the official bulletins of news,
and he was to lose the *Gazette* : but he had another post as Com-
missioner of Stamped Papers.   Swift was concerned to keep his
friend in this employment, and went to see Addison " as the dis-
creeter party ".   But Addison too " talked as if he suspected me,
and would not fall in with anything I said. . . .   When shall I
grow wise ? " he cries out to Stella.   " I endeavour to act in the
most exact points of honour and conscience and my nearest friends
will not understand it so ; what must a man expect from his
enemies ? "

No doubt Addison and Steele were saying that Swift had ratted,
and for his own interest ; and other eminent and less excusable
persons have since then been full-mouthed in that cry.   Swift has

een ably defended by other biographers, and it is superfluous to
o into detail, beyond what is necessary to clear his credit as a
.an. The facts show, first, that on the change of administration
e came to England reluctantly and upon the business of his Church
-an errand pressed on him by the ablest and best of the
ish bishops. The chance to throw all the weight of his genius
to public affairs was wholly unforeseen. It was a temptation,
most irresistible, just as is the offer of a vast audience to orator,
nger or actor—the chance to know mastery, to mould the minds
f other men and—(this would always be present to Swift)—the
.ance to serve his friends and hurt his enemies. No one blames
.e orator or artist for feeling the lure as a lure, provided the thing
. be done involves no compromise of honesty. We have Swift's
.ind before us, disclosed with a frankness of which there are few
ther examples, for this period of time; and I cannot see the
.ast trace of scruple. To go back upon his friends because they
ere not of Harley's party, to look cold on them, to avoid their
.mpany as compromising his reputation for zeal, this indeed would
.ave dishonoured him in his own eyes; but a year or so later,
hen Swift was pestered like a minister by seekers after preferment,
e find St. John complaining that he " never came to them without
Whig in his sleeve "; and there is instance after instance in which
e almost forced Addison's company upon the men in power.
he only Whig friend that he lost was Steele, and the quarrel was
f Steele's making.

But as to principles, in that age, where were they? It is not
.sy at any given moment for an outsider to define the real differ-
.ces of view between leaders of the two main parties into which
.e English property-owning classes are divided, though on some
.articular measure the cleavage may be clear enough. In Queen
.nne's day, the essential criterion of a Whig was to be for the
.rotestant succession and against the divine right of absolute mon-
.chy; and upon these points no man was stauncher than Swift,
.ho for that matter declared later that he had always been a Whig.

For him personally the dominant issue was the Church. He
.as citizen no less than churchman, but as with a soldier, the call
f his profession came first: in his choice between parties he felt
.ound to give his support to that one from which the Church would
.et fair play. How the Whigs of that day felt towards the Church
.ight be judged from the prominence of Wharton, who was their
.arty manager. Now Wharton had expressed his attitude towards
.ligion by doing with some of his companions what drunken

soldiers would hardly do in carelessness ; he had deliberately b
fouled a church in pulpit and altar. This was the man whom th
Whigs had sent over to govern Ireland, the country in which Swi
was a beneficed clergyman ; and in the *Examiner* the first of a seri
of furious personal attacks was aimed at Wharton.

But the larger issue for Swift and for every citizen at that tin
was peace or war ; and on this he took his stand from the firs
honestly convinced, as he told Stella, that those with whom l
worked were " pursuing the true interest of the public." It wa
the teaching of his first master Temple, that the interest of th
public should always come before the interest of party, and tha
no man should let himself be bound by any ties against his bett
judgment in politics ; and the first words that Swift wrote in th
Examiner express Temple's spirit :

> It is a practice I have generally followed, to converse in equal freedor
> with the deserving men of both parties ; and it was never without som
> contempt, that I have observed persons wholly out of employmen
> affect to do otherwise.

But, he says, since several of his Whig acquaintances wer
" grown so unutterably peevish and splenetic," he must give hi
grounds for supporting the Tory measures. War had bred wha
it always breeds—profiteers ; and he quotes Lucan :

> *Hinc usura vorax, avidumque in tempore foenus,*
> *Hinc concussa fides, et multis utile bellum.*

The Latin authors were always to Swift a source of wisdom rathe
than of beauty and refreshment. *Multis utile bellum* had produce
a race of the new rich ; and administration had become too closel
linked to the stock-jobbing interest (though in that day, on th
principles which Marlborough practised, the new rich consisted o
" generals and colonels " as well as those " whose whole fortune
lie in funds and stocks "). The true interest of the public la
therefore in a change of ministry who would assist the Sovereig
in " extricating herself as soon as possible out of the pupillage o
those who found their accounts only in perpetuating the war "—
the many for whom *bellum* was *utile*.

Swift never disputed Marlborough's supreme ability as a soldier
but military glory made no appeal to his imagination. The abilit
that he admired was that of a statesman who can make prosperit
at home rather than conquests abroad ; and in regard to Marl
borough, he sincerely believed, as he told Stella, that the man i

imself was bad. The worst badness to Swift was pecuniary
orruption, and no man who had acquired money as Marlborough
id could be unsuspect. On the other hand, those to whom he
ow gave his allegiance, Harley and St. John, were completely
ree from this reproach; and Harley, careless in all else, was a
erce guardian of the public purse. On this ground perhaps more
han any other, Swift was proud of his association with them, and
roud that he could be as disinterested as they.

This was soon clear. Intimacy had grown very close; just
efore Christmas Swift went to the levee which Harley, like all
ther great men of that day, held in his house for general acquaint-
nce. " He came and asked me what I did there and bid me come
nd dine with him on a family dinner." From that time out Swift
vas the familiar of the whole household, and both Harley and St.
John put him in anxiety by insisting that he should sit up till mid-
ught with them, and drink vastly more than was good for him.
ndeed their easy conviviality alarmed him when a disaster to British
rms in Spain was followed by the loss of several ships from Virginia;
he ministers, the *Journal* says, " seem to value all this as nothing,
nd are as easy and merry as if they had nothing in their hearts or
on their shoulders."

He had constant access to them and was bound to have it, for
the *Examiner* was written under their " advice and direction." Yet
he never limited himself, nor was asked to limit himself, to being
a mere mouthpiece: he was a companion and counsellor. A
passage on January 18, 1711, suggests the relationship:

Mr. Secretary and I went together from his office to Mr. Harley's,[1]
and thought to have been very wise; but the deuce a bit: the company
staid, and more came, and Harley went away at seven, and the Secretary
and I staid with the rest of the company till eleven; I would then have
had him come away, for he was in for't; and though he swore he would
come away at that flask, there I left him. I wonder at the civility of these
people; when he saw I would drink no more, he would always pass
the bottle by me, and yet I could not keep the toad from drinking himself,
nor he would not let me go neither, nor Masham, who was with us.

No other private individual till Delane could have had any such
relations with ministers; but Delane as editor of *The Times* was
director of a great independent concern. Swift was nothing but
himself and his pen; yet he was determined that he and his pen
should be independent. The crucial moment came early. On

[1] Harley's house, as a memorial tablet shows, was at the bottom of Buck-
ingham Street, next to the Embankment Gardens, now the Charing Cross
Underground.

February 5, 1711, he had dined with Harley; they did not sit down till six and stayed till eleven; and on that day the *Journal* complained of these engagements. "I will dine with him no more, if I can help it." Next day: "Mr. Harley desired I would dine with him again to-day; but I refused him, for I fell out with him yesterday, and will not see him again till he makes amends." On the 7th:

I was this morning early with Mr. Lewis of the Secretary's office and saw a letter Mr. Harley had sent to him, desiring to be reconciled but I was deaf to all entreaties, and have desired Lewis to go to him and let him know I expect farther satisfaction. If we let these great ministers pretend too much, there will be no governing them. He promises to make me easy, if I will but come and see him; but I won't and he shall do it by message, or I will cast him off. I'll tell you the cause of our quarrel when I see you, and refer it to yourselves. In that he did something, which he intended for a favour, and I have taken it quite otherwise, disliking both the thing and the manner, and it has heartily vexed me, and all I have said is truth, though it looks like jest.

Harley had made his one error in tact, and the woman who knew Swift did not need to be told what it was. A month later in the *Journal* is his reply to hers: "Stella guesses right as she always does. He gave me"—and then follows in cypher—"a bank bill for fifty pound." There was no overt breach, for on February 12 the *Journal* notes, "I went to the Court of Requests at noon, and sent Mr. Harley [1] into the House to call the Secretary, to let him know I would not dine with him if he dined late." But plainly, though the quarrel was still alluded to as if in jest, behind the jest was reality. It is on the 16th that the *Journal* notes how, after calling on Congreve and dining with him and Estcourt, the actor, and laughing till six, Swift went to Harley's.

"There I staid till nine, and we made up our quarrel."

The next words make it clear what amends Harley made for treating him as a hired writer.

"He has invited me to dinner to-morrow, which is the day of the week (Saturday) that Lord-Keeper (Harcourt) and Secretary St. John dine with him privately, and at last they have consented to let me among them on that day."

This was admission, not to the Cabinet but to the inner committee of the cabinet, and Swift held this privilege continuously,

---

[1] This has been rather absurdly taken as a piece of arrogance, but since access to the House when sitting is not permitted, it is natural enough for a person in the lobby to send in a message to one member by another, even nowadays when there is an elaborate service of messengers.

hough its quality altered and depreciated; two years later (January,
1713) we find him writing:

I dined with Lord-Treasurer, and shall again to-morrow, which is
his day when all the ministers dine with him. He calls it whipping-day.
It is always on Saturday, and we do indeed usually rally him about his
faults on that day. I was of the original club, when only poor Lord
Rivers, Lord-Keeper, and Lord Bolingbroke came; but now Ormond,
Anglesey, Lord-Steward, Dartmouth, and other rabble intrude, and I
scold at it; but now they pretend as good title as I; and, indeed, many
Saturdays I am not there.

It is necessary to say to those not familiar with Swift's manner
that these words are not to be taken literally; it was part of his
' humour," his special pose, to insist on being treated as a person
of more consequence than those whose consequence came from
titles. They must be presented to him, not he to them; and the
higher the rank, the more the punctilio; here is an illustration
from May, 1711, when he was at Chelsea:

I staid at home till five o'clock, and dined with Dean Atterbury: then
went by water to Mr. Harley's, where the Saturday club was met, with
the addition of the Duke of Shrewsbury. I whispered Lord Rivers,
that I did not like to see a stranger among us: and the rogue told it
aloud: but Mr. Secretary said, the Duke writ to have leave: so I appeared
satisfied, and so we laughed. Mr. Secretary told me the Duke of Buck-
ingham had been talking to him much about me, and desired my acquaintance. I answered, it could not be: for he had not made sufficient
advances. Then the Duke of Shrewsbury said, he thought that Duke
was not used to making advances. I said I could not help that; for
I always expected advances in proportion to men's quality, and more
from a Duke than other men. The Duke replied, that he did not mean
anything of his quality; which was handsomely said enough; for he
meant his pride.

This was carrying into a new sphere the principle he had laid
down for his relations with women during the years from 1703
on, when he was a wit and the fashion in London. Ladies must
seek to be presented to him, not he to them; indeed, as soon as
he had got to London in this later visit, we find him writing:
" The Duke of Ormond's daughter is to visit me to-day at a third
place by way of advance and I am to return it to-morrow." September 20: " To-day I returned my visits to the Duke's daughters;
these insolent drabs came up to my very mouth to salute me."
Swift had early made friends with the Ormond household and no
doubt knew the Ladies Mary and Betty when they wore short
clothes: he calls them insolent drabs, just as he calls Dingley and
Stella naughty sluts, and so forth.

It is needless to go on construing Swift's language; it is how
ever necessary to construe his pose—for it was one—in genera
society. For those with whom he felt himself naturally on ar
equality, Addison, Congreve, Pope, Arbuthnot, and the rest, there
was none of this play-acting; he was the easiest of men, free from
all petty jealousies, spleen and affectations. But in fashionable
society and in the political world, he recognized that those who
had wealth or rank would consider themselves his superiors, and
would treat him as an inferior, instinctively and automatically
above all, as an impecunious country clergyman, he would be in
a class habitually ridiculed in the English society of that time
Accordingly, he determined from the outset to confer rank upor
himself and approach society on terms of his own making. Oscar
Wilde did the same—with a difference—at the end of the nineteentl
century as Swift at the beginning of the eighteenth. So for tha
matter did George Bernard Shaw, though again with a difference
But in all three cases the essential procedure was the same; because
they did not want to be treated with insolence, they assumed the
right to be insolent in virtue of their wit; and because they were
able to make good their pretensions, they were accepted on their
own terms.

In his dealings with ministers, Swift might play the game of
rating Harley and St. John in public and giving them orders; or
again, when he needed to assert himself more seriously, he did
as for instance in May, 1711:

Mr. Secretary had too much company with him to-day; so I came
away soon after dinner. I give no man liberty to swear or talk b——dy
and I found some of them were in constraint, so I left them to themselves

Or again, more decisively, in the April of that year, after a dinner
when St. John had been sulky, he writes:

I called at Mr. Secretary's, to see what the D—— ailed him on Sun
day; I made him a very proper speech, told him I observed he was
much out of temper: that I did not expect he would tell me the cause,
but would be glad to see he was in better; and one thing I warned him
of, never to appear cold to me, for I would not be treated like a schoolboy; that I had felt too much of that in my life already, (meaning from
Sir William Temple), that I expected every great minister, who honoured
me with his acquaintance, if he heard or saw any thing to my disadvantage,
would let me know in plain words, and not put me in pain to guess by
the change or coldness of his countenance or behaviour; for it was
what I would hardly bear from a crowned head, and I thought no subject's
favour was worth it.

But apart from such rare occasions it is plain that his habitual

one with these men, and more specially with Harley, was one of
deference, and of compliment—put in his own inverted fashion.
For instance, when Swift had been railing against some proposed
envoy for " a most covetous cur," Harley asked him to " name
some who understood business, but did not love money ; for
he could not find them.   I said, there was something in a Treasurer
different from other men ; that we ought not to make a man a
bishop who does not love divinity, or a general, who does not
love war ; and I wondered why the Queen would make a War
Lord Treasurer who does not love money. He was mightily
pleased."

No other man got so much of this deference, for Swift had
already begun to make a hero of Harley even before a dramatic
thing happened.   At the opening of March the Ministry was " on
very narrow bottom," between the Whigs on one side and the
violent Tories on the other ; and the Queen was not tractable,
having been so much cautioned, by these very ministers when out
of office, against being " governed."   Then on March 8 a secret
agent, the Marquis de Guiscard, detected in treasonable correspondence with the French, was under examination before the Cabinet ;
he made a sudden rush at the Lord Treasurer and stabbed him
in the chest with a penknife which broke on the breast-bone.
Swift's dismay and concern, written down in the intimacy of his
Journal, were violent beyond all common measure and for days
he has little to say of anything else.   By the 25th he is reporting
of the would-be murderer, on whom the lords of the council fell
at once with their swords.

We have let Guiscard be buried at last, after showing him pickled
in a trough this fortnight for twopence a piece ; and the fellow that
showed would point to his body, and, See, gentlemen, this is the wound
that was given him by his Grace the Duke of Ormond ; and this is the
wound, &c., and then the show was over, and another set of rabble
came in. 'Tis hard that our laws would not suffer us to hang his body
in chains, because he was not tried ; and in the eye of our law every
man is innocent till then.   Mr. Harley is still very weak, and never out
of bed.

Meanwhile the House of Commons missed its leader ; " they cannot
stir an inch without him in their most material affairs " ; and public
sympathy swung sharply to the side of the wounded statesman.
By May he was on his way to receive the Earldom of Oxford :

This man has grown by persecutions, turnings out, and stabbing.
What waiting, and crowding, and bowing will be at his levee ! yet, if

human nature be capable of so much constancy, I should believe he will be the same man still, bating the necessary forms of grandeur he must keep up.

Swift was perfectly right. Harley never changed and was the same genial, over-convivial, trifling loiterer, the same good economist of public funds, and the same despiser of money for himself; what was more, he was the same friend who loved Swift's company, listened to his advice and did not take it, wished him well, and took no steps to do him service, yet, when shipwreck came, counted no less unreservedly on Swift's loyalty than when he himself rode the crest of the wave.

By June the change in public feeling was so marked that Swift decided to discontinue writing for the *Examiner*. He told Stella of the change, obscurely as usual : after the next week she would not find the paper so well written as heretofore. His first task was done : but there was still no escape from ties, which, with one side of his complex nature, he felt as entanglements. I turn back to the *Journal* for that side, which wished to be out of it all.

Nothing could exceed the tenderness : on June 4 he came back from a long day in the city and—

at eleven got to bed ; and all the while I was undressing myself, there was I speaking monkey things in air, just as if MD had been by, and did not recollect myself till I got into bed.

Closing up his budget on January 15, here is what he says :

It will be just three weeks when I have the next letter, that's to-morrow. Farewell, dearest beloved MD, and love poor, poor PDFR, who has not had one happy day since he left you, as hope saved. It is the last sally I will ever make, but I hope it will turn to some account. I have done more for these, and I think they are more honest than the last ; however, I will not be disappointed. I would make MD and me easy ; and I never desired more. Farewell, &c. &c.

Throughout there is not only the implication, but the acknowledgment that their lives are completely linked. I am not sure that he seeks to reassure her about rival attractions : still, there are phrases that would have that effect. After dinner at the house of one Lady Lucy, a connection of the Berkeleys, certain ladies had been disparaging about his " Shower " and " Sid Hamet," though they took Prior (who was also there) to be the author :

Don't you wonder I never dined there before ? But I am too busy and they live too far off ; and besides, I do not like women so much as I did. [MD you must know, are not women.]

Lady Kerry was one of his favourites and he went " trapesing " with her to see sights ;

Lady Kerry, Mrs. Pratt, Mrs. Cadogan, and I in one coach ; Lady Kerry's son and his governor, and two gentlemen in another ; maids and misses, and little master, (Lord Shelburn's children), in a third, all hackneys, set out at ten o'clock this morning from Lord Shelburn's house in Piccadilly to the Tower, and saw all the sights, lions, etc. then to Bedlam ; then dined at the chophouse behind the Exchange ; then to Gresham College, (but the keeper was not at home), and concluded the night at the puppet-show, whence we came home safe at eight, and I left them. The ladies were all in mobs ; how do you call it ? undressed ; and it was the rainiest day that ever dripped ; and I'm weary, and 'tis past eleven.

But he takes occasion to tell her that Lady Kerry was " most egregiously ugly : but perfectly well bred and governable as I please."

Yet the house in which he was most often did not belong to one of his grander acquaintances. So far back as 1708 he had made acquaintance with Mrs. Vanhomrigh, the widow of a Dutch merchant who had been employed by William in Ireland, settled and prospered there, and died in 1703, leaving his widow with a fortune and four children. They moved to London and the lists of letters which Swift kept show that in 1709 he wrote letters to Mrs. Vanhomrigh and also that he received two from " Mishessy." This was Esther Vanhomrigh the eldest girl, of whom he was, after his fashion, making a pupil and a pet. When he came to London in 1710, the lodgings that he took in Ryder Street, St. James's, were only a few doors from the " Vans " ; it is likely that he fixed himself there to be near them.

The first mention of Esther in the *Journal* is the story of a practical joke played on him. Word was sent in, as from Mrs. Vanhomrigh, " that her eldest daughter was taken suddenly very ill and desired I would come and see her. I went and found it was a silly trick of Mrs. Armstrong, Lady Lucy's sister, who, with Moll Stanhope, was visiting there : however, I rattled off the daughter." Manifestly these ladies felt they knew how to get a visit from the gentleman who was so busy with his papers. It looks as if Stella had said something disparaging about these friends, for on February 26 he writes :

You say they are of no consequence ; why, they keep as good female company as I do male ; I see all the drabs of quality at the end of the town with them.

The intimacy grew. At the end of April Swift decided to move to Chelsea for the good of his health, to get more walking; he left his books with a friend (he was always buying books, at sight of them "my fingers itch as yours would at a china shop"); but a chest of Florence wine which St. John had given him was deposited with Mrs. Van: so also were his best gown and periwig, into which he must change before he went to pay visits: "Out of mere listlessness I dine there very often as I did to-day," he tells Stella.

But if constant thought proves anything, his inner constancy was untouched in 1711. Here is retrospect that tells of his other life, so unlike the London one.

Feb. 21.—Morning. Faith I hope it will be fair for me to walk into the city, for I take all occasions of walking.—I should be plaguy busy at Laracor if I were there now, cutting down willows, planting others, scouring my canal, and every kind of thing. If Raymond goes over this summer, you must submit, and make them a visit, that we may have another eel and trout fishing; and that Stella may ride by and see PDFR in his morning-gown in the garden, and so go up with Joe to the Hill of Bree, and round by Scurlock's Town. O Lord, how I remember names! Faith it gives me short sighs: therefore no more of that if you love me.

Again, one of the few touches that show an eye for beauty.

March 26th.—Don't you begin to see the flowers and blossoms of the field? How busy should I now be at Laracor.

Somebody said there was only one line in Molière with romantic feeling: "*La campagne en ce mois n'est pas beaucoup fleurie.*" This is Swift's equivalent.

But these are only passing glances: here is the very language of the heart:

April 5th.—Morning. Now let us proceed to examine a saucy letter from one Madam MD. God Almighty bless poor dear Ppt, and send her a great many birthdays, all happy and healthy and wealthy, and with me ever together, and never asunder again, unless by chance. When I find you are happy or merry there, it makes me so here, and I can hardly imagine you absent when I am reading your letter, or writing to you. No, faith, you are just here upon this little paper, and therefore I see and talk with you every evening constantly, and sometimes in the morning, but not always in the morning, because that is not so modest to young ladies.

There follows gossip, and then this:

I am pleased that Ppt the conjuror approves what I did with Mr. Harley; but your generosity makes me mad; I know you repine inwardly at PDFR's absence; you think he has broken his word, of coming in three months, and that this is always his trick: and now Ppt says, she does not see possibly how I can come away in haste, and that MD is satisfied, &c. An't you a rogue to overpower me thus ? I did not expect to find such friends as I have done. They may indeed deceive me too. But there are important reasons [Pox on this grease, this candle tallow !] why they should not. I have been used barbarously by the late ministry ; I am a little piqued in honour to let people see I am not to be despised. The assurances they give me, without any scruple or provocation, are such as are usually believed in the world ; they may come to nothing, but the first opportunity that offers, and is neglected, I shall depend no more, but come away.

The theme recurs :

You say you are not splenetic ; but if you be, faith you will break poor PDFR's —— I won't say the rest ; but I vow to God, if I could decently come over now, I would, and leave all schemes of politics and ambition for ever. I have lived a scurvy, dull, splenetic day, for want of MD : I often thought how happy I could have been, had it rained eight thousand times more, if MD had been with a body.

What schemes exactly were in his mind we cannot say : but one passage is more explicit. He wrote from his lodging at Chelsea to Wexford, where Stella had gone (with money provided by him) to drink the waters.

O faith, I should be glad to be in the same kingdom with MD, how-ever, although you were at Wexford. But I am kept here by a most capricious fate, which I would break through, if I could do it with decency or honour.—To return without some mark of distinction, would look extremely little : and I would likewise gladly be somewhat richer than I am. I will say no more, but beg you to be easy, till Fortune take her course, and to believe that MD's felicity is the great end I aim at in my pursuits. And so let us talk no more on this subject, which makes me melancholy, and that I would fain divert. Believe me, no man breathing at present has less share of happiness in life than I : I do not say I am unhappy at all : but that everything here is tasteless to me for want of being as I would be. And so a short sigh, and no more of this.

And again :

O Madam Stella, welcome home ; was it pleasant riding ? did your horse stumble ? how often did the man light to settle your stirrup ? ride nine miles ? faith you have galloped indeed. Well, but where's the fine thing you promised me ? I have been a good boy, ask Dingley else. I believe you did not meet the fine-thing-man : faith you are a cheat. So you'll see Raymond and his wife in town. Faith that riding to Laracor gives me short sighs, as well as you. All the days I have passed here have been dirt to those. I have been gaining enemies by the scores, and friends by the couples, which is against the rules of wisdom, because they say one enemy can do more hurt than ten friends can do good. But I have had my revenge at least, if I get nothing else. And so let fate govern. . . .

Farewell my dearest lives and delights, I love you better than ever, if possible, as hope saved, I do, and ever will. God Almighty bless you ever, and make us happy together; I pray for this twice every day; and I hope God will hear my poor hearty prayers. Remember, if I am used ill and ungratefully, as I have formerly been, 'tis what I am prepared for, and shall not wonder at it. Yet, I am now envied, and thought in high favour; and have every day numbers of considerable men teazing me to solicit for them. And the ministry will use me perfectly well, and all that know them say they love me. Yet I can count upon nothing, nor will, but upon MD's love and kindness. They think me useful; they pretended they were afraid of none but me; and that they resolved to have me; they have often confessed this: yet all makes little impression on me. Pox of these speculations! they give me the spleen; and that is a disease I was not born to.—Let me alone, sirrahs, and be satisfied: I am, as long as MD and PDFR are well:

> Little wealth,
> And much health,
> And a life by stealth;

that is all we want; and so farewell, dearest MD; Ppt, Dingley, PDFR, all together, now and for ever all together. Farewell again and again.

It is very hard to know what to make of all this: but at least, whatever he wanted, he wanted for them jointly. He wanted dignity; he wanted as much money as would " make them easy "; and he wanted, through pride, to attain these things without the need to solicit. But I cannot see the least indication that he wanted to vary in any essential way his relation to Stella. Critics have tried to read meaning into that tag of a rhyme " a life by stealth " —not recognizing that Swift constantly in these letters amused himself by making up scraps which he gravely represented as old popular sayings—and if a rhyme would not come naturally, it must come as it could. Here I think that, as so often, he had Horace running through his head: " What shall be your object? rank, or treasure hoarded, or the hidden way and the path of a life unnoticed "—*fallentis semita vitæ*. In any case, Swift's whole plan of existence excluded anything furtive from his relation with Stella; and he was still far from thinking it possible that he should be drawn into an entanglement where concealment was necessary.

It seems, however, that as the months went on, Stella grew uneasy, and thought him backward in the effort to secure a material settlement.

Soft and fair, Madam Stella, how you gallop away in your spleen and your rage about repenting my journey, and preferment here, and sixpence a dozen, and nasty England, and Laracor all my life. Hey dazy, will you never have done? I had no offers of any living. Lord-

Keeper told me some months ago, he would give me one when I pleased ; but I told him, I would not take any from him : and the Secretary told me t'other day, he had refused a very good one for me ; but it was in a place he did not like ; and I know nothing of getting any thing here, and, if they would give me leave, I would come over just now.

For by this time, July, 1711, his task on the *Examiner* was done ; and the purposes for which the ministry wanted to keep him were not yet clearly defined.

Meanwhile, through May and most of June, he had been at Chelsea in furiously hot weather, which he hated ; the opportunities of walking were not all he hoped for, because the way back was through open country (five fields) where people were often beset, and there was special reason to fear that attempts might be made on him. He often went and came by water ; the Thames was a crowded highway, and when he had the notion of going to swim in the hot nights on his return, " that puppy Patrick," his servant, would let the boats come within a yard or two of the swimmer before he warned them and then would only " call sneakingly." He went with Lady Kerry to hear the nightingales at Vauxhall, but they were " almost past singing." On the whole, Chelsea was not a success, though Atterbury had a house and garden opposite Swift's lodging and was hospitable ; and Swift liked that turbulent Jacobite. But he liked any cleric who would stand up to his superiors and there was no better bishop-baiter than Atterbury.

On the 9th of June, when he had written his last *Examiner*, there came a holiday of ten days at Lord Shelburn's house, Wycombe, " in a delicious country " between Oxford and London where he " disengaged himself from all public thoughts."

On returning he found that a new dining club had been started, to meet weekly, with Secretary St. John for its chief promoter and Swift for its layer-down of laws. Its end was " to advance conversation and friendship and to reward deserving persons with our interest and recommendation. We take in none but men of wit or men of interest ; and if we go on as we begin, no other club in this town will be worth talking of." The Lord Keeper and the Lord Treasurer (Harcourt and Harley) had been proposed, but " I was against them and so was Mr. Secretary, though their sons are of it : but we design to admit the Duke of Shrewsbury." In short, it was not to be too ministerial. Prior of course was among the chosen, and Arbuthnot, who now begins to appear in the *Journal*. The main practical purpose was to get money for needy men of letters, a matter always near Swift's heart : and moreover it gave reality to that close alliance between the " men of wit and men of interest " which he always desired to establish.

Since the next day's entry in his *Journal* contained notes of a visit to Congreve (whom Harley at Swift's desire had confirmed in his office) concerning a proposal to " erect a society or academy for correcting and settling our language," it is not surprising that Stella saw little indication of an early return ; or indeed that she should have scolded him, as seems to have been her habit, for minding other people's business more effectively than his own.

It is difficult to know where to stop in gathering up materials from the *Journal* for a picture of the man at this time—especially in this first twelvemonth of the three years, when the record is fullest. One seems to be looking into a glass crowded with images of all that is passing about him. He conjures them up for Stella : yet often enough he turns the glass, to show to himself those who are at home in Dublin :

Now, Madame Stella, what say you ? you ride every day ; I know that already, sirrah ; and if you rid every day for a twelvemonth, you would be still better and better. No, I hope Parvisol [1] will not have the impudence to make you stay an hour for the money ; if he does, I'll un-parvisol him ; pray let me know. O Lord, how hasty we are ; Stella can't stay writing and writing ; she must write and go a cockhorse, pray now. Well, but the horses are not come to the door ; the fellow can't find the bridle ; your stirrup is broken ; where did you put the whips, Dingley ? Marg't, where have you laid Mrs. Johnson's ribband to tie about her ? reach me my mask ; sup up this before you go. So, so, a gallop, a gallop ; sit fast, sirrah, and don't ride hard upon the stones. Well, now Stella is gone, tell me, Dingley, is she a good girl ? and what news is that you are to tell me ?

And sometimes what we see is his own face and gesture :

'Tis three weeks, young women, since I had a letter from you ; and yet, methinks, I would not have another for five pound till this is gone ; and yet I send every day to the coffeehouse, and I would fain have a letter, and not have a letter : and I don't know what, nor I don't know how ; and this goes on very slow ; 'tis a week to-morrow since I began it. I am a poor country gentleman, and don't know how the world passes. Do you know that every syllable I write I hold my lips just for all the world as if I were talking in our own little language to MD. Faith, I am very silly ; but I can't help it for my life.

That was the first of his letters from Chelsea. It seems to me that there is a change to be noted in them after July, when for the first time he went to Windsor, and his ambitions took a more definite shape.

---

[1] Parvisol was the agent who collected his tithes.

CHAPTER X

WINDSOR AND LONDON, 1711–13

ON July 5 Swift left Chelsea and spent the evening with " the Society."

We dined at Lord-Keeper's with young Harcourt, and Lord-Keeper was forced to sneak off, and dine with Lord-Treasurer, who had invited the Secretary and me to dine with him ; but we scorned to leave our company, as George Granville did, whom we have threatened to expel.

However, in the evening Swift went to join Lord Oxford (as Harley was now) and spent that and other evenings with him in the next few days. Except for the Lord Treasurer, London was empty now, for the Court was at Windsor ; and as a consequence most of Swift's time was spent at " neighbour Van's," till on July 20 he got his wish and was carried down to Windsor in the Lord Treasurer's coach, on a sudden invitation—short of linen and the rest; he had to borrow one of St. John's shirts next day to go to Court in. From that time on till October he was oftener than not at Windsor, in the lodgings of a prebendary which had been put at St. John's disposal. " Windsor is a delicious place," he writes. His heart was set on a prebend there, out of London, with an avenue two miles long to walk in, yet so near as to be close in touch with ministers.

There seemed at that time no reason why this or any ambition of his within reason should not be gratified, for his position was extraordinary. Taking small things first, on his second visit to Windsor (this time travelling down with the Secretary), one of the Lord Treasurer's servants gave him a letter, from a person whose name is suppressed ; the writer offered a present of fifty pounds " because, he said, he desired to be well with me."

I was in a rage : but my friend Lewis cooled me, and said, it is what the best men sometimes meet with ; and I have been not seldom served in the like manner, although not so grossly. In these cases I never demur a moment ; nor ever found the least inclination to take any thing.

Or again in quite another way, at Court he found himself " generally acquainted with about thirty in the drawing-room; and am so proud I make all the lords come up to me." For he maintained his humour in all its pretensions, against fine ladies, as well as fine gentlemen. The Duchess of Shrewsbury, a beautiful and flirtatious Italian, met him walking with St. John and asked, " Was not that Dr. —— Dr. ——, and she could not say my name in English, but said Dr. Presto." [1] A couple of months later we find her reproaching him for not dining with her.

I said, that was not so soon done; for I expected more advances from ladies, especially duchesses: she promised to comply with any demands I pleased; and I agreed to dine with her to-morrow, if I did not go to London too soon, as I believe I shall before dinner.

In point of fact, next day he drove up early with the Lord Treasurer.

For these affectations disguised, or did not disguise, a very real importance, which rested on two facts; first, that his pen was needed more than it ever had been: and secondly, that his personality was a cement to the Ministry which threatened to fall asunder. Again we may begin with jesting references. In October he and St. John were supping with Oxford and there was " old laughing " against the anger of Sir John Walters, Comptroller of the Board of Green Cloth, because Swift dining there had thought the Queen's wine 'something small.' " I said nothing grieves me but that they would take example and get out of my government; but that I thought I was not obliged to govern bears, though I governed men." Next day the Lord Keeper, Harcourt, warned Walters to be careful how he railed, " for, said he, Dr. Swift is not only all our favourite, but our governor."

In fact, the Ministry was in great danger and depended for its continuance on some notable success. " A peace," Swift wrote on August 27, " is all we have to preserve us "; and Prior had been despatched on a mysterious journey to France. But already there were whisperings that St. John was about to retire; and if so, Swift was clear that the whole combination must crumble. " Do you know," he had written on August 15, " that I have ventured all my credit with these great ministers, to clear some understanding between them; and, if there be no breach, I ought to have the merit of it ? 'Tis a plaguy ticklish piece of work, and a man hazards losing both sides."

As to his other function, of publicist, he writes at the end of that same long letter,

[1] This is the origin of the " Presto " in Deane Swift's reprint of the *Journal* where the original read PDFR.

There is now but one business the ministry wants me for; and when that is done, I will take my leave of them. I never got a penny from them, nor expect it. In my opinion, some things stand very ticklish; I dare say nothing at this distance. Farewell, dear sirrahs, dearest lives: there is peace and quiet with MD and nowhere else. They have not leisure here to think of small things, which may ruin them; and I have been forward enough. Farewell again, dearest rogues: I am never happy, but when I write or think of MD. I have enough of courts and ministers; and wish I were at Laracor; and if I could with honour come away this moment, I would.

The " one business " of which there is mention again and again, the task " that lies on my hands and will take up a great deal of time "—was to write something which would alter the current of popular feeling from the channel into which Marlborough's long success had made it flow. As late as November the manuscript was still under revision; Swift dined at the Secretary's house along with Prior, then back from France. The result was seen when " The Conduct of the Allies " came out and turned the anger of the British people against Dutch selfishness.

Yet even while this was on the anvil he had to be busy with the other part of his task. On October 20 he recounts what had passed during a sitting with St. John that lasted till two in the morning.

The Secretary told me last night, that he had found the reason why the Queen was cold to him for some months past; that a friend had told it him yesterday; and it was, that they suspected he was at the bottom with the Duke of Marlborough. Then he said, he had reflected upon all I had spoken to him long ago; but he thought it had only been my suspicion, and my zeal and kindness for him. I said I had reason to take that very ill, to imagine I knew so little of the world as to talk at a venture to a great minister; that I had gone between him and Lord-Treasurer often, and told each of them what I had said to the other, and that I had informed him so before: he said all that you may imagine to excuse himself, and approve my conduct. I told him I knew all along that this proceeding of mine was the surest way to send me back to my willows in Ireland, but that I regarded it not, provided I could do the kingdom service in keeping them well together. I minded him how often I had told Lord-Treasurer, Lord-Keeper, and him together, that all things depended on their union, and that my comfort was to see them love one another; and I had told them all singly that I had not said this by chance, &c. He was in a rage to be thus suspected; swears he will be upon a better foot, or none at all; and I do not see how they can well want him in this juncture. I hope to find a way of settling this matter. I act an honest part; that will bring me neither honour nor praise. MD must think the better of me for it: nobody else shall ever know of it.

It is not the business of Swift's biographer to elucidate the complex and shifting relations between Harley and St. John. What he must make clear is Swift's attitude to them, and theirs to him. It can be said without reserve that neither of them ever questioned Swift's perfect loyalty to them as ministers, or complained that he was partisan of the one against the other; for both realized that to him the only hope for the common course lay in their acting harmoniously together. A day came when Swift, after using his best efforts to reconcile them, saw that it was impossible, and therefore withdrew from all contact with public affairs, while the struggle between these two former allies continued. When it ended, and Oxford fell, Swift had lost no fraction of his ground in either man's esteem; and Bolingbroke, the winner, appealed for his help and had much to offer in return for it. But Oxford, defeated and insulted, asked for his friend's company in retirement; and Swift did not hesitate a moment. He followed his affection, and pitched interest and ambition to the winds.

In these years, even before the series of events had completed themselves, he wrote characters of the two rivals in his *History of the Four Last Years of Queen Anne*. Yet we get nearer the inwardness of his feeling about them if we study his letters of the moment. Harley is nowhere described in the *Journal to Stella*, but from his first appearance in it, he figures on every second page and a picture of the man builds itself up—genial, jovial, a great lover of talk far into the night; always the boon companion, no good friend to sobriety, yet devotedly and happily a family man; in public life, apparently careless and really dilatory, yet compensating these defects by cheerful courage and a refusal to be rushed into precipitate action. A very frank and full appraisement of him is to be found in a letter from Swift to Archbishop King, written from Windsor in August, 1711.

The Treasurer is much the greatest Minister I ever knew; regular in life, with a true sense of religion, an excellent scholar, and a good divine, of a very mild and affable disposition, intrepid in his notions, and indefatigable in business, an utter despiser of money for himself, yet frugal, perhaps to an extremity, for the public. In private company, he is wholly disengaged, and very facetious, like one who has no business at all. He never wants a reserve upon any emergency, which would appear desperate to others; and makes little use of those thousand projectors and schematists, who are daily plying him with their visions, but to be thoroughly convinced, by the comparison, that his own notions are the best.

It would be interesting to scrutinize the passages in the *Journal* where Swift is almost talking to himself) which have to do with these two men, and try to distinguish how he is affected towards each. For there is a difference—naturally, since in the first place Harley was the acknowledged chief; secondly, he was as much senior in years to Swift as Swift was to St. John. There is through-out a note of deference to Harley's position; in the other case, homage is paid to genius—a word that Swift would never have used in speaking of the Lord Treasurer. The homage is masked as usual under a show of roughness. " I would have you to know, sir," Swift writes in the earliest letter of his to St. John which survives, " that if the Queen gave you a dukedom and the Garter to-morrow, with the Treasury at the end of it, I would regard you no more than if you were not worth a groat." That is his way of saying that no accidents of fortune could add distinction to such talents as St. John possessed by nature. But to Stella he is more explicit.

I think Mr. St. John the greatest young man I ever knew; wit, capacity, beauty, quickness of apprehension, good learning, and an excellent taste; the best orator in the House of Commons, admirable conversation, good nature, and good manners; generous, and a despiser of money. His only fault is talking to his friends in way of complaint of too great a load of business, which looks a little like affectation; and he endeavours too much to mix the fine gentleman, and man of pleasure, with the man of business. What truth and sincerity he may have I know not: he is now but thirty-two, and has been Secretary above a year. Is not all this extraordinary?

In this case there was no possibility, as in Harley's, of admiring a happy family circle, and entering into it; for St. John was dis-solute, and by his intemperance no less of a trial to Swift than the Lord Treasurer. Many are the references to attempts at restricting his consumption of burgundy and champagne; though to his credit should be put various gifts of wine—notably, a chest of Florence which was deposited at the Vanhomrighs so that Swift could make his contribution to that hospitable board. Students of the matter may be distressed to hear that this consignment mostly went sour, " though what the Secretary has himself is the best I ever drank," says Swift ruefully. Indeed from another passage, this gift would seem to have been only some poor amends, for Peterborough on one of his flying passages through Europe sent St. John twelve dozen flasks of Burgundy on condition that Swift should have his share; but " the toad was never quiet till he had finished the whole. I tell him he owes me thirty-six pounds "; which means that Peterborough, as was to be expected, had sent of the best—perhaps

Corton Clos du Roy, which was then commended to Louis XIV
for his special drinking. But on the whole Swift was a moderating
influence in this boon companionship, and records with pride in
April, 1711, that he had found the Secretary " drinking tea while
the rest were at champagne." This was in a moment of penitence
induced by " gravel and pains in his back," brought on by
indulgence added to sitting up all night at business.

I have chid him so severely, that I hardly knew whether he would
take it well : then I went and sat an hour with Mrs. St. John, who is
growing a great favourite of mine ; she goes to Bath on Wednesday,
for she is much out of health, and has begged me to take care of the
Secretary.

During his first stay at Windsor in August he went off with
the couple to the lady's house at Bucklebury, on the high ground
between the Kennet and the Pang, and saw Mr. Secretary playing
the perfect country gentleman :

He smoked tobacco with one or two neighbours ; he inquired after
the wheat in such a field ; he went to visit his hounds, and knew all their
names ; he and his lady saw me to my chamber just in the country fashion.

In short, the two chief men in the ministry not only made Swift
in all possible ways " the companion of their pleasures," to use
his own phrase, but gave him full liberty to admonish them. Yet
I do not think he used this so freely with the elder man as with
the one who was ten years his junior. All the scoldings of Lord
Treasurer that are noted have to do with his practice of being
late on the road to Windsor, which Swift held to be a needless
risk. The more serious admonitions on the danger of dissension
are not reported even to Stella.

Naturally, the world was much concerned with this unofficial
colleague. He was indeed not the only one. " Prior and I are
called ' the two Sosias,' in a Whig newspaper," he notes in November of 1711 ; and in London the Sosias were often together
in St. John's company. Both owed their position in great measure
to their social gifts, for Prior too was as witty in talk as on paper
—though Swift says of him that " he did not leave elbow-room in
conversation." This is a charge that no one brought against Swift
himself in that society—though it may have been different later
when he was the autocrat of Dublin, a big fish in a little pond.
He had no desire to shine at other men's expense. It matters
more, however, that Prior's relation to ministers, apart from his
pleasantness, was that of a specialist in foreign affairs. He was a

ried diplomatic agent. Swift stood nearer to the centre. His
commanding ability and his weight of character imposed him as
counsellor. Dictatorial affectations masked a real disposition to
govern, wherever he found himself; and the best tribute to his
worth is that it was not resented.

Yet as we know now, he was not in the innermost secret. He
never knew, and never even suspected, that both Harley and
St. John were repeatedly in negotiation with the Pretender. So
far as can be ascertained, Prior, then chief British agent in all dealings
with France, knew no more than Swift. But for this there was
good reason. All such traffickings—inspired by a very natural
dislike of the idea of seeing a German princeling on the English
throne—were conducted at the risk of men's lives. With Prior,
there was the danger that compromising papers should be seized
on him while abroad. With Swift the case was different. No
minister in his senses would even hint at such a project unless to
willing ears. Swift was an Irish Protestant, and he must have let
Harley and St. John know that virtually every Irish Protestant
regarded the return of the Stuarts as meaning forfeiture of Protestant
estates in Ireland.

But on the main drift of policy, which was to secure a peace,
and for this purpose, to overthrow the combined power of the
Marlboroughs and the profiteers, it is clear that ministers took
Swift into their fullest confidence; and that he even took part in
shaping the details of policy. He was not completely alone in his
position; up till the summer of 1714 there was what he himself calls
" a triumvirate of honest counsellors." One of them was Erasmus
Lewis, Dartmouth's secretary, but personally as devoted as Swift
to " the Dragon "—their nickname for the Lord Treasurer. From
the spring of 1711 all Swift's correspondence was addressed to
Lewis at Lord Dartmouth's office, " for," he writes, " I never go
to the coffee-house nowadays." Lewis, as his letters show, was
a man of wit as well as an experienced courtier. The other triumvir
was Arbuthnot, that wise physician, humorist and man of abstruse
learning, and Swift valued no man more. Intimacy between them
had begun before the move to Windsor, but there they had closer
companionship.

One privilege was denied to Swift in all his stay at Court; he
never met the Queen; and there is a perceptible note of disappointment on this head. It is noteworthy that in August, 1711,
when Oxford and St. John talked of their friend to Anne, she
said " she had never heard of him." The ministers " thought

to mortify me," Swift says : "I told them that was their faul
and not hers, etc., and so we laughed." But in truth the les
Anne had heard of the author of *A Tale of a Tub*, the better for hi
interest ; and it looks as if the literary offences of his past woul
never have risen up against him, had he not committed new an
graver imprudences. *Deorum offensa diis curæ* was a Latin sayin
that he often quoted ; but he forgot the other tag which shoul
have reminded him *furens quid femina possit*. The Duchess o
Marlborough was out of office and Mrs. Masham full in favour
but the Duchess of Somerset was Mistress of the Robes and n
friend to ministers. Her Duke, Master of the Horse, propose
one day to attend the Council meeting, and St. John refused t
meet him there ; the cabinet was adjourned till next day when
there was a race meeting at which the Duke would be indispensable.
So opened a feud into which Swift must needs venture his hand,
attacking not the Duke but his more formidable partner.

That, however, came later : meanwhile he had made acquaintance with the reigning favourite. Mrs. Masham seemed to him
"extremely like one Mrs. Malolly" (presumably Mullaly) "that
was once my landlady at Trim" ; but at the Lord Treasurer's
table she was "used with great kindness and respect." Swift,
who seldom failed to win women, succeeded with her also, and
when the final break-up came, after she had quarrelled with Oxford,
her first promoter, she had nothing but good words for the man
who had, she said, been always the Ministry's best and most loyal
adviser.

A couple of glimpses of the court, indoors and out, may suggest
the background for this time.

Aug. 8th, 1711.—There was a drawing-room to-day at court : but
so few company, that the Queen sent for us into her bed-chamber, where
we made our bows, and stood about twenty of us round the room,
while she looked at us round with her fan in her mouth, and once a
minute said about three words to some that were nearest her, and then
she was told dinner was ready, and went out. I dined at the Green
Cloth, by Mr. Scarborow's invitation, who is in waiting. It is much
the best table in England, and costs the Queen a thousand pounds a month
while she is at Windsor or Hampton Court ; and is the only mark of
magnificence or hospitality I can see in the Queen's family : it is designed
to entertain foreign ministers, and people of quality, who come to see
the Queen, and have no place to dine at.

Two days later :

Mr. Vice-Chamberlain lent me his horses to ride about and see the
country this morning. Dr. Arbuthnot, the Queen's physician and

favourite, went out with me to show me the places : we went a little after the Queen, and overtook Miss Forester, a maid of honour, on her palfrey, taking the air : we made her go along with us. We saw a place they have made for a famous horse-race to-morrow, where the Queen will come. We met the Queen coming back, and Miss Forester stood, like us, with her hat off while the Queen went by. . . . I was tired with riding a trotting mettlesome horse a dozen miles, having not been on horseback this twelvemonth. And Miss Forester did not make it easier ; she is a silly true maid of honour, and I did not like her, although she be a toast, and was dressed like a man.

Among such scenes Swift's life now passed (though they are not often sketched with so pictorial a touch) and as early as May, 1711, he notes for Stella the alteration :

Prithee, don't you observe how strangely I have changed my company and manner of living ? I never go to a coffeehouse ; you hear no more of Addison, Steele, Henley, Lady Lucy, Mrs. Finch, Lord Somers, Lord Halifax, &c. I think I have altered for the better.

Yet, though the others dropped out, he clung to Addison, only less constantly than to his absent but perpetual companion. Here is a characteristic passage in September, 1711, on one of his returns to London from Windsor :

This evening I met Addison and Pastoral Philips in the Park, and supped with them at Addison's lodgings ; we were very good company ; and yet know no man half so agreeable to me as he is. I sat with them till twelve, so you may think 'tis late, young women ; however, I would have some little conversation with MD before your PDFR goes to bed, because it makes me sleep and dream, and so forth. Faith this letter goes on slowly enough, sirrahs, but I can't write much at a time till you are quite settled after your journey you know, and have gone all your visits, and lost your money at ombre. You never play at chess now, Ppt. That puts me in mind of Dick Tighe ; I fancy I told you he used to beat his wife here : and she deserved it ; and he resolves to part with her ; and they went to Ireland in different coaches. O Lord, I said all this before, I'm sure. Go to bed, sirrahs.

Meetings with Addison were not always so pleasant : here is another entry :

I met Mr. Addison and Pastoral Philips on the Mall to-day, and took a turn with them ; but they both looked terrible dry and cold. A curse of party ! And do you know I have taken more pains to recommend the Whig wits to the favour and mercy of the ministers than any other people. Steele I have kept in his place. Congreve I have got to be used kindly, and secured. Rowe I have recommended, and got a promise of a place. Philips I could certainly have provided for, if he had not run party mad, and made me withdraw my recommendation ; and I set Addison so right at first, that he might have been employed, and have partly secured him the place he has ; yet I am worse used by that faction than any man. Well, go to cards, sollah Ppt, and dress the wine and olange, sollah MD, and I'll go seep. 'Tis rate. Nite MD.

But that was at a moment when party ran fiercest, as will have to be shown. At all times, however, Addison was one to whom Swift's door was never refused : a very small list, drilled into the mind of another personage, who figures prodigiously in the *Journal*. This was Patrick, the servant whom Swift had brought with him from Ireland and whom a dozen times he says he would dismiss at once, if he were in Ireland. It is a fair presumption from what we know of Swift that he thought the man might have difficulty in finding another place ; but the provocations were excessive. Patrick got drunk three times a week (gin in those days was of extraordinary cheapness) and what was worse he got drunk at critical moments. But he had one merit ; he learnt to be so valiant in denying the door to unwelcome callers that Swift put him almost on a level with Harley's porter, whose talent in this respect was famous ; indeed, when Harley's man left, Swift had thoughts of recommending Patrick. Otherwise, the mentions of him are far from proper for a good character. Patrick's hand shook so much that he could not shave his master's head one morning (heads as well as faces had to be shaven in those days of periwigs) ; Patrick was away with the key when his master came home and could not be found—this happened again and again, and there was then no such instrument as a latch-key. When St. John on a sudden picked up Swift to take him to Windsor, Patrick was missing and the doctor must go without his portmanteau. The climax came one day at Windsor :

I sat with Lady Oglethorp till eight this evening, then was going home to write ; looked about for the woman that keeps the key of the house ; she told me Patrick had it. I cooled my heels in the cloisters till nine, then went in to the music meeting, where I had been often desired to go ; but was weary in half an hour of their fine stuff, and stole out so privately, that every body saw me ; and cooled my heels in the cloisters again till after ten : then came in Patrick. I went up, shut the chamber door, and gave him two or three swinging cuffs on the ear, and I have strained the thumb of my left hand with pulling him, which I did not feel until he was gone. He was plaguily afraid and humbled.

Patrick lasted into a second year and then they parted, to Swift's relief ; and when after some months he came soliciting to be taken back, he was refused though his successor was " not such an artist at denying me." Yet it is to Patrick and not to his respectable successor that we owe glimpses of that life below-stairs which always attracted Swift, as we know from his " Directions to Servants." When the new Parliament met in November, 1710, and a Speaker was chosen, the footmen, according to usage, formed themselves into a debating society :

Pompey, Colonel Hill's black, designs to stand speaker for the footmen. I am engaged to use my interest for him, and have spoken to Patrick to get him some votes.

Hill was Mrs. Masham's brother, and Pompey therefore represented the interest of Harley's party.

There was another underworld with which Swift had constant intercourse—that of the printers and their myrmidons. When he went to see them in the city, he had a chop at their houses, or ate by himself at a " hedge tavern." He trusted them ; John Barber in particular was his man of confidence ; and he needed one whom he could trust, for he and they were concerned with business that might bring them not only into trouble but danger ; in London, as later in Dublin, it came close to them. But neither in London nor in Dublin did Swift's agents let him down. After all, they had good reason : the profit to be made from his writings was theirs, he never took a penny of it ; and in London when he had the power, he got them government contracts and they clamoured for more, till he complained that he must " grease fat sows." Yet I think that Barber anyhow, if not Tooke also, would have gone to jail for him uncomplaining, as his Dublin printer did when the need came.

I must now trace the course of events as they affected the anonymous pamphleteer.

His great pamphlet *The Conduct of the Allies* was finished on November 24, 1711, ready to be published " in three or four days when the Parliament begins sitting." It was out on the 27th and by the 28th " begins to make a noise. I was asked by several whether I had seen it, and they advised me to read it, for it was something very extraordinary. I shall be suspected ; and it will have several paltry answers." Next day a new edition was wanted, and " Lord Treasurer made out one or two small additions. It will do a world of good ; it tells abundance of most important facts which were not at all known."

About its doing good to himself, he was not sanguine. " Dilly " Ashe, one of the College set, was back in Dublin and had made his report :

'Tis right what Dilly says ; I depend upon nothing from my friends, but to go back as I came. Never fear, Laracor will mend with a peace, or surely they'll give me the Dublin parish.

The object of the pamphlet (really a little book, sold at a shilling) was to turn public opinion in favour of a peace; to represent the war as carried on solely in the interest of a family (the Marlborough-Godolphin clan), and of a faction—the Whigs and the stockjobbers. Yet these things are not insisted on, nor does the attack on English opponents of the Ministry appear violent : a moderate tone becomes that studious marshalling of argument. Where the true purpose lies, apparent to any student of controversial methods, is in veiled appeal to deep-seated prejudices. It is never hinted that well within living memory the Dutch had been England's determined foe in war; it is never recalled how their fleet insulted and triumphed almost to the port of London. But no Londoner would need to be reminded of Van Tromp with a besom at his masthead; nor was it necessary to dwell on Dutch competition in the carrying trade. All that Swift wanted was to make the English people feel that they had been duped and exploited by the Dutch; had been led to make war in the manner most profitable to their old rivals and enemies, and least profitable to themselves. Because the Duke of Marlborough's genius was not for naval war, all England's victories had been obtained on land, with the result of giving to the Dutch enlarged territory and new commercial advantages. The navy had been used, not in oversea conquests, but in conveying from one country to another mercenary troops for whom England had to pay. The Emperor had gone back on his contracts and left England to make good; was it really essential to carry on the war in order that Spain should be added to the Emperor's dominions ? But the Emperor is a side issue. The pith of the argument is directed against the Dutch, and against those who wanted to swamp England's credit and resources with a war by which the Dutch were to be the gainers.

Results did not come at once, though edition followed edition and the Whigs were " resolved to bring the pamphlet into the House of Lords to have it condemned. But the printer will stand to it and not own the author." There were defections ; Nottingham, a famous Tory, went over to the Whig side. The Lord Treasurer held that a ballad on " Dismal " (so they called him for his looks) would be useful, and by next day one was ready, " two degrees above Grub Street." The Society met that day and before they parted, the printer came with copies " which made them laugh

[1] This means that his tithes would improve.

very heartily a dozen times." It was easy to turn the laugh against Nottingham, but he had his revenge next day when the Lords on his motion voted that no peace should be made unless the Bourbon King were put out of Spain : " a mighty blow and loss of reputation to Lord Treasurer and may end in his ruin." The next day the Lords renewed the vote by an increased majority, and omens seemed to show that the Queen had deserted her ministers. Swift was with Mrs. Masham when Oxford came in " and appeared in good humour as usual, but I thought his countenance was much cast down. . . . I told him I should have the advantage of him for he would lose his head and I should only be hanged and so carry my body entire to the grave." Next day the *Journal* tells of a resolution to get abroad somewhere for several months " for I should hardly trust myself to the mercy of my enemies while their anger was fresh." So it went on through December. Lewis was no more hopeful than Swift ; Secretary St. John was reassuring ; but it was only Oxford who kept up a cheerful face. " Says he, you had better keep company with me, than with such a fellow as Lewis who has not the soul of a chicken, nor the heart of a mite." On the 6th :

> I took courage to-day, and went to court with a very cheerful counten-ance. It was mightily crowded ; both parties coming to observe each other's faces. I have avoided Lord Halifax's bow till he forced it on me ; but we did not talk together. I could not make less than fourscore bows, of which about twenty might be to Whigs.

So the *Journal* goes on, marking time through the crisis ; meanwhile the " Conduct," now in a sixpenny form, was being dis-tributed all through the country by " great men who subscribe for hundreds. . . . The Tory Lords and Commons argue all from it ; and all agree that never anything of the kind was of so great consequence, or made so many converts." Meanwhile, the Society met on the 20th :

> That odious Secretary would make me president next week ; so I must entertain them this day se'nnight at the Thatched House Tavern, where we dined to-day ; it will cost me five or six pounds ; yet the Secretary says he will give me wine.

Swift never liked expense, but this dinner was to cost him more than money. His main fear for the Ministry concerned the Duchess of Somerset ; her Duke was out, but she remained Mistress of the Robes, and to pass the time on December 23 he wrote a " Prophecy." " I like it mightily. I don't know how it will pass." It was a furious lampoon on the Duchess and there must have been talk about it; on the 26th Mrs. Masham begged him not to let it be published for fear of angering the Queen. So he wrote to the printers to stop them; but next day when he entertained his brethren at the Thatched House, the printer brought up dozens apiece of the " Prophecy." " But I ordered him to part with no more." A hopeful precaution when over a hundred copies were loose on the town, and " people mad for it."

Two days after this, December 29, he broke open his *Journal* after it was sealed : " We are all safe." The Queen had made twelve peers to have a majority. " Three of the new lords are of our society. I want nothing now but to see the Duchess out. But we shall do without her." They did not see the back of the Duchess of Somerset, but there was triumph ; even Marlborough was " turned out of all," an extreme measure which Swift disapproved : " I do not love to see personal resentment mix with public affairs." He set to work, this time on his own prompting, to make a plea for moderation in a " Letter to the October Club," the dining club which grouped together all the extreme Tory landed interest. It was not at all so popular as the " Conduct," at which he felt some spleen : " it is finely written and like a true author I grow fond of it because it does not sell."

But there was no limit to the success of the " Conduct." On January 4 :

The House of Commons have this day made many severe votes about our being abused by our allies. Those who spoke, drew all their arguments from my book, and their votes confirm all I writ ; the court had a majority of a hundred and fifty : all agree that it was my book that spirited them to these resolutions.

And again :

The Resolutions printed t'other day in the Votes are almost quotations from it ; and would never have passed, if that book had not been written.

Yet there was no news of his personal advancement. " I will set out in March," he wrote on January 25, " unless the ministry desire me to stay till the end of the session ; but I believe they will not ; for I suppose the peace will be made and they will have no farther service for me. I must make my canal fine this summer, as fine as I can. I am afraid I shall see great neglect among my quicksets. I hope the cherry trees and the river walk are fine things now. But no more of this." A few days before he had received an ugly fright about his small savings, £400, which he had left with his city friend Stratford to be invested in South Sea stock ; and news came that Stratford was on the point of breaking :

I came home reflecting a little ; nothing concerned me but MD. I called all my philosophy and religion up ; and, I thank God, it did not keep me awake beyond my usual time above a quarter of an hour.

He was secure when he wrote this, for the stock had been bought and transferred in due form ; yet it gives a pleasant glimpse of the real man. Bolingbroke used to call Swift " an inverted hypocrite " ; there is less of that disguise in the *Journal* than elsewhere ; but even in the *Journal* he seldom speaks with this grave sincerity. About his personal hopes he keeps his counsel, though it is clear that at this time they ran high. On February 9, 1712, he writes :

I have not been with any of the Ministry these 2 or 3 days. I keep out of their way on purpose, for a certain Reason, for some time, thō I must dine with the Sec^y to-morrow, the choosing of the Company being left to me.[1]

The fact was that the Deanery of Wells was vacant and there was universal expectation that Swift would be chosen. By March the rumour had reached Stella and he answers :

No—if you will have it—I am not Dean of Wells, nor know anything of being so ; nor is there any thing in the story ; and that's enough.

Yet in July, Archbishop King was congratulating him—though with reserve—on the intended preferment ; and steps were actually taken in Ireland to fill up his living at Laracor.

I cannot but think that two letters in the Correspondence are misdated.

Swift to the Earl of Oxford

Jan. 5th, 1712–13.

I most humbly take leave to inform your Lordship that the Dean of Wells died this morning at one o'clock. I entirely submit my poor fortunes to your Lordship.

Lord Bolingbroke to Swift. Thursday morning, Two o'clock.

January 8, 1712–13.

Though I have not seen you, I did not fail to write to Lord Treasurer. *Non tua res agitur*, dear Jonathan. It is the Treasurer's cause ; it is my cause ; it is every man's cause, who is embarked in our bottom. Depend upon it, that I will never neglect any opportunity of showing that true esteem, that sincere affection, and honest friendship for you, which fill the breast of your faithful servant,

BOLINGBROKE.

Surely this should be 1711–12.

However that may be, I have little doubt that the reason why

---

[1] One of the two he had engaged was Lord Carteret, then a brilliant young man of five-and-twenty, and a Whig. His path and Swift's crossed later, notably as will be seen. Another sentence here is worth quoting : " If I like anybody at Court to-morrow, I may perhaps invite them."

Swift kept out of the way of Ministers in February, 1712, was that his hope of this deanery, if it had not been actually intimated by him, was known to them.

But nothing happened: the session lasted; negotiations about the peace dragged on, and on March 26 he writes:

> I believe I shall lose credit with you, by not coming over at the beginning of April; but I hoped the session would be ended, and I must stay till then; yet I would fain be at the beginning of my willows growing. Percival tells me, that the quicksets upon the flat in the garden do not grow so well as those famous ones on the ditch. They want digging about them. The cherry trees, by the river-side, my heart is set upon. Nite MD.

I wonder if he knew how charming a ballad verse was that last line; anyhow, Laracor was the only place that ever made Swift lyrical. But April brought a violent attack of shingles which left him for the whole of the month "in no danger of life, but in miserable torture"—"the most pain I ever bore in my life," he writes on May 10, when he was well enough to return visits of kind inquiry. The *Journal* is replaced here by occasional letters, and they are ambiguous enough as to his own affairs.

> I protest it is impossible for one, who has any thing to do with this ministry, to be certain when he fixes any time. There is a business, which, till it take some turn or other, I cannot leave this place in prudence or honour. And I never wished so much as now, that I had staid in Ireland; but the die is cast, and is now a-spinning, and till it settles, I cannot tell whether it be an ace or a sise. I am confident by what you know yourselves, that you will justify me in all this. The moment I am used ill, I will leave them; but know not how to do it while things are in suspense. The session will soon be over, (I believe in a fortnight,) and the peace, we hope, will be made in a short time; and there will be no farther occasion for me; nor have I any thing to trust to but court gratitude; so that I expect to see my willows a month after the Parliament is up: but I will take MD in my way, and not go to Laracor like an unmannerly spraenekich ferrow.

This recalls his rush for solitude when he returned in 1709—a "splenetic fellow." But splenetic he was during a great part of that year, 1712, partly because there was no outlet for his energy. He wrote nothing of consequence; his only business was to wait and watch, and keep the peace among ministers. June and July he spent at Kensington for his health—and it is evident that the ladies in Dublin grew uneasy. "I wish I had never come here as often and as heartily as Ppt. What had I to do here?" he answers. Then he went to Windsor and got a letter that for once

ade him angry—it must have assumed that he was keeping them
the dark about the deanery.

I just read it, and immediately sealed it up again, and shall read it no
ore this twelve month at least. The reason of my resentment at it
, because you talk as glibly of a thing as if it were done, which, for
ught I know, is farther from being done than ever, since I hear not a
ord of it, though the town is full of it, and the court always giving
e joy and vexation. You might be sure I would have let you know
soon as it was done; but I believe you fancied I would affect not to
ll it you, but let you learn it from newspapers and reports.

nd again from Windsor, September 15, 1712:

I never was so long without writing to MD as now, since I left
em, nor ever will again while I am able to write. I have expected
om one week to another that something would be done in my own
fairs; but nothing at all is, nor I don't know when any thing will,
whether ever at all, so slow are people at doing favours. I have
een much out of order of late with the old giddiness in my head. . . .
ne is kept constantly out of humour by a thousand unaccountable
ings in public proceedings; and when I reason with some friends,
e cannot conceive how affairs can last as they are. God only knows,
ut it is a very melancholy subject for those who have any near concern
it. I am again endeavouring, as I was last year, to keep people from
reaking to pieces upon a hundred misunderstandings. One cannot
ithhold them from drawing different ways, while the enemy is watching
destroy both. See how my style is altered, by living and thinking
d talking among these people, instead of my canal and river-walk and
illows. . . .

Pray God preserve MD's health, and Pdfr's, and that I may live far
om the envy and discontent that attends those who are thought to have
ore favour at courts than they really possess. Love Pdfr, who loves
D above all things.

gain on October 11 in reply to a request that he should do
mething for Stella's brother-in-law:

I tell you what, as things are at present, I cannot possibly speak to
rd-Treasurer for any body. I need tell you no more. Something or
thing will be done in my own affairs; if the former, I will be a solici-
r for your sister; if the latter, I have done with courts for ever.
pportunities will often fall my way, if I am used well, and I will then
ake it my business. It is my delight to do good offices for people who
ant and deserve, and a tenfold delight to do it to a relation of Ppt,
hose affairs she has so at heart. . . .

Oct. 29.—I have helped to patch up these people together once more.
od knows how long it may last. . . .

Oct. 30.—The Duke of Ormond will not be over these three or four
ys. I design to make him join with me in settling all right among our
ople. I have ordered the Duchess to let me have an hour with the
uke at his first coming, to give him a true state of persons and things.

Swift's intimacy with the Ormonds was different from that with either Oxford or Bolingbroke; he loved Ormond and his whole family, but instinctively had the tone of a leader with him rather than of an ally. It was his constant endeavour to keep Ormond and Oxford in close contact: for if the contest between the two leaders came to a breach, Swift was Oxford's man, not Bolingbroke's.

A chance made the bond closer—the " bandbox plot." Swift was with the Lord Treasurer when an odd-looking parcel was brought in and he advised cutting the string instead of untying it. The technique of such enterprise has considerably improved, but Swift believed that he had saved both their lives, " for there was a bullet apiece " in a double barrelled pistol with string tied to the triggers.

Meantime he had found occupation for himself, partly in his project for an Academy to reform the English language, which he set out in an open letter to the Lord Treasurer as early as May—and continually pressed for a grant of funds. But his main work was the preparation of a full history of the events leading up to the peace then in negotiation. It vexed him that Stella should think he stayed from choice.

What a stir is here about your company and visits! Charming company, no doubt; now I keep no company, nor have I any desire to keep any. I never go to a coffee-house nor a tavern, nor have touched a card since I left Windsor. I make few visits, nor go to levees; my only debauching is sitting late where I dine, if I like the company. I have almost dropped the Duchesses of Shrewsbury and Hamilton, and several others. Lord-Treasurer, the Duke of Ormond, and Lady Orkney, are all that I see very often. O yes, and Lady Masham and Lord Bolingbroke, and one or two private friends. I make no figure but at court, where I affect to turn from a lord to the meanest of my acquaintance, and I love to go there on Sundays to see the world. But, to say the truth, I am growing weary of it. I dislike a million of things in the course of public affairs; and if I were to stay here much longer, I am sure I should ruin myself with endeavouring to mend them. I am every day invited into schemes of doing this, but I cannot find any that will probably succeed. It is impossible to save people against their own will; and I have been too much engaged in patch-work already. Do you understand all this stuff? No. Well then, you are now returned to ombre and the Dean, and Christmas; I wish you a very merry one; and pray don't lose oo money.

Lady Orkney, King William's mistress, was a friend he had made while at Windsor in the autumn of 1711 and he had a great opinion of her sagacity. A picture of her by Kneller was one

JOURNAL TO STELLA

This is a letter, written when Swift was ill. The Journal proper is written on sheets twice as wide, and crammed to the very edge of the paper

(*In the British Museum*)

of those he had got together to bring home : the Ormonds had given theirs : Bolingbroke and Lady Masham had promised : and he hoped for a copy of one of the Lord Treasurer : " Then I shall have all the pictures of those I really love here—just half a dozen." But his position grew absurd and painful. On Christmas Day, 1712, he dined " with Lord Treasurer, who chid me for being absent three days. Mighty kind, with a p——; less of civility, and more of his interest ! " In February, 1713, it is the same story. " My grandmother used to say, ' More of your lining, And less of your dining.' " Yet meanwhile " the foreign ministers have got a trick of employing me to speak for them to Lord Treasurer and Lord Bolingbroke ; which I do when the case is reasonable." Even men high in office like Ormond asked for his influence : it was a lesser matter that the Duke of Hamilton and Lord Abercorn, head of the Irish Hamiltons, each asked him to press rival titles to the French duchy of Chatelhérault. He was called in to help in drafting the Queen's speech ; in short he was a sort of minister without office or department ; and still nothing was done for his advancement.

Evidently his letters were full of the subject. " I did not write to Dr. Coghill that I would have nothing in Ireland, but that I was soliciting nothing anywhere, and that is true," he tells Stella. Nevertheless he had engaged Ormond (the Lord-Lieutenant) to decide no Irish appointment without letting him know ; and he had pressed the claims of Dean Stearne to a bishopric.

Parliament met, the peace was decided, the Government had at last the victory to which Swift had so greatly contributed ; but on April 13, 1713, Lewis came to him with a warrant for filling up three deaneries then vacant, and none of them for him :

I bid Mr. Lewis tell Lord-Treasurer, that I take nothing ill of him, but his not giving me timely notice, as he promised to do, if he found the Queen would do nothing for me. At noon, Lord-Treasurer hearing I was in Mr. Lewis's office, came to me, and said many things too long to repeat. I told him I had nothing to do but go to Ireland immediately ; for I could not, with any reputation, stay longer here, unless I had something honourable immediately given to me. We dined together at the Duke of Ormond's. He there told me, he had stopped the warrants for the deans, that what was done for me might be at the same time, and he hoped to compass it to-night ; but I believe him not. I told the Duke of Ormond my intentions. He is content Stearne should be a bishop, and I have St. Patrick's ; but I believe nothing will come of it, for stay I will not ; and so I believe for all . . . may see me in Dublin before April ends. I am less out of humour than you would imagine : and if it were not, that impertinent people will condole with me, as they used to give me joy, I would value it less. But I will avoid company, and muster up my baggage, and send them next Monday by the carrier to Chester, and come and see my willows, against the expectation of all the world.—Hat care I? Nite deelest logues, MD.

He prepared to pack up his belongings, send his baggage ahead and walk to Chester in company with his man—a fortnight's march. "It will do my health a great deal of good." But his ultimatum had swift effect. The warrants were stopped: Oxford made promises: Bolingbroke had Swift to dine with him on the 15th and swore the Queen should settle that night. "The dispute is, Windsor or St. Patrick's." Lady Masham wept at the idea of his leaving England, and Lord Treasurer was all for a prebend at Windsor. But by the 19th the Queen had agreed to the Dublin deanery, subject to Ormond's approval. Ormond however disliked Stearne, "so now all is broken again." Yet next day after a meeting at Swift's, Ormond with great kindness said he would consent, "but would do it for no man alive but me." And so after perplexities—during which Swift refused to meet ministers and "dined at an ale-house with Parnell and Berkeley"—the warrants were signed on the 23rd.

"And I suppose MD malicious enough to be glad, and rather have it than Wells," is the comment in the *Journal*. For Stella was used to Ireland and liked Dublin and her friends there; Swift had a feeling for Laracor, but none for the city; and on entering on his new dignity, he must pay, what with one thing and another, a thousand pounds in all. "So I shall not be the better for the deanery for this year." He hoped for a grant to cover his expenses; "Lord Treasurer rallies me on it, and I believe intends it; but, *quando?*" The last page in the *Journal* is dated from Chester on June 6. He had ridden down in six days, only to find that all the ships had gone and he must ride to Holyhead, another three days' journey.

That is how after almost three years' absence Swift came back to Dublin, as Dean of St. Patrick's—an ecclesiastical title which since his day and for his sake, is, to put it moderately, not less widely known than Dean of Westminster or Dean of St. Paul's.

CHAPTER XI

SWIFT'S RETURN TO COURT

ANOTHER strand in the complex web of Swift's life must now be traced out. We become aware of its importance first in the close of 1711.

A certain Mrs. Anne Long was so famous as a beauty that in 1708 she refused to make the usual advances for which Swift stipulated, on the ground that "a toast" could not so derogate from her dignity. She was intimate with the Vanhomrighs. Shortly after Swift came to London in October, 1710, he heard news of certain troubles about money which led her to seek an obscure lodging at King's Lynn under an assumed name; and he continued to write to her till she died in the following year. We have a letter of hers, written a month before she died, in which she makes jesting reply because apparently he had written that Esther Vanhomrigh had a man's tastes rather than a woman's. " My poor cousin is taken for a hermaphrodite," is Mrs. Long's comment. We have also Swift's reply, for it was enclosed under cover to " little Misessy," and was never forwarded, perhaps because within a week after it was written news of Mrs. Long's death reached the Vanhomrighs. But there is some reason to think it had in reality reached its address; for it came with two covering letters, one of which was intended to be shown. The other was for Misessy's private eye, and it certainly points to much familiarity.

I have writ three or four lies in as many lines. Pray seal up the letter to Mrs. L[ong], and let nobody read it but yourself. I suppose this packet will lie two hours till you awake. And pray let the outside starched letter to you be seen, after you have sealed that to Mrs. L[ong]. See what art people must use, though they mean ever so well. Now are you and Puppy lying at your ease, without dreaming anything of all this. Adieu till we meet over a pot of coffee or an orange and sugar in the Sluttery, which I have so often found to be the most agreeable chamber in the world.

But the letter which she was invited to read contains these observations :

Mishessy is but like her neighbour—she is a politician because every
body else is so, and a Tory out of principle, without hopes of an employ
ment. The poor girl, between sickness, domestic affairs and Stat
speculations, has lost a good deal of her mirth. But I think there i
not a better girl upon earth. I have a mighty friendship for her. Sh
had good principles, and I have corrected all her faults ; but I canno
persuade her to read, though she has an understanding, memory an
taste that would bear great improvement. But she is incorrigibly idl
and lazy—thinks the world made for nothing but perpetual pleasure
and the deity she most adores is Morpheus. Her greatest favourites a
present are Lady Ashburnham, her dog and myself. She makes me o
so little consequence that it almost distracts me. She will bid her siste
go downstairs before my face, for she has " some private business wit
the Doctor." In short, there would never be an end of telling yo
the hardships she puts on me, only because I have lived a dozen o
fifteen years too much.

That may have been intended to convey that the intimacy shoul
not be paraded ; or it may have been written to please her. A
all events, it was not likely to make the intimacy less.

Although there are very many references to Mrs. Vanhomrig
in the *Journal* (though noticeably fewer in the latter part) Esther i
only twice or thrice mentioned ; and for what we know of th
relationship, we must depend on Swift's poem, " Cadenus an
Vanessa." This it must be remembered was written for no ey
but Vanessa's ; the name probably was invented for it, along wit
Cadenus, which is Decanus (dean) anagrammatized. We know
from a letter of much later date that he wrote it at Windsor ; an
since in 1712 he was not decanus but doctor, 1713 is the year. More
over his method is so literal that the outline of the relation may b
taken as authentic in essentials.

He had a passion for amateur pedagogy of the other sex ; an
he began with no thought but simply to indulge his delight i
forming a plastic mind. In a sense it was Stella over again :

> Cadenus, common forms apart,
> In ev'ry scene had kept his heart ;
> Had sigh'd and languish'd, vow'd and writ,
> For pastime, or to shew his wit.
> But time, and books, and state-affairs,
> Had spoil'd his fashionable airs :
> He now could praise, esteem, approve,
> But understood not what was love.
> His conduct might have made him styl'd
> A father, and the nymph his child.
> That innocent delight he took
> To see the virgin mind her book,

Was but the master's secret joy
In school to hear the finest boy.
Her knowledge with her fancy grew;
She hourly press'd for something new;
Ideas came into her mind
So fast, his lessons lagg'd behind;
She reason'd without plodding long,
Nor ever gave her judgment wrong.

Finally, however, there came a change; he found an absent-minded pupil,

At first he modestly conjectures
His pupil might be tir'd with lectures;

and though mortified, politely offers to withdraw. But then the pupil turned upon him and said she would show how she had profited:

That I can vulgar forms despise
And have no secrets to disguise.

In short, she made a declaration; and his first feeling was dismay.

The town would swear he had betray'd
By magic spells the harmless maid:
And ev'ry beau would have his jokes,
That scholars were like other folks;
That, when Platonic flights were over,
The tutor turn'd a mortal lover.
So tender of the young and fair!
It shew'd a true paternal care—
Five thousand guineas in her purse!
The Doctor might have fancy'd worse.

The debate between tutor and pupil goes on; and it is admitted that Cadenus found the preference flattering

'Tis an old maxim in the schools,
That vanity's the food of fools;
Yet now and then your men of wit
Will condescend to take a bit. . . .
Cadenus, to his grief and shame,
Could scarce oppose Vanessa's flame;
Where hot and cold, where sharp and sweet,
In all their equipages meet;
Where pleasures mix'd with pains appear,
Sorrow with joy, and hope with fear;
Wherein his dignity and age
Forbid Cadenus to engage,
But friendship in its greatest height,
A constant, rational delight,

On virtue's basis fix'd to last,
When love's allurements long are past,
Which gently warms, but cannot burn,
He gladly offers in return.

Vanessa however proposes an exchange of stations. She

Will have her turn to be
The tutor; and the pupil, he:

The story breaks off on a question:

But what success Vanessa met,
Is to the world a secret yet
Whether the nymph, to please the swain,
Talks in a high romantic strain;
Or whether he at last descends
To act with less seraphic ends;
Or, to compound the bus'ness, whether
They temper love and books together;
Must never to mankind be told,
Nor shall the conscious muse unfold.

Stripped of the mythological imagery which makes this poem of nearly nine hundred lines one of the most beguiling compliments ever addressed to woman, that is the documentary core. The letters to Vanessa begin again in August, 1712, with a note from him saying that he is tired of Windsor " and will take a little Grub Street lodging and dine with you thrice a week; and will tell you a thousand secrets provided you will have no quarrels to me." The secrets were of high politics; no doubt, he flattered her by confidences; and indeed his head was too full of them for him to avoid such talk where he was intimate. A fortnight later, he is back at Windsor and suggests that " you all " should come down for three or four days. Meanwhile she is bidden to walk in the Park and not sit moping at home, " you that can neither work nor read nor play, nor care for company."

I long to drink a dish of coffee in the Sluttery, and hear you dun me for secrets, and: " Drink your coffee—why don't you drink your coffee ? "

Coffee was a speciality of that house; it came to be so associated with visits to the Sluttery that it passed into a sort of symbolic expression.

In September two letters of raillery from her make it plain enough that they were still tutor and pupil, though the pupil thought herself entitled to be kept in frequent remembrance and to have the proof in letters. But before that month was out, something had happened. "Misessy" had come down to Windsor to see him: and his letter is purposely mysterious, though no doubt intelligible to her.

> I did not forget the coffee, for I thought you should not be robbed of it. John does not go to Oxford, so I send you back the books as you desire. I would not see you for a thousand pounds if I could, but am now in my nightgown, writing a dozen letters and packing up papers. Why, then, you should not have come, and I knew that as well as you. My service to Molkin. I doubt you do wrong to go to Oxford, but now that is past, since you cannot be in London to-night; and if I do not inquire for acquaintance, but let somebody in the inn go about with you among the colleges, perhaps you will not be known. Adieu.

"John" is his confidential printer, Barber. "Molkin" is her sister, who presumably was with her on the expedition. In the last sentence it seems to me certain that "I" is a slip for "you." I do not think that the reference to coffee means more than that they had brought some down to make a brew for him, as part of the adventure. But the other sentences seem to imply that he had been shaken out of his usual poise. Ten years after this, when he is writing to try and convince her of his attachment, twice over he calls up old memories and Windsor comes in both. "Go over the scenes of Windsor, Cleveland Row, Ryder Street, St. James's, Kingston, the Sluttery, etc., Cad thinks often of these, especially on horseback, as I am assured."

We have no more of these letters till the end of May, 1713, when he was leaving England to take up his Deanery, and from his first stage at St. Albans he wrote:

> I promised to write to you; and I have let you know that it is impossible for anybody to have more acknowledgments at heart, for all your kindness and generosity to me. . . . I have hardly time to put my pen to paper, but I would make good my promise. Pray God preserve you and make you happy and easy—and so adieu, brat.

But he wrote a line also from Dunstable to her sister and from Chester to Mrs. Vanhomrigh.

Letters poured after him all the faster because she had heard from Lewis (who forwarded her letters under cover) that he was ill: and then, when she learnt he was well, because he had not written: "If you are very happy, it is ill-natured of you not to tell me so, except it is what is inconsistent with mine. . . . Pray let me hear from you soon which will be an unexpressible joy to her that is always ——"

It seems certain that she then knew nothing of Stella.

He wrote at last on July 8 and the manifest purpose was to discourage letters; he was keeping her at armslength; she, just as evidently, endeavouring to get always nearer. But at this time Swift wanted nobody near him. He wrote from Laracor:

> I stayed but a fortnight in Dublin, very sick, and returned not one visit of a hundred that were made me—but all to the Dean, and none to the Doctor. I am riding here for life, and think I am something better, and hate the thoughts of Dublin, and prefer a field-bed and an earthen floor before the great house there, which they say is mine. I had your last spleenatic letter. I told you when I left England, I would endeavour to forget everything there, and would write as seldom as I could. I did indeed design one general round of letters to my friends, but my health has not yet suffered me. I design to pass the greatest part of the time I stay in Ireland here in the cabin where I am now writing, neither will I leave the Kingdom till I am sent for; and if they have no further service for me I will never see England again. At my first coming I thought I should have died with discontent, and was horribly melancholy while they were installing me; but it begins to wear off, and change to dulness.

There follow a sentence or two about politics, in which one thing only stands out—his spleen that ministers had not consented to let him publish the " History " on which he had spent so much labour and which he thought would have had a good effect:

> But I am now fitter to look after willows, and to cut hedges, than meddle with affairs of state. . . . And I must go and take my bitter draught to cure my head, which is spoilt by the bitter draughts the public hath given me.

The rest is detail about his country neighbours, and then, " Nay, if you do not like this sort of news, I have no better." It is a letter meant to convey that he has no wish to write, and there is no word of tenderness in it; there is no trace of happiness, either remembered or anticipated. But there is implicit in it a very great intimacy. In a sense it is more intimate than any of the *Journal*, where the assumption of a third person present is always felt. He kept his black moods from Stella; they were out of place in that equable relation, so full of the happy gaiety that is reflected in so many pages of the *Journal*. That reflection grows fainter, certainly, as the months of absence grow into years; but the memory of it, and the desire for it, never die out.

Yet it is evident that Stella had not been able to soothe and quiet the turmoil that was raging in an angry, disappointed spirit. Before he came over, he could write that though he was angry about the difficulty in getting the fulfilment of so many pledges, people told him he should be proud that he had "made a bishop, in spite of all the world, to get the best deanery in Ireland." For Stearne seems to have had many enemies. Yet the anger came back when Swift found the new bishop no way disposed (as he thought) to make return of good offices. Two Dublin livings which he had held in his control as Dean, Stearne now disposed of, instead of leaving this privilege to his successor: and he was exacting about payment for the house he had built. It cannot have mended matters that Stearne had been so closely a friend of Stella; for Swift's rage would certainly find expression, and Stella was not the one to agree merely for agreement's sake. The disorder in his head made everything worse; and he simply bolted into solitude at Laracor.

But the plain truth is that he had been living for nearly three years among constant strong excitements, and though he had often spoken of a desire for tranquillity, habit had inevitably bred a craving. Varied and brilliant society, the sense of social success, and above all the contact with the holders of power, the partnership in manipulation of power, had been his daily portion; it is no wonder if he missed these. The companionship to which he returned, though it renewed an old and cherished affection, lacked that physical solace which has been so many million times healing medicine, and which he had chosen, in his great wisdom, to cut out. So far as the end that he professed again and again in the first year of the *Journal*, "only to make MD and me easy," it was achieved; his deanery was an ample provision both of means and dignity; but it did not satisfy now. He had come to crave for more.

"The prints will tell you that I am condemned to live again in Ireland," he wrote just before he left London to one of the young men of letters whom he had served; "and all the Court and Ministry did for me was to let me choose my station in the country where I am banished." It was banishment not only from the scene of power but from hopes of a station to which his cloth was no bar. In 1711 Robinson, Bishop of Bristol, who had been already Envoy to Sweden, was made Lord Privy Seal: a step of the Lord Treasurer's which Swift applauded: "It will bind the church to him for ever." Again, he himself was man of letters as much as clergyman; and Prior, another of the craft, was named plentipotentiary for concluding the peace of Utrecht, along with Bishop Robinson and Lord Strafford. But Strafford, who was

169

"proud as Hell," refused to be associated with one of Prior's mean birth and the mere professional diplomat had to be superseded. Swift was entitled to believe that if he, whether as dean or bishop, was named to any political post, the proudest man in England dare not refuse to be his colleague. I am certain that such visions passed through his mind repeatedly in the days when he was learning to believe himself as apt for the handling of power as any man in England. A prebend at Windsor might well seem a step on the road; but banishment to an Irish deanery looked like an end to all that.

There is not the least indication that while in Ireland he missed his intimacy with Esther Vanhomrigh, and desired to return to it. Yet she had been part of the excitement. He had drifted into the intimacy out of "pure idleness"; and then something that was new to him, that he had neither thought of nor desired, sprang at him. Passion had been outside of his reckoning. Ironically enough, it is in "Cadenus and Vanessa" we can find his description of what ideally love should be:

> A fire celestial, chaste, refined,
> Conceived and kindled in the mind.

In his long intimacy with Stella, the friendship between a young man and a lovely child, tutor and pupil, had gradually and insensibly developed into an attachment for which love is the only word; yet, under the moulding influence of a mind strongly prepossessed against "the gross desire," it had avoided all the physical element; and as Stella grew to maturity, her lover had fenced himself and her about by precautions which were the less felt because they merely kept things on the same footing as they had been for more than half the woman's life. It was quite otherwise in the case of Esther Vanhomrigh, who was twenty when she first met Swift and four years older when, during his long London stay the "sluttery" became one of his constant resorts. Yet he was enough her elder—twenty years between them—to think himself secure—if indeed he thought about it. Forty-four seemed older than, and indeed was older, than it is now; and there is no reason to doubt that what came of it took him by surprise. But when it came, if the facts must be faced, he did not play fair. It is evident that he kept Vanessa as ignorant of his relation to Stella as Stella of his affair with Vanessa. Vanessa had no reason to know that he might have a happiness which she would have called "inconsistent with mine." There was no reason (setting

aside traditions of feminine behaviour) why she should not aspire
to marry him : and no doubt she used all the weapons with which
a determined young woman is provided. She was good to look
at ; she pleased his fastidiousness by a sweetness in her person ;
and she argued boldly for the right to declare her love. No doubt
he should at once have told her of his obligations ; no doubt he
should have realized that it was playing with fire to attempt to
turn passion into platonics. But, as he says in the poem, he was
flattered ; it was a new and different example of his power to please
fair ladies ; and he forgot how Homer says that in leisure spent
with a woman there is a snare of dalliance and desire which plays
tricks with the wisest understanding.

I think the avowal of her passion took place at Windsor in
1712 ; and his letter of ten years later contains a phrase which
suggests (Ball notes it) that passion got its way, for that once.
It seems however that up to the time when he left England to
take up his deanery in 1713, she had accepted the discipline he
imposed. At all events he was willing that Lewis should know
of her correspondence with him.

But it does not seem of much importance what degree of
physical realization was given to Vanessa's passion ; the vital
fact is that knowing of the passion, he allowed their intimacy to
continue. It was an infidelity to the woman who had linked her
life to his, under conditions far harder than those of marriage.

Yet I do not believe that his unhappiness in the summer of
1713 was connected either with absence from Vanessa, or with
the fear of trouble from Stella. It was simply the rage of disappointed ambition and resentment : and to gratify his hurt pride
he deliberately prolonged his trouble. Before he left London he
had declared (in a letter of April 3) his intention to return in
October ; but in July he tells Vanessa that he will not return until
he is sent for. Yet that letter crossed in the post an urgent appeal
from Lewis. " We are all running headlong into the greatest
confusion imaginable. . . . I heartily wish you were here ; for
you might certainly be of great use to us, by your endeavours to
reconcile, and by representing to them the infallible consequences
of these divisions." Again ten days later Lewis wrote : " My
Lord Treasurer desires you will make all possible haste over, for
we want you extremely." Yet Swift continued spleenful, writing
for instance to Atterbury that he was " here in a way of sinking
into utter oblivion." But Lewis wrote yet again, appealing to
an old allegiance.

You and I have already laid it down for a maxim, that we must serve Lord Treasurer, without receiving orders or particular instructions ; and I do not yet see a reason for changing that rule. His mind has been communicated more freely to you than any other ; but you will not understand it. The desires of great men are commands, at least the only ones, I hope, they ever will be able to use.

That gave the impulse. On August 29 Swift left Dublin and was in London on September 9. There, it is evident that the familiar whirl received him joyfully ; and his presence was effectual once more in patching things up.

I make no attempt to follow the shifting politics of the time : but, broadly, Queen Anne's health was precarious ; the Whigs who had failed to prevent the peace, now raised the issue of the succession, clamouring fear of Popery and the Pretender. Meanwhile the ministry was divided. As between Oxford and Boling-broke, the difference was mainly that Oxford had always leanings towards a coalition ; and this would have been congenial to Swift's mind which disliked party. None the less, his friendship with Bolingbroke remained as close as ever.

Still, the world was left in no doubt that Swift regarded Oxford as his patron : and the first of several poems describing himself and his own case—all in the humorous Horatian manner—belongs to the end of 1713. He tells, in imitation of Horace's Epistle to Mæcenas, how one day " Harley, the nation's great support," on his way back from court,

> Observed a parson near Whitehall,
> Cheap'ning old authors on a stall.
> The priest was pretty well in case,
> And show'd some humour in his face ;
> Look'd with an easy, careless mien,
> A perfect stranger to the spleen ;
> Of size that might a pulpit fill,
> But more inclining to sit still.

Accordingly " friend Lewis ", being sent out to inquire,

> Found out that it was Dr. Swift,
> A clergyman of special note
> For shunning those of his own coat ;
> Which made his brethren of the gown
> Take care betimes to run him down :
> No libertine, nor over nice,
> Addicted to no sort of vice ;
> Went where he pleas'd, said what he thought ;
> Not rich, but owed no man a groat.

And so, this parson is asked to dinner; shies off at first, but on encouragement " soon grows domestic," is carried down to Windsor, and

> Much admires the place and air,
> And longs to be a Canon there;
> In summer round the place to ride,
> In winter—never to reside.

Here with his habitual frankness Swift lets us know what he had wanted. But he is put off with the pomp of a deanery—

> Two dozen canons round your stall,
> And you the tyrant o'er them all.

That is the promise: the fulfilment is sketched:

> Dues, payments, fees, demands, and cheats.

till the unlucky dean comes posting back to Harley's gate and begs to be left once more a simple parson.

Still, that is joking: the dean came back more in favour than ever; a sketch shows him at the height of his ascendancy; the scene is Windsor in October, 1713. Bishop Kennett, who wrote it, was a vehement Whig.

Dr. Swift came into the coffee-house, and had a bow from everybody but me. When I came to the ante-chamber to wait before prayers, Dr. Swift was the principal man of talk and business, and acted as a Master of Requests. He was soliciting the Earl of Arran to speak to his brother the Duke of Ormond, to get a chaplain's place established in the garrison of Hull for Mr. Fiddes, a clergyman in that neighbourhood, who had lately been in gaol, and published sermons to pay fees. He was promising Mr. Thorold to undertake with my Lord Treasurer, that, according to his petition, he should obtain a salary of two hundred pounds per annum, as minister of the English church at Rotterdam. He stopped F[rancis] Gwyn, Esq., going in with the red bag to the Queen, and told him aloud he had something to say to him from my Lord Treasurer. He talked with the son of Dr. Davenant to be sent abroad, and took out his pocket-book and wrote down several things, as memoranda, to do for him. He turned to the fire, and took out his gold watch, and telling him the time of the day, complained it was very late. A gentleman said, he was too fast. " How can I help it," says the Doctor, " if the courtiers give me a watch that won't go right ? " Then he instructed a young nobleman, that the best poet in England was Mr. Pope (a Papist), who had begun a translation of Homer into English verse, for which he must have them all subscribe. " For," says he, " the author shall not begin to print till I have a thousand guineas for him." Lord Treasurer, after leaving the Queen, came through the room, beckoning Dr. Swift to follow him; both went off just before prayers.

That tells spitefully the like of what is told in fifty passages of the *Journal*. We need not deny that Swift paraded his own import-ance; but we should remember that when he promised help he was always as good as his word. Long lists could be made of those whose fortunes he served, and in some cases with a very touching solicitude.

The chief name of these comes here. Pope indeed was no way indigent; but Swift served his interests with passion. He fell in love with that mordant genius, that exquisite mastery of words; at the beginning of 1713, we find him writing to Stella: "Mr. Pope has published a fine poem, 'Windsor Forest.' Read it." The poem would have pleased Swift because he always loved Windsor and its amenities: but all the more because it ended with a really noble pæan to the peace. Yet in March, 1713, Pope was still a member of Addison's Whig circle. When the two met first, is not known. Swift was almost a score of years older than this young man of five-and-twenty. The first letter that passed between them which we have is dated December 8, 1713, and is Pope's reply to the Dean's handsome offer of twenty guineas if he would change his religion. The part of this elaborate pleasantry which concerns us is that Pope insists on his desire to be able to offer masses for the salvation of certain persons:

There is but one man whose salvation I insist upon. . . . Dr. Swift, a dignified clergyman, but one, who, by his own confession, has composed more libels than sermons. If it be true, what I have heard often affirmed by innocent people, that too much wit is dangerous to salvation, this unfortunate gentleman must certainly be damned to all eternity. But I hope his long experience in the world, and frequent conversation with great men, will cause him, as it has some others, to have less and less wit every day. Be it as it will, I should not think my own soul deserved to be saved, if I did not endeavour to save his; for I have all the obligations in nature to him. He has brought me into better company than I cared for, made me merrier when I was sick than I had a mind to be, and put me upon making poems on purpose that he might alter them, etc.

It is of course a little artificial, or it would not be Pope; but twenty years were to test and attest the constancy of that affection. Yet of all his contemporaries Pope was the most dangerous to friends and Swift, though of constant loyalty, was not difficult to quarrel with.

One man out of his circle of literary allies had contrived to do this very completely—that impulsive Whig, Richard Steele. Just before Swift left London to take the oath for his deanery, the *Guardian*, a daily paper which Steele had launched, replied angrily to an attack made by the *Examiner* on Lord Nottingham, the Tory who had ratted from Oxford on the question of a peace. Steele signed the article, which imputed authorship of the *Examiner* to Swift, and used words which could be construed as an accusation of infidelity in the matter of religion. Swift's protest was made to Addison, as a judicious friend; but Addison, ignoring the implied request for intervention, sent the letter on to Steele, who replied contemptuously that Swift was only being laughed at if men led him to believe that his influence had kept Steele still in his office as comptroller of stamps. The angry correspondence was carried on to a third exchange of letters, and it is worth observing that Steele says, with evident candour, that he attempts explanation " not out of terror of your wit, or my Lord Treasurer's power, but pure kindness to the agreeable qualities I once so passionately delighted in in you "; and that Swift recalls how " in the only thing he ever published with his name," and in a Letter addressed to the Lord Treasurer, he had " taken care to celebrate as much as he could " Steele's services to English prose literature.

Certainly Swift's denial of responsibility for the article in the *Examiner* should have been accepted; but his general direction of the Tory press must have been notorious; and though he says in the Journal that he deliberately avoided all personal contact with Oldsworth, the editor of the paper, he did also at times supply " hints " for it. Moreover, his direct claim to have used a kind of indirect patronage on Steele's behalf would have been galling to a man less sensitive than that hot-tempered gentleman. But Steele had chosen to quarrel instead of apologizing, and Swift was not the man to let a quarrel lie. One of the burning questions then was the demolition of Dunkirk, which had been stipulated in the Treaty of Utrecht; and the French were slow to destroy the port. Steele plunged in with charges that the Tory government was neglecting a vital interest. He had been elected member for Stockbridge and re-issued his criticisms (first published in the *Guardian*) in a pamphlet: *The Importance of Dunkirk Considered: a Letter to the Bailiff of Stockbridge*. Swift answered with another —*The Importance of the " Guardian " Considered: being a Second Letter to the Bailiff of Stockbridge. By a Friend of Mr. St . . le.* It opens with a character describing Mr. Steele as

the author of two tolerable plays (or at least of the greatest part of them) which, added to the company he has kept, and the continual conversation and friendship of Mr. Addison hath given him the character of a wit. . . . He hath no invention, nor is master of a tolerable style; his chief talent is humour, which he sometimes discovers both in writing and in dis-

course; for after the first bottle he is no disagreeable companion.
never knew him taxed with ill nature which hath made me wonder ho
ingratitude came to be his prevailing vice.

More serious developments came later. The Queen's illnes
at the close of 1713 revived panic about the Pretender, and Steel
after much preliminary advertisement, issued a pamphlet calle
The Crisis. It was for Swift to reply, and he wrote *The Publ.
Spirit of the Whigs*, which opened with a contemptuous survey c
the opposition propaganda. In it he employed his familiar metho
of bracketing the author he attacked with others generally despised

The third and principal of this triumvirate is the author of the *Crisis*
who, although he must yield to the *Flying Post* in knowledge of th
world, and skill in politics, and to Mr. Dunton [1] in keenness of satire an
variety of reading, hath yet other qualities enough to denominate hir
a writer of a superior class to either; provided he would a little regar
the propriety and disposition of his words, consult the grammatical par
and get some information in the subject he intends to handle.

But the attack did not stop there. One of the Whig manœuvre
had been to attempt repeal of the Union with Scotland, and the
came within a single vote of defeating the Ministry. Swift hate
the Scotch with a fervour that should have mitigated Dr. Johnson'
unfriendliness to him, and he detested the Union—which, as h
pointed out in this pamphlet, was really brought about from
fear of having again two kings in the island. He let his spleer
dictate words about "a poor fierce northern nation," and abou
a nobility "so numerous that the whole revenues of their countr
would be hardly able to maintain them according to the dignit
of their titles"; some of whom, though they "affected to appea
very vigorous for dissolving the Union," had under it "gatherec
more money than ever any Scotsman who had not travelled coulc
form an idea of."

This was too much for the House of Lords, where Whigs hac
the mastery; the pamphlet was voted "a false, malicious anc
factious libel," and its publisher and printer were taken into custody
Oxford immediately and secretly sent Swift £100 "to answer sucl
exigencies as the case may immediately require." The prisoner:
were let go on the 9th, but a proclamation calling for the discovery
of the author was issued, with a reward of £300, of which nothing
came but an anonymous letter to Oxford asking for assurance tha
payment would be made if information were given—and the lette
reads very much like the style of Jonathan Swift. Steele on th

[1] This was the editor of *The Athenian Mercury* which printed Swift's Ode.

ontrary—whom Swift had pelted with verse as well as prose, dedicating two imitations of Horace to the subject—had to face an angry House of Commons for his authorship of the *Crisis*, which deprived him of his seat in Parliament and sent him to the Tower.

Apart from this feud, Swift's literary alliances, in this last period of his London life, seem to have been closer than ever. Unfortunately, though his lists of letters show that he wrote as regularly as ever to MD, we have not this continuation of the *Journal* and consequently have not the record of his doings and must gather as we can. The Society of Brothers was on the wane; yet the Duchess of Ormond kept up the tradition of intimacy, (extended even to families), and wrote to Swift as " Brother." A new association however had been formed, not of a few men of letters mixed up with a growing number of peers willing to help on needy talent, but this time of four or five leading writers who decided to make a sort of round game of satiric literature, and allowed Oxford and Bolingbroke the privilege of attending. This was the Scriblerus Club, though whether it ever explicitly received that name is uncertain. At all events, Swift, Arbuthnot, Pope, Gay and Parnell put their heads together to compile the *Memoirs of Martinus Scriblerus* and Oxford and Bolingbroke got invitations to the meetings. A handful of verses survive, with two invitations to Oxford written by the Dean, and replies, one by Gay, the other by Oxford, dated April 14, 1714; and not one is worth quoting. Nor for that matter is it very easy to read nowadays this erudite jesting, to which Arbuthnot probably made the chief contribution; for it has much to do with fantastic theories of medicine and science. Pope's concern was with the satire on literature, and later he carried out his idea singly in the *Dunciad*; while Swift, who was to have contributed the Travels of Martinus, wrote instead those of Lemuel Gulliver. Not much came of the joint stock, except the pleasantness of a club which made a great part of Swift's London diversions.

The correspondence makes us aware of the cares belonging to him as adviser to the Ministry in Irish church concerns. One of great importance arose at this moment : the Primacy fell vacant, and beyond doubt Archbishop King had the best claim to it, in point of standing and of ability. Swift agreed profoundly with King that Irish claims should count most for Irish appointments ; but it was a difficult period in politics ; King's correspondence of this period shows his Whig leanings very strong ; and in December Swift wrote to King's close friend, Bishop Stearne, that he should

be " a very vile man " if he recommended his own brother " if h
were the least disinclined to the present measures of her Majest
and Ministry." Briefly, he had decided to back Lindsay, Bisho
of Raphoe, a strong Tory, an able speaker and High Churchman—
who was accordingly promoted over King's head; and the relation
between the Dean of St. Patrick's and his " great neighbour " wer
for long embittered.

It is, however, hardly to be supposed that Swift looked forwar
to spending the rest of his life in Dublin.   Chances of prefermen
seemed many to a man who was so near to the affection of Anne'
Prime Minister ; how near, two letters in the Correspondence prove
In November, 1713, Oxford's daughter, Lady Carmarthen, recentl
married to the eldest son of the Duke of Leeds, died in childbirth
Swift was passionately moved, and it is evident that he poured ou
his grief at once to Arbuthnot, who replied saying that he di
not " love to irritate a fresh wound," and therefore did not writ
direct to the stricken man.   The office of doing what could b
done in the way of consolation he left, as of right, to Swift
nothing could imply more strongly his sense of the special intimacy
But he did not refrain from counsel :

> I have a true sense of his present condition for which I know philo
> sophy and religion are both too weak, and I believe it is the will of Go
> that it should be so.   I have lost six children.   If I am not deceive
> I believe I could have been content to have ransomed the lives of ever
> one of them even at the hard terms of begging their bread.   I know m
> Lord has the sentiment of humanity and paternal affection very strong
> and I should not love him so well if he had not ; therefore, my dear frienc
> I question not but you will upon this occasion do these offices of humanit
> that are incumbent upon you upon many accounts, which you will fin
> will succeed better by turning his thoughts to other objects than by th
> most rational reflections upon the present affliction.

But already Swift, yielding, as his last words put it, " to a
impulse upon me that I should say something," had written ou
of his heart.   Here is the main part of this letter, which has bee
much and justly praised for its sincerity and its beauty :

> My Lord, whoever had the honour to know her, wants a comforte
> as much as your Lordship : because, though their loss is not so grea
> yet they have not the same firmness and prudence, to support the wan
> of a friend, a patroness, a benefactor, as you have to support that of
> daughter.   My Lord, both religion and reason forbid me to have th
> least concern for that lady's death, upon her own account, and he mus
> be an ill Christian, or a perfect stranger to her virtues, who would no
> wish himself, with all submission to God Almighty's will, in he
> condition.   But your Lordship who has lost such a daughter, and w

who have lost such a friend, and the world which has lost such an example, have, in our several degrees, greater cause to lament than, perhaps, was ever given by any private person before : for, my Lord, I have sat down to think of every amiable quality that could enter into the composition of a lady, and could not single out one, which she did not possess in as high a perfection as human nature is capable of. But as to your Lordship's own particular, as it is an unconceivable misfortune to have lost such a daughter, so it is a possession which few can boast of, to have had such a daughter. I have often said to your Lordship, that I never knew anyone by many degrees so happy in their domestic as you, and I affirm you are so still, though not by so many degrees ; from whence it is very obvious, that your Lordship should reflect upon what you have left, and not upon what you have lost.

It will be seen that he had done the very thing against which Arbuthnot advised him ; and I think whoever compares these two letters, in both of which there is evident the same warmth and spontaneity of feeling, must be struck by differences not less essential. Arbuthnot wrote as a man who knew in his own person the loss of children ; that lay outside Swift's human experience. Yet more than this : in every line of Arbuthnot's letter there is present the mind of one for whom Christianity is real—though he does not invoke the consoling belief in a future life. Swift, in the passage I have quoted and again in the conclusion, employs that argument ; he knew that to Oxford that belief would be a reality. Yet when his own time of bereavement came, it is not easy to trace in his prayers and meditations on Stella any evidence that it was a reality to him. Conscientious in the discharge of his clerical office though he never failed to be, Swift was always ' more an ancient Roman than a '—dean. There is little in this letter of consolation which Cicero might not have signed.

But neither Cicero nor any Roman of them all outdid Swift in the excellence of manly friendship ; and his feeling for Oxford is only one example. In that case there was always present an attitude of deference and of personal allegiance imposed by Oxford's position, and maintained consistently with complete independence. It was no blind devotion, as events were soon to prove. The service which he sought to render to Oxford's ministry in the last period of association with it was that of keeping ministers together. Up to the spring of 1714 he succeeded, but by the month of May it was clear to him that the divisions between Oxford and Bolingbroke were irreconcilable. It is unnecessary to consider what these were or how they were occasioned : Swift himself deliberately has left no account of them. Whether he agreed more with Oxford

or with Bolingbroke we have no means of knowing. He only too
a side when the choice could be no longer avoided, and then it wa
to range himself, not for combat but for comfort, beside a falle
man.

Yet an earlier decision had to be made, and it was purely nega
tive. Since he could not maintain union between the two chiefs
he would withdraw from the scene. As early as April he wa
preparing his retreat. The Reverend John Geree, from the tow
of Farnham, had some connection with Temple's household; h
was an Oxford man, a fellow of Corpus, and now held the colleg
living of Letcombe Bassett near Wantage in Berkshire. Swift
who had endeavoured to get him further advancement, now aske
to be taken into the Rectory as a paying guest. His first step wa
characteristic; he sent down a hamper of Florence wine as a presen
to the household, which was acknowledged by Mr. Geree on
April 24. A month later, Swift was still in London and friend
tried to persuade him against running away; but on June 1 h
went by coach to Oxford, stayed there a couple of days, and set ou
for Letcombe Bassett, taking with him (so one of the Christ Church
canons wrote to young Harley) a portmanteau big enough to
contain his library as well as his equipage. For he was still a
work on his History of the period he had been concerned with, and
he was an applicant for the post of Historiographer to the Queen

But the emotions which he would not express in prose burs
out into verse and he wrote those lines, " The Author upon Him
self," which come down to us with a broken beginning :

> By an old —— pursued,[1]
> A crazy prelate, and a royal prude ;
> By dull divines, who look with envious eyes
> On ev'ry genius that attempts to rise ;
> And pausing o'er a pipe, with doubtful nod,
> Give hints, that poets ne'er believe in God.
> So clowns on scholars as on wizards look,
> And take a folio for a conj'ring book.
>   Swift had the sin of wit, no venial crime ;
> Nay, 'twas affirm'd, he sometimes dealt in rhyme ;
> Humour and mirth had place in all he writ ;
> He reconcil'd divinity and wit :
> He moved, and bow'd, and talk'd with too much grace ;
> Nor show'd the parson in his gait or face ;
> Despised luxurious wines and costly meat ;
> Yet still was at the tables of the great ;

[1] The Duchess of Somerset ; the word left out was " murderess "—and
further on " murdered ".

> Frequented lords ; saw those that saw the queen ;
> At Child's or Truby's, never once had been ;
> Where town and country vicars flock in tribes,
> Secured by numbers from the layman's gibes ;
> And deal in vices of the graver sort,
> Tobacco, censure, coffee, pride, and port.

Using for this graver tone the couplet of which Dryden had shown the power, he sketches his own rise and the gathering jealousies : he tells how *The Tale of a Tub* was brought against him :

> York is from Lambeth sent, to show the queen
> A dang'rous treatise writ against the spleen. . . .

> Now angry Somerset her vengeance vows
> On Swift's reproaches for her —— spouse :
> From her red locks her mouth with venom fills,
> And thence into the royal ear instils.

And so he recapitulates the story till he reaches this conclusion :

> By faction tired, with grief he waits awhile,
> His great contending friends to reconcile ;
> Performs what friendship, justice, truth, require :
> What could he more, but decently retire ?

The touch is neither so deft nor so light as when he uses the familiar octosyllable ; seemingly, he recovered his good humour and wrote in this retirement an imitation of Horace which is in his happiest vein :

> I often wish'd that I had clear,
> For life, six hundred pounds a-year,
> A handsome house to lodge a friend,
> A river at my garden's end,
> A terrace walk, and half a rood
> Of land, set out to plant a wood.
>   Well, now I have all this and more,
> I ask not to increase my store ;
> But should be perfectly content,
> Could I but live on this side Trent,
> Nor cross the Channel twice a-year,
> To spend six months with statesmen here.

He goes on to sketch gaily what lay behind that appearance of importance which Kennett spitefully described :

> 'Tis (let me see) three years and more
> (October next it will be four)
> Since Harley bid me first attend,
> And chose me for an humble friend ;

Would take me in his coach to chat,
And question me of this and that;
As "What's o'clock?" And, "How's the wind?"
"Whose chariot's that we left behind?"
Or gravely tried to read the lines
Writ underneath the country signs;
And mark at Brentford how they spell
Hear is good Eal and Bear to cell.
Or, "Have you nothing new to-day
To shew from Parnell, Pope and Gay?"
Such tattle often entertains
My lord and me as far as Staines,
As once a-week we travel down
To Windsor, and again to town;
Where all that passes *inter nos*
Might be proclaim'd at Charing-cross.

This is no more than the versifying of a passage in his *Journal* where he told Stella that this Lord Treasurer is "a pure trifler." But again, what else but a transcript from many letter endings in the *Journal* is the close?

Thus in a sea of folly toss'd,
My choicest hours of life are lost:
Yet always wishing to retreat,
O, could I see my country-seat!
There leaning near a gentle brook,
Sleep, or peruse some ancient book;
And there in sweet oblivion drown
Those cares that haunt the court and town.

CHAPTER XII

QUEEN ANNE DIES

ON June 8, 1714, Swift wrote from Berkshire " to Mrs. Esther Vanhomrigh, at her lodgings over against the Surgeon's in Great Rider Street, near St. James's Street ":

You see I am better than my word, and write to you before I have been a week settled in the house where I am. I have not much news to tell you from hence, nor have I had one line from any body since I left London, of which I am very glad. But, to say the truth, I believe I shall not stay here so long as I intended. I am at a clergyman's house, an old friend and an acquaintance, whom I love very well ; but he is such a melancholy thoughtful man, partly from nature, and partly by a solitary life, that I shall soon catch the spleen from him. Out of ease and complaisance, I desire him not to alter any of his methods for me ; so we dine exactly between twelve and one, at eight we have some bread and butter and a glass of ale, and at ten he goes to bed. Wine is a stranger, except a little I sent him, of which, one evening in two, we have a pint between us. His wife has been this month twenty miles off, at her father's, and will not return these ten days. I never saw her, and perhaps the house will be worse when she comes. I read all day, or walk, and do not speak as many words as I have now writ, in three days ; so that, in short, I have a mind to steal to Ireland, unless I feel myself take more to this way of living, so different, in every circumstance, from what I left. This is the first syllable I have writ to anybody since you saw me. I shall be glad to hear from you, not as you are a Londoner, but a friend ; for I care not threepence for news, nor have heard one syllable since I came here. The Pretender, or Duke of Cambridge, may both be landed, and I never the wiser. But if this place were ten times worse, nothing shall make me return to town while things are in the situation I left them. I give a guinea a week for my board, and can eat anything. I hope you are in good health and humour. My service to Moll. My cold is quite gone.

A vous, etc.

Here, first of all, we have the man, in one of the moods such as made him on his return from England go and bury himself at Laracor. It would be folly to add touches to this portrait where every line is bitten in. But here also we have the fact that Vanessa claimed to hear from him early and that she was the first who heard.

Such intimacies cannot remain stationary. They increase their hold. Manifestly enough, Vanessa is being kept at arm's-length : but such a gruffness is in itself a mark of intimacy. There is no suggestion of an elderly man writing to a pretty young girl : this is simply a letter from a moody man to a woman who will, he knows, put up with his moody humour. " Mishessy " had gone by the board : she was Vanessa now.

Some biographers have held that on his return from Ireland the lady surprised him by the avowal of her passion which is discreetly described in the poem ; but this is an absurd conjecture. If there was a surprise at any time, it must be dated back to that visit to Windsor in the autumn of 1712 when his letter shows traces of some upheaval : for after the letters which she wrote to him when he left London to take up his deanery, no man could have been surprised by a declaration that the writer of them desired a happiness with which Swift's preference for any other woman would be " inconsistent."

It is possible that while he was in Ireland, in the period when he stopped writing to her, he resolved to break off this intimacy : possible that his reluctance to return to London had something to do with a desire to avoid this entanglement : but this is mere sup- position. One thing, however, is clear. Seduction is a word that has no place here ; an ardent young woman violently in love did her best to make this elder man—free, so far as she knew for mar- riage—answer her own passion : and beyond all doubt the initiative was hers. Beyond all doubt, too, she was never ashamed of it. We have the poem and the correspondence because she deliber- ately left them to pass into the hands of her executors.

This does not excuse Swift in so far as he was blameable ; and he stands plainly convicted to disloyalty to Stella. Yet the facts should be fairly stated. He was not married, at this time ; whether he was later married to Stella is uncertain, and the marriage was at most one of form. He belonged to a Church which did not enjoin celibacy on its priests, and he thought himself fully entitled to indulge the pleasure which he felt in women's society, so far as was lawful to any layman. Beyond that, he would certainly have drawn a distinction. Some of his intimates, notably Bolingbroke and Prior, were men of very loose lives, and he tolerated what he was fully aware of, as passages in the *Journal* show. But in his esteem for Oxford and for Arbuthnot there is a quality of respect for men of happy family life. In the matter of drunkenness, as to which there was little to choose between Oxford and Bolingbroke, he simply disapproved as a hindrance to efficiency what in one of his own cloth would have been a disgrace to his cloth. " People will say when they see his red face," he writes to Stella about one of their intimates, " there goes a drunken parson, and what is worse they will say true." It was an age ' tolerant to the point of coarseness,' even of loose living and of drunkenness in the clergy, but Swift was well aware that for himself any lapse would mean a loss of dignity in the world's eyes, and what mattered no less, in his own. He had, I think, always counted on his dislike of this to assist a temperament in which physical desire appears to have been less than normally strong; there is more than a bitter jest in the witticism which figures among his *Thoughts on Various Subjects* : " What they do in Heaven, we are ignorant of ; what they do not, we are told expressly, that they neither marry, nor are given in marriage." Neither he nor any Protestant clergyman of his day, though determined on celibacy for secular reasons, had the least thought of observing that " custody of the eyes " and the rest, which is inculcated as matter of discipline on a professedly celibate clergy. It was definitely Swift's view that a clergyman of his Church should live freely in the world like any other gentleman ; he resented and disapproved, as his writings show, any disposition in the clergy to behave as a class apart, or to keep aloof from the laity ; and he trusted, for himself and for others, to a sense of propriety rather than of severe principle to keep them from giving offence, where it was their duty to set an example.

In his relations with Vanessa the whole tone of his letters shows that he was ill pleased with himself from the time when there entered into it an element of concealment. He indulged her foolishness first, and then her passion, against his better judgment ; but he also indulged his own inclinations. He had beyond common measure the craving for excitement ; that was the lure of London and of politics for him as it had been for so many ; and part of the excitement, the game, was to shine in the society of women. That in itself was no danger to a man of his temperament : Lady Bolingbroke disturbed his tranquillity no more than the plain Lady Kerry, or the old Lady Orkney, or any other of the ladies with whom he professed himself " in love." Vanessa was in a different category.

Women's companionship, intercourse with women in all the varying senses of the words, is to men both a stimulant and a sedative, and the man who drives his brain hard is specially apt to crave for one or other. Swift's nature, both complex and violent, needed many satisfactions, and Stella could give many of them, when he was with her. She was a woman who had wit to match his own and one to whom he could talk sense or nonsense as the humour took him, and get the response he needed. She stands for all that tranquillized : she and the willows at Laracor. " There is peace and quiet with MD, and nowhere else," he wrote in the early days of the *Journal*, when she was still his confidant, before whom he tumbled out pell-mell whatever was in his mind. But a confidant on paper is a shadowy consolation, and as weeks grew into months and months into years, the young woman near by, who sat so eagerly waiting to be told " secrets," got inevitably the first of his mind's disburdenment. She could be at least the ready listener, proud to be trusted ; and while things were on this footing, Swift was evidently quite happy about them.

Then—at whatever point we date it—there came the surprise of her declaration ; and I see no reason to doubt the truth of the poem's account, that it was to Swift a thing unexpected, undesired and unlooked for. Neither do I doubt that the man of wit was flattered by a new kind of triumph. It was a new stimulus, an added flavour to the zest of London, not altogether pleasing, yet one that he did not care to deny himself—still less, because, to do so, he must be harsh with the young woman he had learned to be fond of. In all this story, one must make allowance for Swift's dislike of giving pain, to which no one has given testimony so strongly as Vanessa, when he had hurt her to the heart. Innumerable men have hurt women by yielding to this kind of good nature in ambiguous relationships.

He was now, in 1714, under an added difficulty if he wished to break off ; for Mrs. Vanhomrigh had died in the previous winter, leaving her affairs in much confusion ; and Vanessa not unnaturally demanded advice and guidance from her friend.

However we take it, the intimacy in this month of June, 1714, was certainly no less than before, and Swift by writing as he did conceded Vanessa's claim to a special status. Yet the lists of his correspondence show that the fortnightly budget to MD went off as punctually as ever.

He was busy now, writing the things which he found it useless to say by word of mouth, in the pamphlet entitled *Some Free Thoughts on the Recent State of Affairs*—and he was deliberately secluded. All his affairs were in the hands of his confidential printer, John Barber : neither Oxford nor Bolingbroke heard from him. " I was six weeks compassing the great work of leaving London and did it at last abruptly enough," he wrote to Archdeacon Walls who acted for him in Dublin. "I care not to live in storms when I can no longer do service in the ship and am able to get out of it." But his friends found him out. The first to write was Gay, who had been named secretary to Lord Clarendon, then going as Envoy Extraordinary to Hanover, and who acknowledged this as wholly owing to Swift. "The many favours I have received from you purely out of your love for doing good, assures me you will not forget me in my absence," the poet added, and subjoined a copy of the "epigrammatical petition" which he had sent to Oxford by way of Arbuthnot. For Gay was never in funds, and amused his friends by a passion for fine clothes. Here is a verse of it—

> I'm no more to converse with the swains,
>   But go where fine people resort :
> One can live without money on plains,
>   But never without it at Court.
> If, when with the swains I did gamble,
>   I array'd me in silver and blue ;
> When abroad, and in Courts I shall ramble,
>   Pray, my Lord, how much money will do ?

Swift, beginning with his usual affectation of gruffness (" I wonder how you could have the impudence to know where I am ") replied that he had taken steps to help to fit him out ; and in the correspondence with Arbuthnot which followed, we find him solicitous to know whether Gay got his money in time—as, rather surprisingly, he did.

Arbuthnot's first letter gave news of " the Dragon " (their pet name for Oxford, " so called by contraries," Swift notes, " for he was the mildest, wisest and best Minister that ever served a Prince"). Oxford had been at the Scriblerus party, " after having sent us really a most excellent copy of verses," ending thus :

> He that cares not to rule, will be sure to obey,
> When summon'd by Arbuthnot, Pope, Parnell, and Gay.

For Parnell the poet, like Swift a clergyman in Ireland, was over also, Scriblering with the other wits. Pope wrote on June 18 a letter which, after his usual elaborate persiflage, has a serious ending.

> I cannot name Mr. Gay, without all the acknowledgments which I shall ever owe you on his account. . . . Of all the world, you are the man without flattery, who serve your friends with the least ostentation.

But for the heart of the matter, it is to the correspondence with Arbuthnot, close and frequent in those days, that one must turn ; for Arbuthnot was the live pivot of the Scriblerus group, yet also like Swift passionately interested in politics. Here is Swift to him on June 16:

DEAR BROTHER,

My stomach is prouder than you imagine, and I scorned to write till I was writ to. I have already half lost the ideas of Courts and Ministers. . . . I did not know till last night that the Princess Sophia [1] was dead, when my landlord and I chanced to pay a visit to a farm in a neighbouring village, and was told so over a mug of ale, by a brisk young fellow just come from London, who talked big and looked on us with great contempt. . . . Writing to you much would make me stark mad; judge his condition who has nothing to keep him from being miserable but endeavouring to forget those for whom he has the greatest value, love, and friendship. But you are a philosopher and a physician, and can overcome by your wisdom and your faculty those weaknesses which other men are forced to reduce by not thinking on them. Adieu, and love me half so well as I do you.

Arbuthnot's answer (after assurances that Gay "went away a happy man" and that both Oxford and Bolingbroke had been pressed to get preferment for Parnell) goes at large into his own projects for Scriblerus, excellent subjects of ridicule from German physicians, and the like. Pope meanwhile is on the literary side "collecting high flights of poetry; they are to be solemn nonsense." But Swift's reply put the truth of it:

To talk of Martin in any hands but yours, is a folly. You every day give better hints than all of us together could do in a twelvemonth; and to say the truth, Pope who first thought of the hint has no genius at all to it, in my mind. Gay is too young; Parnell has some ideas of it, but is idle; I could put together, and lard, and strike out well enough, but all that relates to the sciences must be from you. I am a vexed unsettled vagabond, and my thoughts are turned towards some papers I have, and some other things I would fain get from you and Lady Masham and would have had from the Dragon, but that is impossible till he is out and then I will go to him to Herefordshire and make him give me hints.

His mind was set on history in these days; his application for the post of Historiographer was actually before the authorities; and it vexed him that it should not be promptly granted: so he turned off into "to lament with my neighbours the want of rain, and dryness of hay." There follows one of the swift sketches, like an artist's scribble in a letter, showing how his observation of detail never rested:

Farmer Tyler says, the white mead at Chawdry has not been so bad in the memory of man, and the summer barley is quite dried up; but

[1] Mother to the Elector of Hanover, soon to be George I.

JOHN ARBUTHNOTT, M.D.

*Engraved from a scarce print in the collection of S*ʳ *Will*ᵐ *Musgrave, Bar*ᵗ.

LONDON : *Published, Jan*ʸ. *1798, by* Robert Wilkinson.

No. 58 Cornhill.

Iconographia Scotica, London, 1798   [*By the courtesy of* SIR ROBERT WITT.

we hope to have a pretty good crop of wheat. Parson Hunsdon it is thought must stick to his bargain, but all the neighbours say the attorney was an arrant rogue. We cannot get a bit of good butter for love or money. I could tell you more of the state of our affairs, but doubt your taste is not refined enough for it.

Arbuthnot answered with court news: the Dragon " holds fast with a dead gripe " his badge of office. Lady Masham is concerned about the post of historiographer, but thinks it " not a fit season to speak of it." Meanwhile he exhorts Swift not to be " so dogged " but come up to town for a while.

The other confederates had decided to do like Mahomet and come to the mountain; on Sunday, July 4, Pope and Parnell arrived at Letcombe Bassett and " having received the usual chidings on the part of the Dean," were brought in and drank " a pint of Lord Bolingbroke's Florence."—Swift's wealthier friends did not forget his creature comforts: John Barber had attacked Bolingbroke, who immediately ordered the despatch of " two dozen of red French wine and one dozen of strong Aaziana white wine." Ford [1] offered claret, " old or new," he being overstocked in both; and the Duke of Ormond, when things were at their blackest, sent a consignment of Burgundy, " very good to cure the spleen." Harley, Oxford's heir, despatched a horse from Herefordshire to be at the Dean's disposal. The report of the Scriblerus envoys speaks of other commodities.

There was likewise a sideboard of coffee, which the Dean roasted with his own hands in an engine for the purpose, his landlady attending all the while that office was performing. He talked of politics over coffee, with the air and style of an old statesman, who had known something formerly, but was shamefully ignorant of the last three weeks. When we mentioned the welfare of England he laughed at us, and said Muscovy would become a flourishing empire very shortly.

But with Arbuthnot matters were not on a foot of jesting. Swift was at this time hard pressed for money, and Arbuthnot urged this on Bolingbroke, as well as Swift's application to be historiographer. He received protestations of zeal, but no more; accordingly he himself put at Swift's disposal two hundred pounds which he was " in hopes to have."

Swift's answer was written after he had spent three days in

---

[1] Ford was a rich bachelor with a big place near Dublin; at this time employed in Irish administration; lettered in tastes, and in London a pillar of several coffee-houses. He is almost the only man who belonged both to Swift's Irish circle and his English one; and he was a lasting friend.

Oxford with young Harley, and had learnt that the desired post had been " disposed of these three weeks to one Madox."

So there is an end of that, and of twenty reflections one might make upon it. . . . And so you will lend me all your money. The mischief is, I never borrow money of a friend. You are mightily mistaken : all your honour, generosity, good nature, good sense, wit, and every other praiseworthy quality, will never make me think one jot the better of you. That time is now some years past, and you will never mend in my opinion. But really, Brother, you have a sort of shuffle in your gait ; and now I have said the worst that your most mortal enemy could say of you with truth.

There is no more perfect example to show how Swift gave emphasis to praise by appearing to disparage. It was always when most moved that he had recourse to this inverted irony. Even these few extracts should give to any reader some conception of the friendship between these two men who were at their most lovable in their relation to each other.

But in truth the whole correspondence of these few weeks spent by Swift in his retirement shows the man in his most characteristic development. Everywhere there is a sort of valedictory note, as if he felt an end approaching to his life while his powers were at their strongest. Premonitions did not deceive him ; his *Thoughts on the Present State of Affairs* was meant to be a last word ; yet it was a last word that did not get spoken. Ford, to whom he sent it, handed it with the usual affectation of anonymity to Barber, and Barber thought it wise to take Bolingbroke's advice. Bolingbroke read it, desired to make some alterations, and kept it till things had happened which made it entirely out of date : it was only published long after when it could have no political effect.

It had been Swift's opinion before he withdrew that Oxford could do no service by continuing in office and should resign, in which event he too would leave the court and follow his friend. The advice had been disregarded, and his pamphlet contained strictures on Oxford's administration. So when the manuscript was despatched, Swift wrote a letter to the Lord Treasurer which should make his personal feelings clear.

When I was with you, I have said more than once, that I would never allow quality or station made any real difference between men. Being now absent and forgotten, I have changed my mind. You have a thousand people who can pretend they love you, with as much appearance of sincerity as I, so that according to common justice I can have but a thousandth part in return of what I give. And this difference is wholly owing to your station. And the misfortune is still the greater, because I always loved you just so much the worse for your station. For in your public capacity you have often angered me to the heart, but, as a private man, never once. So that if I only looked towards myself, I could wish you a private man to-morrow. For I have nothing to ask, at least nothing that you will give, which is the same thing, and then you would see whether I should not with much more willingness attend you in a retirement, whenever you pleased to give me leave, than ever I did at London or Windsor. From these sentiments I will never write to you, if I can help it, otherwise than as to a private person, nor allow myself to have been obliged by you in any other capacity.

The memory of one great instance of your candour and justice, I will carry to my grave, that having been in a manner domestic with you for almost four years, it was never in the power of any public or concealed enemy to make you think ill of me, though malice and envy were often employed to that end. If I live, posterity shall know that and more, which, though you, and somebody that shall be nameless, seem to value less than I could wish, is all the return I can make you. Will you give me leave to say how I would desire to stand in your memory; as one, who was truly sensible of the honour you did him, though he was too proud to be vain upon it; as one, who was neither assuming, officious, nor teasing, who never wilfully misrepresented persons or facts to you, nor consulted his passions when he gave a character; and lastly, as one whose indiscretions proceeded altogether from a weak head, and not an ill heart? I will add one thing more, which is the highest compliment I can make, that I never was afraid of offending you, nor am now in any pain for the manner I write to you in. I have said enough; and, like one at your levee, having made my bow, I shrink back into the crowd.

It was then not sure that Oxford would be worsted in the struggle. A fortnight later, Erasmus Lewis thought it still uncertain, even though Lady Masham had told the Minister to his face that he had never done the Queen any service nor was capable of doing one. As late as July 25 Swift had no reply to his letter, though he had heard that the " Dragon " was vastly pleased with it and was showing it round. Swift wrote now for directions. His licence for absence was nearly out, but if Oxford resigned in a few days, as he was told was intended, he could go with him to his seat in Herefordshire; or else could return later, " if you please to command me." Answer came at last, written on July 27:

To-morrow morning I shall be a private person. When I have settled my domestic affairs here, I go to Wimpole; thence alone to Herefordshire. If I have not tired you *tête-à-tête*, fling away so much time upon one who loves you. And I believe, in the mass of souls ours were placed near each other.

That was a Monday night. Bolingbroke had won; and Erasmus Lewis wrote that same evening to describe " the pride of the conqueror," and the brutality with which the Queen's reasons for dismissing Oxford were stated. "They rail to the pit of hell. I am ready to burst for want of vent," he adds.

On the 29th, Swift, in a letter written to Archdeacon Walls asking him to arrange for extension of the licence to be absent, ended :

> I shall lose all favour with those now in power by following Lord Oxford in his retreat. I am hitherto very fair with them, but that will be at an end.

Bolingbroke had promised to fulfil the pledge given a year earlier by Oxford of paying Swift £1,000 to clear off the expenses of entering on the Deanery : he had expressed his determination not to let his friend continue in what they both accounted to be his Irish banishment ; and he was by far less dilatory than his predecessor. Meanwhile Lady Masham, the Queen's favourite, was entreating Swift to join Bolingbroke for the Queen's sake :

> I know you take delight to help the distressed ; and there cannot be a greater object than this good lady, who deserves pity. Pray, dear friend, stay here ; and do not believe us all alike to throw away good advice, and despise everybody's understanding but their own.

With this alternative open to him, Swift decided to follow into retirement a broken and disgraced minister ; feeling perhaps all the more bound to comply because Oxford could not but know that he asked a sacrifice ; feeling certainly the prouder because the proof of friendship which he had offered was demanded of him when it could be most indisputable.

Yet Swift never had the satisfaction of fulfilling the gesture on which he was determined ; for on the Sunday following the Tuesday on which Oxford was dismissed, Queen Anne died. Bolingbroke might well write to Swift, " What a world is this and how does Fortune banter us ! "

Ford, who was in the inner circle, thought that Swift's chances had been great.

> I really believe Lord Bolingbroke was very sincere in the professions he made of you, and he could have done anything. No minister was ever in that height of favour ; and Lady Masham was at least in as much credit as she had been in any time of her life.

He himself wrote to Vanessa, who had great expectations for him from Bolingbroke, " I cannot rely on his love for me." Yet his motive was simpler than calculation, and he let her see it :

> I told Lord Oxford I would go with him when he was out, and now

he begs it of me, and I cannot refuse him. I meddle not with his faults, as he was a Minister of State; but you know his personal kindness to me was excessive. He distinguished and chose me above all other men while he was great, and his letter to me the other day was the most moving imaginable.

While he still lingered in Berkshire, Bolingbroke wrote asking for his presence in London. A phrase in that letter led Swift to believe that there was still possiblity of a reunion between the Tory leaders; but Lewis urged him to abandon such thoughts. Oxford, in fact, was staying on, with some thought of being included in a new coalition. On August 15 Swift wrote to him the last letter which we have of this Berkshire period, announcing his enforced departure to renew the oaths. "I shall have no thoughts of returning," he says, "unless some juncture of affairs shall make my friends think it may be of any use." No other communication passed between these two for nearly a year, and then Swift broke his resolution of waiting to be asked to return. For Oxford was in the Tower, under impeachment, in danger of his life, and Swift wrote to solicit the privilege of affording him his "poor service and attendance." Nothing, surely, in Swift's life as a courtier became him like his leaving it.

We have not the letter in which he bid farewell to Arbuthnot, but we have Arbuthnot's reply—much more concerned for Lady Masham's misfortunes than his own, though he lamented a kind mistress, and found a sorry scene about him:

I have an opportunity calmly and philosophically to consider that treasure of vileness and baseness, that I always believed to be in the heart of man; and to behold them exert their insolence and baseness; every new instance, instead of surprising and grieving me, as it does some of my friends, really diverts me, and in a manner proves my theory. . . . Dear friend, the last sentence of your letter quite kills me. Never repeat that melancholy tender word, that you will endeavour to forget me. . . . That hearty sincere friendship, that plain and open ingenuity in all your commerce, is what I am sure I can never find in another man. I shall want often a faithful monitor, one that would vindicate me behind my back, and tell me my faults to my face. God knows I write this with tears in my eyes.

It would be well if the chapter could close with that. Were Swift to be judged by his dealings with men only, few could face the assize so boldly. But the other tangled skein of his existence has to be followed: for in it there is no breaking off.

No letters survive to let us know how the news of events affected Stella and her companion, though Swift was writing to

hem ; but Vanessa kept hers. On July 8 Swift wrote to her
solely about money affairs ; she was in difficulties, and he told
her to borrow from one of his publishers, Tooke, on his security.
This, it should be observed, was at a moment when he was himself
embarrassed for money.)   On August 1, he tells her that he had
intended to leave for Ireland on the 2nd, but had to postpone
his departure to stay with Oxford.   There followed a consequence
that he little expected ; she posted down to visit him in Berkshire,
and let him know that she proposed to follow him to Ireland,
where she had property.   He wrote on August 12 after this visit:

I think since I have known you, I have drawn an old house upon
my head.   You should not have come by Wantage for a thousand
pounds.   You used to brag you were very discreet : where is it gone ?
It is probable I may not stay in Ireland long, but be back by the beginning
of winter.   When I am there, I will write to you as soon as I can conveniently, but it shall always be under a cover ; and if you write to
me, let some other direct it ; and I beg you will write nothing that is
particular, but what may be seen ; for I apprehend letters may be opened,
and inconveniences will happen.   If you are in Ireland while I am there,
I shall see you very seldom.   It is not a place for any freedom, but where
everything is known in a week, and magnified a hundred degrees.
These are rigorous laws that must be passed through ; but it is probable
we may meet in London in winter, or, if not, leave all to fate, that seldom
cares to humour our inclinations.   I say all this out of the perfect esteem
and friendship I have for you.   These public misfortunes have altered
all my measures, and broke my spirits.   I shall, I hope, be on horseback
in a day after this comes to your hand.   I would not answer your
questions for a million, nor can I think of them with any ease of mind.
Adieu.

Construe that as one may, it means more than common friendli-
ness.   It means also that then, as always, she had brought dis-
turbance, not tranquillity.   Yet many years later, proposing that
" a history of Cad and ——" should " be written through all its
steps from the beginning of time," he sketches a list of chapters.
Most of the titles are unintelligible, but one is " The Berkshire
Surprise."   It is fair to assume that after the usual " chiding," the
visitor was made welcome enough to be reminded of it, after six
years.

But the essence of the facts is that Vanessa had made up her
mind to follow the Dean to Ireland, and that, willing or unwilling,
he had acquiesced.   That part of his London life stuck fast to
him, for a matter of nine years.

CHAPTER XIII

DUBLIN: 1714-20

TRADITION says Swift was mobbed in the streets when he came back to Dublin. If this be true there is no trace of it in his letters : unless it be his observation on October 20, George I's coronation day, that he lit a bonfire "*par manière d'acquit,* and to save my windows." For Dublin was demonstrating enthusiastic Whig loyalty and throwing up its hats for the Hanoverian ; and Swift, though he could write later to Archbishop King, " I have always been a Whig," and was a convinced supporter of the Protestant succession, yet hated the triumphant faction and at this period conversed only with Tories. All his loyalty and all his affection went out to the men who had been his associates when they were in power, and who now were in disgrace and even in danger. We see him, as Arbuthnot wrote to Pope, " with a stern countenance and still aiming a blow at his enemies." Yet he knows that the blows cannot reach their mark ; he is like one of those whom poets have often imagined cut off in their strength by violent death, still full of the passion of the struggle, still craving for the old comradeship, *tendentemque manus ripæ ulterioris amore.*

Partir c'est mourir un peu, a Frenchman has written ; but for Swift, severance from England was to die many deaths. " There I made my friendships, and there I left my desires," he wrote long after ; there he had " drunk delight of battle with his peers " in the field of combat which was peculiarly his own. Now the weapons for which his hands were itching must lie unmastered, the shafts unsped. Since the days of his Moor Park apprenticeship, he had never written without the stimulus of equal companionship, he had never worked except in a team. Far ahead was the time when he would become more formidable as a lone hand champion (like Cuchulain of the Irish epic) than ever in the picked battalion. Now his friends were out of the fight, and he raged companionless. One thing he did write in those first months which ranks with his best, and it is precisely the cry of his bereavement:

IN SICKNESS

Written in October, 1714

'Tis true—then why should I repine
To see my life so fast decline?
But why obscurely here alone,
Where I am neither loved nor known?
My state of health none care to learn;
My life is here no soul's concern:
And those with whom I now converse
Without a tear will tend my hearse,
Removed from kind Arbuthnot's aid,
Who knows his art, but not his trade,
Preferring his regard for me
Before his credit, or his fee.
Some formal visits, looks, and words,
What mere humanity affords,
I meet perhaps from three or four,
From whom I once expected more;
Which those who tend the sick for pay,
Can act as decently as they:
But no obliging, tender friend,
To help at my approaching end,
My life is now a burthen grown
To others, ere it be my own.

For the first three years of his London life, we have so free
and full access to Swift's domestic relations (if they can be called
domestic) that in studying him at this period there is danger of
misunderstanding. That door is shut to us; we know nothing
of how he greeted or was greeted by the woman for whom so long
he wrote his daily budget. That central figure disappears; yet,
though we may be certain that he had his welcome, none the less
it is clear that her society had not power to charm like David's
harping. What Stella was worth to him we must only guess at,
but it should be remembered always that she belonged to " the
scene he was condemned to." The first letter that we have after
his return was to Bolingbroke, now in retirement—" the only
honourable post that those who gave it you were capable of con-
ferring." He himself would retire too if he could, but his cabin
at Laracor had fallen down, and he lacked mud to rebuild it, and
straw to thatch it.

I live a country life in town, see nobody, and go every day once to
prayers; and hope, in a few months, to grow as stupid as the present
situation of affairs will require. Well, after all, parsons are not such bad
company, especially when they are under subjection; and I let none
but such come near me. However, pray God forgive them, by whose

indolence, neglect, or want of friendship, I am reduced to live with twenty leagues of salt water between your Lordship and me.

Bitter words. The only friendship that he formed in this period is significant, for Knightley Chetwode was that rare thing, an Irish landlord of large property who held to the Tories. His approaches were flattering. "I thought I was at Court again, and that the bearer wanted a place," Swift writes. There were many invitations to Chetwode's home, Woodbrooke near Portarlington; and before the autumn was over, he was on his way there across country from Trim, where he had been staying, to make Laracor habitable.

On that journey a messenger met him to say that Vanessa had arrived and taken up her abode at Kildrought, now known as Celbridge, on the Liffey, eleven miles from Dublin, in a house she had inherited from her father. She had asked him to visit her, but he answered:

I would not have gone to Kildrought to see you for all the world. I ever told you you wanted discretion. I am going to a friend upon a promise, and shall stay with him about a fortnight, and then come to town, and I will call on you as soon as I can, supposing you lodge in Turnstile Alley, as your servant told me. . . .

Does not Dublin look very dirty to you, and the country very miserable? Is Kildrought as beautiful as Windsor, and as agreeable to you as the Prebend's lodgings there? Is there any walk about you as pleasant as the avenue, and the Marlborough Lodge?

The strongest card that Vanessa held was that she belonged to the scene he had left. Yet she had another, for she appealed to his compassion; and she played it unsparingly:

You cannot but be sensible, at least in some degree, of the many uneasinesses I am slave to: a wretch of a brother, cunning executors, and importunate creditors of my mother's, things I can no way avoid being subject to at present, and weighty enough to sink greater spirits than mine without some support. Once I had a friend that would see me sometimes, and either commend what I did, or advise what to do, which banished all my uneasiness. But now when my misfortunes are increased by being in a disagreeable place, among strange prying deceitful people, whose company is so far from being an amusement, that it is a very great punishment, you fly me, and give me no reason, but that we are amongst fools, and must submit. I am very well satisfied we are amongst such, but know no reason for having my happiness sacrificed to their caprice. You once had a maxim, which was, to act what was right, and not mind what the world said; I wish you would keep to it now. Pray what can be wrong in seeing and advising an unhappy young woman? I cannot imagine. You cannot but know that your frowns make my life insupportable.

His answer (conjecturally dated by Ball Dec. 6, 1714) was this:

I will see you in a day or two, and believe me it goes to my soul not to see you oftener. I will give you the best advice, countenance, and assistance I can. I would have been with you sooner if a thousand impediments had not prevented me. I did not imagine you had been under difficulties. I am sure my whole fortune should go to remove them. I cannot see you, I fear, to-day, having affairs of my place to do ; but pray think it not want of friendship or tenderness, which I will always continue to the utmost.

Here is her rejoinder—if not to this, to some similar admonition :

Well! now I plainly see how great a regard you have for me. You bid me be easy, and you would see me as often as you could ; you had better have said as often as you could get the better of your inclinations so much, or as often as you remembered there was such a person in the world. If you continue to treat me as you do, you will not be made uneasy by me long. It is impossible to describe what I have suffered since I saw you last ; I am sure I could have borne the rack much better than those killing, killing words of yours. Sometimes I have resolved to die without seeing you more, but those resolves, to your misfortune, did not last long ; for there is something in human nature that prompts one so to find relief in this world, I must give way to it, and beg you would see me, and speak kindly to me, for I am sure you would not condemn anyone to suffer what I have done, could you but know it. The reason I write to you is, because I cannot tell it you, should I see you ; for when I begin to complain, then you are angry, and there is something in your look so awful, that it strikes me dumb. Oh! that you may but have so much regard for me left, that this complaint may touch your soul with pity. I say as little as ever I can. Did you but know what I thought, I am sure it would move you. Forgive me and believe me, I cannot help telling you this, and live.

We may assume that some stay was put on Vanessa's importunity for the time ; except for a brief note from him, belonging probably to 1715, or 1716, and again emphasizing discretion (" I hate anything that looks like a secret "), we have no more of the correspondence till 1719. But the intimacy—whatever form it took—continued, and certainly did not lessen.

However, in the six months after his return, Swift had other thoughts to occupy him than those feminine importunities. Proceedings against the Tory party had begun ; Erasmus Lewis wrote warning him to hide his papers. In Ireland, Knightley Chetwode had himself been put out of the Commission of the Peace, and was uneasy for his friend. This was not groundless. The Whigs, not content with grasping all offices under the new King, began to inquire into the conduct of those who made the Peace of Utrecht. Bolingbroke, who had been dismissed from office in August 1714, stood his ground till March, but then fled to France. Prior, the chief agent in negotiation with France, was seized. Meantime Swift was actually in correspondence with Ormond, who already meditated following Bolingbroke. Ormond's letter, as well as one from Swift's confidential agent, Barber the printer, were seized on the person of a private individual who carried them, and came into the hands of the Lords Justices—of whom Archbishop King, no friend to Swift at this time, was one. By June Oxford, who refused to fly, was impeached, and Bolingbroke, certain to be attainted in his absence, was actually joining the Pretender's court. Swift soon found himself obliged to check his friend Chetwode from involving himself with the Jacobite schemes of which Ormond was the centre. His frame of mind is depicted with even more than his usual energy in a letter to Pope, who had reproached him for silence :

I am naturally no very exact correspondent, and when I leave a country without a probability of returning, I think as seldom as I can of what I loved or esteemed in it, to avoid the *desiderium* which of all things makes life most uneasy. But you must give me leave to add one thing, that you talk at your ease, being wholly unconcerned in public events : for if your friends the Whigs continue, you may hope for some favour ; if the Tories return, you are at least sure of quiet. You know how well I loved both Lord Oxford and Bolingbroke, and how dear the Duke of Ormond is to me. Do you imagine I can be easy, while their enemies are endeavouring to take off their heads. *I nunc et versus tecum meditare canoros.*

Later he speaks of some inclination to come to England.

But truly I must be a little easy in my mind before I can think of Scriblerus. . . . You are to understand that I live in the corner of a vast unfurnished house. My family consists of a steward, a groom, a helper in the stable, a footman, and an old maid, who are all at board wages, and when I do not dine abroad, or make an entertainment, which last is very rare, I eat a mutton-pie, and drink half a pint of wine. My amusements are defending my small dominions against the Archbishop, and endeavouring to reduce my rebellious choir. *Perditur hæc inter misero lux.*

The project of going to England for his own comfort took no shape : but on July 19, when news reached Dublin that Oxford had been committed to the Tower, Swift wrote the letter to which reference has been already made, asking leave to give him there his " poor service and attendance." . . .

It is the first time I ever solicited you in my own behalf, and, if I am refused, I think it will be the first request you ever refused me. I do not conceive myself obliged to regulate my opinions by the proceedings of a House of Lords or Commons; and therefore, however they may acquit themselves in your Lordship's case, I shall take the liberty of thinking and calling you the ablest and faithfulest minister, and truest lover of your country that this age hath produced. And I have already taken care that you shall be so represented to posterity in spite of all the rage and malice of your enemies.

There was no reply till two years later when Oxford, discharged at last and without trial, wrote that his son " keeps the letter as a family monument." He answered at the same time another letter in which Swift expressed the hope " that during this glorious scene of your life—I do not mean your discharge, but your two years' imprisonment—you have sometimes found a minute to remember an inconsiderable man who ever loved you above all things." Yet if Oxford's answer showed all the old affection, it had also the old dilatoriness. The two men never met again. But in these years Swift was continually busy on his projects for a historical justification of the ministry whose chief had inspired in him so lasting a devotion.

None of these works was published till after his death and none has capital interest. I am concerned here only to note that, although the habit of writing did not easily leave one who had so greatly acquired it, yet what he wrote at this time was a kind of continuance of that life which he no longer lived, and that gradually, little by little, he ceased to write. Any man who has been used to journalism will understand how the conditions of that craft are bound up with quick issue. The journalist, unlike the writer of books needing long meditation or study, counts instinctively on the stimulus of seeing at once the result of his labour; and it is scarcely conceivable that a worker in this kind should continue writing without prompt publication. In spite of *Gulliver*, Swift was a journalist at heart and by choice.

I must now try and track out the beginnings of the new life, during the period in which he was practically lost to the public view.

Arbuthnot wrote to him, in the first year of their separation, while the interchange of letters was still frequent: " You are certainly some first minister of a great monarch, who, for some misbehaviour, are condemned, in this revolution of things, to govern a Chapter, and a choir of singing-men." That was not far from Swift's own view: but—" My notion is," he wrote to Chetwode, " that if a man cannot mend the public, he should mend old shoes, if he can do no better; and therefore I endeavour in the little sphere I am placed to do all the good it is capable of. I hear they think me a smart Dean." The ablest of his successors, the late Dr. Bernard, Dean of St. Patrick's, and afterwards Archbishop of Dublin, fully confirms that estimate. Chapter and choir were never more ably handled ; and in all that related to church preferment the Dean was active to the utmost of his power, seeking to serve his friends and the men whom he thought worth serving. One was his friend Archdeacon Walls, and there were difficulties ; but "nobody is so stiff as an easy man put upon his mettle," he told Walls, and finally he wrote a formal protest to Archbishop King, pressing certain changes of livings in which Walls was concerned, and complaining that it appeared as if his support were likely to hinder rather than help those who cultivated his acquaintance. The letter ended with a dignified appeal for better relations.

In those days the Deanery was, as it is now, a great oblong of small dull bricks with a wide plain flight of stone steps fronting the street, while its other side, on which were the principal rooms, looked towards the south side of the cathedral : but no public way then ran, as now, between them. All was part of the close ; and just beyond the cathedral's east end rose the library founded by King's predecessor, Archbishop Marsh, and beyond this, in contact with it, was the great seventeenth-century palace. It is now a police barrack, and only the wide stone gateway is obvious : but in the barrack there is still a reception room with coved ceiling some sixty feet long communicating with another apartment of noble proportions. King's letters give the impression of a Puritan simplicity ; but when he went to England he travelled with a coach and eight. The archbishops of that day were great potentates, and George I's administration had named King one of the Lords Justices who in the Lord-Lieutenant's absence were responsible for the country. Normally this would have been the Primate's office ; but Archbishop Lindsay had been chosen by Oxford in 1714 in preference to King because he was a Tory. Swift had supported that choice and King knew it ; it made a breach in their long alliance.

This had never been quite a friendship, in spite of many protestations on both sides of good will. As far back as 1711, when Swift was in full career of successful journalism, King had propounded the advisability of earning reputation by some serious theological work, and spoke with disparagement and even contempt of the volume of Miscellanies which had then just appeared. Swift was very angry about it in his budget to Stella ; but there was no breach. Now, in 1716, King answered Swift's letter by assuring him that he was misinformed by busybodies and expressed a hope for hearty co-operation. Then correspondence was renewed; but within three months a casual word set Swift on flame. " We have a strong report that my Lord Bolingbroke will return here and be pardoned," King wrote from London, " certainly it must not be for nothing. I hope he can tell no ill story of you." The implication, whether in jest or earnest, was firstly that Bolingbroke was about to betray his former allies (and Swift fiercely resented this) ; secondly, that Swift might after all have been compromised in Jacobite intrigue.

Cordial friendship was, in short, temperamentally impossible between these two neighbours whose dwellings were barely a stone's throw apart ; yet King was the only man in Ireland whose intellect and judgment, setting aside the special gifts of genius, put him on a level with Swift. But he was too fair-minded not to bestow respect when he found Swift, in those first years while his finances were still embarrassed, making provision of a glebe of twenty acres to be attached to the living of Laracor, at the cost of some £250 from his own pocket.

The old circle of friends continued: Dr. Raymond of Trim was a chief figure : the Chetwodes were always anxious to have the Dean for a guest, and he became now very intimate at Belcamp, five miles north of Dublin, the seat of the Grattan family—a numerous brotherhood—one of whom, Henry, had for grandson the first patriot who rivalled Swift's fame in Ireland. The correspondence shows a gradual slacking of ties to England, though both the Duchess of Ormond and Lady Bolingbroke, in sore distress and anxiety, wrote to him such letters as women only write to a man they like, trust, and respect. A letter from Swift to Pope, of August, 1716, has more wit in it than friendship, but is famous because of the suggestions in it for Gay's benefit : " a set of Quaker pastorals, for the pastoral ridicule is not exhausted. . . . Or what do you think of a Newgate Pastoral among the whores and thieves there ? " Here was the germ of the " Beggars' Opera."

In return, the wits set their absent colleague raking Ireland for subscribers to the edition of Prior's poetical works, for that poet was likely to " end his days in as forlorn a state as any other poet has done before him, if his friends do not take more care of him than he has done of himself." Swift taxed his acquaintance to the utmost and Prior's acknowledgments were heartfelt.

One must suppose that by 1716 his " great house " was less bare, and his cellar also. The furnishing of this was among his first cares : on October 20, 1714, he had bought forty-six dozen bottles and " wanted nothing but the circumstance of wine to be able to entertain a friend." However, " a great vessel of Alicant " lay there waiting to be bottled : it will be remembered that he avowed a vulgar preference for Spanish white wine. But the custom of the country encouraged him to ship from Bordeaux, and whatever else he economized on, he was (he tells Pope once) " never thrifty in wine." Later he says that he got through half a dozen hogsheads yearly, and generally had eight or nine in his cellar.[1]

I cannot say whether the forty-six dozen bottles were made to his order ; but in 1727 he provided himself with flagons of blackish green glass, bearing his name and the date stamped ; two are preserved in the National Museum of Ireland.

A quatrain attributed to Delany contrasts the two deans, Stearne and Swift :

In the time of Dean John, if you came here to dine,
You had choice of good meat, but no choice of wine.
In Jonathan's days those that come here to eat,
Have good wine enough, but no choice of good meat.

Swift's relations with his predecessor were strained for some time and it did not mend matters that much of Stearne's plenishing remained. This included " a great cat, who by her perpetual noise and stink must certainly be a Whig," he wrote to the Tory Chetwode. However, Chetwode preserved and transmitted a letter in which Swift himself confessed leniency towards another animal of this tribe. He was still in Dublin lodgings, had ridden up from Laracor, twenty Irish miles, and arrived on a dark winter evening, cold, wet and hungry—asking for dinner. The old woman muttered that she had had no fire ; he stormed after his fashion, till she admitted the truth. Her cat had kittened that day in the empty kitchen grate and could not be disturbed. Swift submitted and went to bed without his dinner.[2]

In the deanery he provided himself with a cook-housekeeper, " as old and ugly as that the Dean left : the ladies of my acquaintance would not allow me one with a tolerable face though I most earnestly interceded for it," he says. She was always addressed as " sweetheart."

[1] There were eight when the inventory of his goods came to be taken in 1742.
[2] Unhappily the letter has been lost, but Chetwode's heir declared " by the honour of his ancestors' blood " that he had seen the story in Swift's own handwriting—adorned doubtless with many terms of contumely for both cat and old woman.

" The ladies " supervised in all such matters. " I am as help-less as an elephant," Swift writes once in his *Journal* : and it is probable that this inability to cope with small domestic emergencies was a great part of his appeal to the sex. When he entertained mixed company, they always made the arrangements, and Stella, though never officially, did the honours of the house. Knightley Chetwode's reply in October, 1714, to this announcement about the cook is worth noting. " The ladies are I confess a little hard upon you in regard to faces. But you know best if it be not just "— and then followed the words : " Since the world says you may command a very agreeable one and yet defer it." Chetwode thought better to strike these out, but they remain legible.

Such comment was inevitable, and not less inevitably Stella would have been aware of it. That it never grew to scandal is the proof of her amazing loyalty and discretion. But unless all Swift's intimates were mistaken, her uneasiness at this time was grave ; and it must have been quickened by the presence of Vanessa. The story transmitted is that St. John Ashe, Bishop of Clogher, Swift's oldest friend, and a dear friend of hers, noticed her bearing as unlike herself, questioned her, and was told she felt herself slighted : that he went to Swift, who agreed to marriage on con-dition of secrecy and of continuing the existing way of life ; and that they were married by him at Clogher in County Tyrone.

There is no certain proof of the marriage and Stella in her will described herself as " Esther Johnson, Spinster." But Sheridan and Delany, who from 1718 were Swift's intimates, accepted the story—first put into public print by Orrery—without question ; Berkeley is quoted (at second-hand) for the same belief; and Bishop Evans, who knew and hated Swift, wrote of it as a fact to the Archbishop of Canterbury four years before Stella died.

I must discuss the matter more fully later : here it is only necessary to say that if the marriage took place, as seems probable, it was at the close of that period of which Swift wrote later to Gay : " I was three years reconciling myself to the scene to which I had been condemned and stupidity was what I had recourse to." Only after 1716 do we find him forming new friendships and turning back to literature as a pursuit and recreation, in the company of a circle in which Stella was a central figure.

But the marriage altered nothing in their relations, except that it gave Stella a guarantee that Swift would not marry Vanessa. None the less that other intimacy continued as before, though furtively, while Stella's special position was made as public as ever.

CHAPTER XIV

SWIFT'S IRISH CIRCLE

IN the year after that to which his marriage to Stella is dated
Swift's life took on a new shape. It is the end of his deliberate
seclusion and the beginning of friendships, not with men whom
he regarded as of his own calibre, but with minds congenial to
at least a side of his character. He loved scholarship and he loved
wit, and these new associates were both wits and scholars. They
were also, and this was new to him, very much his juniors. Of
his English circle only Bolingbroke was markedly younger than
he, and Bolingbroke's position in the State did away with all sense
of inequality. But the Rev. Thomas Sheridan and the Rev. Patrick
Delany were only entering Dublin university when Swift, already
forty, was the frequent guest of Halifax and Somers, and the close
ally of Steele and Addison. Delany was a junior Fellow of the
College: Sheridan had set up a school in Dublin in which the
classics were taught through English, not through Latin, and
teaching in English style was carefully given. The first known
fact about the Dean's relationship with the two friends is that in
December 1717 he attended a Greek play, probably—for even this
is not certain—performed by Sheridan's scholars. We do not
get on to firm ground till October 10, 1718, when Swift writes
a long epistle in verse to Delany, and the opening indicates sufficiently that of the two young men Delany had most of his esteem :

> To you whose virtues, I must own
> With shame, I have too lately known ;
> To you, by art and nature taught
> To be the man I long have sought,
> Had not ill Fate, perverse and blind,
> Placed you in life too far behind :
> Or, what I should repine at more,
> Placed me in life too far before.

Discoursing on wit and humour, he distinguishes the two : " that gives surprise, and this delight "; he makes his acknowledgments to Voiture who " in various lights displays That irony which turns to praise "; but the purpose of the discussion is made plain at the conclusion. Delany is to admonish Sheridan—" who full of humour, fire, and wit, Not always judges what is fit." For Sheridan after a bare three months' acquaintance had permitted himself to compose a lampoon, chaffing Swift because his muse was dead and solemnly buried with asses and owls.

The reproof did not check a friendship, which had its main bond in the cult of verses, mostly nonsensical. Sheridan adored clever trifling, and Swift had always a leaning that way. Evidently he had written of his diversions to Prior, who replies (in a letter about the subscription to his poems), " If you are once got into *la bagatelle*, you may despise the world." And for a score of years at least, Swift never got out of it. In the latest collected edition of his Poems, ' Trifles ' occupy ninety pages; ' Riddles ' thirty more, and the majority of these were addressed to Sheridan, whose replies go to swell the volume. One ' trifle ' by its date, 1718, shows that the admonition through Delany was not seriously meant or taken :

My offers of peace you ill understood ;
Friend Sheridan, when will you know your own good ?

Part of the joke lies in that the letter was written with Swift's left hand, because the other " was employed at the same time writing some letters of business." Sheridan answered with the left hand, in the same clumsy metre, but went on with his right in a fashion which shows both the freedom he used and the wit which made it acceptable :

Alas, thy numbers failing all,
Poor Jonathan, how they do fall !
Thy rhymes, which whilom made thy pride swell,
Now jingle like a rusty bridle :
Thy verse, which ran both smooth and sweet,
Now limp upon their gouty feet :
Thy thoughts, which were the true sublime,
Are humbled by the tyrant, Time :
Alas ! what cannot Time subdue ?
Time has reduced my wine and you ;
Emptied my casks, and clipp'd your wings,
Disabled both in our main springs ;
So that of late we two are grown
The jest and scorn of all the town.

But yet, if my advice be ta'en,
We two may be as great again;
I'll send you wings, you send me wine;
Then you will fly, and I shall shine.

One may add here this sentence from a letter of February 12, 1722, to Archdeacon Walls, Swift's vicegerent in most affairs :

My crew has drank near three hogsheads since I came to town [in October] and we must take up new when I come down.

Sheridan doubtless had more than his share, Delany a sober portion ; the Grattans and their kinsfolk the Jacksons were others of the band ; but it included the ladies.   There is a most characteristic letter to Stella in which the Dean pretends that she and Dingley have proposed to come and spend the afternoon at the Deanery bringing their provisions :

Jack Grattan said nothing to me of it till last night ; it is none of my fault, how did I know but you were to dine abroad ?   You should have sent your messenger sooner ; yes, I think the dinner you provided for yourselves may do well enough here, but pray send it soon.   I wish you would give a body more early warning, but you must blame yourselves.   Delany says he will come in the evening, and for aught I know, Sheridan may be here at dinner.   Which of you was it that undertook this frolic ?   You may be sure if there be a good bottle you shall have it.   I am sure I never refused you, and therefore that reflection might have been spared.   Pray be more positive in your answer to this.

Margoose, and not Mergoose ; it is spelt with an *a*, simpleton.   No, I am pretty well after my walk.   I am glad the Archdeacon got home safe, and I hope you took care of him.   It was his own fault ; how could I know where he was, and he could have easily overtaken me ; for I walked softly on purpose, I told Delany I would.

Stella endorsed this : ' An Answer to No Letter.'   She and Dingley were probably then lodging with Archdeacon Walls.   It was one of Swift's amusements to find blunders in Stella's spelling, and here he supposes her to have made a bad shot at Margaux— the vintage of all Bordeaux which seems to have been then most reputed in Ireland.

Or again, we find the " crew " in the country.   Writing to Archbishop King from Chief Baron Rochfort's house of Gaulstown in Meath, Swift says on September 28, 1721 :

My Lord, I row after health like a waterman, and ride after it like a post-boy, and find some little success ; but *subeunt morbi tristisque senectus*.   I have a receipt to which you are a stranger ; my Lord Oxford and Mr. Prior used to join with me in taking it, to whom I often said, when we were two hours diverting ourselves with trifles, *vive la bagatelle*. I am so deep among the workmen at Rochfort's canals and lakes, so dextrous at the oar, such an alderman after the hare——

That is the graver aspect of it; but " The Country Life," a long poem, tells " how George, Nim, Dan, Dean, pass their days " in company with Delany and Sheridan. George and Nim are the sons of the Lord Chief Baron; Dan is the Rev. Daniel Jackson— a lazy member. " You can sit in your nightgown now till noon without any reproaches and have nobody to tease you to the oar or the saddle," says a letter to him. But the poem gives us detail:

> At seven the Dean, in night-gown drest,
> Goes round the house to wake the rest;
> At nine, grave Nim and George facetious,
> Go to the Dean to read Lucretius;
> At ten my Lady comes and hectors
> And kisses George, and ends our lectures;
> And when she has him by the neck fast,
> Hauls him, and scolds us, down to breakfast.
> We squander there an hour or more,
> And then all hands, boys, to the oar;

At two the bell warns all for dinner and Lady Betty " soundly chides " the loiterers.

> Now water brought, and dinner done;
> With " Church and King " the ladies gone.
> Not reckoning half an hour we pass
> In talking o'er a moderate glass.
> Dan, growing drowsy, like a thief
> Steals off to doze away his beef;
> And this must pass for reading Hammond—
> While George and Dean go to backgammon.
> George, Nim, and Dean, set out at four,
> And then, again, boys, to the oar.

So it goes on till sunset and then:

> We go to prayers and then to play,
> Till supper comes; and after that
> We sit an hour to drink and chat.
> 'Tis late—the old and younger pairs,
> By Adam lighted, walk up stairs.
> The weary Dean goes to his chamber;
> And Nim and Dan to garret clamber.

Then come other details, telling " how the Dean delights to vex the Ladies and lampoon their sex." And so on, with an excursus upon that good Tory, the Chief Baron, and "how little weight he sets on all Whig papers and Gazettes."

All these trifles together do not add a pennyweight to Swift's permanent literary baggage : indeed they encumber his fame. But they show us a man returning to the uses of life and laughter, and they were superficial signs of health. Except letters, and whatever was done on his History, he had written nothing since his return, save only that desperate cry of loneliness " In Sickness " in the first months, and in 1716 a characteristic string of verses, " Phyllis, or the Progress of Love," whose theme is a young lady's elopement with her groom and the succeeding stages of their relation. Yet even this is related to his English time and the familiar road to Windsor :

> They keep, at Staines, the Old Blue Boar,
> Are cat and dog, and rogue and whore.

The first sign of general animation resulting from the stimulus of friendship with lively young brains may be found in a paraphrase of Horace addressed to Archbishop King, in whom he began to recognize a man " ready to defend With life his country or his friend." But even in the year when he wrote that, he was telling Knightley Chetwode :

I am the only man in this kingdom who is not a politician, and therefore I only keep such company as will suffer me to suspend their politics, and this brings my conversation into very narrow bounds. Joe Beaumont is my oracle for public affairs in the country, and an old Presbyterian woman in town.

Joe Beaumont was a shopkeeper in Trim with inventive brains and occasional lapses into lunacy ; the old Presbyterian was Mrs. Brent, housekeeper at the Deanery and a personage of mark in the saga.

But by 1720 there came a mighty change. A whole batch of verses dates from November : " The Progress of Beauty," " Progress of Marriage," " Progress of Poetry," and another sheaf, in which Apollo is made to appoint Swift vicegerent in his empire. The chief interest of these is that Stella figures and figures for the first time under that name. The " crew " must have insisted that its leading lady should have a title suitable—for Stella was immensely popular with the young men—and Swift chose the Latin for Esther. Lines headed " Apollo to the Dean " indicate that Stella has been caught writing verses (abetted by that traitor Delany) on a window-pane in the Deanery, a window " direct to the north where I never once went." For in that grim house, dining-room, drawing-room and the dean's study faced north across the close to the grey cathedral; and it was possibly on the dining-room window that Stella and Delany wrote their complaint that Apollo's deputy

> Leaves Phœbus to treat
> With the thoughts he inspires, regardless of meat;
> Hence they that come hither expecting to dine
> Are always fobbed off with sheer wit and sheer wine.

Delany held the pencil : but Apollo testifies

> That Stella was helping, abetting and aiding;
> And still as he writ, stood smiling and reading :
> That her eyes were as bright as myself at noon-day,
> But her graceful black locks were all mingled with grey.

Apart from these local railleries, Swift had got back into political themes. The South Sea Project inspired him in 1721 to a savage ballad—with one verse in it too good to leave unquoted. Why is it that in that " dangerous gulf profound, Fools chiefly float, the wise are drown'd ? "

> So have I seen from Severn's brink
> A flock of geese jump down together;
> Swim where the bird of Jove would sink,
> And, swimming, never wet a feather.

But this lies off the line of his true development, which he struck in 1720 when he wrote the first of his Irish tracts. It was a *Proposal for the Universal Use of Irish Manufactures* and the proposal has been summed up in one sentence—" Burn everything that comes from England except the coal." This was his answer to the English policy of denying to the Irish (Anglo-Irish and native, Protestant and Catholic alike), the opportunity of competing with English manufacturers. Woollen fabrics were and had been for centuries an Irish speciality : the country abounded with wool. All exportation of woollens was therefore prohibited. The incidence of this measure was specially apparent to Swift because the weavers' quarter lay round St. Patrick's in the " Liberties " of the cathedral ; and over these streets the Dean had (by survival from the original Anglo-Norman foundation) rights and duties as a magistrate. In April, 1721, the weavers numbered nearly 1,700; their families brought this to a total of 6,000, and they were in appalling distress, largely because of the general consequences of the South Sea failures. They sold and pawned household stuff, looms and tools and having nothing else left but to starve, they petitioned government, who ordered them a hundred pounds and a collection in the churches, but at the same time prosecuted the printer of Swift's pamphlet. When the jury disagreed and twice refused to give a verdict, Chief Justice Whitshed refused to let them go until, after being eight times sent back, they had brought in a special verdict leaving the question to his decision. But the public indignation was so great that the verdict was postponed until the Duke of Grafton, arriving as Lord-Lieutenant, ended the affair by dropping the prosecution.

Swift as usual was known for the author and as usual could not be reached; but he was not idle nor discomfited. A fund was raised for the weavers, the playhouse gave a performance for their benefit; Sheridan on that occasion wrote the prologue— and the Dean the epilogue, exhorting Irish heroes and heroines, on the stage or off it, to be clad in Irish stuff.

But the Dean took more practical measures and set apart five hundred pounds to be lent in small sums to the needy weavers and other tradesmen at a nominal interest, only sufficient to pay an accountant's fee; for the plan was carefully thought out, loans were made only to men who had a reasonable hope to repay by a shilling a week; and the steward of the whole was the Presbyterian Mrs. Brent. There are different accounts as to how the scheme fared: Johnson says it soon collapsed because Swift was too punctilious a creditor; but then Johnson disliked Swift and disliked punctilious creditors: Sheridan's son says that the plan worked admirably so long as Swift was able to oversee it. One thing, however, is certain beyond yea and nay, that from this time forward Swift was adored by his subjects in the Liberties. He was a hard man in many ways; but he won the love and the trust of the Irish poor, and their blessings attend his memory.

It is strange to think that underneath all the gaiety which his " crew " had reawakened in him, and underneath this active bene-ficence, his mind, stirred again to energy, was busy with the deep down gestation and gradual moulding of a work in which satire, ceasing to concern itself with individuals, becomes universal and takes on at least the mask of misanthropy. For 'Gulliver' was on the way. As early as September, 1721, Bolingbroke writes— "I long to see your Travels," and a letter from Vanessa in June or July, 1722, shows that she had either read or heard of the Voyage to Brobdingnag. Swift was never an uncommunicative artist.

It is notable that at this point in his Irish period there comes a reopening of communications with his English circle. Prior indeed had frequently written to him, because of the business concerned with the subscriptions to his Poems ; but that tie ended in September, 1721 : the letter from Swift to Archbishop King, cheerfully describing the way of life at Gaulstown, and referring to Prior's easy philosophy, breaks off in the middle of a phrase :

I am just now told from some newspapers, that one of the King's enemies, and my excellent friend, Mr. Prior, is dead ; I pray God deliver me from many such trials. I am neither old nor philosopher enough to be indifferent at so great a loss ; and therefore I abruptly conclude.

There is no mistaking the wrench there : yet Prior was never a true intimate. Of those who were, Arbuthnot had written twice in 1718, the second time very largely to suggest prescriptions for Swift's tortures of deafness and giddiness which throughout all this period gained on him : Bolingbroke from his elegant exile had sent at intervals long and elegant meditations in praise of his own philosophy : and Swift had replied, as always, with an admiration which it is not easy for those who did not know Bolingbroke to share. But from Pope, or to Pope, there had been no word written, till in the beginning of 1722 Swift sent him an immense letter which is in essence an appeal for help. Pope stood outside party, was admired by all parties, and had influence to obtain a hearing in the quarters where it could be effective.

Swift reviews his whole career since his leaving England ; declares himself to have lived " in the greatest privacy and in utter ignorance of those events which are most commonly talked of in the world " : and to have abstained completely from all writing of a partisan character. But he admits the writing of a discourse " to persuade the wretched people to wear their own manufactures instead of those from England," and that the treatise " soon spread very fast, being agreeable to the sentiments of the whole nation, except of those gentlemen who had employments, or were expectants." For this he says, the writer had been accused of " a design of setting the two kingdoms at variance " ; and when the printer was prosecuted, " the Chief Justice among other singularities, laid his hand on his breast, and protested so solemnly that the author's design was to bring in the Pretender."

Having avowed his pamphlet, Swift proceeds first to protest against the ascription to him of miscellaneous writings, disgraceful to " any man of common sense and literature " ; and he proceeds to show cause why he should find " at least tolerable quarter from the other party." He recalls his friendship with Addison ; his constant opposition to a Popish successor, and his justification of

JOHN GAY

Mezzotint by MILVUS *from painting by* AIKMAN *in the British Museum*

MATTHEW PRIOR

Mezzotint by FABER *from the painting by* KNELLER *in the British Museum.*

the revolution principle in cases such as that of the Prince of Orange's expedition, when it seemed the lesser of two evils. Then after a review of his mortal antipathy to standing armies, his desire for annual parliaments, and his detestation for setting up "a moneyed interest in opposition to the landed," his dislike for suspension of the Habeas Corpus Act and in general for whatever leads to "military power," he concludes:

These are some of the sentiments I had relating to public affairs, while I was in the world ; what they are at present, is of little importance either to that or myself ; neither can I truly say I have any at all, or if I had, I dare not venture to publish them ; for, however orthodox they may be while I am now writing, they may become criminal enough to bring me into trouble before midsummer. And indeed I have often wished, for some time past, that a political catechism might be published by authority four times a year, in order to instruct us how we are to speak, write, and act during the current quarter. I have by experience felt the want of such an instructor ; for, intending to make my court to some people on the prevailing side, by advancing certain old Whiggish principles, which it seems had been exploded about a month before, I have passed for a disaffected person.

It is to my mind the letter of a man who announces his intention no longer to stand aloof from politics and who makes an appeal for reasonable fair play. By its appeal to the past, it indicates an intention to reopen connections with that English scene to which he had been so long a stranger.

We have not Pope's answer, if indeed he ever replied to what was, unlike Swift's letters in general, impersonal and meant for other eyes than those of the friend to whom he wrote. But at the close of that year Gay, on some impulse, broke a silence of eight years with a warmhearted note to which Pope joined his grateful remembrances : and it let loose a flood of impulses in Swift :

January 8.

Coming home after a short Christmas ramble, I found a letter upon my table, and little expected when I opened it to read your name at the bottom. The best and greatest part of my life, until these last eight years, I spent in England : there I made my friendships, and there I left my desires. I am condemned for ever to another country ; what is in prudence to be done ? I think to be *oblitusque meorum, oblivi- scendus et illis.* What can be the design of your letter but malice, to wake me out of a scurvy sleep, which however is better than none ? I am towards nine years older since I left you, yet that is the least of my alterations ; my business, my diversions, my conversations, are all entirely changed for the worse, and so are my studies and my amuse- ments in writing. Yet, after all, this humdrum way of life might be passable enough, if you would let me alone. I shall not be able to relish my wine, my parsons, my horses, nor my garden, for three months, until the spirit you have raised shall be dispossessed. I have sometimes wondered that I have not visited you, but I have been stopped by too many reasons, besides years and laziness, and yet these are very good ones. Upon my return after half a year amongst you, there would be to me, *Desiderio nec pudor nec modus*. I was three years reconciling myself to the scene, and the business, to which fortune has condemned me, and stupidity was what I had recourse to. Besides, what a figure should I make in London, while my friends are in poverty, exile, distress, or imprisonment, and my enemies with rods of iron? Yet I often threaten myself with the journey, and am every summer practising to ride and get health to bear it; the only inconvenience is, that I grow old in the experiment.

The rest is full of inquiries and projects as to Gay himself. Why not come over to Ireland as secretary to the next chief governor?

The wine is good and reasonable; you may dine twice a week at the Deanery House; there is a set of company in this town sufficient for one man; folks will admire you, because they have read you, and read of you; and a good employment will make you live tolerably in London, or sumptuously here.

Then (after prudential admonition), comes a demand for regular correspondence. Gay answered promptly, a letter of news; but in August, Pope, with excuses for delay, made his reply.

It is an honest truth there is no one living or dead, of whom I think of oftener or better than yourself. I look upon you to be as to me in a state between both. You have from me all the passions and good wishes that can attend the living, and all the respect and tender sense of loss that we feel for the dead. Whatever you seem to think of your withdrawn and separate state, at this distance, and in this absence, Dean Swift lives still in England, in every place and company where he would choose to live; and I find him in all the conversations I keep, and in all the hearts in which I would have any share. We have never met these many years without mention of you.

The letter went on to say that all his friends of a later date —Oxford, Harcourt, Oxford's son, Lord Harley—were men to whom he had been bequeathed by Swift: and Bolingbroke too was now returned " as, I hope, to take me with all his other hereditary rights."

A letter from Bolingbroke accompanied this—even more literary than the poet's. But Bolingbroke had throughout an extraordinary hold on Swift's admiring imagination; and henceforth he was a constant member of the group, of which Swift henceforward might be called a corresponding member. For there was truth behind Pope's fine phrases: and indeed Swift was a man not easily forgotten. He on his part was continually thinking of going to England, drawn to it less by the desire to renew his literary friendships than to see Oxford again. In 1719 he wrote to that dilatory creature begging for his picture: in 1722 he wrote once more complaining:

I have now been ten years soliciting for your picture, and if I had solicited you for a thousand pounds, I mean of your own money, not the public, I could have prevailed in ten days. You have given me many hundred hours, can you not now give me a couple?

The end of that letter asks for leave to come over and stay at Brampton, that the Memoirs might be completed: and again in 1723 the same reproaches and the same request are renewed with the same affectionate half-jesting flattery. But no answer came; and indeed Swift's health was then ill-suited for a journey.

Yet in that summer of 1723 he had ridden over half of Ireland, among strange scenes, and without company; for he shunned company. An end had come to a long painful story which no one who respects his memory can willingly dwell on, and which to him must have caused anguish.

There is a great gap in the correspondence between Swift and Vanessa: nothing can be certainly assigned to any date between 1714 and 1719. But we can gather some things with certainty. Vanessa had a lodging in Dublin, and Swift never went to her house at Cellbridge till 1720. In Dublin she was known to people no less prominent than Archbishop King and the Provost of Trinity, Dr. Pratt. She had the name of a wit, but she went very little into society: a letter from Swift in the later period reproaches her for this.

We are told by Deane Swift—(who could only have known of the facts by distant report)—that for the first two years of her stay in Ireland Swift visited her frequently—chiefly to see " what progress she had made in literature "—but " observing that her passion for him rather increased than diminished, became from the year 1716 abundantly more sparing of his visits," and endeavoured to encourage the idea of her marrying a certain Dean Winter who was " her professed admirer."

Now, 1716 was the year in which the marriage to Stella is said to have taken place. All this is uncertain; but certainly in January, 1718, Vanessa and her sister consulted the Archbishop on a project of selling their Irish estate and returning to live in London. It is noticeable that King advised against this, and one may fairly assume that if the gossip about Swift was becoming serious, he might have encouraged the design. Ball inclines to believe that a letter from Swift to Vanessa, undated but generally assigned to 1714, belongs to this period.

I received your letter when some company was with me on Saturday night; and it put me in such confusion that I could not tell what to do. I here send the paper you left me. This morning a woman who does business for me, told me she heard I was in love with one, naming you (and twenty particulars), that little master and I visited you, and that the Archbishop did so, and that you had abundance of wit, etc. I ever feared the tattle of this nasty town, and told you so, and that was the reason why I said to you long ago, that I would see you seldom when you were in Ireland, and I must beg you to be easy, if for some time I visit you seldomer, and not in so particular a manner. I will see you at the latter end of the week if possible. These are accidents of life that are necessary, and must be submitted to, and tattle, by the help of discretion, will wear off.

However we take it, plainly Swift endeavoured, for a period longer or shorter, to keep the relation on the footing which he desired. But no less plainly, in a later stage he had abandoned all attempt to check the expression of her passion and struggled only for secrecy. The first dated letter which we have from this period was written as he left Trim in May, 1719, on a journey to a house he did not know; possibly to Thomastown in County Kilkenny, where Mr. Mathew (ancestor of the Earls of Llandaff and of the more famous Father Mathew) offered extraordinary hospitality, treating his house as a hotel in which the guests did or ordered what they pleased, and might do anything but pay. According to Sheridan, Swift enjoyed this entertainment for four months. The important part to note, however, is that having to trust to local posts he wrote in French (as usual, competent but inaccurate.) The letter abounds in compliment; it is here that he reproaches her seclusion; " en vous cachant comme vous faîtes, le monde ne vous connoit peu, et vous perdez l'eloge des millions de gens." There is however a sentence at the opening which goes far beyond the language of compliment—

Croyez moy, s'il y a chose croyable au monde, que je pense tout ce que vous pouvez souhaiter de moy, et que tous vos desirs seront toujours obèi comme de commandmens qu'il sera impossible de violer.

From this on, the letters are frequent. There is raillery from her :

Is it possible that again you will do the very same thing I warned you of so lately ? I believe you thought I only rallied when I told you the other night I would pester you with letters. Did not I know you very well, I should think you knew but very little of the world, to imagine that a woman would not keep her word whenever she promised anything that was malicious. Had not you better a thousand times throw away one hour, at some time or other of the day, than to be interrupted in your business at this rate ?

She goes on to threaten him with black magic, and Swift's answer, praising her wit, does little indeed to discourage love-making.

But raillery apart, I think it inconvenient for a hundred reasons that I should make your house a sort of constant dwelling-place. I will certainly come as often as I conveniently can, but my health and the perpetual run of ill weather hinders me from going out in the morning ; and my afternoons are so taken up, I know not how, that I am in rebellion with a dozen people beside yourself, for not seeing them. For the rest, you need make use of no other black art besides your ink. 'Tis a pity your eyes are not black, or I would have said the same of them.

Next, she complains because promised letters do not come ; he answers that he will promise no more. " I choose rather to be better than my word, than worse." But at the end he proposes a new technique for discretion :

I wish your letters were as difficult as mine ; for then they would be of no consequence if they were dropped by careless messengers. A stroke thus — — — — signifies everything that may be said to Cad — at beginning or conclusion.

His letter ends with four dashes : no ostrich was ever better hidden. Her next begins :

— — — — Cad — you are good beyond expression and I will never quarrel again if I can help it ; but, with submission, 'tis you that are so hard to be pleased, though you complain of me. I thought the last letter I wrote you was obscure and constrained enough : I took pains to write it after that manner. It would have been much easier for me to have wrote otherwise.

She ends :

I am mightily pleased to hear you talk of being in a huff. 'Tis the first time you ever told me so. I wish I could see you in one. I am now as happy as I can be without seeing — — — Cad. I beg you'll continue happiness to your own Skinage.

Then follow jesting interchanges, playing with allusions to the past —and an offer from him to come and see her at Cellbridge. But then we have violent passionate letters from her. " 'Tis not in the power of art, time or accident to lessen the inexpressible passion which I have for ———. Nor is the love I bear you only seated in my soul, for there is not a single atom of my frame which is not blinded with it. For heaven's sake, tell me what has caused this prodigious change which I have found in you of late."

She was pitiable, and all the more so because her sister was far gone in consumption; she spared no appeal.

Believe me 'tis with the utmost regret that I now complain to you, because I know your good nature such, that you cannot see any human creature miserable without being sensibly touched. Yet what can I do? I must either unload my heart and tell you all its griefs, or sink under the unexpressible distress I now suffer by your prodigious neglect of me. 'Tis now ten long, long weeks since I saw you, and in all that time I have never received but one letter from you, and a little note with an excuse. Oh, how have you forgot me!

And again in another, after crying out for his presence:

I firmly believe, could I know your thoughts (which no human creature is capable of guessing at, because never any one living thought like you), I should find that you have often in a rage wished me religious, hoping then I should have paid my devotions to heaven. But that would not spare you, for was I an enthusiast, still you'd be the deity I should worship. What marks are there of a deity but what you are to be known by? You are present everywhere; your dear image is always before eyes; sometimes you strike me with that prodigious awe, I tremble with fear; at other times a charming compassion shines through your countenance, which revives my soul. Is it not more reasonable to adore a radiant form one has seen, than one only described?

Her sister died in March, 1721. He wrote on the first shock of the news:

For God's sake get your friends about you, to advise and to order everything in the forms. It is all you have to do. I want comfort myself in this case, and can give little. Time alone must give it to you. Nothing now is your part but decency. I was wholly unprepared against so sudden an event, and pity you most of all creatures at present.

This loss left her more than ever dependent on the man she adored, and he was not always at hand, and his letters could only preach philosophy. But here and there were words to be found that she would get by heart:

I can say no more, being called away, mais soyez assurée que jamais personne du monde a ete aimée, honorée, estimée, adorée par votre ami que vous. I drank no coffee since I left you, nor intend to till I see you again. There is none worth drinking but yours, if myself may be the judge.

This reference to coffee, whatever it stood for, comes again and again :

> God send you through your law and your reference ; and remember that riches are nine parts in ten of all that is good in life, and health is the tenth. Drinking coffee comes long after, and yet it is the eleventh ; but without the two former you cannot drink it right ; and remember the china in the old house, and Ryder Street, and the Colonel's journey to France, and the London wedding, and the sick lady at Kensington, and the indisposition at Windsor, and the strain by the box of books at London.

I do not see how any one can dispute that these letters of his, though deliberately obscure in their expression, are love letters as well as hers. What is this but a recalling of old love passages—of whatever kind ? and as to the coffee, it is plain enough that it is a symbol. Beyond yea or nay the aspiration of her whole nature was to be his mistress : beyond yea or nay, he fell into a clandestine relationship with her ; she was his secret woman ; and half a dozen phrases could be emphasized to show that—to put the facts bluntly —she got her way. For if ever there was a case in which man was the pursued, not the pursuer, this was it.

The essential character of her attachment is conveyed in the conclusion of the letter which, though undated, Mr. Freeman in his edition of the correspondence between them puts, I think rightly, at the end of her series :

> For the pleasure of writing to you, the satisfaction I have in you remembering me when you read my letter, and the delight I have in expecting one from — — — Cad, makes me rather choose to give you some uneasiness then to add to my own.

Passion always commands a certain respect in proportion to its intensity, and Vanessa was as passionately in love as woman can be. But she was in love with a great man, and in love with his greatness, yet no thought for his name in the world ever weighed against her own desire. She was even ready to exploit what she knew lay behind his angry fierceness, a good nature that could not bear to give pain. Whatever she brought him was never heartsease ; what she gave him was passion, never loyalty. She was the exact opposite of Stella ; and in the long run she forced Swift to choose between them. As Orrery tells the story, she wrote to Swift demanding that he should either break off or make her his wife ; the younger Sheridan says that she wrote to Stella asking to know whether she was married to the Dean or no. The latter seems to me the likelier, for Vanessa never in her letters

hints at a refusal to see the man she loved. She talks of kill
ing herself : but she never puts his affection really to the tes
by an ultimatum, as a passionate woman will who respects he
passion.

The story is that Swift rode out to Cellbridge, flung her lette
down before her and went away without a word. All that w
know for certain is that a breach came, between August 22, 1722
when his last letter was dated, and May 1, 1723, when she made
her will, in which Swift's name is not mentioned, though there ar
bequests to nearly a score of persons, and the chief of them to :
stranger. She died on June 2, 1723, leaving her property betweer
her two executors, of whom one was Bishop Berkeley—knowr
to her only by repute—to whom this windfall of £30,000 came a
a " providential event," to aid his scheme for founding a university
in the Bermudas. The other, Robert Marshall, afterwards a judge
was then a young man about to be called to the bar. It is saic
that Marshall saw her on her deathbed and that she confided to
him the " Cadenus and Vanessa " poem and the correspondence
with instructions that they should be published. The younge
Sheridan tells us that the printer was busy on the letters when hi
father, hearing of this, applied to the executors, who stopped the
printing but retained the manuscript.

If so, Sheridan acted on behalf of an absent man, for Swif
had gone on a long southern journey into parts of Ireland where
he was not " acquainted with one Christian among them." Or
May 10, that is, ten days after Vanessa made her will, and therefor
some time after the breach had occurred, he wrote to his frienc
Robert Cope, saying that he would start in ten days. On Saturday
June 1, the day before she died, he wrote again to Cope saying
that he would set out on the Monday :

> I go where I was never before, without one companion, and among
> people where I know no creature, and all this to get a little exercise
> for curing an ill head. . . . Your friend Ford keeps still in Ireland
> and passes the summer at his country house with two sober ladies of hi
> and my acquaintance.

Ford, whose house Woodpark lay on the road between Dublir
and Trim, was the only one of Swift's intimates who was also
intimate both with the Vanhomrighs and " the ladies." In April
Swift had stayed with him, and Ball conjectures that the quarrel
with Vanessa had then broken out; that Swift, foreseeing a publi
scandal, decided to withdraw himself, and that Ford arranged fo
a hospitality which should remove Stella from the danger of Dublir

gossip. In fact, neither he nor the ladies set foot in Dublin during the four months of the Dean's absence.

It is impossible to be certain whether the news of Vanessa's death reached Swift before he set out on the journey which was to carry him down the wild cliffs of Carberry in County Cork. Tradition makes him a visitor to the deep and lovely inlet of Glandore, and associates his Latin verses "Carberiæ Rupes" with this scene. But we know nothing definite of his movements till August 3, when he was at Clonfert in East Galway, a guest of the Bishop, and wrote to Sheridan that he expected to be in Dublin by the end of the month. "Are the ladies in town or in the country?" he asks. "If I knew I would write to them." The break had therefore been very complete. Another detail shows it extended to all his correspondents, and was even longer than he first designed; for on September 20 he writes to Pope that, returning after a summer expedition of four months on account of his health, he had found Pope's long letters with the longer appendix from Bolingbroke, which were posted in August.

That letter to Pope shows his mood at its blackest:

If I could permit myself to believe what your civility makes you say, that I am still remembered by my friends in England, I am in the right to keep myself here. *Non sum qualis eram.* I left you in a period of life when one year does more execution than three at yours, to which if you add the dulness of the air, and of the people, it will make a terrible sum. . . . Your notions of friendship are new to me; I believe every man is born with his *quantum*, and he cannot give to one without robbing another. I very well know to whom I would give the first places in my friendship, but they are not in the way. I am condemned to another scene, and therefore I distribute it in pennyworths to those about me, and who displease me least, and should do the same to my fellow prisoners, if I were condemned to jail. . . . I have often endeavoured to establish a friendship among all men of genius, and would fain have it done. They are seldom above three or four contemporaries, and if they could be united, would drive the world before them. I think it was so among the poets in the time of Augustus; but envy, and party, and pride, have hindered it among us. . . . I would describe to you my way of living, if any method could be called so in this country. I choose my companions among those of least consequence and most compliance. I read the most trifling books I can find, and whenever I write, it is upon the most trifling subjects; but riding, walking, and sleeping take up eighteen of the twenty-four hours. I procrastinate more than I did twenty years ago, and have several things to finish which I put off to twenty years hence.

And in fact the next letter in the Correspondence, some nonsense mixture of English and Latin addressed to Sheridan, suggests an exchange of pennyworths. But in England Arbuthnot set to work to rouse him from his vapours and vertigo, holding the pen for the group:

> Your friends here wish to see you, and none more than myself; but I really do not advise you to such a journey to gratify them or myself; but I am almost confident, it would do you a great deal of good.

He added that Swift had no idea how well he stood with those in power. " I myself have been at a great man's table and have heard, out of the mouths of violent Irish Whigs, the whole table turn upon your commendation."

The atmosphere in Dublin must have been hard to bear in that year for a man so proud and sensitive. " Cadenus and Vanessa," though not published, was handed round in copies,—" by particular malice," Swift thought—though Berkeley was always his friend and there is no reason for believing that Marshall was his enemy. There were however men who hated him, and one was Evans, Bishop of Meath, an importation of the new brand which Walpole brought into fashion. About 1718 Evans held a visitation at Trim, which Swift attended as rector of Laracor. The bishop spoke rudely to one of the clergy and Swift rose up and made a fiery speech, in which he declared that he would never appear again at a visitation. This, he said, writing to the Bishop in 1719, was " not from any contempt of your Lordship's jurisdiction, but that I would not put you under the temptation of giving me injurious treatment, which no wise man, if he can avoid it, will receive above once from the same person." If, however, he should be forced to attend, " I hope," he adds, " that in such a case your Lordship will please to remember in the midst of your resentments that you are to speak to a clergyman, and not to a footman."

Naturally the feud did not end there, and scandal offered a chance. Bishop Evans wrote gleefully, on July 27, 1723, to Archbishop Wake of Canterbury:

> I think it not improper for me to acquaint your Grace with a passage lately happened here wherein Jonathan Swift is said to be pretty much concerned. A young woman, Mrs. Van Omrig (a pretended vain wit), and ye Dean had great friendships, many letters and papers passed betwixt them (the subject of which I know nothing of); they give out there was a marriage promise between them, but this I can't affirm. However it be, she designed to give him all her fortune, which was about £5,000. In April last she discovered the D. was married to Mrs. Johnson (a nll. daughter of Sir W. Temple, a very good woman), upon which she expresses in her illness great indignation, making a new will and leaving

all to Dr. Berkeley of this College (who never had seen her but about twice), and to one Mr. Marshall, who was charged by her (on her death bed) to print all the letters and papers which had passed between D. and herself. 'Tis generally believed she lived without God in ye world. When Dean Price (the Minister of her Parish) offered her his services in her last minutes : she sent him word no Price no Prayers, with a scrap out of the Tale in the Tub . . . and so she dyed. If anything like this should have fallen to an Englishman he would have been peppered with lampoons, etc. (as ye Bishop of Ferns and others were, without the least colour on grounds most undeservedly). Ye Archbishop of Dublin and ye whole Irish posse have (I fear) prevailed with Mr. Marshall (ye lady's executor) not to print the papers, etc., as she desired, lest one of their own dear joys should be trampled over by the Philistines.

Undoubtedly any ordinary clergyman would have been treated as the Bishop suggests ; indeed, a few years later we find Swift himself inditing a ballad on one of the clergy sent over from England (a dean too), who was tried for committing a rape. But even in 1723 Swift's public action had made him regarded as a champion of the Irish people and not a safe subject for peppering. A year later he had reached the position which may be defined by one sentence : When the English government wished to take him into custody, they were asked if they would provide ten thousand men to carry out the arrest. But the next chapter shall give details.

CHAPTER XV

THE DRAPIER

IN 1722 complaints came from Ireland that there was a shortage of copper coins. On all previous occasions the coinage had been done in Ireland; but under Walpole's Whig rule it was definitely the policy to leave no profit to Ireland which could be secured to Englishmen; and a patent for coining £108,000 worth of halfpence and farthings was granted to one William Wood, a bankrupt ironmonger. The reason for the choice of the patentee was that he had paid the Duchess of Kendal, George I's German mistress, ten thousand pounds for her influence. Much indignation was felt in Ireland and both Houses of Parliament protested, Whig and Tory uniting.

Swift was a man concerned always about the business of government; he disliked the Whigs, and as an Irishman he was increasingly resentful of the growing tendency to despoil Ireland for the benefit of England. The Irish for whom he was concerned were the Protestant settlers—with whom he would have included such of the native stock as had adopted the state religion and identified themselves with the ruling class. The English, however, made no discrimination where economic questions were concerned. They gratified the Protestant Irish with every device of penal law that could reduce the Catholics to helotry; but when money or trade was at stake, all Irish interests were lumped together and sacrificed to English convenience. The result was a great impoverishment of the country. It had neither freedom to export its own manufactures, nor to maintain its own shipping, since all trade must be carried in English bottoms.

Swift cannot in any ordinary sense be called an Irish nationalist; but he became a nation-builder. He realized more clearly than others of his time how bad in principle was this system of government; moreover, he had an Englishman's dislike of unfair treatment in the abstract, added to the universal resentment which is felt by the sufferer. He was moved, too—and in this as in so many things he was before his time—by the instinct which has led Englishmen settled across the seas to desire freedom in the management of their local affairs ; and he perceived in the general indignation caused by this introduction of a suspected coinage (for it was believed that Wood's coins were far below the ordinary percentage of copper) a means to unite the oversea population in an assertion of their local right. Since coinage knew no distinction of Protestant and Catholic, all might be brought into one movement. If, in answer to the oppressive domination of England, he had made an abstract proposal of united action, either between the rival political parties, Whig and Tory, or between the privileged Protestant minority and the disfranchised Catholics, bickering would have begun at once. But now a single concrete injustice gave a common impulse. To realize this was a mark of supreme political insight ; yet I am not certain whether Swift understood that he had set his hand to the building of a nation, which by its very definition should not be English.

Another impulse was perhaps stronger than political vision. Misgovernment is partly due to blundering and partly to corruption. Swift despised blundering, but he loathed corruption ; and the corruptness of this job stank to heaven.

In April, 1724, there was published by one Harding a pamphlet in the form of a letter " To the Tradesmen, Shopkeepers, Farmers and Country People in General of the Kingdom of Ireland." It was signed " M. B., drapier " ; the writer described himself as having " a pretty good shop of Irish stuffs and silks " ; and it was an appeal to common folk to reject Wood's halfpence with one accord. The general argument was that bad money will necessarily drive out good ; and of course Swift exaggerated wildly the possible consequences. This first letter is the classic example of demagogic argument because about a core of truth it builds up a structure of intimidating invention. But as in *Gulliver's Travels*, once you grant Swift his premise, he leads you on through a series of developments, each springing so naturally from the last that reason is carried off its footing. As in *Gulliver*, the language is of studied simplicity. Here is a typical passage :

Suppose you go to an ale-house with that base money, and the landlord gives you a quart for four of those half-pence, what must the victualler do ? his brewer will not be paid in that coin, or if the brewer should be such a fool, the farmers will not take it from them for their bere (barley), because they are bound, by their leases, to pay their rents in good and lawful money of England, which this is not, nor of Ireland neither, and the 'squire, their landlord, will never be so bewitched to take such trash for his land ; so that it must certainly stop somewhere or other, and wherever it stops, it is the same thing, and we are all undone.

The common weight of these half-pence is between four and five to an ounce; suppose five, then three shillings and four-pence will weigh a pound, and consequently twenty shillings will weigh six pounds butter weight. Now there are many hundred farmers, who pay two hundred pounds a year rent; therefore when one of these farmers comes with his half year's rent, which is one hundred pounds, it will be at least six hundred pound weight, which is three horses load.

If a 'squire has a mind to come to town to buy cloaths, and wine, and spices for himself and family, or perhaps to pass the winter here, he must bring with him five or six horses loaden with sacks, as the farmers bring their corn; and, when his lady comes in her coach to our shops, it must be followed by a car loaded with Mr. Wood's money.

Having shown by artful suggestion how universal would be the damage, he goes on to argue that to refuse is no offence, since the King's right can only enforce the acceptance of coin made of lawful metal. But soon, leaving the legal argument, he returns for a special appeal to " the poorer sort of tradesmen "—those who swarmed in the Liberties. He talks their own dialect to them; tells them it will " ruin even the beggars ":

For when I give a beggar a half-penny, it will quench his thirst or go a good way to fill his belly; but the twelfth part of a half-penny will do him no more service, than if I should give him three pins out of my sleeve.

Yet after this plain talk comes a concluding paragraph, with applications from Scripture and from classical mythology, which looks very much as if Swift had determined to set his signature legible for all persons of intelligence. But the last word of all goes direct to the groundlings.

N.B.—The author of this paper is informed by persons, who have made it their business to be exact in their observations on the true value of these half-pence, that any person may expect to get a quart of two-penny ale for thirty-six of them.

So the heather was set on fire; all Dublin ran wild for the Drapier: and now matters took a new development. When Wood got his patent, the Duke of Grafton was Lord-Lieutenant; but in the spring of 1724 a struggle in the ministry was ended by recalling Grafton and sending Carteret to this post of dignity, where he would have less opportunity to intrigue against Walpole. Now Carteret was a man of the Bolingbroke type, wit and scholar as well as statesman. So far back as December, 1710, Mr. Secretary St. John asked Swift to dine and choose his own company. Carteret

—then a man of five-and-twenty—was one of those chosen ; and, Whig though he was, this friendship had continued. Now on April 28, 1724, Swift wrote to the newly appointed Lord-Lieutenant (who was still in London) calling his attention to the general opposition to this " ruinous project." He enclosed two pamphlets, of which he added, as if dropping the mask before an old friend, " one is entitled to a weaver and suited to the vulgar, but thought to be the work of a better hand."

The letter closed affectionately and respectfully : " I hope your Excellency will forgive an old humble servant, and one who always loved and esteemed you, for interfering in matters out of his province." But the Viceroy did not answer and on June 9 there went to him a letter very different in tone :

I have been long out of the world, but have not forgotten what used to pass among those I lived with while I was in it, and I can say, that during the experience of many years, and many changes in affairs, your Excellency, and one more, who is not worthy to be compared to you, are the only great persons that ever refused to answer a letter from me, without regard to business, party, or greatness ; and if I had not a peculiar esteem for your personal qualities, I should think myself to be acting a very inferior part in making this complaint.
. . . I know not how your conceptions of yourself may alter, by every new high station ; but mine must continue the same, or alter for the worse.

Carteret, whom nobody can help liking, sent the soft answer, in which a rebuke was most delicately conveyed.

I am convinced . . . that you still retain some part of your former friendship for me, of which I am the more confident from the agreeable freedom with which you express yourself.

Swift cried " *Touché* " like a fencer, and gave to his apology the charm of his own methods as a courtier.

After all my rattling, you have brought me down to be as humble as the most distant attender at your levee. It is well your Excellency's talents are in few hands ; for, if it were otherwise, we who pretend to be free speakers in quality of philosophers, should be utterly cured of our forwardness, at least I am afraid there will be an end of mine, with regard to your Excellency. Yet, my Lord, I am ten years older than I was when I had the honour to see you last, and consequently ten times more testy. Therefore I foretell that you, who could so easily conquer so captious a person, and of so little consequence, will quickly subdue this whole kingdom to love and reverence you.

But this was only the exchange of courtesy between high opponents ; Swift had no intention of abandoning the combat. Five weeks later, there appeared a second Drapier: a third on August 25, and then on October 13, the famous Fourth. It is needless to summarize them; but Swift had dropped all affectation of writing as the plain shopkeeper. Every living soul in Dublin knew who 'the Drapier' was; and since the second letter was a reply to a semi-official defence of Wood, and the third an answer to the Report of the committee of the Privy Council, it was necessary to argue like a scholar. As the controversy goes on, the issue broadens, till in the Fourth the Irish at large are taught that a national right is at stake and must be defended:

A people long used to hardships lose by degrees the very notions of liberty; they look upon themselves as creatures at mercy, and that all impositions laid on them by a stronger hand are, in the phrase of the report, legal and obligatory. Hence proceed that poverty and lowness of spirit, to which a kingdom may be subject, as well as a particular person. And when Esau came fainting from the field at the point to die, it is no wonder that he sold his birth-right for a mess of pottage.

The Lord-Lieutenant who had not yet resided was reported to be coming over to " sell Wood's half-pence," which the public persisted in refusing. Naturally (since the private correspondence had continued in the most flattering terms), 'the Drapier' eulogizes Carteret, on the assurance of " a gentleman that hath known him from his first appearance in the world " (here Swift, one may say, signs his own civility) and hopes that " from such a governor this kingdom may reasonably hope for as much prosperity *as under so many discouragements* it can be capable of receiving." The argument proceeds to examine the methods by which government may hope to elude this opposition; and Swift enumerates the possible additions to " good words, burgundy and closetting," by which Irish gentlemen could be bribed to believe that " Ireland is a depending kingdom." But, says the pamphlet, " Ireland is, on the contrary, called in some statutes, an imperial crown, as held only from God " :

I, M. B. drapier, declare, next under God, I depend only on the king my sovereign, and on the laws of my own country. And I am so far from depending upon the people of England, that, if they should ever rebel against my sovereign, (which God forbid) I would be ready at the first command from his majesty to take arms against them, as some of my countrymen did against theirs at Preston. And if such a rebellion should prove so successful as to fix the pretender on the throne of England, I would venture to transgress that statute so far, as to lose every drop of my blood to hinder him from being king of Ireland.
It is true indeed, that within the memory of man the parliaments of

England have sometimes assumed the powers of binding this kingdom by laws enacted there ; wherein they were at first openly opposed (as far as truth, reason, and justice are capable of opposing) by the famous Mr. Molineux, an English gentleman born here, as well as by several of the greatest patriots and best whigs in England ; but the love and torrent of power prevailed. Indeed the arguments on both sides were invincible. For in reason, all government without the consent of the governed is the very definition of slavery : but in fact, eleven men well armed will certainly subdue one single man in his shirt.

No matter ; if they attempt, as Walpole was said to have threatened, to ram their half-pence down the throats of the Irish,—

The remedy is wholly in your own hands ; and therefore I have digressed a little in order to refresh and continue that spirit so seasonably raised amongst you ; and to let you see, that by the laws of God, of Nature, of Nations, and of your Country, you are, and ought to be, as free a people as your brethren in England.

Then, once more assuming the popular style, Swift discusses the possibility of administering this dose in the shape of molten fire-balls, and remarks significantly that " there cannot be fewer than fifty thousand *operators* "—allowing one operator to every thirty patients : " Now under correction of better judgment, I think the trouble and charge of such an experiment would exceed the profit."—For " operators " read " troops," and the innuendo is plain.

When Carteret arrived, this pamphlet was in all hands, and it was decided to proceed against it. His first act was to offer three hundred pounds for discovery of the author, whom he knew to be his friend. Meanwhile, the printer Harding was imprisoned and preparation made for his indictment. But a letter of seasonable advice reviewing the whole history (of course from Swift's pen) was sent to each member of the Grand Jury, who were addressed as being themselves " merchants and principal shopkeepers." They refused to find a bill for the indictment ; whereupon Whitshed, the same Lord Chief Justice who had formerly bullied a jury into submission over the prosecution of *A Proposal for the Use of Irish Manufacturers*, discharged them. Immediately Swift circulated a copy of the Resolution of the English House of Commons in 1680 which described such discharging as arbitrary and illegal. When a second jury was empanelled, it sent in a presentment, declaring all those who sought to impose Wood's half-pence to be enemies to his Majesty's government, and acknowledging the services of " such patriots as have been eminently zealous in detecting the fraudulent imposition." Finally, there appeared a fifth Drapier, dated "from my shop in St. Francis Street" (which leads direct to the Deanery) dated December 14. In this 'the Drapier' gave an account of himself, of which the parable was easily interpreted.

He had been bred at a free-school where he got some little knowledge of the Latin tongue; had served his apprenticeship in London and there set up with good success "until *by the death of some friends, and misfortunes of others*," he returned to this Kingdom, and began to employ his thoughts in cultivating the *woollen manufacture* through all its branches. Yet when he had produced "*a piece of black and white stuff* just sent from the dyer," some said the people in England would be offended if Irish manufactures were made to equal theirs. (This of course refers to the condemnation of his tract in 1720.) None the less, "considering that the lower and poorer sort of people wanted *a plain, strong coarse stuff* to defend them against *cold easterly winds*, which then blew very fierce," he contrived one on purpose, and a second and a third; and then was incited to make a fourth "of the best Irish wool he could get"; and "thought it grave and rich enough to be worn by the best lord and judge of the land." One more passage must be quoted to show how completely Swift indicated his authorship —and how he drove home the main conclusion, to which the question of Wood and his brass was a paltry subsidiary:

This habit of writing and discoursing, wherein I unfortunately differ from almost the whole kingdom, and am apt to grate the ears of more than I could wish, was acquired during my apprenticeship in London, and a long residence there after I had set up for myself. Upon my return and settlement here, I thought I had only changed one country of freedom for another. . . . I have been likewise told, and believe it to be true, that liberty and property are words of known use and signification in this kingdom; and the very lawyers pretend to understand, and have them often in their minds' mouths. These were the errors, which have misled me.

As everybody knows, the half-pence had to be withdrawn, Wood getting a matter of £20,000 in compensation for the profits of his job (the English are honest dealers); and though the printer died in prison, Swift walked the streets, no man daring to lay hand on him. Two other letters of the series written at the time were not published till ten years later: in one he plainly designed to acknowledge the authorship openly, for it is dated from the Deanery. But he probably thought it needless. There is indeed a story that when Carteret had issued his proclamation, Swift came to Court, broke into the circle, and with his bushy eyebrows drawn down,

and eyes like blue fire, exclaimed : " Soh, my lord, what is this
about your persecuting a poor printer ? " Whereupon Carteret
turned away with a dexterous quotation, " Res dura et regni novitas
me talia cogunt moliri." It may have been then, at least memory
of that adroit parry must have been in Swift's mind, when he burst
out, " What brings the like of you here ? Get home and send us
back our boobies."

There is, however, a story better authenticated and more
significant. All the letters were sent in copied by an amanuensis,
who was Swift's butler. Shortly after the reward was announced
this man got drunk and stayed out all night. Swift sent for him,
and said, " You think you have me in your power ; get out of the
house." The man begged, but made no effect, and he went and
stayed out till the whole affair was over. Swift took him back,
left him for some time in his place, then sent for him again and
ordered him to strip off his livery. The man pleaded, Swift insisted,
and when the livery was off, sent for the other domestics. " This,"
he said, " is no longer your fellow servant ; this is Mr. Robert
Blakeney, verger of the cathedral."

Another story may be referred to the passages quoted from
the Fifth letter. One of the maids under Mrs. Brent's jurisdiction
had earned his praise ; he gave her a guinea and told her to go
and buy a piece of good Irish stuff. Seeing no alteration in her
dress, he asked her what she had done with the guinea ; whereupon
she disappeared and reappeared with a lapful of his books. " These
were the best Irish stuff I could buy, your Reverence."

In short, ' the Drapier ' had become the idol of Ireland, and
more particularly of the Dublin shops and workshops ; but through
the Kingdom, the " Drapier's Head " was a popular sign. Even
he himself, when he wrote an epitaph that was to keep his name
remembered on the walls of St. Patrick's, chose to be remembered
as " the defender of liberty."

What he had done, though it concerned a small matter, was
of far-reaching importance. He had led the Irish people to beat
the government. It was an Englishman who taught Ireland that
under the English jury system penalties of law cannot be inflicted
if the law is against public conscience. He had shown the possibilities of a combination, even unarmed, to defeat the machinery
of law and of power. This was the beginning of constitutional
agitation in Ireland ; and the extraordinary fact is that it was an
agitation conducted by one man. The Drapier letters were the
main artillery ; but the pulpit also thundered. He preached a

sermon " On Doing Good " in praise of " what is called public spirit in the people. . . . When I say the people, I mean the bulk or mass of the people, for I have nothing to do with those in power." He thanked God that " when an open attempt is made and far carried on to make a great Kingdom one large poor-house, only to enrich one obscure, ill-designing projector and his followers," that there had been raised " such a spirit of union among us, at least on this point."—Then there was a swarm of pasquinades in prose and verse : for instance, in prose, " A full and true account of the solemn Procession to the Gallows at the Execution of William Wood "; in verse, a dozen or so of lampoons on Wood, and others, more stinging, on " The Upright Judge who condemned the Drapier's Printer." One is on Whitshed's motto :

> *Libertas et natale solum :*
> Fine words : I wonder where you stole 'em.
> Could nothing but thy chief reproach
> Serve for a motto on thy coach ?

Or this amenity—

> In church your grandsire cut his throat ;
>   To do the job too long he tarried ;
> He should have had my hearty vote
>   To cut his throat before he married.

In all this, however, there was not a word against Carteret, whom Swift liked and admired, whom he knew to be a scarcely concealed enemy of Walpole, and in whom he saw possibilities for his friends. And so, after the Drapier effusions, we find quite a number of poems in praise of Carteret and his lady. The first (and the only one with any merit) tells amusingly enough how Lady Carteret sent to ask him to dine ; how he was astonished by the message, but accepted ; and how when he got into the Castle yard, he suddenly turned shy, was afraid to face such company as he had not frequented for ten years, and in short, bolted ; was rounded up and ordered to write an account of the whole. It ends most dexterously : " Is he criminal who flies The living lustre of your eyes ? "

Here was a fantastic situation. Within four months after a reward was offered for the Drapier, Swift was not only asked to Court, but encouraged to invite Lady Carteret to his Deanery—where, as the poem tells us, he took her to visit ' Naboth's Vineyard '— a field at a short distance, which he had begun to enclose as a paddock for his horses, and then was tempted to turn into a garden, with espaliers in the best Moor Park tradition.

He was also, at this time, writing to Carteret to beg a living for Sheridan—who, he says, was agreed " to have done more public service by many degrees in the education of lads than any five of his vocation." " His greatest fault," the letter adds, " is a wife and four children, for which there is no excuse, but that a wife is thought necessary for a schoolmaster." (Swift had a dislike of Mrs. Sheridan which her husband seems to have fully shared). By July of that year Carteret had complied with this request, and Swift in thanking him submitted a list of other clergy suited for preferment. At the head stood Delany, and Carteret was soon a guest at this fortunate man's agreeable villa Delville. " Dr. Delany is a perfect courtier," Swift wrote in November to another favourite protégé, Stopford. Yet there was some delay, and next year Swift was quarrelling with the Lord-Lieutenant because his friend had been passed over. However, by the beginning of 1727 Delany was Chancellor of Christ Church and fairly launched on a career of prosperity which led through two rich marriages to the Deanery of Down.

But the unlucky Sheridan came back on Swift's hands; and of all the crew he was Stella's special friend. His country house was always at the disposal of the Dean and his ladies, and Swift could indulge his taste with planning and delving about that " wild place " at Quilca, on the south border of Cavan, eight miles from the post town at Kells. They must have spent the Christmas of 1722 there, for Sheridan wrote a " New Year's poem " that year—describing the Dean's sad downfall:

> From settling governments and thrones,
> To splitting rocks, and piling stones.
> Instead of Bolingbroke and Anna,
> Shane Tunnally and Bryan Granna;
> Oxford and Ormond he supplies
> In every Irish Teague he spies:
> So far forgetting his old station,
> He seems to like their conversation;
> Conforming to the tatter'd rabble,
> He learns their Irish tongue to gabble;
> And, what our anger more provokes,
> He's pleased with their insipid jokes;
> Then turns and asks them, who do lack a
> Good plug, or pipefull of tobacco. . . .
> Bright Stella, Quilca's greatest pride,
> For them he scorns and lays aside;

And Sheridan is left alone
All day, to gape, and stretch, and grown;
While grumbling, poor, complaining Dingley,
Is left to care and trouble singly.

In the spring of 1725 they were back again as tenants in Sheridan's absence; they spent the whole summer there. Swift wrote:

I live in a cabin and in a very wild country; yet there are some agreeablenesses in it, or at least I fancy so, and am levelling mountains and raising stones, and fencing against inconveniences of a scanty lodging, want of victuals, and a thievish race of people.

Stella took a hand and was given a light pickaxe, with handle of cherry-wood, bearing a Latin verse to say that the country-side laughs to see her shifting rubble. Here is Swift's report to Sheridan in June:

Mrs. Johnson swears it will rain till Michaelmas. She is so pleased with her pickaxe, that she wears it fastened to her girdle on her left side, in balance with her watch. The lake is strangely overflown, and we are desperate about turf, being forced to buy it three miles off, and Mrs. Johnson—God help her—gives you many a curse. Your mason is come, but cannot yet work upon your garden, neither can I agree with him about the great wall. . . . You would wonder what carking and caring there is among us for small beer and lean mutton, and starved lamb, and stopping gaps, and driving cattle from the corn. In that we are all to be-Dingleyed. The ladies' room smokes; the rain drops from the skies into the kitchen. . . . I write on till Molly comes in for the letter. O what a draggletail she will be before she gets to Dublin!

The end is in verse.

The Blessings of a Country Life

Far from our debtors,
No Dublin letters,
Not seen by our betters.

The Plagues of a Country Life

A companion with news,
A great want of shoes;
Eat lean meat, or choose;
A church without pews.
Our horses astray,
No straw, oats, or hay;
December in May,
Our boys run away,
All servants at play.

While they were at Quilca, a letter brought the great news that Carteret had given Sheridan the living of Rincurran, near Cork.

Swift dashed off a reply, full of practical advice about the letting of tithes and so forth. Next day, there followed a letter of more general counsel, urging

a great appearance of temperance while you are abroad. But Mrs. Johnson and I go further, and say, you must needs observe all grave forms, for the want of which both you and I have suffered. . . .

I must desire that you will not think of enlarging your expenses ; no, not for some years to come, much less at present ; but rather retrench them. You might have lain destitute till Antichrist came, for anything you could have got from those you used to treat ; neither let me hear of one rag of better clothes for your wife or brats, but rather plainer than ever. This is positively Stella's advice as well as mine. She says now you need not be ashamed to be thought poor.

We compute you cannot be less than thirty days absent ; and pray do not employ your time in lolling abed till noon to read Homer, but mind your business effectually ; and we think you ought to have no breaking up this August, but affect to adhere to your school closer than ever, because you will find that your ill-wishers will give out you are now going to quit your school, since you have got preferment, etc. Pray send me a large bundle of exercises, good as well as bad, for I want something to read. I would have you carry down three or four sermons, and preach every Sunday at your own church, and be very devout. . . . Keep very regular hours for the sake of your health and credit ; and wherever you lie a night within twenty miles of your living, be sure call the family that evening to prayers. I desire you will wet no commission with your old crew, nor with any but those who befriend you, as Mr. Tickell, etc.

That letter gives us both the men and the relation between them. It is imperious even to bullying : but in the phrase " both you and I have suffered " Sheridan is put implicitly on a level with this powerful senior who had just got him an addition of £200 to his narrow income ; and it is written hot-foot on another by a man who, for instance, had kept the Lord-Lieutenant waiting three months for an answer to very graceful civilities.

As first fruits, Sheridan sent down a horse for Stella's riding. She took kindly to the life : but Dingley " would rather live in a Dublin cellar than a country palace." They were still at Quilca on September 11 when the news came that in spite of good advice Sheridan had miscarried. He was asked to preach in the city of Cork and either did not know or forgot that it was the day of thanksgiving for George I's accession : and he gave out as his text : " Sufficient unto the day is the evil thereof." Since he was known to be a Tory, the blunder was promptly delated, and Carteret felt obliged to forbid him the Court—though he had delighted in this merry companion.

Swift's letter is full of character:

> It is safer for a man's interest to blaspheme God, than to be of a
> party out of power, or even to be thought so. And since the last was
> the case, how could you imagine that all mouths would not be open
> when you were received, and in some manner preferred by the govern-
> ment, though in a poor way? I tell you there is hardly a Whig in Ireland,
> who would allow a potato and butter-milk to a reputed Tory. . . .
> Too much advertency is not your talent, or else you had fled from
> that text, as from a rock. For as Don Quixote said to Sancho, what
> business had you to speak of a halter in a family where one of it was
> hanged? . . . Therefore sit down and be quiet, and mind your business
> as you should do, and contract your friendships, and expect no more
> from man than such an animal is capable of, and you will every day find
> my description of Yahoos more resembling.

But that was not the end. Swift wrote to Tickell, the poet,
Addison's biographer whom Carteret had made Chief Secretary,
claiming from him, as " Mr. Addison's friend and in the most
honourable part his heir," favour for Sheridan. Meanwhile, since
the disappointed man was planning revenge on Richard Tighe, the
officious Whig who rode post to Dublin with the news of that
unlucky text, Swift gave encouragement:

> I do think it is agreed, that all animals fight with the weapons natural
> to them, which is a new and wise remark out of my own head, and the
> devil take that animal, who will not offend his enemy when he is provoked
> with his proper weapon. . . . I will kill that flea or louse which bites
> me, though I get no honour by it.

And for many months thereafter lampoons rained on Tighe, not
only from Sheridan, but from his more formidable backer.

All this part of the correspondence gives insight into what is
the relations between Swift and Stella. She was always, except
when he went to stay at some big house like the Rochforts', at
the centre of the picture—taking a hand even in the ditching and
delving. But we have other documents. From 1719 onwards
Swift sent her birthday verses, and whether in verse or prose he
wrote always with his eye on the object. Indeed these verses
were, as Horace says of his own satires and epistles, *Sermoni propiora*,
nearer to prose than poetry. The first of them is the neatest and
the shortest:

> Stella this day is thirty-four,
> (We shan't dispute a year or more :)
> However, Stella, be not troubled,
> Although thy size and years are doubled
> Since first I saw thee at sixteen,
> The brightest virgin on the green;

So little is thy form declined;
Made up so largely in thy mind.
  O, would it please the gods to split
Thy beauty, size, and years, and wit!
No age could furnish out a pair
Of nymphs so graceful, wise, and fair;
With half the lustre of your eyes,
With half your wit, your years, and size.
And then, before it grew too late,
How should I beg of gentle fate,
(That either nymph might have her swain)
To split my worship too in twain.

That tells us nothing precise except, a little mercilessly, that she was grown stout; but he is lenient on the age, for she was eight-and-thirty, having been born on March 13, 1681. She is thirty-six in the next tribute, and here the opening must be quoted:

All travellers at first incline
Where'er they see the fairest sign,
And if they find the chambers neat,
And like the liquor and the meat,
Will call again, and recommend
The Angel Inn to every friend.
And though the painting grows decay'd,
The house will never lose its trade:
Nay, though the treach'rous tapster, Thomas,
Hangs a new Angel two doors from us,
As fine as daubers' hands can make it,
In hopes that strangers may mistake it,
We think it both a shame and sin
To quit the true old Angel Inn.

If that be not an allusion to Vanessa, it is very like one; but if it is, it stands by itself. The main point in the poem, however, is the tribute to Stella's social gift—

See, at her levee crowding swains,
Whom Stella freely entertains
With breeding, humour, wit, and sense,
And puts them to so small expense,
Their minds so plentifully fills,
And makes such reasonable bills,
So little gets for what she gives,
We really wonder how she lives!
And had her stock been less, no doubt
She must have long ago run out. . . .
  Then, Chloe, still go on to prate
Of thirty-six and thirty-eight;

Pursue your trade of scandal-picking,
Your hints that Stella is no chicken. . . .
All men of sense will pass your door,
And crowd to Stella's at four-score.

There follows in that same year a long poem that begins with
acknowledgment for her labour in collecting and transcribing his
verses, and then passes to tribute :

Thou, Stella, wert no longer young,
When first for thee my harp was strung,
Without one word of Cupid's darts,
Of killing eyes, or bleeding hearts ;
With friendship and esteem possest,
I ne'er admitted Love a guest.
In all the habitudes of life,
The friend, the mistress, and the wife,
Variety we still pursue,
In pleasure seek for something new. . . .
But his pursuits are at an end
Whom Stella chooses for a friend.

Then, characteristically enough, the praise turns to admonition.
Stella had a temper (the *Journal* says somewhere of Bolingbroke
" he is like Ppt and will not be governed ")

Your spirits kindle to a flame,
Moved by the lightest touch of blame ;
And when a friend in kindness tries
To show you where your error lies,
Conviction does but more incense,
Perverseness is your whole defence. . . .
And, what is worse, your passion bends
Its force against your nearest friends,
Which manners, decency, and pride
Have taught you from the world to hide.

The end of it runs : " When you copy next, Will you keep strictly
to the text ? " But there was no fear of her : she was too long
used to admonition and instruction. I think conscious discipleship
dates from the last period of Swift's stay at Moor Park : at all
events, he writes in 1711, that if she comes to certain conclusion
about certain verses—" then I have spent fourteen years " (since
1697) " to no purpose in trying to form your mind." We have her
acknowledgment under her own hand, when she writes verses to
Swift for his birthday, November 30, 1721, calling herself " your
pupil and your humble friend " :

When men began to call me fair,
You interposed your timely care:
You early taught me to despise
The ogling of a coxcomb's eyes;
Show'd where my judgment was misplaced;
Refined my fancy and my taste.
You taught how I might youth prolong,
By knowing what was right and wrong;
How from my heart to bring supplies
Of lustre to my fading eyes. . . .
Your lectures could my fancy fix,
And I can please at thirty-six.

She was then in fact forty: who would not like her the better for
the lapse from strict arithmetic, which proves that she was not too
severely modelled to her Mentor's pattern? The last lines of this
must be given, for the accent of sincerity comes through their
formal design:

Long be the day that gave you birth
Sacred to friendship, wit, and mirth;
Late dying may you cast a shred
Of your rich mantle o'er my head;
To bear with dignity my sorrow,
One day alone, then die to-morrow.

Let it be remembered to her that even in the year when she wrote
this she was a jealous woman and had cause for jealousy. But she
was never at any time left uncertain of her value to the man who
in his own way loved her as women are not often loved, and who
could say of her things that carried conviction with a force that
few men have given to language.

In 1720 were written lines "to Stella visiting me in Sickness":
and these begin with praise of her honour:

The world shall in its atoms end,
Ere Stella can deceive a friend.
By honour seated in her breast
She still determines what is best:
What indignation in her mind
Against enslavers of mankind!
Base kings, and ministers of state,
Eternal objects of her hate!

Then the praise turns to her courage:

For Stella never learn'd the art
At proper times to scream and start;
Nor calls up all the house at night,
And swears she saw a thing in white.

Indeed, she once gave dreadful proof of her man-mindedness; Swift himself told the story while he sat recalling her life when she was a-burying. She and Dingley were at a lonely house in the suburbs with only a boy among their servants; a gang of men tried to break in; Stella ran down with a pistol and shot one through the window. She can have been little over twenty-three, for it was when Ormond was Lord-Lieutenant; Swift says he often toasted her for the deed. Yet she was none the less a woman; and here Swift's verses become an example of his poetry at its best:

> When on my sickly couch I lay
> Impatient both of night and day,
> Lamenting in unmanly strains,
> Call'd every power to ease my pains;
> Then Stella ran to my relief,
> With cheerful face and inward grief;
> And, though by Heaven's severe decree
> She suffers hourly more than me,
> No cruel master could require
> From slaves employ'd for daily hire
> What Stella, by her friendship warm'd
> With vigour and delight perform'd:
> My sinking spirits now supplies
> With cordials in her hands and eyes:
> Now with a soft and silent tread
> Unheard she moves about my bed.
> I see her taste each nauseous draught,
> And so obligingly am caught;
> I bless the hand from whence they came,
> Nor dare distort my face for shame.
>   Best pattern of true friends! beware;
> You pay too dearly for your care,
> If, while your tenderness secures
> My life, it must endanger yours;
> For such a fool was never found,
> Who pull'd a palace to the ground,
> Only to have the ruins made
> Materials for a house decay'd.

One need not go through all these poems, but it is impossible to pass by the one which celebrated Stella's birthday in 1723, for it brings in the whole " crew " and the household. The poet complains that the God of Song had been stingy with inspiration:

> I told him what the world would say,
> If Stella were unsung to-day:
> How I should hide my head for shame,
> When both the Jacks and Robin came;

How Ford would frown, how Jim would leer,
How Sheridan the rogue would sneer,
And swear it does not always follow,
That *semel'n anno ridet Apollo.*

The God, invoked, suggested a sovereign means for inspiration :

You must apply to Mrs. Brent ;
For she, as priestess, knows the rites
Wherein the god of earth delights,
   First, nine ways looking, let her stand
With an old poker in her hand ;
Let her describe a circle round
In Saunders' cellar on the ground :
A spade let prudent Archy hold,
And with discretion dig the mould.
Let Stella look with watchful eye,
Rebecca, Ford, and Grattans by.
   Behold the bottle, where it lies
With neck elated toward the skies !
The god of winds and god of fire
Did to its wondrous birth conspire ;
And Bacchus for a poet's use
Pour'd in a strong inspiring juice.
See ! as you raise it from its tomb,
It drags behind a spacious womb,
And in the spacious womb contains
A sov'reign med'cine for the brains. . . .

   From thence a plenteous draught infuse,
And boldly then invoke the Muse ;
But first let Robert on his knees
With caution drain it from the lees ;
The Muse will at your call appear,
With Stella's praise to crown the year.

We may presume it was a Jeroboam of Margaux—which Stella (wise in that also) affected. Saunders, Archy and Robert were the butler, footman and valet : on such an occasion the whole strength was turned out. One of the Jacks was Dan Jackson, the other Jack Grattan ; Robin another Grattan, and Jim, the Rev. James Stopford, a young fellow of Trinity, for whom Swift had a special liking.

Another set of verses chaffs Stella on her love of delicacies : it was written when she and Dingley came back from their long stay at Woodpark with " Ford who thinks of nothing mean "—

She look'd on partridges with scorn,
Except they tasted of the corn ; . . .
Through candle-light she view'd the wine,
To see that ev'ry glass was fine.

But now arrives the dismal day;
She must return to Ormond Quay.
The coachman stopt; she look'd, and swore
The rascal had mistook the door:
At coming in, you saw her stoop;
The entry brush'd against her hoop:
Each moment rising in her airs,
She curst the narrow winding stairs.

So it goes on, lampooning Stella's lodging that overlooked "the Liffey's stinking tide"; telling how she "sent for company to sup," until at last regretfully:

She fell into her former scene,
Small beer, a herring, and the Dean.

But then, her poet abandons this raillery, which he says cannot hurt, as having not the least pretence to truth.

Your table's neat, your linen fine;
And, though in miniature, you shine:

and for a last word he adds:

For though my raillery were true,
A cottage is Wood Park with you.

There are others of them; and the one belonging to 1725 has a charming turn. If she (at forty-three), is reputed to be no longer young, he will not believe it:

For nature, always in the right,
To your decay adapts my sight;
And wrinkles undistinguish'd pass,
For I'm ashamed to use a glass:
And till I see them with these eyes,
Whoever says you have them, lies.

Dingley has her share of verses too—and they show us a bustling, good-natured busybody, not very wisely full of cares for herself and her friends:

For, though philosophers maintain
The limbs are guided by the brain,
Quite contrary Rebecca's led;
Her hands and feet conduct her head;
By arbitrary power convey her,
She ne'er considers why or where:
Her hands may meddle, feet may wander,
Her head is but a mere by-stander:
And all her bustling but supplies
The part of wholesome exercise.

STELLA

VANESSA

Both portraits are in the possession of Dr. R. R. Leeper at Swift's Hospital. The artists are unknown. The Stella came from Lord Monck's house at Enniskerry, Co. Wicklow.

The centre of her life was a lap-dog, Tiger: her delight was gossip;
but as to the sort of conversation over which Stella presided, neither
she nor her ally, Mrs. Brent, ever " minded a word that was spoke ":

> You tell a good jest,
> And please all the rest;
> Comes Dingley, and asks you, what was it?
> And, curious to know,
> Away she will go
> To seek an old rag in the closet.

The last of all the poems to Stella must be mentioned in its sad
place; but there is another of 1724 which renews the theme of
sickness:

> When indecently I rave,
> When out my brutish passions break
> With gall in every word I speak.

Such avowal as this lends credit to a report transmitted by Delany.
Swift, he says, had once " earnestly desired that she should be
publicly owned as his wife." " I well knew a friend," Delany
says, " to whom she opened herself upon that head, declaring that
the Dean's temper was so altered and his attention to money so
increased, her own health at the same time so impaired, that she
could not take upon herself the care of his house and economy."

This resolution was, he says, " fully confirmed and I fear
embittered," by the publication of " Cadenus and Vanessa," which
was already current in manuscript while she was Ford's guest at
Woodpark in 1723, and the Dean wandering among the cliffs of
Carberry. Strangers came in, began to talk of the poem: " One
of them said, surely that Vanessa must be an extraordinary woman
that could inspire the Dean to write so finely of her. Mrs. Johnson
smiled and answered that was not quite so clear; for it was well
known the Dean could write finely upon a broomstick." That
no doubt falls short of perfect behaviour; there are claws in the
stroke. Vanessa did not bring out the best side of Swift: it
would be asking too much that she should elicit the best in Stella.

The portraits of her are not very helpful: they show a lady
sitting very erect, with long neck, sloping shoulders, a fully
developed bust; the face is a long oval, the eyes very large and
dark, the mouth well formed but expressionless, except in the
picture which is here for the first time reproduced, by the courtesy
of Dr. R. R. Leeper, director of Swift's hospital. It was bought
by him from Lord Monck's house in County Wicklow, and the

painter is not known. But it suggests that vivacity of wit by which she was distinguished, and perhaps also the touch of temper with which Swift taxes her. All the rest one may be tempted to read into it; for we know the record; and if it is not a picture of courage and utter loyalty, then it cannot be a true likeness.

CHAPTER XVI

ENGLAND REVISITED

" YOU desire me to return home, and you promise me in that
case to come to London, loaden with your Travels." So
Bolingbroke wrote to Swift in September, 1724, from France;
and again from London in July, 1725, of "travels into those
countries of giants and pygmies," about which presumably he
had heard in detail from Ford. At all events, the *Travels* were
in progress—and as has been seen already, Sheridan had heard of
Yahoos in 1725. About that same time Swift wrote to Pope (July
19, 1725), "I am so full of grand designs that I believe I shall never
bring them to pass, but to your comfort, *grandia loquimur*, they are
all in prose." This means that Swift realized to the full the value
of what he was doing; that it would ("I speak grandiloquently ")
put him into competition with Pope, then recognized as the head
of English literature.

Plainly also, come to London he would not till they were
finished: the only motive that might have hastened his journey
had been withdrawn a year before, when Oxford died. But on
September 29, 1725, when the long stay at Quilca was closing, he
wrote to Pope a letter which tells how those months had been
spent—from which we may infer with certainty that Stella heard
or read the whole while they were being copied for press.

The letter is almost too well known to quote, yet too perfect
an example of Swift's writing to be omitted:

I have employed my time, besides ditching, in finishing, correcting,
and amending, and transcribing my Travels, in four parts complete,
newly augmented, and intended for the press, when the world shall
deserve them, or rather when a printer shall be found brave enough to
venture his ears. I like the scheme of our meeting after distresses and
dispersions; but the chief end I propose to myself in all my labours is
to vex the world rather than divert it; and if I could compass that
design, without hurting my own person or fortune, I would be the
most indefatigable writer you have ever seen, without reading. I am
exceedingly pleased that you are done with translations. Lord Treasurer
Oxford often lamented that a rascally world should lay you under a

necessity of misemploying your genius for so long a time. But since you will now be so much better employed, when you think of the world, give it one lash the more at my request. I have ever hated all nations, professions, and communities, and all my love is towards individuals : for instance, I hate the tribe of lawyers, but I love Counsellor Such-a-one, and Judge Such-a-one : so with physicians—I will not speak of my own trade—soldiers, English, Scotch, French, and the rest. But principally I hate and detest that animal called man, although I heartily love John, Peter, Thomas, and so forth. This is the system upon which I have governed myself many years, but do not tell, and so I shall go on till I have done with them. I have got material toward a treatise, proving the falsity of that definition *animal rationale*, and to show it would be only *rationis capax*. Upon this great foundation of misanthropy, though not in Timon's manner, the whole building of my Travels is erected.

Then he replies to Pope's promise of introduction to a lady " who is as deaf, though not as old, as yourself. What you will most wonder at, she is considerable at Court, yet no party woman ; and lives in Court, yet would be easy and make you easy." This, as Swift of course knew, was Mrs. Howard, afterwards Countess of Suffolk, official mistress to George, Prince of Wales. But he affected not to understand :

The lady whom you describe to live at court, to be deaf, and no party woman, I take to be mythology, but know not how to moralize it. She cannot be Mercy, for Mercy is neither deaf, nor lives at Court. Justice is blind, and perhaps deaf, but neither is she a Court lady. Fortune is both blind and deaf, and a Court lady, but then she is a most damnable party woman, and will never make me easy, as you promise. It must be Riches, which answers all your description. I am glad she visits you, but my voice is so weak that I doubt she will never hear me.

For the perfection of English prose, it would be hard to beat that passage, so exquisitely finished, yet with the rhythm perpetually varied as is the shifting key of actual speech. And indeed, except for the opening sentence, the same is true of the paragraph which follows :

Mr. Lewis sent me an account of Dr. Arbuthnot's illness, which is a very sensible affliction to me, who, by living so long out of the world, have lost that hardness of heart contracted by years and general conversation. I am daily losing friends, and neither seeking nor getting others. Oh ! if the world had but a dozen Arbuthnots in it, I would burn my Travels. But, however, he is not without fault. There is a passage in Bede highly commending the piety and learning of the Irish in that age, where, after abundance of praises he overthrows them all, by lamenting that, alas ! they kept Easter at a wrong time of the year. So our Doctor has every quality and virtue that can make a man amiable or useful ; but, alas ! he has a sort of slouch in his walk. I pray God protect him, for he is an excellent Christian, though not a Catholic, and as fit a man either to live or die as ever I knew.

It would be imbecile to suppose that a man who writes such a letter does not know that he is writing literature: or that Swift at the height of his fame, writing to Pope, did not know that the letter might probably be preserved. Yet in him there was a curious prodigality of his talent: he threw things from him and cared little where they went. But the essential (if indeed anyone needs to be impressed with it) is that a letter like this is no less spontaneous, no less heartfelt, because it is well written; and I should be surprised if there was even a draft of it made. Prose-writing is an art of which mastery becomes so complete that the master in it makes the perfect movements, attains the perfect rhythm and timing, almost as a cricketer or billiard player makes the particular stroke which he has never made before, but for which he has years of practice. The medium is ready there to convey thought or emotion in a cadence which varies like the shapes of a running stream. In a sense this letter is not improvised: it lets go the thoughts that had been gathering for months: and what he says of Arbuthnot is saying again with more amplitude what he wrote to Arbuthnot himself ten years before. But the whole comes with a jet, in a steady yet infinitely varied flow.

Pope's letters to Swift offer a complete contrast: for one thing, Pope never let the idea of future publication drop out of his mind, and for another he never understood like Swift the technique of prose. In his own medium, constant revision was necessary; lasting verse cannot be improvised verse, any more than a dancer can improvise a perfect dance. One is conscious of unduly laboured expression in Pope's familiar letters. Yet such depth of feeling as Swift communicates itself, and in Pope's reply a reassuring passage about Arbuthnot ends with a sentence that rings completely true:—"I knew it would be a pleasure to you to hear this and in truth that made me write so soon to you."

The correspondence was active through that winter—Bolingbroke joining in with Pope: and there was a better account of Arbuthnot, who "loves mischief the best of any good-natured man in England" (it is Pope's phrase). Arbuthnot himself wrote to Swift that rather than let the *Travels* go unpublished, "I will set the letters myself." He added that when Swift did come over he would be so "much courted and taken up by the Ministry that unless your friends meet you at their tables, they will have none of your company. . . . I know of near half a year's dinners where you are already bespoke." In short, all the world was agog to see the famous wit, and Ministers were mighty curious to meet the Drapier who had beaten them single-handed. But Swift was in little case for society. He writes to Tickell (still at Dublin Castle) on November 12, 1725 :

> I have got slowly out of a feverish disorder, that hath confined me these ten days. I shall dine to-morrow at home, after a sort of *en famille* with the two ladies my nurses. And if you please to be a fourth, I shall take care that no unacceptable fifth be of the company. And pray let me know to-night or to-morrow morning, for as to Sunday [1] I look on you as a guest when you please.

The next letter in the series that we have is to Stopford, "Dear Jim" (he was one of the very few to whom Swift used the Christian name in writing) ; it is dated from "Wretched Dublin, in miserable Ireland," and a review of the circle and their occupations ends with "the Dean of St. Patrick's sitting like a toad in a corner of his great house with a perfect hatred of all public actions and persons."

Yet the move was made early in March, 1726. When he reached London—in good case, for we may believe one who was himself a habitual invalid—Pope, summoned at once to join the Dean at his lodgings in Berry Street, wrote to Oxford, " He is in perfect health and spirits to the joy of all who know him as he was eleven years ago [2] and I never received a more sensible satisfaction than in having been here now two days with him." After that, Pope says, Arbuthnot took charge and " led him a course through the town to Lord Chesterfield, Mr. Pulteney, etc. Lord Bolingbroke and Lord Harcourt propose to carry him to Sir Robert Walpole, and I to Mrs. Howard." On March 26 he went to stay with Bolingbroke at Dawley for some days, and then to Pope at Twickenham. On April 12 we find Arbuthnot conveying an invitation from the Princess of Wales to visit her. Whether that command was obeyed we do not know, but Swift, according to his own often-repeated story, raised his special standard in proportion to her Royal Highness's rank and made her send for him a matter of ten times before he consented to appear at Leicester House. The result was eminently successful : Caroline of Anspach had brains beyond most women of the day and they were of the kind to appreciate Swift's force as well as wit.

---

[1] He always received on Sunday evenings.
[2] It should be twelve.

His first encounter was characteristic. London in that month of April was all agog to see a " wild boy " who had been found in a German forest : Arbuthnot had the keeping of him and showed him with such success at Court that the Princess of Wales had to wait for a view, and apparently Swift and he appeared at Leicester House on the same evening. " I told her," Swift writes six years later, " that having sent for a wild boy from Germany, she had a curiosity to see a wild Dean from Ireland." On several other occasions Swift's presence was commanded, either to Leicester House or Richmond, and Mrs. Howard usually transmitted the summons. For Swift had made close alliance with this lady, whom Pope called in compliment " a thing that's most uncommon —A reasonable woman, Handsome and witty, yet a friend." Her one defect made a bond of sympathy with Swift :

> " Has she no faults," then Envy says, " sir ? "
> " Yes, she has one, incline your ear :
> When all the world unites to praise her,
> The woman's deaf and will not hear."

We are told repeatedly by Swift that in this year and in the next when he returned, it was conveyed to him that the occupants of Leicester House desired to see him settled in England ; and it is plain that this revived in him desires—rather than ambitions, for what he hoped was transfer, not advancement. But it was not his own interest that he pressed on Caroline ; the Dean did not forget ' the Drapier.' Much talk passed upon the subject of Ireland, when, says Swift (writing to Lady Suffolk in 1731, long after George II's accession) " she appeared so much to pity this distressed kingdom, and gave me leave to write to her, if ever I lived to see her Queen, and promised that in such a case she would use all her credit to relieve us ; whereupon I asked Dr. Arbuthnot who was present to be witness of what she said, and her Majesty confirmed it."

Nor did Swift leave the matter in Caroline's hands. Walpole, desiring to meet him, asked him to dinner, after which Swift asked for a private discussion. On April 28 he reported the result in a long letter to Peterborough, who had arranged the interview. He had " no other design in desiring to see Sir Robert Walpole than to represent the affairs of Ireland to him in a true light." He had failed because he saw Walpole had conceived opinions, " from the example and practices of the present and former governors," which " I could not reconcile to the notions I had of liberty." As there had been no room for debate, he set down his grounds for complaint which he begged Peterborough to forward to Walpole.

Firstly, persons of English descent born in Ireland " are treated as Irishmen," though they ought to be " on as good a foot as any subjects of Britain." Secondly, they are denied the natural liberty of exporting their manufactures. Thirdly, the University, " where youth are instructed with a much stricter discipline than either in Oxford or Cambridge," is discouraged by the filling of all employments with persons from England. Fourthly, several of the bishops sent over "having been clergymen of obscure condition " job the best preferments to their kindred ; and the same is true of the judges and all others in civil employment, " if they have a cousin, a valet, or footman, in their family, born in England." As a result the Irish gentry, unable to provide for their younger sons, have no choice but to rack their tenants, " which they have done to such a shocking degree that not one farmer in a hundred can afford shoes or stockings to his children or eat meat."

These meetings were known and much talk followed : Swift was to have a vacant Irish bishopric. But, writing to Stopford, he said : " I was neither offered, nor would have received, except upon conditions which would never be granted. For I absolutely broke with the First Minister and have never seen him since, and I lately complained of him to the Princess because I knew she would tell him." The fair construction to put on this is that Swift insisted on a cessation of the policy which was being deliberately carried out by the government's main agent in Ireland, Archbishop Boulter of Armagh.

There was, however, one matter which Swift certainly had in mind : he held that the English government owed him the promised thousand pounds which Oxford by neglect, and Bolingbroke by lack of time, had failed to pay. " Tell Archdeacon Walls," he wrote to Sheridan on July 8, " that I never asked for my thousand pounds, which he hears I have got, though I mentioned it to the Princess the last time I saw her ; but I bid her tell Walpole, I scorned to ask him for it." This is to be mentioned " to no one except the ladies, because I know Mrs. Johnson would be pleased with it." It would, however, appear that Walpole decided to make the offer, and that even so Swift decided to refuse : for after his return to Dublin he says (in some affectionate raillery to Pope on the matters of giving and taking between them) : " I have not half your pride ; witness what Mr. Gay says in his letters that I was censured for begging presents, though I limited them to ten shillings, and although I forgave Sir Robert Walpole a thousand pounds, *multa gemens*." If anything were needed to give credibility to this, it would be the *cri du cœur*; no doubt it cost him a groan or two.

But there is not the least evidence to show that Swift asked Walpole for preferment or sought an interview on any but public grounds.

Meantime he was enjoying the pleasures of friendship: not always hilariously. On May 16 Pope wrote to his friend Fortescue that his was a sad house, for his mother was dangerously ill. " There is nobody with me but the Dean of St. Patrick's, who would hardly be here if he were not the best natured and most indulgent man I know; it is so melancholy a way of passing his time." Yet Mrs. Pope must have mended, for Pope and Swift, with Gay for a pleasant third, went off for a riding tour as far as to Lord Bathurst's house at Cirencester. After that, most of the time was spent at Twickenham, where Swift writes that Pope took complete charge: " Mr. Gay and I find ourselves engaged for three or four days and we neither of us dare dispute his pleasure."

A letter of Pope's to Mrs. Howard on June 20 gives one suggestion of their diversions. She had just put her Twickenham house (the Prince of Wales's gift) at his disposal and he writes to say that they had gone there to celebrate a birthday: for a calf (" of the right sex, yours ") had been born to the establishment. " We had a cold dinner at Marble Hill. Mrs. Susan offered us wine upon the occasion and upon such an occasion we could not refuse it. Our entertainment consisted of flesh and fish and the lettuce of a Greek island named Cos. We have some thoughts of dining there to-morrow to celebrate the day after the birthday, and on Friday to celebrate the day after that when we intend to entertain Dean Swift: because we think your hall the most delightful room in the world, except that where you are."

On another day Bolingbroke and Congreve made up five at dinner at Twickenham. There is no question but Swift enjoyed all this, except for his constant anxiety about Pope.

I had rather live in forty Irelands than under the frequent disquiets of hearing you are out of order. I always apprehend it most after a great dinner; for the least transgression of yours, if it be only two bits and one sup more than your stint, is a great debauch; for which you certainly pay more than those sots who are carried dead drunk to bed.

But these gaieties prevented one of his purposes, which was to go into papers for the completion of his historical memoir of Oxford's administration, in company with Oxford's heir.

This vexed him. It was a worse annoyance that "Cadenus and Vanessa" should be published at this moment. Knightley Chetwode wrote to him of it, and he answered, testily enough, that he was indifferent :

I never saw it since I writ it. Neither do I believe the gravest character is answerable for a private humoursome thing which by an accident inevitable and the baseness of particular malice, is made public. . . . I have borne a great deal more ; and those who will like me less, upon seeing me capable of having writ such a trifle so many years ago, may think as they please, neither is it agreeable to me to be troubled with such accounts, when there is no remedy, and only gives me the ungrateful task of reflecting on the baseness of mankind which I knew sufficiently before.

Tickell touched on this sore spot again in letters from Dublin and was told it was "a thing no friend would publish. . . . Folly, malice, negligence, and the incontinence in keeping secrets (for which we want a word), ought to caution men to keep the key of their cabinets."

But already when he wrote this, a terrible anxiety had hold of him : A letter to Sheridan on July 8 says that he had for two months been uneasy about Stella's health and " as is usual, feared the worst that was possible and doubted all the good accounts that were sent me." Now, serious illness was admitted : " I pray God her danger may warn her to be less wilful."

Still, there was yet no imminent apprehension. In that same letter he tells Sheridan how he had received—presumably from some private patron of a living—" the fairest offer of a settlement here that one can imagine, within twelve miles of London, and in the midst of my friends." But he felt " too old for new schemes and especially such as would bridle me in my freedoms and liberalities " (a notable sentence from one who had the name of a miser). Another and a stronger temptation had been Bolingbroke's offer of " a fine house and garden and park and wine-cellar in France, to pass away the winter in " ; and " if Mrs. Johnson were not so much out of order I would certainly accept of it, and I wish she could go to Montpelier at the same time. You see I am grown visionary."

A week later, there was an end to visions ; a letter from his sub-dean, Worrall, warned him of the worst. It is best to give his reply in full : the precautions are not less characteristic than the emotions :

What you tell me of Mrs. Johnson I have long expected, with great oppression and heaviness of heart. We have been perfect friends these thirty-five years. Under my advice they both came to Ireland, and have been ever since my constant companions; and the remainder of my life will be a very melancholy scene, when one of them is gone, whom I most esteemed, upon the score of every good quality that can possibly recommend a human creature. I have these two months seen through Mrs. Dingley's disguises. And indeed, ever since I left you, my heart has been so sunk, that I have not been the same man, nor ever shall be again; but drag on a wretched life, till it shall please God to call me away.

I must tell you, as a friend, that if you have reason to believe Mrs. Johnson cannot hold out till my return, I would not think of coming to Ireland; and in that case, I would expect of you, in the beginning of September, to renew my licence for another half year; which time I will spend in some retirement far from London, till I can be in a disposition of appearing after an accident that must be so fatal to my quiet. I wish it could be brought about that she might make her will. Her intentions are to leave the interest of all her fortune to her mother and sister, during their lives, and afterwards to Dr. Steevens's Hospital, to purchase lands for such uses there as she designs. Think how I am disposed while I write this, and forgive the inconsistencies. I would not for the universe be present at such a trial of seeing her depart. She will be among friends, that upon her own account and great worth, will tend her with all possible care, where I should be a trouble to her, and the greatest torment to myself. In case the matter should be desperate, I would have you advise, if they come to town, that they should be lodged in some airy healthy part, and not in the Deanery, which, besides, you know, cannot but be a very improper thing for that house to breathe her last in.[1] This I leave to your discretion, and I conjure you to burn this letter immediately, without telling the contents of it to any person alive.

Pray write to me every week, that I may know what steps to take; for I am determined not to go to Ireland, to find her just dead, or dying. Nothing but extremity could make me so familiar with those terrible words, applied to such a dear friend. Let her know I have bought her a repeating gold watch, for her ease in winter nights. I designed to have surprised her with it; but now I would have her know it, that she may see how my thoughts were always to make her easy. I am of opinion that there is not a greater folly than to contract too great and intimate a friendship, which must always leave the survivor miserable.

Three days later he wrote of his feelings in almost the same words to Stopford, but with even less restraint, and adding:

Besides, this was a person of my own rearing and instructing from childhood, who excelled in every good quality that can possibly accom-

---

[1] Apparently the understanding still was that in Swift's absence the ladies used his house as theirs, though when he was at home they never slept under the same roof with him.

plish a human creature. They have hitherto writ me deceiving letters, but Mr. Worrall has been so just and prudent as to tell me the truth; which, however racking, is better than to be struck on the sudden. Dear Jim, pardon me, I know not what I am saying; but believe me that violent friendship is much more lasting, and as much engaging, as violent love.

And again on July 27 to Sheridan, when all hope seemed gone:

I have yours just now of the 19th, and the account you give me, is nothing but what I have some time expected with the utmost agonies, and there is one aggravation of constraint, that where I am I am forced to put on an easy countenance. It was at this time the best office your friendship could do, not to deceive me.

We know exactly where he was, and before whom he must put on an easy countenance; for on the very day he wrote this, he would have had his share of a letter from Bolingbroke addressed " To the three Yahoos of Twickenham, Jonathan, Alexander, John." It ends with the hope that Jonathan's "imagination of business, will be succeeded by some imagination more becoming a professor of that divine science, *la bagatelle*. . . . Mirth be with you."

These were the men whom alone he counted his equals, whom he esteemed above all others; and from them his heart was hidden, at the very time when he laid it bare to those to whom he gave his friendship (it is his own word) in pennyworths. But the younger men, neither his equals in genius nor in experience, were part of Stella's life. To them he showed himself as he was; not ashamed even to let it be seen how far his passions were beyond his control. The letter to Sheridan goes on:

I look upon this to be the greatest event that can ever happen to me; but all my preparations will not suffice to make me bear it like a philosopher, nor altogether like a Christian. There hath been the most intimate friendship between us from her childhood, and the greatest merit on her side, that ever was in one human creature to another. Nay, if I were now near her, I would not see her; I could not behave myself tolerably, and should redouble her sorrow. Judge in what a temper of mind I write this. The very time I am writing, I conclude the fairest soul in the world hath left its body. Confusion! that I am this moment called down to see a visitor, when I am in the country, and not in my power to deny myself.

I have passed a very constrained hour, and now return to say I know not what. I have been long weary of the world, and shall for my small remainder of years be weary of life, having for ever lost that conversation, which could only make it tolerable. I fear while you are reading this, you will be shedding tears at her funeral; she loved you well, and a great share of the little merit I have with you, is owing to her solicitations.

POPE

BOLINGBROKE

From drawings by JONATHAN RICHARDSON, *in the British Museum*

Yet in the end the ordeal which he shrank from was deferred. He left London on August 15, having bidden Worrall to send him further news at Chester; and within a week he was in Dublin— where for a climax of irony, he found the city beflagged in his honour and the leading citizens coming out in boats to welcome the Drapier home.

Stella had recovered somewhat. She was to last out through another change of season, and in another absence Swift was to renew the same torment. But in these few extra months accorded to her, she saw the launching of the work which made Swift's fame universal.

CHAPTER XVII

GULLIVER'S TRAVELS

IT is a commonplace of observation that a man's brain will work
normally when the spirit is in torture ; and Swift, who deferred
the publication of the first tract by which he set store till he was
leaving London, and did the same with his *Tale of a Tub*, now took
precisely the same course about his *Travels*. The book had been
kept a secret among the band at Twickenham ; not even Arbuthnot
had seen it ; and only Pope was involved in the business of finding
a publisher. Even Pope's privity is only a matter of inference ;
but Swift says that he never got money from any of his works but
this one and that " only by Mr. Pope's good management." Whatever hand was employed, Benjamin Motte [1] received a parcel with
a letter signed " Richard Sympson," who, writing on behalf of
his " cousin, Mr. Lemuel Gulliver," offered the manuscript for a
sum of £200, with the proviso that if the sale did not justify this
price, any amount considered due would be refunded. Motte
answered on August 11 that he could only offer payment at the
end of six months. " Richard Sympson " stipulated on August 13
that the book must appear by Christmas as farthest ; and Motte
undertook the same day to get it out within a month of receiving
the manuscript. Thus before Swift left London on August 15,
he knew that the affair was complete. But he saw no proof sheets.
The book appeared in November, for on the 8th Arbuthnot writes :
" *Gulliver's Travels* will have, I believe, as great a run as John
Bunyan." It was an odd collocation, but a sound one ; except
the *Pilgrim's Progress*, what other book in English is so well known ?
The next sentence sounds even more oddly : " Gulliver is a happy
man that at his age can write such a merry book." Remembering
Swift's own description of his intentions, it sounds odder. Yet
in point of fact most of the people who have read *Gulliver* have
read it for fun.

But we do not get the same kind of fun out of it as London
society did in that winter of 1726 ; and Arbuthnot's letter illustrates

---

[1] He had succeeded to the business of Tooke, Swift's old publisher.

this. He had seen the Princess of Wales and found her reading the *Travels* : she " was just come to the passage of the hobbling Prince, which she laughed at." At the end of this letter he adds :

Lord Scarborough, who is no inventor of stories, told me, that he fell in company with a master of a ship, who told him, that he was very well acquainted with Gulliver, but that the printer had mistaken, that he lived in Wapping, and not in Rotherhithe. I lent the book to an old gentleman, who went immediately to his map to search for Lilliput.

Swift on his part wrote to Pope : " A Bishop here said that book was full of improbable lies, and for his part, he hardly believed a word of it." All these stories have been repeated by many critics as authentic (I cannot except myself) ; and Lord Scarborough may have been as literal as Arbuthnot made him out to be. Yet I have doubts ; for certainly these two masters of humour contrive to convey in parables the perfect commendation of Gulliver's amazing gift for making the strangest tale appear simple nature ; and Swift surely had a design at the back of his mind—to convey what he thought about the intellect of bishops, as supplied to Ireland under Sir Robert Walpole's rule.

The passage concerning the hobbling prince is one of those which were specially likely to amuse, since a particular application could be fixed. Of the two parties in his Majesty's Empire of Lilliput, one wore high heels, the other low, and although " the high heels " (according to the principal secretary) " were most agreeable to ancient constitution, his Majesty hath determined to make use only of low heels in the administration of the government." Consequently the King wore the lowest heels in his palace ; but the Heir apparent, having " some tendency towards the high heels, had one heel higher than the other, which gave him a hobble in his gait." Now under George I was clearly established the usage that each Hanoverian Prince of Wales should always be in opposition to his parent, and the future George II showed some inclination to the Tories, while his father lay in Walpole's Whig pocket.

On the whole, however, Pope reported that though the book might be thought too bold and general a satire, " none that I hear of accuse it of particular reflections." Yet certainly part of its vogue was due to hints which no uninstructed modern would seize : for instance, the flight of Gulliver from Lilliput to the neighbouring and hostile kingdom of Blefuscu was meant to recall the case of Bolingbroke, flying lest he should be condemned for not having pushed the French to complete destruction in 1712. Again, Lady

Louisa Stuart tells us that the passage in which Gulliver denies the charge of scandalous intercourse with the Lord Treasurer's wife, was taken ironically, since the laxity of Walpole's lady was generally known.

But such personal strokes are to be found only in the first part, where Gulliver moves among laughable replicas of humanity, who have their parties and their wars and their badges of distinction, that seem absurd where everything is reduced to microscopic scale. But in Brobdingnag it is normal humanity which is held up to be viewed from the standpoint of beings whose rats are big as our mastiffs : and here Swift inverts his method. For although among the pygmies Gulliver describes how ministers qualify for office by agile feats on the tight-rope, and earn ribbons, red, blue or green, by jumping and creeping like trained dogs, yet it is explained that these were modern corruptions, imposed on the original institutions of their state ; and in describing the primitive fashions, Swift gives his book the character of a Utopia. Thus in Lilliput, informers convicted of false testimony are put to ignominious death ; theft is treated with moderate leniency, but fraud and breaches of trust are capital crimes. Moreover, the law-abiding citizen of long standing is pensioned by the State, for justice, the Lilliputians think, should not only punish but reward. And in the choice of ministers to be employed, they have more regard to good morals than to great abilities ; believing that " providence never intended to make the management of public affairs a mystery to be comprehended only by persons of sublime genius." Also " the disbelief of a divine providence renders a man uncapable of holding any public station."

These were peculiarly Swift's own Utopian ideas, and perhaps also this other, that ingratitude is made a capital crime, because " whoever makes ill returns to his benefactor must needs be a common enemy to mankind." But when he comes to principles of education, we are reminded of Plato's Republic. Parents are the last to be trusted with the education of their own children ; there are public nurseries for males and females, according to their degree (for in Swift's Utopia there is no levelling) ; and in the nurseries for girls cowardice is as much a reproof as among the boys.

The children of cottagers and labourers are left to grow up at home, " their business being only to till and cultivate the earth ; but the old and diseased are supported by hospitals ; for begging is a trade unknown in this empire."

Thus for the positive side of Swift's philosophy we must look where it is set into a narrative so diverting, so ingenious, so fantastic, and yet so credible, that the reader is unaware of contact with speculations like Plato's. All that is excellent is here described as existing among a race of creatures contemptible to us by their stature, yet governing themselves according to true reason. The negative side comes in the sequel, where Gulliver, brought after another series of adventures to Brobdingnag, and presented as a curiosity to the King of this gigantic race, ventured to tell his Majesty that human worth cannot be measured by bulk of body, and so was given the chance to explain how reason operated in the government of his own dear native country.

He expatiated with joy upon the house of peers, the highest court of judicature from whom there can be no appeal; on the holy bishops, the freely chosen Commons, the venerable judges, the prudently managed trading and the rest. When he had finished the King began to question—and his questions began with education; they went on to the methods by which persons were chosen for employment; and so, by a series of awkward inquiries, to which no answer is supplied, there is suggested a devastating criticism of the whole system. And when Gulliver, dismayed at the King's summing up, answers by citing some of mankind's notable inventions, especially their destructive artillery, His Majesty only expresses amazement "that so impotent and grovelling an insect should entertain such inhuman ideas."

There is another touch of Utopia in the comments upon Brobding-nagian law. Here also it is held that government should be a simple matter; and no law must be more than two-and-twenty words long. Learning for them consists of morality, history, poetry and mathematics, but the last only as applied to what may be useful to agriculture and all mechanized arts. "As to ideas, entities, abstractions and transcendentals, I could never drive the least conception into their heads," Gulliver adds.

These were matters in which Swift himself had no interest, and in the third part he went on to satirize those who had. By common consent this is where he failed. "I tell you freely the part of the projectors is the least brilliant," Arbuthnot wrote at once. In the earlier parts, Swift is dealing with things perfectly familiar to him, human actions, human systems of behaviour and of government; he can at will make these familiar things look strange (and frequently ridiculous or disgusting) by supposing them magnified or reduced in the proportion of a foot to an inch;

or again by the art of his narrative he can make a thing so strange as a promenade of court carriages on a man's handkerchief, pass for a natural occurrence. But in Laputa he becomes fantastic. It is only when Gulliver reaches the island Maldonado, where he can converse with the illustrious dead, that we meet passages of interest; yet of these only one stands out, that desperate account of the Struldbrugs who are born by chance exempt from death.

A very characteristic part of this often escapes notice. Gulliver, on hearing of these fortunate persons (as he conceives them to be), sketches how he would proceed, if he were one. First, he would acquire riches and so might hope within a couple of centuries to be the richest man in the kingdom. Next, he would study so that he must become by seniority pre-eminent in learning, and by recording events would be a living treasury of knowledge. Then comes a sketch of an existence, not altogether unlike what might have been conceivably possible to the Dean of St. Patrick's:

I would never marry after threescore, but live in an hospitable manner, yet still on the saving side. I would entertain myself in forming and directing the minds of hopeful young men, by convincing them from my own remembrance, experience and observation, fortified by numerous examples, of the usefulness of virtue in public and private life. But my choice and constant companions should be of a sett of my own immortal brotherhood, among whom I would elect a dozen from the most ancient down to my own contemporaries. Where any of these wanted fortunes, I would provide them with convenient lodges round my own estate, and have some of them always at my table, only mingling a few of the most valuable among you mortals, whom length of time would harden me to lose with little or no reluctance, and treat your posterity after the same manner; just as a man diverts himself with the annual succession of pinks and tulips in his garden, without regretting the loss of those which withered the preceding year.

From this fancied outline we pass to the reality, as Swift conceives it, of beings who must outlive the usual life. They have no distinction of taste, but eat and drink without relish and appetite; cannot amuse themselves with reading, because their memory will not carry them from the beginning of a sentence to the end; and they are dead in law. Their property is taken from them, all but a pittance, since otherwise, as avarice is the necessary consequence of old age, these immortals would become proprietors of the whole kingdom.

Fifteen years after Swift wrote this, he was in the case he had described. Is it possible that he foresaw it?

The fourth part is the adventure in a country where men are loathsome brutes, enserfed by the ruling race of horses. It is the

tremendous climax to his satire and cannot by any s
be called " merry "—though Gulliver's attempts t
with the superior animals and keep aloof from
humour of the grimmest sort. My concern here
point out Swift's philosophy, of which the ' Travel
dious expression : and here again is a positive and a
the first conveyed through a description of the instit
among the Houyhnhnms, who live purely by natur   ason,
have neither diseases nor doctors, laws nor criminals, wars nor
soldiers. Here mating is carried out only in obedience to orders
of authority, and here—as in Lilliput—the progeny are in no special
relation of fondness to their parents.

Their language has no word for lying ; they express it by ' saying
the thing which is not.' Swift's detestation of untruthfulness
was formidable : and no doubt he was much lied to ; ungovern-
able temper with a bullying disposition breeds lying wherever it
is found.

The negative side is given, as in Brobdingnag, by the device
of making Gulliver describe to his master the customs prevailing
among his own human kind ; and here with savage irony Swift
lets loose his abhorrence of war. A few sentences may give an
idea of it :

Alliance by blood, or marriage, is a frequent cause of war between
princes ; and the nearer the kindred is, the greater is their disposition
to quarrel : *poor* nations are *hungry*, and *rich* nations are *proud*; and
pride and hunger will ever be at variance. For these reasons, the
trade of a *soldier* is held the most honourable of all others ; because a
soldier is a *Yahoo* hired to kill in cold blood as many of his own species,
who have never offended him, as possibly he can.

Law and medicine are treated in the same way. But to satirize
lust, he takes another method and shows us the advances made to
Gulliver by a female Yahoo.—It is strange to consider this lurid
work of the intellect and imagination, all operating in powerful
alliance, and contrast it with the sanity, the easy humour, and not
rarely the tenderness, of his private letters, which show us the
man as he was in relation to other men. But the artist expresses
that inner self which moves in solitude ; and no one can put down
this fourth book of ' Gulliver ' without feeling that Swift's mind
in loneliness suffered a kind of demoniac possession.

If we were to consider ' Gulliver ' as a work of instruction—and
every satirist in his way is a moralist, an advocate of the opposite
to what he lashes—it must be said that it defeats its own object.

nd will not learn from a philosopher in a rage, for then he
es to be a philosopher. Lilliput may teach something, Brob-
ingnag may at least set us thinking, but there is an instinctive
recoil from this final exaggeration. Yet it would be foolish to
suppose that Swift had any serious purpose of making his fellow
creatures better. In Lilliput perhaps he wrote to please himself,
to delight in witty and copious invention ; perhaps there is a
similar enjoyment even in Brobdingnag ; but when we come to
the Yahoos, the artist is deaf and blind to all but the need of his
own impulse ; it is a savage chant of detestation and enmity towards
the world into which he has been born, the cry of a tortured soul
seeking the relief it can only find in a repose *ubi sæva indignatio
ulterius cor lacerare nequit.*

Since my purpose is only biographical, I do not attempt even
to summarize the study which has been made of the sources from
which Swift drew suggestions. Rabelais of course is never out
of his mind : but he laid under contribution a whole world of
writers, including certainly Cyrano de Bergerac.[1] One fact, however, is too curious to be omitted : Swift was no seaman, yet set
out deliberately to write in the character of an experienced navi-
gator ; and Mr. Churton Collins discovered a technical treatise on
the Mariner's Art by Samuel Sturmy which contained elaborate
directions for the handling of a ship in a hurricane. Swift simply
annexed this bodily, and when Mr. Sturmy says, for instance, " Get
the starboard tacks aboard, cast off anchor, braces and lifts," Swift
writes, " We got the starboard tacks aboard," and so forth, till as
Mr. Sturmy directed, " they kept her full and by as near as she
would lie."

I do not suppose that these lines conveyed any meaning to a
man, whose only experience of the sea was that of a passenger
between Chester or Holyhead and Dublin—though he saw a deal
of foul weather. But it is not sufficiently noted by Dr. Eddy
that from early days Swift was an indefatigable reader of
" Voyages " ; the list of books read by him in 1697 at Moor
Park comprises the *Voyage de Syam*, the *Histoire d'Éthiopie*, the
Voyage de Maroc, *Histoire des Côtes* amongst other items ; and he had
mastered to absolute perfection the simple narrative English of
Dampier and other early mariners, which is so full of sap. Throughout his life he seems to have read these tales of adventure as men
nowadays divert themselves with detective fiction.

[1] Elaborate study will be found in the work by Dr. W. A. Eddy published
by the Princetown University Press.

One other observation should be made. He writes of horses as one familiar with them, yet without ever conveying that he had an eye for a horse. He used riding all his life, but nothing in his letters, which abound in references to his efforts to suit himself, conveys that he had any feeling for a horse except as a more or less convenient creature to carry him. Riding was exercise which he valued ; it was a means of travel ; but I cannot find a trace of delight in horsemanship, or of interest in any quality of a horse except as a hack.

This, however, is by the way. As to the book's success, it is enough to say that Lilliput and Brobdingnag have made adjectives in half a dozen European languages—if indeed there is any tongue where they are not understood. " Yahoo " is, I think, only in English speech. Yet how useful! It exemplifies Swift's feeling for the sound of words, just as does the quick patter of syllables in Lilliput and the lumbering march of Brobdingnag—which, however, he meant to be Brobdingrag, as appears from the letter prefixed to the second edition, in which certain alterations (made by the publisher, fearing for his ears) were replaced by the original.

There had doubtless been several impressions before this : the first sold out within a week, so Pope and Gay reported in a joint letter. " From the highest to the lowest it is universally read, from the cabinet council to the nursery." Even the Duchess of Marlborough (then on friendly terms with Pope), " says she can dream of nothing else since she read it—and that if she knew Gulliver, though he had been the worst enemy she had ever had, she should give up her present acquaintance for his friendship."

Of course she knew who Gulliver was. " It is generally said that you are the author," the same letter says : and of course she knew that Swift had lampooned her and her duke ; but this amazing woman, now rich with all Marlborough's accumulations and her own, vigorous and combative as ever, did not, one fancies, find it hard to forgive a hard hitter, when she saw the knocks so widely distributed. A fortnight later, Pope writes that he had gone to London for the first time since Swift's departure, simply in order to observe " how every single man looks upon it," and that the diversion had fully answered his anticipations.

Meantime, the author was receiving compliments from those who were officially highest in the land. Close alliance had sprung up between him and Mrs. Howard, who gave him a ring before he left England ; and he retorted by sending her " a piece of Irish plaid made in imitation of the Indian "—and begged her to show this Dublin poplin to the Princess of Wales and suggest that "another such piece will be offered to her Royal Highness if she will descend to honour Ireland by receiving and wearing it; and in recompense, I who govern the vulgar will have her Royal Highness's health drunk by five hundred Irish weavers as an encourager of the manufactury." The Princess, however, did not wait for another to be woven, but seized on Mrs. Howard's, and moreover ordered a new piece to measure, "the height of the Brobdingnag dwarf multiplied by two and a half." Various formulæ followed, for the explication of which he was referred to the academy of Lagado. Thereupon, Swift sent Mrs. Howard a singular jewel—the crown of Lilliput, which had been thrust into a corner of Gulliver's waistcoat pocket when the palace was on fire, and had been by mistake carried to England.

Peterborough added his tribute, saying that he had hoped to write in Houyhnhnm, but the lady to whom he applied for instruction how to draw sounds out of consonants was a professed friend to the Italian language, and so he must fall back on Yahoo : though "a neighing duetto" was promised for the next opera. "The greatest lady in the land resolves to send a pair of shoes without heels to Captain Gulliver : she takes *vi et armis* the plaid from the lady it was sent to, which is soon to appear upon her royal person : and now, who but Captain Gulliver ? . . . Verily, verily I believe he was never in such imminent danger of preferment." Lady Bolingbroke wrote, in French, of her delight about the French translation. So it is little wonder that by February Swift tells Knightley Chetwode that Captain Gulliver's book, though "much censured" in Ireland, "in England hath made a bookseller almost rich enough to be an alderman."

That, however, was a vulgar test of success. If ever a man had applause in the choicest form, it was the author of *Gulliver*. A whole literature of imitation began from the first and outlasted his life by decades ; but the best tribute came from his friends, Pope, Gay and Arbuthnot, who clubbed together in verses that celebrate the three great books of the *Travels* : Gay probably devising the Lilliputian couplets to "the Man Mountain" :

> In amaze
> Lost I gaze.
> Can our eyes
> Reach thy size ?

Pope probably did most of Mistress Glumdalclitch's "Lamentation for the Loss of Grildrig," and the very clever verses in which Mary

Gulliver bewails her returned husband's coldness and his preference for the sorrel mare. The latter in particular has Pope's
signature in a sly indecency, for which there is no parallel in
Gulliver ; Swift, often unbearably disgusting, is never lewd.

So fame beat at the doors of a deaf, diseased and failing man,
who (as the reference to Irish censure shows) was angrily conscious
of any hostile criticism, yet had little enjoyment of even the most
discerning applause ; a man by his own choice lonely and homeless,
over whom hung in these months the constant certainty that such
ties as he had allowed himself to form, his poor substitute for a
home, must before long be broken, and while they still held, could
bring him little but painful premonitions of ultimate anguish.

CHAPTER XVIII

SWIFT'S LAST VISIT TO ENGLAND AND STELLA'S DEATH

SWIFT had left England in 1726 under a firm promise to return in spring. The main attraction was certainly Pope, who pursued him after his departure with letters whose elaboration does not conceal the reality of feeling. Swift answered in a spirit that recalls the *Journal to Stella*; no other creature drew from him such affection, such dwelling on the object of it, such re-creating of the environment.

> You have taught me to dream, which I had not done in twelve years further than by inexpressible nonsense; but now I can every night distinctly see Twickenham, and the Grotto, and Dawley, and Mrs. Blount, and many *et ceteras*, and it is but three nights since I beat Mrs. Pope.

That last touch about his games of backgammon with the old lady is exquisite.

The letter goes on with chidings, entirely characteristic of Swift among his intimates. He had given Pope two silver cups with the inscription " *Pignus amicitiæ exiguum ingentis* " : and Pope spoke of returning in kind this " little token of a vast friendship." Swift answered :

> I knew thy pride and the naughtiness of thy heart. I remember when it grieved your soul to see me pay a penny more than my club at an inn, when you had maintained me three months at bed and board; for which, if I had dealt with you in the Smithfield way, it would have cost me a hundred pounds, for I live worse here upon more. Did you ever consider that I am for life almost twice as rich as you, and pay no rent, and drink French wine twice as cheap as you do port, and have neither coach, chair, nor mother ?

It was in such ways that his eternal preoccupation with money broke out. Pope told Young a story, how he and Gay once went to call on the Dean at his lodging—" you know how intimate we were "—and how Swift met them with his usual railing : What, they had come away from their fine lords and ladies to call on a poor Irish dean ? Well, since they were there, they must dine.—

But they had dined.—Very well, he would not be a gainer by them : let us see : a lobster. Yes, that would have done very well ; two shillings : a couple of tarts, a shilling : a bottle of wine, two shillings ; that's five shillings. There's half a crown for you, Pope —and for you, Gay.—" And would you believe," Pope ends, " he forced us to take it."

There was correspondence in that autumn and winter with Walpole's chief antagonist, Pulteney, who expressed and doubtless felt a great desire to be on good terms with Swift. Nor was royalty allowed to forget him. Over and above the Dean's own correspondence with Mrs. Howard concerning the poplin " plaid," Arbuthnot wrote of " a great deal of discourse with your friend, her Royal Highness. She insisted upon your wit and good conversation. I told her that was not what I valued you for, but for being a sincere, honest man and speaking truth when others were afraid to speak it." This is worth putting alongside of Addison's tribute (several years earlier, March 20, 1718) to " your good nature, which is a very odd quality to celebrate in a man who has talents so much more shining in the eyes of the world."

There were also new contacts with the publishers, through Pope, who had projected a joint edition of their *Miscellanies*—the riskiest venture for any man to embark on with such a collaborator as Pope ; but it went forward, Swift sending over a selection of his verses from which Pope and Gay should choose at will, and also some of his Thoughts and Aphorisms. By February 18, 1728, the first part of it was ready and Pope wrote :

I am prodigiously pleased with this joint volume, in which methinks we look like friends, side by side, serious and merry by turns, conversing interchangeably, and walking down hand in hand to posterity, not in the stiff forms of learned authors, flattering each other, and setting the rest of mankind at naught, but in a free, unimportant, natural, easy manner ; diverting others just as we diverted ourselves.

By April 8 Swift was ready to start, and on the 27th we find " Richard Sympson " demanding that the publisher should fulfil his contract and pay over the two hundred pounds. This meant that, when Swift arrived, Pope set him in motion, for he himself had never before taken such a step.

Practically the whole of this visit was to Pope. The two friends were together at Twickenham, where Pope's mother was too ill to be left. Writing to Caryll in the October of that year, the poet complains of solitude and ill health, but adds : " I had indeed the company here constantly of Dean Swift who made my retirement his own for more than four months and is but just gone to Ireland."

But in June a project long floating in Swift's mind was on the point of interrupting this retirement. He had read immensely in French authors; he wrote French with a competence unusual in one who had seldom the occasion to speak French—although indeed at St. Patrick's, the French Huguenots had leave to hold their services in the Lady Chapel and he speaks of " gabbling French with them on matters of business." But he had never been in France; and at this time Voltaire, who was in England and had met him, offered most flattering letters of introduction, describing Swift as " *un des hommes les plus extraordinaires que l'Angleterre ait produits.*" Bolingbroke had promised others, when suddenly on June 15 there came the news of George I's death on his road to Hanover. Swift wrote to Stella " the day we heard the King was dead and the circumstances of it." If we had that letter, much guessing and piecing-together would be spared. " Since then," he adds to Sheridan, on June 24, " we have been all in a hurry with millions of schemes. I deferred kissing the King and Queen's hands till the third day, when my friends at court chid me for deferring it so long." (" Friends at Court " means principally Mrs. Howard.) " I was just ready to go to France when the news arrived, and I came to town in order to begin my journey, but I was desired to delay it; and I then determined it a second time when, upon some new incidents, I was with great vehemence dissuaded from it by certain persons, whom I could not disobey. Thus things stand with me. . . . Here is a strange world, and our friend " (Stella) " would reproach me for my share in it; but it shall be short, for I design soon to return to the country."

Thus once again the hope of a changed situation sprang up in Swift's breast; and we learn by a side allusion that Stella never shared his desire to leave Ireland, which she had come to love. It seemed, indeed, as if chance had brought him on the scene at the exact lucky moment; for Walpole was out, and Swift was high in favour with the new Queen. But evidently the smart of his former disappointment remained and his inclination was to withdraw from all appearance of competition. One of those who urged him to stay was Bolingbroke: he wrote on June 17, not to " think of such an unmeaning journey " (to France) " when the opportunity of quitting Ireland for England is I believe fairly before you." But the adviser whom he held chiefly responsible was Mrs. Howard, and he never ceased to reproach her with it.

DEAN SWIFT, aged about 65

A mezzotint by MILLER *from the painting by* BINDON *in the British Museum*

Two years later, upon some report that she had fallen out of court favour, he wrote to her, on Pope's suggestion, and reviewed their relations : called her to witness that he had never attended on the Queen till after he "had received her repeated messages," and that he had never asked anything except, upon leaving in 1726, from Mrs. Howard "a present worth a guinea, and from her Majesty one worth ten pounds by way of a memorial." Mrs. Howard gave him a ring ; Caroline promised a medal—but it was not ready when he left, nor when he came back, and it was never given, although as he repeats again and again in letters to Lady Betty Germain (who defended Mrs. Howard) he had spent thirty-five guineas on the web of poplin. But the real sting was the slight. "I never asked anything more than a trifle," he wrote to Mrs. Howard, "as a memorial of some distinction which her Majesty graciously seemed to make between me and every common clergyman ; but that trifle was forgotten according to the usual method of Princes."

He complained also that Mrs. Howard had not been frank with him :

When I sent you a note, conjuring you to lay aside the character of a courtier and a favourite upon that occasion, your answer positively directed me not to go in that juncture ; and you said the same thing to my friends, who seemed to have power of giving me hints that I might reasonably hope for a settlement in England ; which, God knows, was no very great ambition, considering the station I should leave here of greater dignity, and which might have easily been managed to be disposed of as the Crown pleased. If these hints came from you, I affirm, you then acted too much like a courtier.

Undoubtedly in that first fortnight after George II's accession, hopes ran high among Swift's friends. He speaks of "a thousand schemes wherein they would have me engaged, which I embraced but coldly, because I like none of them." Then, as everyone knows, after a fortnight the Tory figurehead, Sir Spencer Compton, was displaced and Walpole back in the saddle. Swift left London to stay with Lord Oxford in Cambridgeshire, for discussion of the projected "History"—which, to his regret, had to be laid aside. Then he went back to Twickenham, and Mrs. Howard pelted him with letters, urging him to go and see the Queen who was now come down to Richmond. But giddiness and deafness had come back on him, and he sent excuses. At the end of August came a letter from Sheridan which made all other considerations trifling.

Swift had been less apprehensive about Stella when he left

than in the previous year. She was indeed an invalid; but on her birthday, March 13, he had offered her once more his tributary verse, and mustered up a touch of gaiety for the opening—

> This day, whate'er the fates decree,
> Shall still be kept with joy by me:
> This day then let us not be told,
> That you are sick, and I grow old.

Yet, he goes on, though " talk of spectacles and pills " may be put off for another time, reason can give consolation:

> From not the gravest of divines
> Accept for once some serious lines.

Suppose then there were no " future happiness and pain," is it possible that virtue:

> Should acting die, nor leave behind
> Some lasting pleasure in the mind? . . .
> Say, Stella, feel you no content,
> Reflecting on a life well spent?

and he recalls its merits:

> Your gen'rous boldness to defend
> An innocent and absent friend;
> That courage which can make you just
> To merit humbled in the dust; . . .
> That patience under tort'ring pain,
> Where stubborn Stoics would complain:
> Must these like empty shadows pass?

The moral argument continues; then comes the poetry, which, like all in Swift that can be called poetry, is as precise as prose—

> O then, whatever Heaven intends,
> Take pity on your pitying friends!
> Nor let your ills affect your mind,
> To fancy they can be unkind.
> Me, surely me, you ought to spare,
> Who gladly would your suff'rings share;
> Or give my scrap of life to you,
> And think it far beneath your due;
> You, to whose care so oft I owe
> That I'm alive to tell you so.

There is in that a tenderness which I do not find elsewhere in him. Evidently their rôles had changed, and he who had so often drawn upon her patience must now bear with the humours of a sick mind.

Yet the mere fact that he proposed a journey to France in June shows how little he was prepared for any sudden break-up in the invalid. We have not Sheridan's letter, but Swift took it as meaning an imminent end. " I expect before you read this to receive another from you with the most fatal news that can ever come to me. . . . Here is a triple cord of friendship broke which hath lasted thirty years, twenty-four of which in Ireland."

Again, as in the previous year, he shrank from returning, if, indeed, return he could.

I am strongly visited with a disease, that will at last cut me off, if I should this time escape ; if not, I have but a poor remainder, and that is below any wise man's valuing.

But he left Twickenham and went into solitude in London. From there he wrote on September 2nd in reply to another letter :

If I had any tolerable health, I would go this moment to Ireland ; yet I think I would not, considering the news I daily expect to hear from you. I have just received yours of August 24th ; I kept it an hour in my pocket with all the suspense of a man who expected to hear the worst news that fortune could give him, and at the same time was not able to hold up my head. These are the perquisites of living long ; the last act of life is always a tragedy at best, but it is a bitter aggravation to have one's best friend go before one. . . . I never was in such agonies as when I received your letter, and had it in my pocket. I am able to hold up my sorry head no longer.

On September 18 he was able to travel : his last act was to write to Mrs. Howard, begging that she should convey to the Queen his regrets that he had been " incapable of attending her as she was pleased to permit me." Horace Walpole says somewhere that Swift was " a brute who would have done anything for a mitre " : but at this moment mitres were little in his mind. He had not even kept his promises to Pope of another meeting ; and there is a note of reproach in Pope's letter :

I was sorry to find you could think yourself easier in any house than in mine, though at the same time I can allow for a tenderness in your way of thinking, even when it seemed to want that tenderness.

Swift's answer, giving as reason for his flight " that unsociable, comfortless deafness " has these moving words :

You are the best and kindest friend in the world, and I know nobody alive or dead to whom I am so much obliged ; and if ever you made me angry, it was for your too much care about me. I have often wished that God Almighty would be so easy to the weaknesses of mankind, as to let old friends be acquainted in another state ; and if I were to write an Utopia for heaven, that would be one of my schemes.

In truth his infirmities grew fast upon him, and if the word 'sane' means one of balanced judgment, there were many moments when he scarcely deserved it. For one instance, in the May of this year he had received a letter from Archbishop King, telling him that in his absence he must supply a proxy for King's visitation. This demand Swift conceived to be an innovation; "I take my Chapter to be my proxy; it is only through them that you visit me, and my sub-dean is to answer for me." Later authorities have held that Swift was justified in his contention, and did his duty by his office; but nothing could justify the outburst of fury, complaining of King's conduct to him for the last six-and-twenty years. There had never been entirely good understanding, and no doubt Swift was hard to bear; a letter from King written in 1713 concerning the few months which Swift had passed in Ireland after his appointment to the deanery says that he had behaved "with contempt" to all—which indeed is probable enough. But a letter of King's which Mr. Ball quotes, written in 1726, certainly suggests that King was disagreeably impressed by 'the Drapier's' amazing popularity. "As to our Irish copperfarden Dean, he has behaved himself very well in his station and been useful to the public, both in his charity and labours; all I wish is that you would not spoil him in London."

The tone of that, with its touch of condescending approbation, would have infuriated a less choleric man of much less admitted eminence than Swift; and if King habitually spoke so, in a small community, about his neighbour across the way, resentment was inevitable. But Swift in possession of himself knew as well as any that ever lived how to strike hard and not strike wildly; yet it appears from King's formal reply that the letter was sent off without date or address given. And that was early in his stay, when his mind was free from anxiety. At the end, when he felt himself too ill to stay even in Pope's house, when he expected from day to day the news of Stella's death, he was not even capable of taking a decision; and it appears that Sheridan, who was nearest to Stella in these months, wrote secretly to Pope urging that he should be urged to come over.

On September 12 Swift wrote to Worrall—"I am in such a condition of health that I cannot possibly travel." On the 18th he set out, and for greater speed pushed on to Holyhead, which he reached on Sunday, September 25, only to find himself delayed there a full week. He was alone, "except for a young fellow who smiles when he meets me and would fain be my companion : but it is not come to that yet." To pass the time, because he could not read by candlelight, he began with verses :

> Lo here I sit at holy head,
> With muddy ale and mouldy bread :
> I'm fastened both by wind and tide,
> I see the ships at anchor ride.
> All Christian vittals stink of fish,
> I'm where my enemyes would wish.
> Convict of lies is every Sign,
> The Inn has not one drop of wine.
> The Captain swears the sea's too rough,
> He has not passengers enough.
> And thus the Dean is forc'd to stay
> Till others come to help the pay. . . .

> I never was in haste before,
> To reach that slavish hateful shore.
> Before, I always found the wind
> To me was most malicious kind,
> But now the danger of a friend,
> On whom my fears and hopes depend,
> Absent from whom all Climes are curst,
> With whom I'm happy in the worst,
> With rage impatient makes me wait
> A passage to the Land I hate.

A long string of couplets lets go his spleen against " this land of slaves, where all are fools and all are knaves " ; but when the vein gave out, he fell to writing a journal of his journey and his stay at Holyhead.

I shall say nothing upon the suspense I am in about my dearest friend ; because that is a case extraordinary, and therefore by way of amusement, I will speak as if it were not in my thoughts, and only as a passenger who is in a scurvy unprovided comfortless place without one companion, and who therefore wants to be at home, where he hath all conveniences there proper for a gentleman of quality. I cannot read at night, and I have no books to read in the day. I have no subject in my head at present to write on. I dare not send my linnen to be washed, for fear of being called away at half an hour's warning, and then I must leave them behind me, which is a serious point. I live at great expense, without one comfortable bit or sup. I am afraid of joining with passengers for fear of getting acquaintance with Irish. The days are short, and I have five hours at night to spend by myself before I go to bed. I should be glad to converse with farmers or shopkeepers, but none of them speak English. A dog is better company than the vicar, for I remember him of old. What can I do but write everything that comes into my head ? But the worst part is my half-hourly longing, and hopes and vain expectations of wind; so that I live in suspense, which is the worst circumstance of human nature. . . .

The master of the pacquet boat, one Jones, hath not treated me with the least civility, altho' Wat [1] gave him my name. In short I come from being used like an Emperor to be used worse than a Dog at Holyhead. . . . Pray pity poor Wat, for he is called dunce, puppy, and liar 500 times an hour, and yet he means not ill, for he means nothing. Oh, for a dozen bottles of deanery wine and a slice of bread and butter. Whoever would wish to live long should live here, for a day is longer than a week, and if the weather be foul, as long as a fortnight. Yet here I would live with two or three friends, in a warm house, and good wine—much better than being a Slave in Ireld. [2]

On the Friday the wind came fair and they got aboard, but within half an hour it began to blow in their teeth and they had to run back to anchor after three or four hours' tossing. When they sailed at last, it was to Carlingford Lough, and here it seems Sheridan met Swift with news that Stella was somewhat better. Moreover, the journey had been good medicine for both giddiness and deafness.

The few letters from Swift that we have belonging to this winter are entirely normal. One of January 18, 1728, to Carteret, shows him using the privilege of old acquaintance to advise, with sound wisdom, against a project of Dublin University to limit the choice of professors to Fellows of the House—a " narrow and partial opinion which can only tend to mend fellowships and spoil professorships," though he would gladly see preference given to the home product " upon equal deserving." A fierce note at the end, concerning the offer made to Gay that he should be gentleman usher to the Queen's two-year-old daughter, shows how constant still was his preoccupation with that little circle of friends. But none of those friends heard from him a word or hint concerning what was, as he had foreseen, " the greatest event that ever befell him."

Stella died on Sunday, January 28; and once more we are in the region of legend.

The only sure evidence that we have is from Swift himself, and it lets us know, first, that he was not present when she died; more than this, that he was that evening receiving company as usual at the deanery, and that when the news came he concealed it and continued to wear the same countenance to his friends.

[1] His servant.
[2] It is an odd comment on Swift's fame that the inhabitants of Holyhead called their square after him, ' Swift Square.' People would sooner be damned by him than not noticed.

Then, he sought relief from disordered thoughts in writing. Here are his words, singularly devoid of emotion:

This day, being Sunday, January 28, 1727-8, about eight o'clock at night, a servant brought me a note, with an account of the death of the truest, most virtuous, and valuable friend, that I, or perhaps any other person, was ever blessed with. She expired about six in the evening of this day; and as soon as I am left alone, which is about eleven at night, I resolve, for my own satisfaction, to say something of her life and character.

Then follows the summary of her birth and life, which has been quoted already, and is matter of fact enough. Yet the last sentence gives the explanation. "Properly speaking, she has been dying six months, but kept alive, almost against nature, by the generous kindness of two physicians and the care of her friends." In such an illness, grief wears itself out. The cry of bereavement that recurs again and again in his letters from London when that first threat reached him, is not to be looked for here. What can be traced is the oppression of a vast weight of sorrow. After the sentence that has just been quoted come these words: "Thus far I writ the same night between eleven and twelve." Yet the entry for that date does not close here: sleep in all probability would not come, and he took up his pen again to sketch her character; how never once he had heard her "make a wrong judgment of persons, books, or affairs"; how she had "a gracefulness somewhat more than human, in every motion, word and action"; how in an afternoon's or evening's conversation, by the agreement of all her friends, "she never failed of delivering the best thing that was said in the company"; yet, "she never mistook the understanding of others; nor ever said a severe word but where a much severer was deserved."

Her servants loved, and almost adored her at the same time. She would, upon occasions, treat them with freedom; yet her demeanour was so awful, that they durst not fail in the least point of respect.

That ends the first night's writing: here is the next day, and the next to that:

Jan. 29.—My head aches, and I can write no more.
Jan. 30.—This is the night of the funeral, which my sickness will not suffer me to attend. It is now nine at night; and I am removed into another apartment, that I may not see the light in the church, which is just over against the window of my bed-chamber.

The burying had to be done at night because she was to lie

in the nave of Swift's cathedral, at the foot of one of the great pillars. The window from which Swift saw, and could not bear to see, the lights, is still there, on the upper floor next the drawing-room, for that side of the house escaped the fire which destroyed much else about 1780.

He wrote long that night, relating that proof of her courage which has been quoted already, and adding that she " was never known to cry out or discover any fears in a coach or on horseback, or any uneasiness by those sudden accidents with which most of her sex either by weakness or affectation appear so much disordered."

She never had the least absence of mind in conversation, or given to interruption, or appeared eager to put in her word, by waiting impatiently until another had done. She spoke in a most agreeable voice, in the plainest words, never hesitating, except out of modesty before new faces, where she was somewhat reserved; nor among her nearest friends, ever spoke much at a time. . . .

She had a true taste of wit and good sense, both in poetry and prose, and was a perfect good critic of style; neither was it easy to find a more proper or impartial judge, whose advice an author might better rely on, if he intended to send a thing into the world, provided it was on a subject that came within the compass of her knowledge.

He praises the skilfulness of her economy, which made her small revenues " pass for much more considerable than they really were," but had always " a stronger bent to the liberal side."

She bought clothes as seldom as possible, and those as plain and cheap as consisted with the situation she was in; and wore no lace for many years. Either her judgment or her fortune was extraordinary in the choice of those on whom she bestowed her charity, for it went farther in doing good than double the sum from any other hand. And I have heard her say, " she always met with gratitude from the poor "; which must be owing to her skill in distinguishing proper objects, as well as her gracious manner in relieving them.

But she had another quality that much delighted her, although it might be thought a kind of check upon her bounty; however, it was a pleasure she could not resist: I mean that of making agreeable presents; wherein I never knew her equal, although it be an affair of as delicate a nature as most in the course of life. She used to define a present, " That it was a gift to a friend of something he wanted, or was fond of, and which could not be easily gotten for money."

The only fault that he finds in her is that—

When she saw any of the company very warm in a wrong opinion, she was more inclined to confirm them in it, than to oppose them. The excuse she commonly gave, when her friends asked the reason, was, " That it prevented noise, and saved time."

Almost at the close comes this observation:

> She loved Ireland much better than the generality of those who owe both their birth and riches to it.

She had indeed reason to love a country where she had "the esteem and friendship of all who knew her, and the universal good report of all who ever heard of her, if I am told the truth by those who keep general conversation."

It is necessary now to say something of the legendary accretions to actual record. According to one story, Swift was overheard to offer on her death-bed public recognition of their marriage, and she to answer, "It is too late." According to another, much more definite, she begged Swift in the presence of Sheridan, who was attending her as a clergyman, to let her die his acknowledged wife. "Swift made no reply, but turning on his heel walked silently out of the room, nor ever saw her afterwards during the few days she lived."

This account, though written long after, comes from Sheridan's son. It seems to me entirely irreconcilable with anything that Swift wrote to Stella, or wrote about Stella, or with the good nature which was so often attributed to him—even by Vanessa. Yet Sheridan writes as an admirer and cannot be suspected of malevolence. But what follows in his story shakes its credit. Mrs. Johnson, he says, roused by indignation, "inveighed against Swift's cruelty in the bitterest terms, and sending for a lawyer made her will bequeathing her fortune by her own name to charitable uses." Now Stella's will was made a full month before she died; further, it conforms exactly to the description of her intentions which Swift sent to Worrall eighteen months earlier. It was in short, at all points, the will he approved her making, and this part of Sheridan's statement is demonstrably untrue. There is even one further point which seems to indicate that Stella's will is a proof of her affection to Swift, and not of estrangement. She directed that her strong-box and all the papers she had in it and elsewhere should be given to him. Now, in the account of her which he wrote after her death, dwelling on her economy, he says that she was never without ready money, "insomuch that on her death when her nearest friends thought her very bare, her executors found in her strong-box about one hundred and fifty pounds in gold." I believe that she intended making a bequest to Swift of about one tithe of her property, yet in such a way as not to publish the fact.

There one must leave it. On the marble slab next to her tomb the epitaph composed by Swift tells how she was " celebrated under the name of Stella in the poems of Jonathan Swift, dean of this cathedral." Yet I think the truest epitaph for her must be sought elsewhere. I do not find any reference to her after her death in any of Swift's letters, of which hundreds are preserved. He spoke of her neither to his English nor his Irish circle : a door was shut. The only glimpse through that door is in a letter to Pope written two years after Stella was buried :

A mischief on it, I find neither prose nor rhyme will come to me as it used ; but that is not the worst, for I am daily harder to please, and less care taken whether I am pleased or not. I dine alone, or only with my housekeeper. I go to my closet immediately after dinner, there sit till eleven, and then to bed. The best company here grows hardly tolerable, and those who were formerly tolerable are now insupportable. This is my life five nights in seven.

" Less care taken whether I was pleased or not." That perhaps was the essential difference between the last period of Swift's life and all that went before it. There was no one to stand between this solitary and his accumulating anger against the whole scheme of things.

CHAPTER XIX

THE IRISH PATRIOT

FOR ten years after Stella's death, Swift was in full activity; some of his most memorable pamphlets date from these years, and so does the plan of that charitable foundation which still witnesses to his enlightened philanthropy. During the first half, at all events, of this period many of his best letters were written; but by an odd irony, the main theme of this Irish patriot is his desire to escape from Ireland, if only for a brief visit, to England. That was the expression of his private mind; his public preoccupations were all Irish. We have a mass of his writings in prose and verse ranging over the whole ten years, but with one notable exception, the lines written by anticipation about his own death, all that has interest belongs to the political literature of Ireland. An exhaustive study of them would need several chapters of Irish history, which are not essential for a study of Swift's life; a very brief outline of the facts will suffice for comprehension of what moved him to action, what he attempted and what he achieved.

The people of Ireland suffered from two sorts of oppression, external and internal. The first came from the English Government, which destroyed the power of the Irish parliament to legislate effectively, and itself passed laws which crippled every form of Irish industry. The second had two forms; oppression of the Catholic people by a system of penal laws; oppression of the tenants by rackrenting landlords, or the middlemen to whom they farmed out the lands.

Swift's agitation was directed against the English control of Irish affairs. It is probable that he was first moved by the plight of those loom-workers by whom his deanery and cathedral were surrounded, and over whom he had jurisdiction in the Liberties; for his first intervention in Irish politics (except on Church matters) was his proposal that Irish people should give a preference to Irish-made wares, and, as we should say, boycott what came from England. This was his reply to England's prohibition of the export of Irish woollens, and other produce. In the affair of

Wood's halfpence he resisted a new encroachment on the privileges of Ireland, which had heretofore minted its own copper, and an affront to the Irish Parliament, whose representations against the contract had been disregarded. With great skill he raised both the question of Parliament's abstract right and of the concrete social injury inflicted by a debased coinage. Thus in the matter of Irish manufactures he spoke for the whole people, since Catholic and Protestant were equally involved; and in that of coinage, though the Parliament whose rights were denied was one in which Catholics had no representation, he made the entire country feel that every man would be cheated even in the price of a pot of ale.

As to the internal oppression, Swift denounced again and again the rackrenting landlords; and here he spoke for the Catholics even more than for the Protestants, since nearly all landlords were Protestant and most tenants Catholic. He did not limit himself to denunciation; he advised all landlords who were his friends to be moderate in their demands; a notable instance is in a letter to his old friend the printer Barber, who had risen to be Lord Mayor of London and so had much interest in the Irish Society, a London company which owned Londonderry and Coleraine with many lands about these places. He preached by example; he himself had found the lands belonging to the deanery let for a bare fifth of their value, had never raised them above twenty per cent, and had been very moderate in exacting fines for renewal.

But on the constitutional question of the penal laws, Swift said no word. As the friend of Pope he was necessarily without strong prejudice against Catholics; and the question of their status was brought before him in a long document by the Chevalier Wogan, an Irish gentleman in the Spanish service, who was a scholar of repute. Swift replied to Wogan's literary compliments with expressions of regard, but avoided the political issue.

Indeed, as a practical politician, he could at that period hardly expect to achieve any result by raising it, especially as he was suspect of Jacobite tendencies; and if he raised it, he would lessen whatever influence he had. Yet I see no ground to believe that he would, if he could, have given equal rights in the State to Catholics.

His only concrete achievement in politics was to enforce the withdrawal of Wood's halfpence; and after a few years a new contract was issued by English authority to an English speculator. But he had made Ireland feel and think. The result was seen a generation later, first when all Ireland turned " American " in sympathy during the war in which the American colonies resented similar though much lighter restrictions on their freedom, and broke away : secondly, in 1782, when Ireland in arms demanded and obtained the restoration of power to its own parliament, and the abolition of restrictions on its commerce.

Yet even after Grattan's triumph there remained the problems for which Swift had proposed no remedy—the excessive power of Irish landlords, and the division of Ireland's people into an ascendancy and a servile class. The consequences of this division led to the rebellion of 1798, the extinction of the Irish parliament at the Union, and then to a revolution, half agrarian, half political, which went on by stages over more than a century and is hardly yet complete. It cannot be said that Swift saw far. But he saw intensely ; and to-day it is not remembered in Ireland that he raised no voice for the Catholics, who were in the main the old Irish. What is remembered is that he, though an Englishman, stood for Ireland against England.

The Drapier letters are the completest expression of his views on Ireland ; but the series of his tracts, greater and lesser, is long. He himself, however, in his letters to his English friends mentions two ; and it may suffice to describe these. The first is called " A Short View of the State of Ireland," and it was published in the beginning of 1728, just after Stella's death.

It is an answer to the assertion that Ireland was prosperous because rents and the price of land were rising. In this pamphlet there is no use of his habitual irony. He sets out " the true causes of any country flourishing," and examines them in relation to Ireland.

In point of soil and climate Ireland is as well situated as England, and " the native productions which both Kingdoms deal in, are very near on equality," excepting mines and minerals. In industry of the people, " our misfortune is not altogether owing to our own fault, but to a million of discouragements. . . . The conveniency of ports and havens which Nature bestowed us so liberally is of no more use to us, than a beautiful prospect to a man shut up in a dungeon." The nation has no shipping of its own, because all trade must be carried in English-built ships sailing from English ports ; and the right to export freely Irish live stock, dead meat, cheese and butter is denied. These things happen because there is denied also the sixth condition of prosperity, that of " being governed only by laws made with their own consent, for otherwise they are not a free People. . . . We are in the condition of patients who have physic sent them by doctors at a distance, strangers to their constitution and the nature of their disease."

Residence of the Princes, concourse of foreigners "for education, curiosity or pleasure or as to a general mart of trade," are all conditions lacking in Ireland. "Those who have the misfortune to be born here, have the least title to employment." One-third part of the rents of Ireland is spent in England, which with the profit of employments "will amount to a full half of the income of the whole Kingdom, all clear profit to England." Then, with a momentary lapse into irony, he says, "Let the worthy Commissioners who come from England ride round the Kingdom, and observe the face of Nature, or the face of the natives, the improvement of the land . . . the vast number of ships in our harbours and docks . . . the roads crowded with carriers laden with rich manufactures. With what envy and admiration would these gentlemen return from so delightful a progress ? . . . But my heart is too heavy to continue, for it is manifest that whatever stranger took such a journey, would be apt to think himself travelling in Lapland or Ysland . . . when he saw . . . the families of farmers who pay great rents, living in filth and nastiness upon butter-milk and potatoes, without a shoe or stocking to their feet, or a house so convenient as an English hog-sty to receive them."

There is not one argument used to prove the riches of Ireland, which is not a logical demonstration of its poverty. The rise of our rents is squeezed out of the very blood and vitals, and clothes, and dwellings of the tenants who live worse than English beggars. The lowness of interest, in all other countries a sign of wealth, is in us a proof of misery, there being no trade to employ any borrower.

It has been said that Swift exaggerated the misery which he saw about him ; and no doubt he painted with a sombre brush. In the old Ireland, as more recently in the old Russia, there were pleasant oases of wealth and even splendour ; but they were set in dreadful swamps of poverty ; and this was true of the capital as of the country. I have seen recently the letters of an English lawyer who came over, a generation after this tract was written, to take up a highly-paid post ; he reported enthusiastically of the profusion of all good things in Dublin and of the security with which rents for land were paid. Yet half a century after his day, an English Parliamentary Commission reported that half the population of Ireland had no food other than potatoes and milk, and that even milk was not available for a greater part of them. Two years after that Report was sent in, the great famine set grim proof on it, reducing the population by two millions out of eight, between 1846 and 1851.

That tragedy was only the awful climax in a series ; and in the year when Swift wrote his view of the State of Ireland, Ireland was in the throes of a lesser famine, which lasted over three years. His correspondence is full of it. Those who read the tract which he published in 1729 do not always realize the circumstances in which he wrote this *Modest Proposal for preventing the Children of Poor People from being a Burden to their Parents and Country, and for making them Beneficial to the Public.*

This time, irony had full sway :

It is true a child, just dropped from its dam, may be supported by her milk for a solar year with little other nourishment, at most not above the value of two shillings, which the mother may certainly get, or the value in scraps, by her lawful occupation of begging, and it is exactly at one year old that I propose to provide for them, in such a manner as, instead of being a charge upon their parents, or the parish, or wanting food or raiment for the rest of their lives, they shall, of the contrary, contribute to the feeding and partly to the clothing on many thousands. . . .

I have been assured by a very knowing American of my acquaintance in London, that a young healthy child well nursed is at a year old a most delicious, nourishing, and wholesome food, whether stewed, roasted, baked, or boiled, and I make no doubt that it will equally serve in a fricassee, or a ragoût. . . .

I have reckoned upon a medium, that a child just born will weigh twelve pounds, and in a solar year if tolerably nursed increaseth to 28 pounds. . . .

I grant this food will be somewhat dear, and therefore very proper for landlords, who, as they have already devoured most of the parents, seem to have the best title to the children.

All the detail of the plan, the reservation of breeding stock, the proportion of males to females so reserved, the advantage of flaying the carcass (the skin of which artificially dressed will make admirable gloves for ladies and summer boots for fine gentlemen) and the provision of shambles, are set out with the same gravity as may be observed in the descriptive passages of *Gulliver*. In the same spirit, imagined arguments against it are dismissed ; for instance, that it does nothing to relieve the nation of the sick or aged poor.

But I am not in the least pain upon that matter, because it is very well known, that they are every day dying, and rotting, by cold, and famine, and filth, and vermin, as fast as can be reasonably expected.

Against these he arrays the advantages, of which it is only necessary to mention the sixth, in which irony culminates :

This would be a great inducement to marriage, which all wise nations have either encouraged by rewards, or enforced by laws and penalties. . . .

Then in his summing up, he gives the irony a new turn.

I can think of no one objection, that will possibly be raised against this proposal, unless it should be urged that the number of people will be thereby much lessened in the kingdom. This I freely own, and was indeed one principal design in offering it to the world. I desire the reader will observe, and I calculate my remedy *for this one individual Kingdom of Ireland, and for no other that ever was, is, or, I think, ever can be upon earth.*

" Therefore," he says, " let no man talk to me of other expedients " —and there follows a rapid enumeration of such things as he had elsewhere proposed—from taxing absentees at five shillings in the pound down to " putting a spirit of industry and skill into our shopkeepers."

A last stroke of irony is the great recommendation that they run no danger of disobliging England by competition in supply :

For this kind of commodity will not bear exportation, the flesh being of too tender a consistence, to admit a long continuance in salt, *although perhaps I could name a country, which would be glad to eat up our whole nation without it.*

The concluding paragraph is a perfect example of the Gulliverian manner :

I profess in the sincerity of my heart that I have not the least personal interest in endeavouring to promote this necessary work, having no other motive than the *public good of my country, by advancing our trade, providing for infants, relieving the poor, and giving some pleasure to the rich.* I have no children, by which I can propose to get a single penny ; the youngest being nine years old, and my wife past child-bearing.

It cannot be said that this tract failed of reaching the English public ; for in February, 1730, a few months after it was printed, Pope's friend, Lord Bathurst, wrote to Swift a letter full of ingenious and witty amplifications on the proposal, which he thought should by no means be limited to Ireland. In short, it is clear that the English enjoyed it as an admirable example of Swift's peculiar humour. The same would appear to be true of all his other writings on Irish themes, except only the Drapier's letters, which produced concrete results by threatening a riot. Neither the weight of argument, nor the sting of irony, had the least effect on English policy or English public opinion in this matter.

But in Ireland it was not so. A distinct nation began to be

conscious of itself as a separate entity; full of internal fissures and cleavages almost irreparable, yet pressed together by a common sense of wrong which this English-Irishman, unwillingly Irish, yet Irish by his resentments, drove home to the apprehension and the spirit of Catholic and Protestant alike.

For a general description of the political tracts and of their effect on the reader, it would not be easy to better what was written in 1730 by Lord Bathurst in imitation of Swift's own ironic way of praise:

You have overturned and supported Ministers; you have set kingdoms in a flame by your pen. Pray, what is there in that, but having the knack of hitting the passions of mankind? With that alone, and a little knowledge of ancient and modern history, and seeing a little farther into the inside of things than the generality of men, you have made this bustle. There is no wit in any of them: I have read them all over, and do not remember any of those pretty flowers, those just antitheses, which one meets with so frequently in the French writers; none of those clever turns upon words, nor those apt quotations out of Latin authors, which the writers of the last age among us abounded in; none of those pretty similes, which some of our modern authors adorn their works with, that are not only a little like the thing they would illustrate, but are also like twenty other things. In short, as often as I have read any of your tracts, I have been so tired with them, that I have never been easy till I got to the end of them. I have found my brain heated, my imagination fired, just as if I was drunk. A pretty thing, indeed, for one of your gown to value himself upon, that with sitting still an hour in his study, he has often made three kingdoms drunk at once.

Thus, the years which followed on Stella's death saw Swift at the height of his intellectual powers and in such fame as few men have attained to; worshipped by the crowd at his doors, and courted by all that was most distinguished in Ireland and in England. Yet everything was dust and ashes to him. There was no pleasure even in the praise of those he valued most, Pope and Bolingbroke, the two other members of what he called " a peculiar triumvirate who have nothing to expect or to fear."

I do profess without affectation, that your kind opinion of me as a patriot, since you call it so, is what I do not deserve; because what I do is owing to perfect rage and resentment, and the mortifying sight of slavery, folly, and baseness about me, among which I am forced to live.

" Does not the corruption of men in high places eat into your heart and corrupt your spirits? " he once asked Delany—who, good, easy, prosperous man (prospering largely through Swift's good offices with Carteret), found the world by no means so bad a place. The mood lasted, and darkened to blackness. " You think as I ought to think," he wrote to Bolingbroke early in 1730, " that it is time for me to have done with the world, and so I would if I could get into a better before I was called into the best, and not die here like a poisoned rat in a hole." Such force of expression does not come without an answering force of the feeling it expresses ; and this man was built too big for ordinary uses. It was purgatory for him, as Arbuthnot saw, to be condemned to " manage a chapter and a choir of singing men." It is easy to sit in judgment. He was arrogant. He lacked above all things humility. " Gentleness and cheerfulness, these are the perfect virtues, these come before all morality," is a saying of Stevenson's that he would have spat upon. Yet who wants to sit in judgment when a Titan writhes on the crag where destiny has fettered him ?

The torment was physical, all the more because his body remained vigorous. " I can walk eight or ten miles a day and ride thirty Irish ones " (close on forty English), he wrote to Pope when he was sixty-four. But the use of his powers alike of mind and body was denied him by the persistent disease. " I have been these ten weeks confined by my old disorders of deafness and giddiness," he wrote to his publisher Motte in February, 1728—a week or two after Stella's death.—He was in Dublin most of that spring, exulting at least in his friends' successes.

" The ' Beggar's Opera ' has knocked down Gulliver, I hope to see Pope's Dulness " (the *Dunciad*) " knock down the Beggar's Opera, but not till it has fully done its job. . . . To expose vice and to make people laugh with innocence does more public service than all the Ministers of State from Adam to Walpole." So he wrote to Gay. Part of the Opera's " job " was to make Gay solvent, and there is much concern about that. " Wealth is liberty, and liberty is a blessing fittest for a philosopher, and Gay is a slave just by two thousand pounds too little," he wrote to Pope, fearing that Gay would return from Bath " with twenty pounds more flesh and two hundred less in money." But delight over Gay's fame, and anticipations for Pope did not fill his time : he must be busy. " Finding it troublesome to read at night, and the company here growing tasteless, I am always writing bad prose or worse verses, either of rage or raillery, whereof some few escape to give offence or mirth and the rest are burnt." So he told Lord Bolingbroke in 1730. A chief outlet was in a weekly *Intelligencer*, written by him and Sheridan, his best ally in pursuit of *la bagatelle*.

But Sheridan knew that a change was needed while the void left by Stella was still aching; and probably by his intervention, Swift was asked to pay a visit to Sir Arthur Acheson, a Tory knight who lived with his lady at Market Hill near Armagh. There Swift went in June, 1728—not only he, but his equipage, three horses and two servants, for so he always went attended; and there he stayed till the end of January. The visit had been a success, as he told Pope when it was over:

> I lived very easily in the country. Sir Arthur is a man of sense, and a scholar, has a good voice, and my Lady a better. She is perfectly well bred and desirous to improve her understanding, which is very good, but cultivated too much like a fine lady. She was my pupil here, and severely chid when she read wrong. With that, and walking, and making twenty little amusing improvements, and writing family verses of mirth by way of libels on my Lady, my time passed very well and in very great order.

Swift was at Market Hill again for three months in 1729 and as many more in the year following. The scattered writings of his stay there—a whole basketful of verses—show us 'the Dean' as Ireland knew him and adored him.

In the first place, before 1728 was out, Sir Arthur was writing triumphantly :

> Happy, O Market-Hill! at least,
> That court and courtiers have no taste :
> You never else had known the Dean,
> But, as of old, obscurely lain ;
> But now your name with Penshurst vies,
> And wing'd with fame shall reach the skies.

The Dean himself was so enamoured of the neighbourhood as to have actually rented a piece of ground from his host and proposed to build on it. Word of this reached Bolingbroke, who, with prudence inspired by his own follies, advised against it; and Swift answered that he had come to a better mind. He had had enough of building; for at the Deanery, "Naboth's vineyard" had cost him a pretty penny with walling it—though it had given him the chance to plant espaliers of his own and to indulge the taste which generally got play on other people's property. Here at Market Hill, an easy-going indolent host, devoid of taste for sport or for improvements, let his guest become overseer in general and set about embellishing. The verses give us a score of pictures : they are mostly written as my lady's complaints against the Dean. He is " all the day sauntering, with labourers bantering, among his colleagues, a parcel of Teagues : hailfellow well met, all dirty and wet, find out if you can, who's master, who's man, who makes the best figure, the Dean or the digger." Like all the great humorists, Swift loved to rub shoulders with low life and to get the tang of rough speech : he scattered largesse among the Teagues, sixpences and plugs of tobacco. For one of his fundamental traits was a love of giving ; he would make a hullabaloo in Dublin about getting in before it rained, to save sixpence on a coach fare, and then, safe at his door, would give the sixpence to one of the old applewomen, Cancerina or Stumpalinda : for he had names for them all.

That was only one side of his diversions ; the other was the planning of improvements, walks, grottoes, caves and what not. Market Hill has changed its name and is now Gosford Castle, but it still shows 'the Dean's Walk,' 'the Dean's Seat.' There he would sit, " perplexing his wit, in search of a motto, to fix on a grotto "—while meantime the master of the house went on with his meditations, letting the guest have sway—and not in the least grateful because the guest showed him how " the cottagers conspire to cut his hedges down for fire " : how his cows are milked surreptitiously and his meadows rooted by their pigs. It was part of the play when you entertained ' the Drapier ' that he should take possession, should direct operations, and even interfere in the cellar " in quality of butler's mate " ; settling with Dennis " what pints may best for bottles pass, just to give every man a glass : when proper to produce the best, and what may serve a common guest."

As to the lady of the house, she had no escape from servitude : she must be dragged out for country walks, " familiar grown to dirt or wet," " through bogs and through briers by the worst of all squires " ; and after all, submit to observations on her highheeled shoes. Even her person does not escape : she must be called Snipe and Skinnybonia, must listen to Rabelaisian comments on what Sir Arthur suffers abed from her elbows ; worse still, she must be put to reading, " instead of new plays, dull Bacon's essays," and face a catechism on her task over breakfast, from a schoolmaster who " rages and frets and his manners forgets." That was the Dean, as Ireland knew and loved him ; a great man who chose to be an original, an eccentric, a great " characther."

All this time, he was being pelted with exhortations to come over to England—from Pope and Bolingbroke, of course ; but evidently he was more tempted by invitations which from 1730 onwards came in the first instance from Gay. That amiable improvident had been taken in hand by a very great lady, the Duchess of Queensberry. The sequel to the " Beggar's Opera " was forbidden production (not very unnaturally, since all the world had clapped and stared " when two great ministers were in a box together " and the song was

> If you mention vice and bribe,
> 'Tis so pat to the tribe.
> Each cries : That was levell'd at me.

Thereupon the Duchess in all her imperious beauty went to court and ostentatiously solicited subscriptions for the publication of " Polly." Sir Robert's master forbad her the court, and she, with her Duke and her poet in tow, went down to live the simple life at Amesbury, near Stonehenge.

Swift had never seen the Duchess since she was a child at the house of her father, Lord Clarendon, whom he knew well. In 1727, when he was at Twickenham, she called one day, but he was out of humour and would only peep through the curtains. Now she sent "her services"; but there was also allusion to the fact that Gay had shocked her by saying that Swift—a great authority on manners—ate with his knife. Swift replied that his custom was to demand definite advances from all ladies ; and that as to the fork, it was the fault of Pope's housekeeping which provided only two-pronged instruments, and that it was " morally impossible with a bi-dental fork to convey a morsel of beef with the encumbrance of mustard and turnips into your mouth at once." Gay replied again that the Dean was really wanted at Amesbury, and would be welcome to a three-pronged fork : and that the Duchess must speak for herself. This is how she did it :

> I would fain have you come. I cannot say you will be welcome, for I do not know you, and perhaps I shall not like you, but if I do not, unless you are a very vain person, you shall know my thoughts as soon as I do myself.
>
> C. Q.

So it went on month after month, long letters coming, in which Gay and the Duchess divided the paper between them; and Swift played with the idea of making his journey.

There was nothing in Ireland that held him. All his descriptions of his existence come to the same ; either he " eats his morsel alone like a King," or else in company with Mrs. Brent. Here is detail to Pope in January, 1730.

I dine *tête-à-tête* five days a week with my old Presbyterian house-keeper, whom I call Sir Robert and so do all my friends and neighbours. I am in my chamber at five, there sit alone till eleven, and then to bed. I write pamphlets and follies merely for amusement, and when they are finished, or I grow weary in the middle, I cast them into the fire, partly out of dislike, and chiefly because I know they will signify nothing. I walk much every day, and ride once or twice a week, and so you have the whole state of my life.

On Sunday evenings he was always at home—"it costs me six bottles of wine to people I cannot keep out. I do not visit one lord temporal or spiritual, nor am acquainted with above three squires and half a dozen parsons." Exception must be made here for the Lord-Lieutenant and his lady, to whom Swift thought it proper to pay some court, but paid it willingly. Carteret, he wrote, had "a genteeler manner of binding the chains of this Kingdom than most of his predecessors"; and six times he had given promotion on Swift's request. Lady Carteret is praised with less reserve, "the best queen we have known in Ireland these many years." She received verses from the Dean, in his best complimentary manner, and paid for them with a tea-caddy of her own workmanship; but her mother, Lady Worsley, outdid this with another, larger and more elegant still, designed to hold writing materials —a fine piece of joinery ornamented with lacquer by her ladyship's hands. It stands in the Deanery to-day.

Yet these great folks were only distinguished acquaintances, and he had constantly the longing for those with whom he had "made his friendships and left his desires"—those whom he counted his equals. But there was always something to hold him back. One impediment was a vexatious and protracted lawsuit that threatened half of his whole savings—some sixteen hundred pounds: yet I think more decisive were his infirmities. "For my own part," he tells Pope, "I think when a man is sick or sickly, great Lords and Ladies, let them be ever so civil, familiar, and so friendly, are not half so commodious as middling folks whom one may govern as one pleases and who will think it an honour and happiness to attend us, to talk or be silent, laugh or look grave, just as they are directed." He wrote in the same sense, though less explicitly, to Gay. If he fell sick at Amesbury, the Duchess could not nurse him, nor her women. The Duchess replied very firmly that she could and would; and it is a pity he never made the experiment. This remarkable lady had transformed the fat, lazy, improvident Gay, who now had three thousand pounds to his name ("and a fence about them," as Swift desired); who had even become a sportsman and wrote with pride of having shot five brace of partridges and four and a half of quails that season (next year it was nineteen brace), and who now drank nothing. This, however, was no inducement for Swift, for, amongst other difficulties, he descanted on the abstemiousness of Pope and Bolingbroke (a recent convert to temperance). Did Gay remember how, when they had had four glasses out of a pint, Pope would retire and say, Gentlemen I leave you to your wine! The Dean drank little, and that little mixed with water and sugar, but he could not bear that there should be a stint of claret.

And so the exchanges went on, always hopefully, till in the end of 1732 Pope wrote announcing Gay's sudden death. So ended these letters. "They made up," Swift wrote to him, "a great part of the little happiness I could have here." That is one milestone on the downward journey. Five years earlier, the death of Congreve, "whom I loved from my youth and who, surely, besides his other talents was a very agreeable companion," had led Swift to wish "almost that I had never had a friend" and to praise the felicity of one of his Dublin allies, Dr. Helsham, a well-to-do, good-natured, scholarly physician, lavish in entertainment to abundance of friends:

They pass the evening with him at cards, with plenty of good meat and wine, eight or a dozen together. He loves them all, and they him. He has twenty of these at command. If one of them dies, it is no more than "poor Tom." He gets another, or takes up with the rest, and is no more moved than at the loss of his cat. He offends nobody, is easy with everybody. Is not this the true happy man?

No wonder Pope said to Swift, "You have a desperate hand at dashing out a character by great strokes, and at the same time a delicate one at fine touches."

None of these losses came light to Swift; and he was always in anxiety for Pope, whom he loved best, and for Bolingbroke, whom he most admired. Characteristically, he is always solicitous for their fortune. One passage addressed to Bolingbroke shows him at his best as an adviser:

My Lord, I have no other notion of economy than that it is the parent of liberty and ease, and I am not the only friend you have who has chid you in his heart for the neglect of it, though not with his mouth, as I have done. For there is a silly error in the world, even among friends otherwise very good, not to intermeddle with men's affairs in such nice matters. And, my Lord, I have made a maxim, that should be writ in letters of diamonds, that a wise man ought to have money in his head, but not in his heart.

Pope indeed never gave him ground for such anxiety; but it was a matter of jubilation when he learnt that his friend could afford to give away a hundred pounds a year. Here for once we have Swift speaking simply without restraint or irony:

> I am under the necessity of some little paltry figure in the station I am, but I make it as little as possible. As to the other part, you are base, because I thought myself as great a giver as ever was of my ability; and yet in proportion you exceed, and have kept it till now a secret even from me, when I wondered how you were able to live with your whole little revenue.

How much that tells of the secret pride in generosity under curmudgeonly airs; and of the ceaseless vigilant eye on a friend's concerns.

Yet separation had its effect. In 1734, almost two years after Gay's death, he says to Mrs. Pendarves (better known as Mrs. Delany), " Madam, it is a very cold scent to continue a correspondence with one whom we never expect to see. . . . Mr. Pope and my Lord Bolingbroke themselves begin to fail me, in seven years." Yet the one man who was most truly like-minded with him, Arbuthnot, wrote repeatedly and got no answers: it is hard to know why, for when at last Swift picked up the thread, his memory had no trace of the letters. By that time, in 1734, he could only talk to Arbuthnot of the prospects of mortality. The reason which he urged against coming over was now one of economy. " I am not in a position to keep horses and servants in London." But then comes a revealing touch. " I could not live with my Lord Bolingbroke or Mr. Pope; they are both too temperate and too wise for me, and too profound and too poor." " Infinitely too philosophical," he adds, on the same theme in another letter to Pulteney. There was too much " Essay on Man " in the atmosphere, and in the end it seems to me that Bolingbroke's sententious and abstract lucubrations had worn out Swift's patience. But writing to Arbuthnot as one unphilosophical human being to another man, he gives other considerations that weighed with his humour:

> And how could I ride over their cursed roads in winter, and be turned into a ditch by every carter or hackney-coach? Every parish minister of this city is governor of all carriages, and so are the two Deans, and every carrier should make way for us at their peril. Therefore, like Cæsar, I will be one of the first here rather than the last among you.

He had grown to need the atmosphere to which as Dean and Drapier he was now accustomed.

But, within a few months, in March, 1735, "the people who read news struck me to the heart," he says, by announcing Arbuthnot's end. It is the last of these English milestones: no other loss came that counted. "The death of Mr. Gay and the Doctor have been terrible wounds near my heart. Their living would have been a great comfort to me, although I should never have seen them, like a sum of money in a bank from which I should at least receive annual interest, as I do from you" ('you' is Pope, of course) "and have done from my Lord Bolingbroke."

These friendships were still left for him to draw on, and were so while anything could give him comfort. But for the rest of his life, England really dropped out of his vision, for he could never get there. The story now has to do solely with Ireland.

CHAPTER XX

THE END

IT was coming to the end of writing-time with Swift: yet in the end of 1731 he tells Gay of several months spent over " near five hundred lines on a pleasant subject . . . only to tell what my friends and enemies will say on me after I am dead. I shall finish it soon for I add two lines every week, and blot out four and alter eight." Nothing else of his work in verse is so well known; but a few passages must be quoted here; first from the introduction, in which with his habitual inversion he praises friends by lampooning himself.

> In Pope I cannot read a line,
> But with a sigh I wish it mine,
> When he can in one couplet fix
> More sense than I can do in six; . . .
> I grieve to be outdone by Gay
> In my own hum'rous biting way;
> Arbuthnot is no more my friend,
> Who dares to irony pretend,
> Which I was born to introduce,
> Refin'd at first, and shew'd its use.
> St. John, as well as Pult'ney, knows
> That I had some repute for prose;
> And, till they drove me out of date,
> Could maul a minister of state.

Then comes a description of public anticipations of his death, rumours, and finally the passing bell: and here we meet old rancours, and old affections:

> Kind lady Suffolk, in the spleen,
> Runs laughing up to tell the queen.
> The queen, so gracious, mild, and good,
> Cries, " Is he gone! 'tis time he should.
> He's dead, you say; why, let him rot:
> I'm glad the medals were forgot.
> I promised him, I own; but when?
> I only was a princess then;
> But now, as consort of a king,
> You know, 'tis quite a different thing."

> Here shift the scene, to represent
> How those I love my death lament.
> Poor Pope will grieve a month, and Gay
> A week, and Arbuthnot a day.
> St. John himself will scarce forbear
> To bite his pen, and drop a tear.
> The rest will give a shrug, and cry,
> " I'm sorry—but we all must die ! "

Not one Irish friend comes into his picture—nor for that matter, one Irish enemy. Nothing could show clearer how little concern he had, *sub specie æternitatis*, with that " land of slaves and fens."

This poem is, with one exception, the last thing he wrote deserving of that name. " My poetical fountain is drained," he told Pope in 1732. But " two great works " in prose occupied him, both " begun almost 28 years ago " (when he was with Berkeley in Dublin, and writing the " Petition of Mrs. Harris "). One of them was a *Collection of Genteel and Ingenious Conversation*, and the other the *Directions to Servants, in about twenty stations from the steward and waiting-woman down to the scullion and pantry boy*. These, when they appeared after his death, set perhaps the first example of realistic dialogue, and so led the way to the novel of ordinary life.

Essentially, however, what he said to his publisher Motte in December, 1732, was true. " I must tell you plainly, I have now done with writing "; nor had he any of that itch to see things in print which led Pope to spin out their joint *Miscellanies* to a third volume, and then angle laboriously to get back his letters from Swift, and finally slip these out also by tortuous methods, protesting all the time as if his sanctuary had been burgled.

What remains to do is to track out the last few years of the great wit and great citizen in his social and civic life.

He had made new friends, some of them women. Dublin at that period boasted three blue-stockings, all citizens' wives. Mrs. Grierson, wife of a bookseller, had dedicated an edition of Tacitus to Carteret; the other two were poetesses, Mrs. Sican and Mrs. Barber; and these two Swift did his best to launch in London. But there were others, who have left us in their debt. One was Mrs. Pendarves, better known as Mrs. Delany, wife of Swift's friend; she met the Dean early in 1733 at Delany's house and noted that he " talks a great deal and does not require many answers : has infinite spirits and says abundance of good things in this common way of discourse." A little later he was calling himself her " master " and correcting her grammar, pronunciation, and behaviour. The brief glimpse she gives is one of the many which suggest that Swift's melancholy black mood was kept for himself and his writing desk, and that in company he was even full of spirits. This is borne out by what we learn from another and much less reputable protégée of this period.

As far back as 1730 he mentions " a little, young poetical parson, who has a little, young poetical wife." These were the Pilkingtons—for whom, five years later, " rogue " and " whore " were the names he selected. But in 1730 he was concerned to push their fortune, and since his old friend Barber the printer was becoming Lord Mayor of London, he secured for Pilkington the post of chaplain, and packed him off with flaming recommendations to Pope and Bolingbroke. Within a month both these friends expostulated and begged him to be carefuller of his introductions— for Pope had asked the creature to stay a fortnight, and could not bear him.

Swift might have passed the reproof on to Delany, who had been the first introducer. Yet Mrs. Letitia had spared Delany trouble by supplying a rhapsody : " While I the Godlike men of old, In admiration rapt behold," so leading up to her contemporary, in whom " the patriot, bard and sage unite." The first meeting was at Delany's house, and Swift's first word was in character : " What, this poor little child married ! God help her, she is early engaged to trouble." Pilkington was asked to preach for the Dean next Sunday, and Mrs. Letitia had the occasion to observe with what becoming piety the Dean went through the Communion service, never needing to glance at his Prayer Book ; how he bowed to the Holy Table, a part of his behaviour censured by some as savouring of Popery ; and how after service he was surrounded by a crowd of poor, to all of whom he gave alms, except one old woman who was told, " water was not so scarce but she might have washed her hands."

Then they went on to the Deanery to dinner ; but first she was taken into the study (Mr. Pilkington being told to stay behind), that he might show her " all the money he got when he was in the Ministry." The Dean opened a cabinet with a lot of empty drawers, crying " Bless me, the money has flown ! " Then he showed her his bureau with trinkets given him by the Oxfords, Lady Masham, Lady Betty Germain and the like. He let her choose a couple of medals, and laughed to see her judging them by weight, not by age. All this rings very true : but there follow stories some of which cannot be taken seriously ; for Swift is made

to say, " I never preached but twice in my life, and then they were
not sermons but pamphlets "—which has not even bowing acquaintance with the facts. But some of the by-play about his making
coffee, and his praises of the lady because she did not seek to interfere, are fully in character, and so is the observation that a compliment from him was always disguised as an affront; and I have
no difficulty in believing that her arms were black and blue from
pinches administered when she used " an inelegant phrase."

There is, however, one story that must either be true or a
deliberate invention. The couple were asked back to supper,
the Dean opened a bottle of claret, then, decanting it and pouring
out the last glass which was muddy, he called to Mr. Pilkington
to drink it. " For ", says he, " I always keep some poor parson to
drink the foul wine for me." Pilkington said he was glad to get
a glass at any rate. " Why, then," said the Dean, " you shan't
drink it; for you are wiser than a paltry curate, who upon my
making the same speech to him, told me he did not understand
such usage, and so walked off without his dinner. By the same
token, I told the gentleman who had recommended him to me
that the fellow was a blockhead."

That is entirely in accord with the traditional picture of Swift,
painted by Thackeray and others, but curiously hard to fit in with
the letters. According to it, Dean Swift used the insolence to
junior clergy which he resented when a bishop attempted it to
them; he treated his own cloth exactly as did the squires, who
expected the parson to go out with the pudding. Again, in Mrs.
Pilkington's book we read that Swift showed her a letter from
Pope in order that she might study Pope's " low and ungentleman-
like reflections " on the Queensberrys. That letter is not trace-
able in the correspondence; and in short, not to delay over it, the
lady is a most untrustworthy witness. But I can believe her
when she says the Dean did not laugh, but " when any pleasantry
passed, he used to suck in his cheeks, as folks do when they have a
plug of tobacco in their mouths, to avoid risibility."

Yet, however sceptical we are about gossip, we must believe
Swift against himself (where there is no use of irony), and one
letter written in 1735 (when he was sixty-eight) makes a painful
impression. Motte had been charged to furnish an allowance of
twenty pounds a year (say £80 to-day), to Swift's sister, Mrs.
Fenton, who had married very unwisely against his advice. She
complained of delay. Swift says he knew nothing of it. " Not
caring one straw whether that woman received one penny, or

what became of her, who had during her whole life disobliged me
in the most circumstances of her conduct, I did not employ one
thought upon her except to her disadvantage. I did not know
Mrs. Fenton had a son, nor will ever believe such a breed had
either worth or honour."

Even the fact that he had maintained this allowance during
his sister's distress does not excuse the lack of human charity.
I do not stress natural ties, for these he disregarded on principle,
as having no foundation in reason. Yet at least it is to be remembered that the Swift of this year was an altered creature. Deafness
and giddiness were more and more frequent, and his former plump-
ness had changed to emaciation. A month after he wrote that
letter he journeyed down to Cavan to stay with Sheridan, whose
school was now established there : he spent four days on a journey
of forty-eight miles and was almost spent with distress ; his skin
and bone could scarcely bear the saddle. The younger Sheridan,
who was there as a boy, says : " His memory was much impaired,
and his other faculties much on the decline : his temper peevish,
fretful, morose and subject to sudden fits of passion." The
disease had worn away that power of self-control which was
necessary to keep so violent a spirit within bounds.

After this journey he does not appear to have risked travelling
farther from his home than he could ride or be driven in a couple
of hours.

Yet the spirit of the man was still indomitable in face of power
and authority. Carteret had been replaced by a new Lord-Lieutenant—the Duke of Dorset, grandson of Prior's patron, and son
to one of Swift's friends. He had been the intimate of Lady
Betty Germain, and Swift renewed his old correspondence with
Lady Betty, using her influence to ask favours of the Duke for
his friends. Good relations were established between Castle and
Deanery. But Dorset, like a good Whig, made one more effort
to induce Ireland to repeal the Test Act; Swift once more went
on the war-path against it and the House of Commons simply
roared the project down. Yet at the same time the same House
was considering a Bill to suppress the tithes from flax and hemp—
putting money into landlord pockets at the cost of the Church ;
and Swift headed a petition against it on behalf of the clergy. One
Bettesworth, Sergeant-at-Law, actively opposed the petition, and
a broadside ballad appeared—" On the Words Brother Protestants
and Fellow Christians, so familiarly used by the Advocates for the
Repeal of the Test Act." This was unsigned, but needed no

signature to fix the author.   It begins with the strange fellowships made by a flood : how " the generous wheat forgot its pride and sail'd with litter side by side " ; how "a ball of new-dropp'd horse's dung " called to the pippin, " See, brother, how we apples swim."   " Thus "—and there follow various applications, chiropodist claiming brotherhood with doctor, ' curate sloven ' writing to a dean, ' your brother loving,' till there comes a double-barrelled shot, lampoon for one mark, compliment for the other.

> Thus at the bar the booby Bettesworth,
> Though half a crown o'erpays his sweat's worth,
> Who knows in law nor text nor margent,
> Calls Singleton his brother sergeant.

The publication was quickly sent to Bettesworth by some kind friend, and, according to Sheridan, was handed to him in company ; whereupon having read it, after a short while of speechless rage, he took out a penknife and swore by God he would crop the Dean's ears.   So, setting out for the Deanery, he learnt that Swift was at Worrall's, proceeded there, and was shown into the front room, where Swift, leaving his friends in the back, entered and asked his business.   " Sir," says he, " I am Sergeant Bettesworth." " Of what regiment, pray ? " asked the Dean.   Getting no avowal of the authorship Bettesworth went on to noisy threats, till Worrall came in, whereupon the angry man went away.   Swift on the advice of his friends wrote an account of the encounter to Dorset, and mentioned that Bettesworth had bullies at the door and a sharp knife in his pocket and had since boasted of intention to do damage. However, says the letter, " he threatened me with nothing but his pen ; and though I may be dispirited enough by sickness and years, yet I have little reason to apprehend any danger from that man ; for his very enemies, and even his ridiculers, who are of the two by far the greater number, allow him to be a peaceable man in all things, except his words, his looks, his rhetorical dictions, his books and his hatred to the clergy."

If it is true, as Sheridan adds, that Bettesworth likened Swift to one of his own Yahoos, using his gown as a screen from whose cover to squirt filth, the hits were not all on one side.   But the gown was not the real shield.   Thirty-one of the principal inhabitants of the Liberty of St. Patrick's bound themselves " to defend the life and limbs of the Dean against a certain man and all his ruffians and murderers."   And since " the jolly boys " of the " Kevin Bail " (Dublin's name for this district) were of such temper that a guard of soldiers was quartered there about this period to restrain their faction fighting, Swift was formidably protected; and three or four other lampoons in verse on the unlucky Sergeant flew about the streets.

All the rabble adored the Dean, and if Sheridan is right, he had only to show himself and a fight subsided. But indeed the admiration reached fat burgesses. In December, 1735, when he was away on a long visit to Sheridan at Cavan, his cousin Mrs. Whiteway wrote:

The Drapier's birthday was celebrated by Mr. Land with a dinner of wild-duck, plover, turkey, and pullet; two bowls of punch, and three bottles of claret. At night Mr. Kendrick gave a supper, with an ocean of punch. Their houses were illuminated, and the bells rung. Several other houses followed their example.

In the following November, to usher in his seventieth year, the celebrations were renewed on a larger scale with bonfires, illuminations and firing of guns. Healths were drunk: "Long life to the Drapier, Prosperity to Poor Ireland and the Liberty of the Press." Pope, who saw this reported in the papers, wrote:

Something better and greater than high birth and quality must go towards acquiring those demonstrations of public esteem and love. I have seen a royal birthday uncelebrated, but by one vile ode and one hired bonfire. Whatever years may take away from you, they will not take away the general esteem for your sense, virtue, and charity.

Even to Pope, one perceives, the Drapier and the Dean were eclipsing Gulliver. Swift answered him:

My popularity that you mention is wholly confined to the common people, who are more constant than those we miscall their betters. I walk the streets, and so do my lower friends, from whom, and from whom alone, I have a thousand hats and blessings upon old scores, which those we call the gentry have forgot. But I have not the love, or hardly the civility, of any one man in power or station. . . . What has sunk my spirits more than even years and sickness, is, reflecting on the most execrable corruptions that run through every branch of public management.

Earlier in that same year, this resentment had flamed out in one searing blast: the last thing of any consequence that he wrote, and in the opinion of Delany, no bad judge, almost the best. It was directed against the Irish landlord gentry who found that it paid them better to clear the tenantry off all land that would stay permanently in grass, and so have cattle instead of men. In order to facilitate this process, they petitioned the House of Commons that land so devoted to grazing should be exempt from tithe (since cattle needed no parsons). The House of Commons decided to give its strongest support to this encouragement of evictions. Thereupon Swift launched his poem, " The Legion Club," which describes the parliament in College Green :

> Not a bowshot from the college,
> Half the globe from sense and knowledge;

This time, iambics are too deliberate; his execration must fly swifter :

> Could I from the building's top
> Hear the ratt'ling thunder drop,
> While the devil upon the roof
> (If the devil be thunder-proof)
> Should with poker fiery-red
> Crack the stones, and melt the lead;
> Drive them down on ev'ry scull,
> While the den of thieves is full;
> Quite destroy that harpies' nest,
> How might then our isle be blest !

Yet, " since the house is like to last," it should be made useful—as a mad-house :

> Let the club have right to dwell
> Each within his proper cell,
> With a passage left to creep in,
> And a hole above for peeping.
>   Let them, when they once get in,
> Sell the nation for a pin;
> While they sit a-picking straws,
> Let them rave of making laws;
> While they never hold their tongue,
> Let them dabble in their dung.

So goes on this vision of Avernus :

> Near the door an entrance gapes,
> Crowded round with antic shapes,
> Poverty, and Grief, and Care,
> Causeless Joy, and true Despair,
> Discord periwig'd with snakes,
> See the dreadful strides she takes.

One by one, in Virgilian fashion, the denizens of hell are summed up : last of all, the chief offender on the tithe question :

> Bless us, Morgan ! are thou there man ?
> Bless mine eyes ! art thou the chairman !
> Chairman to yon damn'd committee !
> Yet I look on thee with pity.

Dreadful fight ! what, learned Morgan
Metamorphos'd to a Gorgon ! . . .
Will you, in your faction's phrase,
Send the clergy all to graze ;
And, to make your project pass,
Leave them not a blade of grass ?

How I want thee, hum'rous Hogarth !
Thou, I hear, a pleasant rogue art ;
Were but you and I acquainted,
Ev'ry monster should be painted :
You should try your graving tools
On this odious group of fools ;
Draw the beasts as I describe them
From their features, while I gibe them ;
Draw them like, for I assure ye,
You will need no car'catura ;
Draw them so, that we may trace
All the soul in ev'ry face.

There is in that poem more than merely its concentrated fury ;
we meet the long preoccupation of a powerful mind with one
peculiar horror. This latest of Swift's noted satires links itself
with his most important public service—which indeed was con-
summated only after his death—and with the long-foreseen tragedy
of his own end.

The *Journal to Stella* describes a visit paid by him to Bedlam.
He does not mention then what appears later, that he became one
of the hospital's governors—presumably in the time while he was
still much in London. It is not certain that insanity had then a
morbid interest for him—though no man could feel the seat of
reason so threatened and not have some apprehension. But one
terribly dramatic saying of his can be fixed to a date not many
years later. In 1717 Young of the "Night Thoughts" was
staying in Dublin and records how, as he and others were walking
with Swift a mile or two outside the city, Swift stopped :

We passed on ; but perceiving that he did not follow us, I went
back and found him fixed as a statue and earnestly gazing at a noble
elm which in its upward branches was much withered and decayed.
Pointing at it he said, " I shall be like that tree : I shall die at the top."

That was in his fiftieth year. In 1732 (when he was sixty-five)
we find a practical outcome of these thoughts. Sir William Fownes
is in correspondence with him concerning a proposal for a hospital
to receive lunatics, " there being no public place for their reception

nor private undertakers, as about London." In 1735 Swift wrote
to Eaton Stannard, Recorder of Dublin, saying that he had determined to leave his whole fortune " to build a hospital for idiots
and lunatics in the city or the suburbs," and requesting his assistance
in acquiring the land.

Everyone in Dublin knew of the proposed bequest: a year
later the " Legion Club " verses alluded to it:

> Yet should Swift endow the schools
> For his lunatics and fools.

In 1739 when the Poem on his own Death was at last published, it
ended with this comment:

> He gave the little wealth he had
> To build a house for fools and mad,
> And show'd by one satiric touch,
> No nation wanted it so much.

Few gibes are better known; yet even in Ireland not one in a
thousand understands the reality. Swift's money, about £7,000,
was wholly inadequate to the purpose; but the feeling on his
death was such that the very Parliament he had lampooned took
the matter generously in hand and erected a building, still an orna-
ment to Dublin, in which handsome corridors and walks were at
the disposal of those who before had been liable to be thrown like
beasts into a barred pit. Provision by Parliament was made for
the maintenance: England had to wait seventy years before (in
1815) a similar institution was set up out of public funds. It is
one concrete proof—and not a small one—how far Swift was
beyond his time in notions of civilized government, and what is
more, how powerfully he prevailed to impart his own views.
From 1745 to the present day, Swift's Hospital, as it is always called
(though officially and by his choice it is St. Patrick's), has continued
its work and under modern conditions sends out more than half
its patients cured. The boardroom where its directors meet is a
sort of Swift museum; his portrait, Stella's and Vanessa's, adorn
the walls; and in a corner stands the escritoire at which he wrote
Gulliver (and how much else) during his life in the Deanery.

There is one more thing to be chronicled; one last blaze of
the fierce old man's Irish patriotism. Another trouble had arisen
over the currency, and Primate Boulter acting as Lord Justice
issued a proclamation reducing the value of gold by threepence
in each guinea. This was confirmed by an Act of the Irish Parliament. Swift was up in arms at once, and a ballad " upon pulling

the gold down" was sent abroad on the streets. At a state dinner given by the Lord Mayor to the Duke of Devonshire, who had succeeded Dorset as Viceroy, the Primate taxed Swift with stirring up the mob. The Dean retorted that, if he had held up his finger, the Primate would have been torn in pieces, but that he deferred doing it, for "it would make an odd figure in history if a Primate was destroyed by the people for doing an odd job—he would give it no other name"; and thereupon he stalked out of the room. Next day the bells of St. Patrick's were muffled and rang funereally, while a black flag flew from the steeple, to the consternation of citizens who at first thought the Dean was dead. But learning the cause, they repaired to a tavern and drank long life to the Dean and confusion to the enemies of Ireland. The Lord-Lieutenant sent for Swift, who returned answer that his health did not allow him to attend; he was sick of "the country's disease."

Of course the story illustrates a violence of temper which had become uncontrollable now that he was turned of seventy. Another episode illustrates his friends' dread of him, but also his own better qualities. One Michael Clancy, a doctor driven out of his profession by loss of sight, heard read to him Swift's savage Epitaph on the notorious Colonel Charteris, and bethought him of a comedy which he called "The Sharper." In hopes that a good word from the Dean would give the piece a chance on the stage, he went to Dr. Helsham and begged him to put the comedy into Swift's hands. "Have you a mind that I should be obliged to go down his stairs faster than I went up?" was Helsham's answer; "not I, I do not care to bring his tongue on me." Dr. Grattan was tried next and answered to the same effect that he would "have it thrown in his face and be called a blockhead for his pains." But another of the Grattan brothers, a parson, said that he would try the experiment of leaving it on the Dean's table and await events. Swift found it, read it, and asked of all his friends, who had brought it? but no one dare own up. At last Helsham, seeing the parcel, asked what it was and when the Dean answered "that it was a villain well painted," he perceived that he might disclose the story. Thereupon Swift went into his closet and wrote a very charming note, praising the work, pitying the loss of sight, and sending five pounds in gold pieces. Clancy's letter of gratitude, even if it sounds extravagant in deference, is pleasant reading. "That approbation which in some more happy period of my life would have made me proud even to vanity, has now in my distress comforted and soothed my misery."

But the rest is only a chronicle, to use Swift's own grim words, of " age, giddiness, deafness, loss of memory, rage and rancour against persons and proceedings." A letter to his cousin, Mrs. Whiteway, on November 27, 1738, says that he hopes to be better on the 30th, his birthday, " because it is a day you seem to regard, although I detest it, and I read the third chapter of Job that morning."

As far back as the days of the *Journal to Stella* we find that he had formed the practice of reading this passage that begins : " Let the day perish when I was born and the night in which it was said there is a man child conceived." But we find also that in the first London winter when he was in full flood of his new activity, hand in glove with Harley and St. John, the day passed and he never remembered it. Again in 1711, he says to Stella (who had written him verses), " Yes, faith, I lamented my birthday two days after and that's all." It was no very deep depression in those times. But now in 1738 he might well take to himself Job's cry :

Wherefore is light given to him that is in misery and life unto the bitter in soul ? for the thing which I greatly feared is come upon me : I was not in safety, neither had I rest, neither was I quiet : yet trouble came.

He was almost friendless now. Sheridan was dead, the man who, it was said, could do for him what the young David did for Saul and lift the gloom off his hours of blackness. Worse still, Sheridan had died estranged from Swift. There had been many quarrels ; inevitably, since the game they habitually played was one of exchanging insults in jest—a game not safe at any time, but least of all with men old and irritable. Pope was far away and the life had gone out of their correspondence. Of the old Dublin circle, Walls and Worrall, associated so closely with all his affairs, seem to have dropped out ; Worrall is set down in a list of those whom he " found ungrateful." But in truth the relations cannot have been easy to maintain when his temper grew more violent ; it was unfortunately not in his nature to forget that he had laid almost all his intimates under some obligation, and owed nothing to any of them but the ordinary offices of friendship. Delany, probably avoiding danger, kept more aloof : and the new friends did not do credit to Swift's discrimination. Among these were the Pilkingtons, and if one may take Mrs. Pilkington's stories as approximating to the truth, especially those in the later instalment of her memoirs, these folk were mixed up in a deal of conviviality that savoured of horseplay. In this " crew " of his, the Dean domineered. He had, however, made one ally of another order, Lord Orrery, whose acquaintance dates from 1732, when Swift was only beginning to decline. The young nobleman's approach was deferential and accompanied by tributary verse. Swift, who liked a lord to be a scholar, was easily propitiated, and this aspirant to culture attached himself closely to the celebrity, was commended to Pope, and in his comings and goings to England was entrusted with various literary commissions. In 1737 Swift wrote to Pope, " Next to yourself I love no man so well." Orrery's letters to Swift show us the fine gentleman amateur in letters ; they do not suggest the personage who stands revealed in his Memoir of Swift. Valets are a slandered class ; many a one has served a great man with a wise dog's devotion ; but there are valets to whom no man is a hero, and the soul of one of them had got into this man of quality, who used his intimacy of access to genius by gathering materials for a work of simpering malice.

Only one piece of good fortune lightened the road's end for Swift. So far back as 1730 he had written a friendly letter to his cousin Mrs. Whiteway, daughter of his uncle Adam Swift. Thereafter he saw her at times, and though she offended against one of his principles by pressing him to eat (as we learn from a letter of Sheridan's), she grew intimate. The old Presbyterian Mrs. Brent who managed all and was generally known as the Dean's ' Sir Robert,' died in 1734 ; and thereafter when Swift left Dublin, Mrs. Whiteway was in charge. Her letters show a woman with some fair pretence to wit, very much in league with the chief mirth-maker Sheridan. This ought to be remembered because she is largely concerned in the painful story of Swift's break with that ally. As the younger Sheridan tells the story, his father had come to the Deanery seriously ill, and there been laid up with an illness lasting months. Recovering at last, he came downstairs and said to Swift, " Mr. Dean, I fear I have been a great expense to you all this time." If he said this, Sheridan blundered characteristically, it was a direct appeal to what had become a monomania of parsi-mony. But it was Mrs. Whiteway who answered promptly, that if he felt so, there was an easy remedy : he could move elsewhere. She spoke ; Swift remained silent ; and Sheridan went to another friend's house at Rathfarnham, where he died. It was a grievous mistake in judgment on Mrs. Whiteway's part, but plainly made because she was thinking first of the sick man whose sickness was now her chief care. In these last years, she often took a hand in his correspondence; and it was she who, in May, 1740, had the painful task of writing to warn Pope that the Dean was no longer in a state to reply to letters, still less to finish his remaining unpublished works, as Pope desired.

For Swift's memory was now completely gone. In June, 1741, he was able to write a note of introduction for his cousin once removed, William Swift, grandson of Godwin, asking the good offices of Eaton Stannard. But the last letter of his that says anything to us is addressed to Mrs. Whiteway, and it is heavy with affliction:

I have been very miserable all night, and to-day extremely deaf and full of pain. I am so stupid and confounded, that I cannot express the mortification I am under both in body and mind. All I can say is, that I am not in torture, but I daily and hourly expect it. Pray let me know how your health is and your family. I hardly understand one word I write. I am sure my days will be very few; few and miserable they must be. I am, for these few days,
Yours entirely,
J. SWIFT.

If I do not blunder, it is Saturday, July 26, 1740. If I live till Monday, I shall hope to see you, perhaps for the last time.

The rest is ugly reading. After Sheridan's death, a certain Dr. Wilson, prebendary of St. Patrick's, established himself as a familiar at the Deanery, and probably was much answerable for the growing estrangement of the Dean's older friends. Matters came to a head in 1742. Swift, no longer able to ride, had refused to buy a coach as long as Walpole remained in power: in 1739, on the rumour of a change, he had bought one, but on Walpole's recovering his ascendancy, declined to use it. In 1742 it was in use again, and while he and Wilson were driving together, there was a violent struggle. Wilson swore that the old man had attacked him; the Dean's servant, Brennan, who rode behind, swore that Wilson had insisted on Swift's making him sub-dean and so in charge of the chapter to the exclusion of the acting deputy, Dr. Wynne. Brennan swore also that he had to rescue his master from blows; at all events Wilson had to leave the coach, and there followed a petition for an inquiry into the state of Swift's mind.[1] The Commission included several of Swift's friends. They found him "not capable of taking care of his person or fortune."

---

[1] Orrery suggests that Wilson habitually scourged the old man, as was then done with lunatics. A man who did that would have been lynched by the Dublin mob; as it was, Wilson appears to have been roughly handled.

He was left in the Deanery under the supervision arranged by the trustees. After the first few weeks he recognized no one and flew into passion at the sight of faces. For three years he lasted on, pacing up and down his room for ten hours a day, eating by snatches the food set out for him. He was shaven weekly down to the chin; below that a long fringe of white beard was allowed to grow. It was said that his servants took money to let people have a sight of him; Mr. Ball disbelieves this; I see no reason to, but what matter? Mrs. Whiteway came in twice a week to ensure

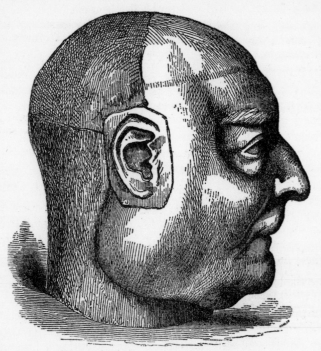

DEATH MASK OF DEAN SWIFT.

that things were done orderly, and in April, 1744, Deane Swift, his cousin, heard a story that, in the month before, he reached out for a knife, and as the housekeeper moved it from him, fell to shrugging his shoulders and rocking himself, repeating the words, "I am what I am."

He may all this time have known what he was, and what he had been.

However complete his misery, death ended it quietly, on October

19, 1745, when he had almost completed his seventy-eighth year. The body lay in state in the Deanery and crowds flocked in, till someone stole a lock of the long white hair, and the public were excluded.

He was buried, as his will desired, in the cathedral, yet not in the place he himself had indicated. Evidently the general sentiment prevailed which desired to associate his grave with Stella's; she lies at the foot of one pillar of the nave to the left of the entrance, he at the foot of the next to the right. Over his grave is inscribed the epitaph which he had composed for himself. All the world knows one line of it; he lies *ubi saeva indignatio ulterius cor lacerare nequit* ("where rage and resentment can no longer eat into the heart)." That is how he shaped for himself Job's aspiration after the quiet places of death : " There the wicked cease from troubling, and there the weary be at rest." But it is not often remembered that his epitaph ends with a challenge, in which there is no downheartedness of defeat. " Go, passer-by and do, if you can, as he did, a man's part in the defence of liberty."

What then did liberty, which he counted it his chief merit to have defended, mean in the mind of this great man ? Certainly not what we understand nowadays by equality : he was no leveller, the whole pith of his philosophy accepted the existence of a governing class. He admitted privilege too, for birth and for honourable wealth; although he held that immorality and infidelity should disqualify even the privileged from public trust. But he claimed privilege also, and equal privilege, for talent irrespective of station; for men like himself or Prior. Genius, to use his own word, had a title, if it chose, to take full part in government. But neither to genius nor to privilege nor to royalty itself would he concede arbitrary power against the spirit of those " gothic " institutions on which the English state was based. The mass of the people must have their word to say. I once heard Mr. Balfour (as he then was) define in the House of Commons what he meant by democracy. He took it to mean ' government by the consent of the governed,' and he added that in his opinion no other form of government was compatible with his notion of civilization. In that sense, and only in that sense, Jonathan Swift, like this other aristocrat, may be called an upholder of democracy.

Yet his true concern was never with abstract principles, but rather applied itself to the conditions which should make good principles workable; and he perceived clearly that the disease fatal to popular government was corruption. The main object of his satire first and last was to stigmatize and sear corrupt preference in the bestowal of employment. He resented the injustice because it was injustice ; but he resented even more the sacrifice of the public good to private machinations.

Broadly, these were the main principles that inspired as sound a mind as ever applied itself to politics. We should dismiss completely the notion that Swift during the working period of his life —even to the full measure of threescore years and ten—was anything less than sane. It is true that before his days were ended, his mind gave way. What then? Walter Scott's mind gave way also, yet no one disputes the sanity of that sagacious and serviceable intelligence, until at last it paid the penalty of overstrain. Scott died at sixty-three ; had Swift's life been no longer, no human being would have ever suggested that he was mad. The cases are different, for Scott's sanguine nature led him to imprudences of outlay, from which there followed his desperate overtaxing of the inventive brain. Swift, a cautious man, lived always within his means ; he never used, much less abused, his faculty of creation to supply the need of money. But from his early years he was beset by disease, not of the brain, but yet affecting the supply of serous fluid so that it produced the torments of giddiness, deafness and roaring in the ears, enough to over-tax the power of any man's self-control. Just as Scott at the bidding of necessity invented too much and took on him too much of the labour which goes to shaping and uttering invention, so Swift indulged and in a sense worked to excess his master faculty, which was of passionate feeling. Rage accumulated in him like water behind a dam. Yet, since it was never his nature to let loose passion in a free flow of words, but rather to convey it tortuously, almost by inversion, in ironic understatement, the mere form of his art involved an effort of constant self-discipline. Except in the *Legion Club*, we never find the direct volcanic outpouring ; and Swift was in the seventieth year when in that instance he gave his passion free flow. He had then got beyond the point where irony could be his weapon. Restraint was going from him.

Yet five years later, on January 28, 1742, only five months before the writ in lunacy was issued, we have a document in his hand, admonishing the sub-dean and chapter to repress certain irregularities of the Vicars choral—who, it is reputed, had pleaded licence to " sing and fiddle " at " a club of fiddlers in Fishamble Street." It concluded in these words—

THE END

And I do further intreat my said Sub-Dean and the Chapter that, the infirmities of age disabling me to attend personally and take the care which I have much at heart, they will keep up the honour and dignity of the Chapter, and not let it suffer in its rights or privileges by the encroachments of any persons nor by the neglects, disobedience, or perfidy of those who are subject to it.

It is a faint shadow of the man, moving even in its weakness; but it is the utterance of a sane mind. Disease had not yet been able to inflict upon that strong nature the last indignities. Yet there are two drafts of this document, and the first exhibits much more petulance of old age (it is from that we have the detail about fiddlers and their club); but also in its conclusion there is a flash of the old fire.

My resolution is to preserve the dignity of my station, and the honour of my Chapter; and, gentlemen, it is incumbent upon you to aid me, and to show who and what the Dean and Chapter of Saint Patrick's are.

These are the last words that come down to us under Swift's own hand. *Mentem mortalia tangunt.* Who can look without compassion on that image of human decay? Those of us who have lived much in Swift's company, receiving such communication as is possible through the stored-up utterance of the dead, hold him, I think, in veneration rather than affection. *Pantagruel, Don Quixote,* the *Pilgrim's Progress*—any one of these may have been or may be the book of books for a thousand readers; I can hardly think that of *Gulliver.* Even in his greatest work, Swift has none of the qualities that endear; yet with him we inevitably feel the presence of one of the master minds in all literature. He uplifts us by a sense of what human power can do. Simply as a writer, he has, I think, no equal in English prose; certainly no one for force. But there is no monotony; it is never the mechanically recurring stroke which Johnson introduced and Macaulay shortened down to the beat of a piston-rod. Neither has it the elaborate cadence by which many admired writers have, I think, modelling themselves too closely on verse-forms, acquired something of a dancing master's deportment. Swift's movement is always free, unhurried but ordered with the natural poise of a strong man walking; it has the dignity of one accustomed to move in good company; he avoids emphasis and never rams his points home like a pile-driver. The stroke, when it is sharpest, often comes by a side glance, accompanied merely by some slight inflection of the voice.

Yet though a writer of whom this can be said must have the admiration of all who seek to write, or love good writing, it is not by such mastery that our hearts are commanded. To move us, a man must have some such skill; yet it is by what he has to say, not by his manner of saying it, that he will win allegiance and affection. All the genial topics of appeal are discarded by Swift. He glorifies no love, he celebrates no glory. Yet his correspondence proves to us how readily his nature rose to enthusiasm of admiration for his friends, and how deeply entwined in his being was an attachment more lasting and more passionate than a million of common loves. There is much in his letters that shows us how he gained the hearts of men and of women; but from his published writings I at least receive only one dominant impression—force. If a record could be kept, who struck the hardest, few indeed could show a blade that bit so deep; and the blow that he dealt was delivered always in the teeth of power—against Marlborough when he was stronger than the ministry who made Swift their champion, against the British Government when the cause that he made his own was that of an impoverished race.

With a government behind him, he brought Marlborough down. On his lone-hand raids in Ireland, he effected little of tangible result; yet what he did was worth more. He showed to a people lamentably misgoverned that there was one who would take risks to claim their rights; he taught them that they had rights to claim; he trusted his safety to them, he gave them a man to whom they could be loyal; and in their loyalty he had the reward that he valued most.

For in spite of all, in spite of our sense that he is of supreme significance in the technical mastery of prose writing, in spite of the undisputed fact that his invention, combined with his irony, gave us one of the world's masterpieces, I come back at last to his own choice of words, and lay one more poor tribute of homage before the grave, next to Stella's, where we are bidden to imitate if we can *strenuum pro virili libertatis vindicatorem.*

INDEX

Academy to reform the English language, 160

Acheson, Sir Arthur and Lady, 291–2

Addison, Joseph, 98, 99; 104–5; 108; 116–17; 151–2, 175

Advice to Servants, 75

Anglo-Irish, Swift's creation of the, 15, 228 *seq.*

Arbuthnot, Dr., 149, 150–1, 178, 179; correspondence with Swift, 36, 187–190, 194; offer of financial help to Swift, 190–1; 204, 216, 226; Swift's letter on his illness, 250, 251, 252; death of, 297; 296, 297

Ashe, Dillon, 96

Ashe, St. George (Bishop of Clogher), 20, 45, 96, 208

Athenian Mercury, The, 39, 41

Atterbury, 28, 84, 85, 111

Bandbox plot, the, 160

Barber, John, 153, 167, 186, 191, 284, 300

Bathurst, Lord, 288–9

Battle of the Books, 59, 60–4, 84

Baucis and Philemon, 104–6

Bedlam, 306

Berkeley, Lord, 70, 73, 74, 75, 78–9, 108–9, 110

Bettesworth, Sergeant, 302–4

Bolingbroke, Lord (St. John), 128, 131, 136, 141–2, 146–7, 148; negotiations with Pretender, 149; 157, 172, 176; Swift's admiration for, 191–2, 218, 295; 184–5; in office, 192–3; failure to help Swift, 193, 194; in retirement, 200, 202, 206, 216; 261, 296

Brent, Mrs., 207, 213, 215, 235, 245, 293–4, 310

Cadenus and Vanessa, 164–6, 226, 247, 256

Capel, Lord, 51, 53

Cartaret, Lady, 236–7, 294

Cartaret, Lord, 157, 230, 231, 232, 233, 236, 294

Chelsea, Swift at, 137–8, 141

Chetwode, Knightley, 201, 202, 203, 206, 207

Conduct of the Allies, 153–5, 156

Congreve, 40; *Double Dealer*, 41; 91, 104, 142, 151; death of, 295

Cowley, 40, 63

Delany, Mrs., 208, 296, 299–300, 309

Delany, Rev. Patrick, 10, 209, 210, 211, 237, 309

Dingley, Mrs. Rebecca, 80, 116, 211, 239, 244, 246–7

Directions to Servants, 153, 299

Dissensions in Athens and Rome, 79, 85

Dorset, Duke of, 302

Drapier Letters, the, 58, 229–37, 285, 288

Dryden, 39, 40, 41, 63, 91

Dunton, James, 38–9, 176

Evans, Bishop of Meath, 80, 226–7

Examiner, The, 126, 130, 131, 136, 141, 174

Fenton, Mrs. (Swift's sister), 301–2

Floyd, Miss Biddy, Swift's verses to, 100

Ford, Charles, 190, 191, 224

Fountaine, Sir Andrew, 96, 104, 116

Gay, John, 75; Swift's service to, 187; 188; the *Beggar's Opera*, 206, 290; 217, 218, 278; and the Duchess of Queensberry, 293, 294; *Polly*, 293, 294–5; 297

Genteel Conversation, 299

Geree, the Rev. John, 180, 183

Germain, Lady Betty, 75, 100, 302

Giffard, Lady, 32, 43, 48, 55, 64

Godolphin, Lord, 107, 123

Grattans, the, 206, 211, 308

Guiscard, Marquis de, 135

Gulliver's Travels, 34, 77, 93, 215, 229, 249–50, 251, 260–9, 270

Halifax, Lord, 78, 79, 80, 104, 110, 111, 118, 124

Harding, Swift's printer, 216, 233, 234–5

Harley, Robert (Lord Oxford), 48, 56, 85, 124, 125–7, 131; Swift's quarrel and reconciliation with, 132; 143, 144; conviviality of, 146, 184–5; Swift's admiration for, 146, 147, 179; negotiations with the Pretender, 149; disgrace of, 155; 157, 159, 172; Swift's poem on, 172–3; death of his daughter, 178–9; breach with Bolingbroke, 179–80; 187, 188; retirement of, 191–2; promise of £1,000 to Swift, 193, 257; in the Tower, 193–4, 203–4; 219, 273

Mrs. Harris's Petition, 77, 299

Helsham, Dr., 295, 308
Henley, Anthony, 104
History of the Four Last Years of Queen
  Anne, 146, 256, 273
Howard, Mrs. (Countess of Suffolk), 250,
  252, 253, 255, 267–8, 271, 272–3

Johnson, Esther, see Stella.
Johnson, Mrs., 48, 80, 81
Jones, Betty, 23, 37, 38, 53
Journal to Stella, 55, 73, 77, 97, 120, 122,
  123, 157, and *passim*

Kennett, Bishop, sketch of Swift, 173
Kerry, Lord and Lady, 101, 137
King, Archbishop, 95–7, 98, 109, 177–8,
  205–6, 213, 276

Legion Club, the, 305–6, 307
Letter to the October Club, 156
Lewis, Erasmus, 149, 155, 171, 192, 194,
  202
Lines Written in a Lady's Ivory Table-
  book, 73–4
Long, Mrs. Anne, 163–4
Lindsay, Archbishop, 178, 205

Macaulay and Swift, 14, 24, 29, 39, 48, 49
Marlborough, Duke of, 126, 130–1, 150,
  154, 156
Marlborough, Duchess of, 150, 267
Marvell, Andrew, his Mr. Smirke quoted,
  92
Masham, Mrs., 150, 155, 156, 162, 192,
  193, 194
Meditations on a Broomstick, 101
Miscellanies, with Pope, 93, 271, 299
Modest Proposal, 91, 287–8
Motte, Benjamin, 260, 299, 301

Ode to Mr. Congreve, 40, 41–2
Ode on Sancroft, 39
Orkney, Lady, 160
Ormond, Duke of, 94, 96, 159–60, 161,
  190, 203
Ormond, Duchess of, 177, 206
Orrery, Lord, 9, 10, 95, 310
Oxford, Lord, see Harley

Parnell, 188, 189
Patrick, Swift's servant, 125, 141, 152–3
Partridge, John, 101, 102
Pembroke, Lord, 96–7
Peterborough, Lord, 147–8, 268
Philips, Ambrose, 98, 99, 151
Phyllis, or the Progress of Love, 213
Pilkingtons, the, 10, 300–1, 309–10
Pope, Alexander, 93, 103, 173, 174, 177,
  190, 216, 218, 251, 252, 255, 267;
  Swift's gift to, 270; Swift's visits to,
  252, 255–6, 258, 271–2; *Miscellanies*
  with Swift, 271; Swift's love for, 275;
  295, 296

Princess of Wales (later, Queen Caroline),
  252; and Irish affairs, 253; 254; and
  Gulliver, 261; 268, 271; 298 (the
  Queen)
Prior, Matthew, 85, 104, 109, 144, 148,
  149, 169–70, 203, 206, 215–16
Problem, The, 73
*Project for the advancement of Religion and the
  Reformation of Manners*, 113–14
Proposal for the Use of Irish Manufactures,
  214, 215–16
Pulteney (Earl of Bath), 271, 296

Queen Anne, 79, 92, 113, 124, 125, 145,
  149, 150, 151, 172, 193
Queensberry, Duchess of, 293, 294

Raymond, Dr., 206
Resolutions for When I come to be Old, 75–7
Rochefort, Chief Baron, 211, 212, 213

Sacramental Test for Dissenters, 81, 107,
  108, 109, 112
St. James's Coffee-house, 103–4
St. John, see Bolingbroke
Scarborough, Lord, 261
Scott, Sir Walter, 9, 24, 90
Scriblerus Club, the, 177, 187, 203
Sentiments of a Church of England Man,
  113
Sheridan, Rev. Thomas, 209, 210, 211;
  237–8, 239–40; Swift's letter of
  advice to, 239; at Cavan, 302, 304;
  309; and Mrs. Whiteway, 310
Sheridan, Thomas, Junior, 10, 290, 302,
  310
" Short View of the State of Ireland,"
  285–7
Society of Brothers, the, 143, 155, 177
*Some Free Thoughts on the Recent State of
  Affairs*, 186, 191
Somers, Lord, 78, 79, 80, 87–8
Somerset, Duchess of, 155–6, 180, 181
Stearne, Dean, 95–6, 169, 177–8, 207
Steele, Richard, 98, 99, 103, 123, 129, 151,
  152; quarrel with Swift, 174–5; the
  Crisis, 176, 177
Stella (Esther Johnson), education by
  Swift, 48; relations with Swift, 48–9,
  55–6, 80, 97, 120, 140, 170, 185–6, 240;
  54; parentage, 80–1; love of fun, 81,
  82; 81; Tisdall's proposal, 82–3;
  95–6, 122, 124; and Vanessa, 166, 170,
  185–6, 200, 208, 223–4, 243, 247; reported marriage with Swift, 208, 209,
  219, 226, 247, 281; her spelling, 211;
  and the " Crew," 213; 226–7; at
  Quilca, 237–8, 239; Swift's verses to,
  240–7, 274; portraits of, 247–8; illness of, 256–8, 273–5; death, 278–80;
  298; her will, 257, 281; her burial,
  279–80; her tomb, 289; Swift's character of, 280–1

INDEX

Stopford, James, 245, 252
Swift, Adam, 19, 52, 71
Swift, Deane, 19
Swift, Deane, the younger, 10, 19, 46, 49, 219
Swift, Dryden, 16
Swift, Godwin, 16, 17, 19, 22, 94
Swift, Jonathan (the Dean's father), 16
Swift, Jonathan, Dean, *Account* of his Family, the, 17, 22, 39; love of anonymity, 79, 85–6, 93, 99, 109, 191; *la bagatelle*, 75, 190, 210, 258; birth, 14; birthday celebrations, 304, 309; burial and epitaph, 313; and Catholics, 21, 112, 284, 285; character and personality, 13–14, 15, 17, 24, 32, 33, 35, 38, 43, 51, 52, 53, 54, 57, 64, 69, 73–4, 76, 77, 84, 99, 118–21, 148–9, 271, 290; and the Church, 21, 129–30; as a clergyman, 77–8, 118–19, 179, 184, 204–5; Dean of St. Patrick's, 162, 199, 204–5; the Deanery, description of and life at, 200–1, 205, 206–7, 208, 225, 252, 294; description of, 65, 106–7; and democracy, 313; the Drapier, 228–48, 253, 304; Dublin life as Dean, 209–14, 225; education, 17, 18, 20, 22, 23, 24; family ties, attitude to, 17, 19, 302; First-fruits for the Church in Ireland, 94–5, 97, 107–8, 109, 125, 302, 303; proposed journey to France, 272, 274; and the French language, 56–7, 272; friendship, genius for, 53, 58, 129, 179, 199, 225; and gardening, 57, 78, 95, 156, 158, 168, 291, 292; Historiographer, application for post of, 117, 180, 188, 190; at Holyhead, 276–7; Swift's Hospital, 307; illnesses, 30, 39, 47–8, 107, 109, 158, 159, 169, 216, 252, 269, 275, 276, 290, 302, 309; Ireland, championship of, 199, 214, 227, 228–9, 253–4, 283–9, 304, 307–8; Ireland, dislike of, 110, 117, 168, 169, 283, 290, 299; Ireland, popularity in, 65, 215, 235, 276, 289, 303–4, 308; and the Irish primacy, 177–8; and the Jacobite intrigue, 206; Kilkenny, school life at, 17, 18, 22; Kilroot, prebend of, 51; Laracor, 70, 78, 80, 94, 98, 116, 117, 120, 122, 123, 139, 156, 158, 200, 201; last days, 312–13; at Letcombe Bassett, 180, 188–90; "little language," 48, 55, 77, 97; M.A. degree, 45, 46; marriage, views on, 37, 38, 72–3, 76, 83, 119–20, 185; reputed marriage to Stella, 208, 209, 219, 226, 247, 281; money preoccupations, 18, 19–20, 93, 270–1; at Moor Park, 21, 24–32, 37, 40–9, 54, 55; nurse, visit to England with his, 21–2; at Oxford, 31, 45–6, 179, 202–3; the pamphleteer, 105, 112–16, 283, 285; Peace, efforts towards the, 154, 161;

penury, fear of, 20, 120; poems and verses, 32, 33–6, 39, 40–4, 59, 60, 61, 63, 73–5, 93, 100, 213–14, 298, 299; politics, attitude to, 313–14; portraits, 106, 160–1; praise by disparagement, 110, 191, 298; preferment disappointments, 69–70, 79–80, 97, 98, 100, 114, 115, 116, 117, 118, 122, 140–1, 157, 158, 161, 162, 253, 272–3; *Principles*, his, 118–19; at Quilca, 237–8, 249; rank, attitude to, 133–4, 144, 252; and the power of Reason, 15, 119; royalist, 17, 21; Scotch, hatred of the, 176; self-portrait, 183; and his servants, 75; and soldiers, 34, 96, 130; as a talker, 148; Temple " penitential letter " to, 50; Temple, legacy from, 69; Temple's literary executor, 58, 69; Trinity College, Dublin, 18–20; Whig, 21, 97, 98, 112, 113, 118, 123, 124, 128–9, 199; at Windsor, 143–4, 148, 158–9, 167; and wine, 57, 99, 147–8, 207, 211, 295; women, love of tutoring, 48, 164, 291, 292, 299–300; the writer, 13, 39–40, 90, 91, 251, 315–16
Swift, Mrs. (the Dean's mother), 21, 22–3, 31, 36, 49–50
Swift, Thomas, the Rev. (the Dean's grandfather), 15
Swift, Thomas (the Dean's cousin), 19, 37, 86
Swift, William (the Dean's uncle), 16, 19, 45
Swift, Willoughby (the Lisbon cousin), 19, 49

Tale of a Tub, 42–3, 59, 83, 84–92, 93, 94, 98, 99–100, 115–16, 181
Tatler, the, 103–4, 128
Temple, Lady (Dorothy Osborne), 23, 31–2, 43, 54
Temple, Sir William, 21, 23, 25; relations with Swift and influence, 24, 25, 27, 33–4, 36, 39, 43, 55, 56, 57, 58, 59, 64, 65, 79, 130; use of French, 25, 56–7; early life, 25–6; in Flanders, 26–8, 29; love of food *and* wine, 27; posthumous memoirs, 27; reputed parentage of Swift, 29–30; 31, 33; Swift's appreciation of, 34, 35, 40, 55, 58, 60, 64; 39–40; illness, 43–4; his garden, 57; *Letters and Miscellanea*, 53, 57, 58, 59, 79; *Ancient and Modern Learning* controversy, 59–63; death of, 64; legacy to Swift, 69
Temple, Sir John, 39
Thackeray on Swift, 14, 301
Tickell, 239, 240, 252, 256
Tighe, Richard, 210
Tisdall, the Rev., 81, 82–3
Tooke, 127, 128, 153

Vanbrugh, Sir John, 104

INDEX

Vanhomrigh, Esther (Vanessa), growth of intimacy with Swift, 137–8 ; 163, 164 ; 166, 167 ; the coffee symbolism, 166, 222, 293 ; character of relations with Swift, 170, 171, 183–6, 220–1, 223 ; and Stella, 168, 170, 223–4, 247 ; visit to Letcombe Bassett, 195 ; at Celbridge, 201 ; 201, 202, 219–23 ; illness and death of her sister, 222 ; death of, 224, 225 ; her will, 224, 226–7, 241

Vanhomrigh, Mrs., 137, 138, 164, 167

Varina, see Jane Waring

Voltaire, 272

Walls, Archdeacon, 95, 120, 186–7, 211, 254

Walpole, Sir Robert, 161, 253–4, 255, 261, 272, 273

Walters, Sir John, 144

Waring, Jane (Varina), 51–3, 70–2

Wharton, Lord, 108, 109, 122, 129–30

Whiteway, Mrs., 304, 310–11, 312

Whitshed, Lord Chief Justice, 233, 234

Wild boy, the, 253

William III, 21 ; Swift's ode to, 40 ; 46–7, 69–70

Wilson, Dr., 311

Winder, Rev. James, 53, 54

Wogan, Chevalier, 284, 285

Wood's Halfpence, 228–34, 284

Wootton, 59

Worrall, the Rev., 203, 309

Worsley, Lady, 294

Printed in Great Britain by Butler & Tanner Ltd., Frome and London